Faulkner's Ethics

"Michael Wainwright's reassessment of William Faulkner's major works in relation to the ethics of Henry Sidgwick and Jacques Derrida—with support from game theory and psychoanalysis—is original, perceptive, and timely. Wainwright provocatively refigures Faulkner's corpus in the light of these hitherto disparate philosophical trajectories, and in doing so acquaints the philosophers with one another in ways which are lucid and suggestive. *Faulkner's Ethics: An Intense Struggle* represents a serious challenge to extant Faulkner scholarship."
—Niall Gildea, Author of *Jacques Derrida's Cambridge Affair: Deconstruction, Philosophy and Institutionality* (2019)

"Early Faulkner criticism often followed the trajectory of Faulkner's life, sometimes simply assuming that life had a moral compass. Later schools, for example historical materialism, sought the 'substratum' of material reality that underpinned the narrative, again only assuming that issues, such as the nature and economics of labor, had moral implications. Psychology, anthropology, mythology—all have had their day, often very useful days, often touching on ethical issues—but what has been lacking is ethics itself. Michael Wainwright's *Faulkner's Ethics: An Intense Struggle* will end that neglect and, I believe, spur a new interest in moral struggle, moral direction as it can be found in Faulkner's life and literature."
—Charles A. Peek, *Professor Emeritus, Department of English, University of Nebraska Kearney*

Michael Wainwright

Faulkner's Ethics

An Intense Struggle

Michael Wainwright
Department of English
Royal Holloway University of London
Egham, UK

ISBN 978-3-030-68871-4   ISBN 978-3-030-68872-1   (eBook)
https://doi.org/10.1007/978-3-030-68872-1

This Palgrave Macmillan imprint is published by the registered company Springer Nature Switzerland AG.
The registered company address is: Gewerbestrasse 11, 6330 Cham, Switzerland

For
Steve and Julie
The innermost good of their seeking
Might come in the simplest of speech

Acknowledgments

Sections of this work have appeared in other publications, and I thank those concerned for granting permission to use this material:

- "Authorial Irresponsibility: Hemingway's 'The Battler' and Faulkner's 'Barn Burning'"; copyright©2018; this material originally appeared in *Faulkner and Hemingway*, ed. Chris Rieger and Andy Leiter (Cape Girardeau, MO: Southeast Missouri State University Press, 2018), 80–102.
- "The Moral Mathematics of Strategic Games in *The Unvanquished*"; copyright©2020 Johns Hopkins University Press; this material originally appeared in *The Faulkner Journal* 31.2 (Fall 2017): 197–228.
- "The Gifted Presence of *Intruder in the Dust*"; copyright©2019; this material originally appeared in *Faulkner and Money*, ed. Jay Watson and James G. Thomas Jr. (Jackson, MS: University Press of Mississippi, 2019), 169–85.
- "William Faulkner's 'A Fable': Buchenwald and Buchwald's Disfiguring of Modernisms"; copyright©2020; this material originally appeared in *Philological Review* 44.2 (2020): 55–87
- "Strains of Attachment: Jon Bowlby's Theory and William Faulkner's *Pylon*"; copyright©2021; this material originally appeared in *Soundings* 104.1 (2021): np; this material is used by permission of the Pennsylvania State University Press.

I also extend my thanks to the following people for their support, friendship, and patience: Molly Beck, Rebecca Hinsley, Petra Treiber, and

Shriram Viswanathan at Palgrave Macmillan; Tim Armstrong, Robert Eaglestone, Juliet John, and Ruth Livesey at Royal Holloway, University of London; and the innumerable scholars I have met at Faulkner and Yoknapatawpha Conferences at the University of Mississippi, including Ann J. Abadie, Houston A. Baker, Jim Carothers, Elizabeth Cornell, John N. Duvall, Jennie J. Joiner, Donald M. Kartiganer, Brian McDonald, Charles A. Peek, François Pitavy, Chris Rieger, Carl E. Rollyson, Terrell L. Tebbetts, Theresa M. Towner, Annette Trevzer, Joseph R. Urgo, and Jay Watson.

Contents

CHAPTER 1

Introduction: The Innermost Good

Experience has frequently shown [...] how light may be shed on one part of the field of knowledge from another apparently remote.
—Henry Sidgwick, *The Methods of Ethics* (401)

On 23 March 1962, Simon Claxton interviewed the American author William Faulkner (b. 1897) at the Nobel laureate's home in Oxford, Mississippi. Asked about his "objective in writing," Faulkner's response was disarming. "I'm telling a story, introducing comic and tragic elements as I like. I'm telling a story—to be repeated and retold." The postscript to this unassuming statement, however, embraced a further objective: these elemental introductions "illustrate Man in his dilemma—facing his environment" (277). Faulkner's unexpected death less than four months after this interview—he suffered a fatal coronary occlusion on 6 July—has made this postscript canonical, reconfirming as it does the summary Judith Sutpen effectively offers of the author's creative project in what is widely regarded as Faulkner's greatest single achievement, *Absalom, Absalom!* (1936):

> You get born and you try this and you dont know why only you keep on trying it and you are born at the same time with a lot of other people, all mixed up with them, like trying to, having to, move your arms and legs with strings only the same strings are hitched to all the other arms and legs and the others all trying and they dont know why either except that the strings are all in one another's way like five or six people all trying to make a rug on

the same loom only each one wants to weave his own pattern into the rug. (105)

The interconnectedness of which Judith speaks amounts to the problematics of coordination; the attendant dilemmas encapsulate the conflicting demands of egoism and universalism; and this encapsulation belongs to the academic domain of utilitarian philosophy. "Since the middle of the eighteenth century," relates John Rawls, "the dominant systematic moral doctrine in the English-speaking tradition of moral philosophy has been some form of utilitarianism" (v). Within the historical context in which Faulkner sets Judith Sutpen's life—she was born in 1841 and dies in 1884—the leading exponent of this doctrine was Henry Sidgwick (1838–1900), the English utilitarian and economist, who would eventually accede to the post of Knightbridge Professor of Moral Philosophy at the University of Cambridge in 1883. Some one hundred years earlier, Jeremy Bentham (1748–1832) had founded modern utilitarianism, extrapolating its principles from the thoughts of his predecessors, especially those of Thomas Hobbes (1588–1679), David Hume (1711–76), and Adam Smith (1723–90), precepts that Sidgwick, initially under the influence of John Stuart Mill (1806–73), was to make so intelligible in *The Methods of Ethics* (1874).

Sidgwick's magnum opus, states Jerome B. Schneewind, "is an acknowledged masterpiece of moral philosophy" (vii), earning this status for offering, as Rawls asserts, "the clearest and most accessible formulation of what we may call 'the classical utilitarian doctrine.'" This guiding principle "holds that the ultimate moral end of social and individual action is the greatest net sum of the happiness of all sentient beings" (v). In forwarding this doctrine, Sidgwick consistently confronts the resulting difficulties, dealing with these issues in an open manner that is at once consistent and thorough. "Sidgwick's *Methods of Ethics*," as Marcus G. Singer chronicles, "was regarded as important on first publication, as is shown by the great amount of discussion, criticism, and controversy it engendered." That significance was "also shown, no doubt, by the fact that it underwent five revisions, for a total of six editions, in the author's lifetime" (421).

Despite his devotion to *The Methods of Ethics*, Sidgwick made time for other projects, and "by modern standards," as Schneewind notes, "his writings are extremely varied" (15). The most notable of these publications are *The Principles of Political Economy* (1883), *Outlines of the History of Ethics* (1886), and *The Elements of Politics* (1891). *The Methods of*

Ethics, however, remains his masterpiece. Commemorating the thirtieth anniversary of Sidgwick's death, the then Knightbridge Professor of Moral Philosophy C. D. Broad thought *The Methods of Ethics* "to be on the whole the best treatise on moral theory that has ever been written" (143). Another three decades later, Brand Blanshard explicitly agreed with Broad's opinion, adding that "for combined subtleness, thoroughness, lucidity, and fairness, I know of no equal to it in ethical literature" (90). Indeed, *The Methods of Ethics* would remain the leading examination of utilitarian principles until the appearance of Derek Parfit's (1942–2017) *Reasons and Persons* in 1984, and its contribution to progressivism in western thought—what James T. Kloppenberg calls the role of "Sidgwick's ideas in the context of that more general transformation of American and European philosophy and political theory" ("Rethinking Tradition" [1992] 369) between the 1870s and the 1920s—must not be underestimated.

As in Britain at the end of the nineteenth century, "social democratic theory in the United States" emerged during this period, as Kloppenberg traces, "from a background of ethical reformism rather than revolutionary political action" (*Uncertain Victory* [1986] 206). Hence, while admired in Britain for "his role in the reformulation of utilitarianism," that role "also played an important part in a broader transatlantic community of discourse" ("Rethinking Tradition" 369), and Sidgwick's American confrères fêted him. William James knew Sidgwick both as a philosopher and as a member of the Society for Psychical Research. Deeply moved by Sidgwick's death, James wrote to his widow, Eleanor Mildred Sidgwick (née Balfour). "Dear Mrs. Sidgwick, you have no idea how many of us mourn with you in this bereavement or what an impression of flawlessness in quality your husband left by his person on all those who knew him, and by his writings on those who never saw him." Her husband was "a spotless man, a wise man, a heroic man" (qtd. in Deborah Blum, *Ghost Hunters* 250). For his part, while reviewing *Henry Sidgwick: A Memoir* (1906), a reminiscence coauthored by Eleanor and Henry's brother Arthur, John Dewey notes how Sidgwick "combined the scientific, inductive and empirical interest with great personal sensitiveness to ideal and spiritual aspirations." Sidgwick "found himself to the last unable satisfactorily to reconcile the two tendencies," adjudges Dewey, but he "remains a monument to all that is best in" the moral tradition established by his utilitarian forebears, a tradition of "simplicity, openmindedness, absolute fairness and sincerity" (244).

Both James and Dewey were drawn to what Kloppenberg calls "Sidgwick's incisive criticism of prevailing options available in late-nineteenth-century thought: idealism and positivism in epistemology, Kantian intuitionism and Benthamite utilitarianism in ethics, and revolutionary socialism and laissez-faire liberalism in political theory" ("Rethinking Tradition" 369), and the resonances (and occasional discords) between Sidgwick, James, and Dewey cannot help but emphasize Sidgwick's transatlantic significance. On the one hand, this emphasis reveals Sidgwick's critical importance to the development of pragmatism and aligns him with the Father of American Pragmatism, his contemporary Charles Sanders Peirce (1839–1914). The main body of Peirce's work, however, was not published in his lifetime, nor was that corpus immediately and widely disseminated thereafter; only by degrees, and finally with the attention of admirers such as Jacques Derrida (1930–2004), has Peirce's philosophy gained importance for its prescience. On the other hand, most importantly, and in the context of Faulkner studies, this emphasis reveals Sidgwick's general influence on the scholarly mind, an epistemological contribution that literary academics have tended to overlook. One of the aims of *Faulkner's Ethics: An Intense Struggle* is to redress this neglect. For, as Rawls notes, *The Methods of Ethics* "is the first truly academic work in moral philosophy which undertakes to provide a systematic comparative study of moral conceptions, starting with those which historically *and by present assessment* are the most significant" (v; emphasis added).

"The Good investigated in Ethics," opines Sidgwick in the seventh, final, and definitive edition of *The Methods of Ethics* (1907), "is limited to Good in some degree attainable by human effort; accordingly knowledge of the end is sought in order to ascertain what actions are the right means to its attainment. Thus however prominent the notion of an Ultimate Good—other than voluntary action of any kind—may be in an ethical system, and whatever interpretation may be given to this notion, we must still arrive finally, if it is to be practically useful, at some determination of precepts or directive rules of conduct" (3).[1] Sidgwick defines ethics, therefore, "as the science or study of what is right or what ought to be, so far as this depends upon the voluntary action of individuals" (4). This ostensibly straightforward definition actually necessitates some unpacking: the individual is an agent; such an agent is neither a derivative of nor naturally substituted by anyone else; the practical deliberations of an agent are first-personal, and the agent is responsible for that agent's deliberate actions.

Moreover, "in opposition to [Immanuel] Kant," as Schneewind notes, "Sidgwick holds that the sense of 'freedom' which concerns the libertarian is" that "in which a man may be just as free when he acts wrongly or irrationally as he is when he acts rightly or rationally." Sidgwick maintains this view "to preserve the connection between freedom and responsibility" (208). For Sidgwick, as Schneewind concludes, "the important aspects of morality are those concerned with decisions about what is to be done, and that retrospective judgements, those essential to feelings of remorse and guilt and to assessments of responsibility, merit, and blameworthiness, are of little moment except in so far as they are logically tied to some set of prospective judgements" (211–12). Unavoidably, environmental considerations cast the remit of agential responsibility, as Faulkner's comparable understanding suggests in the light of Judith Sutpen's hitched strings in *Absalom*, beyond the individual agent. Responsibility for voluntary acts must answer to *reasonable self-love*. "It has been widely held by even orthodox moralists," as Sidgwick avers, "that all morality rests ultimately on the basis of 'reasonable self-love'; *i.e.* that its rules are ultimately binding on any individual only so far as it is his interest on the whole to observe them" (*Methods* 7).

Not every moral deliberation results in an obligation. "Some moral conclusions merely announce that you *may* do something," as Bernard Williams (1929–2003), one of Sidgwick's latter-day successors as Knightbridge Professor of Moral Philosophy, explains in *Ethics and the Limits of Philosophy* (1985). "Those do not express an obligation, but they are in a sense still governed by the idea of obligation: you ask whether you are under an obligation, and decide that you are not." Other moral deliberations, however, do result in obligations. In these cases, "an obligation applies to someone with respect to an action—it is an obligation to do something—and the action must be in the agent's power." The formula "*ought* implies *can*" is well known in this association (175; emphasis original). "I cannot conceive that I 'ought' to do anything," reasons Sidgwick, "which at the same time I judge that I cannot do" (*Methods* 33), and although "as a general statement about *ought* it is untrue," as Williams notes, Sidgwick's proposition "must be correct if it is taken as a condition on what can be a particular obligation, where that is practically concluded" (175; emphasis original). Any deliberation that proposes an impracticable act has failed in its objective; the process of deliberation must be reanimated; and this cycle must be repeated until it posits a practicable act. Moral obligation results in practicable acts that are virtuous or dutiful, and "the terms 'ought,' 'right,' and 'duty,'" as Schneewind concludes, "are used primarily in connection with the demands of reason on action" (222).

Reasonable self-love demands what Sidgwick in *The Methods of Ethics* calls "Prudence" (7); this virtue appreciates universalistic demands; as a result, prudence is an important aspect of goodness in general. Nonetheless, "common moral opinion recognises and inculcates other fundamental rules," including "those of Justice, Good Faith, [and] Veracity." Although these four duties coincidence to some degree with the cardinal virtues of Christianity—those of prudence, justice, temperance, and courage—to the rational mind, all reasonable principles "are only valid so far as their observance is conducive to the general happiness" (8). Sidgwick, despite his religious skepticism, hereby retains his regard for a "Common Sense morality" (243) strongly informed by Christian principles. "As Mill has urged," notes Sidgwick, "in so far as Utilitarianism is more rigorous than Common Sense in exacting the sacrifice of the individual's happiness to that of mankind generally, it is strictly in accordance with the most characteristic teaching of Christianity" (504). Although "Common Sense does not regard moral rules as being *merely* the mandates of an Omnipotent Being who will reward and punish men according as they obey or violate them," continues Sidgwick, "it certainly holds that this is a true though partial view of them, and perhaps that it may be intuitively apprehended. If then reflection leads us to conclude that the particular moral principles of Common Sense are to be systematised as subordinate to that pre-eminently certain and irrefragable intuition which stands as the first principle of Utilitarianism; then, of course, it will be the Utilitarian Code to which we shall believe the Divine Sanctions to be attached" (505; emphasis original). According to that reflection, "all the rules of conduct which men prescribe to one another as moral rules are really—though in part unconsciously—prescribed as means to the general happiness of mankind, or of the whole aggregate of sentient beings" (8).

Sidgwick denotes the two practices that take happiness as an ultimate end as egoistic hedonism and universalistic hedonism. He often terms the former practice simply egoism. He often terms the latter practice simply utilitarianism. While egoism pursues self-interest, utilitarianism mitigates that pursuit. In discussing character traits, and especially those of a hedonistic quality, Sidgwick initially defers to Hume. "No one can read Hume's *Inquiry into the First Principles of Morals* without being convinced of this at least," he remarks in *The Methods of Ethics*, "that if a list were drawn up of the qualities of character and conduct that are directly or indirectly productive of pleasure to ourselves or to others, it would include all that are commonly known as virtues" (424). In Sidgwick's strictest sense, virtuous acts "are always such as we conceive capable of being immediately realised by voluntary effort, at least to some extent; so that the prominent obstacle to virtuous action is absence of adequate motive" (426). On the one hand, "it is easy to see how certain acts—such as kind services—are likely to be more felicific when performed without effort, and from other motives than regard for duty" (429). Disinterested impulses must not be repressed. "Rational Self-love will best attain its end by limiting its conscious operation" (174), and this limitation often expresses itself in benevolence or "the purposive actions called 'doing Good'" (393). Simple acts of giving amount to benevolence, but on some occasions, disinterested impulses will exhort greater deeds of self-sacrifice, and "actions most conducive to the general happiness do not—in this world at least—always tend also to the greatest happiness of the agent" (9–10). On the other hand, "a person who in doing similar acts achieves a triumph of duty over strong seductive inclinations, exhibits thereby a character which we recognise as felicific in a more general way, as tending to a general performance of duty in all departments" (429). Making a duty of virtuous action can help, therefore, to forestall a lack of motive, and "if the duty of aiming at the general happiness is thus taken to include all other duties, as subordinate applications of it, we seem to be again led to the notion of Happiness as an ultimate end categorically prescribed,—only it is now General Happiness and not the private happiness of any individual" (8).

Both reasonable and studied, *The Methods of Ethics* remains the seminal work of modern utilitarianism and, as such, provides a suitable framework for the study of the ethical issues within William Faulkner's canon. "I am not a trained thinker, not a school man," Faulkner professed during his "Interviews in Japan" (1955), but a lack of education in philosophy did not hinder a moral sensitivity from pervading his literature. Indeed, this lack was a boon: no academic doubts undermined his intuitions; the "shame" he might have felt "if I were an educated man and could refer to philosophy" (134) never weighed him down. The ethical simply perfused his literary mind. "Morality is not an invention of philosophers," as Williams observes. "It is the outlook, or, incoherently, part of the outlook, of almost all of us" (174). For, as Faulkner's fiction evinces and as Williams avers, "moral obligation applies to people even if they do not want it to" (178). This "critical view of morality," as Eileen John concludes, is "inescapable" (295); literature "gravitate[s] toward moral concerns" (287);

this irresistible attraction "does not mean that the moral project has to be given priority within the work, but […] it has a kind of implacable presence" (293). Martha C. Nussbaum, in effect, agrees. "If our moral lives are 'stories' in which mystery and risk play a central and a valuable role," she argues in *Love's Knowledge* (1990), "then it may well seem that the 'intelligent report' of those lives requires the abilities and techniques of the teller of stories" (142).

The novelist and philosopher Iris Murdoch produced many such reports. "It is important to remember that language itself is a moral medium, almost all uses of language convey value," she counsels in "Literature and Philosophy" (1997). "This is one reason why we are almost always morally active. Life is soaked in the moral, literature is soaked in the moral." The novel "is particularly bound to make moral judgements in so far as [its] subject-matter is the behaviour of human beings" (27). Put succinctly, the presence of morality within the novel is pervasive, and while "*there is nothing outside of the text,*" as Derrida insists in *Of Grammatology* (1974) concerning the "critical production" of hermeneutics (158; emphasis original), "from the perspective of morality," as Williams asserts, "there is nowhere outside the system, or at least nowhere for a responsible agent" (178). In sum, related economies of inclusiveness inscribe the systems of language and morality, placing serious authors, literary theorists, and moral philosophers within coincidental reserves.

Recognizing this systemic imbrication, as Nussbaum does in "Perceptive Equilibrium" (1987), helps her to identify "the absence, from literary theory, of the organizing questions of moral philosophy, and of moral philosophy's sense of urgency about these questions." For Nussbaum, "the sense that we are social beings puzzling out, in times of great moral difficulty, what might be, for us, the best way to live—this sense of practical importance, which animates contemporary ethical theory and has always animated much of great literature   is absent from the writings of many of our leading literary theorists." Nussbaum cites Derrida as a prime offender. "One can have no clearer single measure of this absence than to have the experience of reading Jacques Derrida's *Éperons* [*Spurs* 1978] after reading Nietzsche." The work of Friedrich Nietzsche "is profoundly critical of existing ethical theory, clearly; but it is, inter alia, a response to the original Socratic question, 'How should one live?'" (243). In Nussbaum's judgment, "Derrida does not touch on that question" (243); and, what is far worse, "if one turns from criticism to more general and theoretical writing about literature, the ethical vanishes more or less altogether" (242). Literary theorists avoid ethical philosophy. "The names of the leading moral and political philosophers of our day—of John Rawls, Bernard Williams, Thomas Nagel, Derek Parfit, Judith Jarvis Thomson, and many others—and also the names of the great moral philosophers of the past—of Mill, Bentham, Henry Sidgwick, Rousseau, of the ethical sides of Plato, Aristotle, Hume, and Kant—do not appear, more or less, at all" (243). For Nussbaum, interpreters of the human condition, whether they are moral philosophers or literary theorists, must be ethically engaged.

"With several prominent contemporary figures—above all Jacques Derrida and Richard Rorty—there is no clear answer to the question, to which profession do they belong?" complains Nussbaum in "Perceptive Equilibrium." "The question, indeed, loses its interest, since the professions share so many issues, and since differences about method are internal to each group, rather than divided simply along disciplinary lines" (242). Yet, owing to the systemic cohabitation of language and morality, as Nussbaum's statement concedes, the thoughts of those who explore these coincidental reserves cannot help but imbricate literary theory and moral philosophy; in consequence, Nussbaum's concern over disciplinary demarcation undermines her criticism of Derrida. Hence, in contradistinction to Nussbaum's "Perceptive Equilibrium," *Faulkner's Ethics* recognizes the ethical significance of Derrida's canon, writings that implicitly share many of Sidgwick's concerns (and that hold a similarly transatlantic importance).[2] For Derrida, "there is no consideration of belief in moral intuitions," as Kevin Hart observes, "and no place assigned to faith regarded as a theological virtue" (181). Even Derrida's hope in a "*justice, which [he] distinguish[es] from right*," a justice "*beyond all 'messianisms,'*" as expressed in "Faith and Knowledge: The Two Sources of 'Religion' at the Limits of Reason Alone" (1998), echoes in its foundation on "*a universalizable culture of singularities*" Sidgwick's hope for the universalistic tempering of self-interest. Derrida's notion of justice relies on a naturalized faith in the other. "*This justice inscribes itself in advance in the promise, in the act of faith or in the appeal to faith that inhabits every act of language and every address to the other*," he states. "*The universalizable culture of this faith, and not of another or before all others, alone permits a 'rational' and universal discourse*" (56; emphasis original). Derrida's reliance on the reasonable, excogitative principles, which underpin a universalizable culture of singularities, resonates with Sidgwick's reasonable approach to utilitarianism. "Some form of utilitarianism," as the existentialistic Murdoch admits in

Metaphysics as a Guide to Morals (1992), "is probably now the most widely and instinctively accepted philosophy of the western world" (47).

Ironically, then, the intuitions that both Sidgwick and Derrida question, but that Faulkner listens to in questioning the human environment, support the currently widespread philosophical desire to promote rational prudence, with the choice of texts from Derrida's prolific oeuvre for the present volume being a matter of convergence between ethical matters of Sidgwickian, Derridean, and Faulknerian concern. Sidgwick's *The Methods of Ethics* displays his deep respect for cognition. When he argues from the particular to the general in seeking a science of ethics that has universal applicability, the connecting thread is human rationality. In "Derrida Degree a Question of Honour" (9 May 1992), formal ontologists, critical rationalists, and formal logicians, including Barry Smith, Hans Albert, and Willard Van Orman Quine, object that "Derrida's voluminous writings [...] stretch the normal forms of academic scholarship beyond recognition" (13), with that expansion bordering on the illogical and the irrational, but Derrida's reasoning is always careful and studied, showing his deep and abiding respect for alterity, a consideration that aims to extend personal horizons so that they overlap one another, a consideration that understands human rationality to facilitate and manifest that imbrication. The present volume, therefore, does not use Sidgwick to interrogate Derrida nor conduct the reverse procedure, but conciliates their moral thoughts in conducting a first parse through the ethics of Faulkner's literature. "At the crossing point of these [three] languages, each of which bears the silence of the other," to appropriate Derrida from "How to Avoid Speaking: Denials" (1989), "a secret must and must not allow itself to be divulged" (94). The three authors' works "cut across each other," but while the resultant interpretations "look at the holes" (Derrida, *Glas* [1986] 210) or interstitial aporia, the interpretive emphasis remains on those ethical intersections, the essential coalescences that delimit aporetic privations.

Resolved to explore the ethical in Faulkner's canon and determined to do so with reference to Sidgwick and Derrida, the chapters that follow nevertheless defer occasionally to related findings that perceptively inform a utilitarian perspective. Other moral and political philosophers of note (as well as psychoanalysts and psychologists of renown) provide these sources. Particularly important in this regard are Parfit's reductionist findings. His contribution to the advancement of moral philosophy is difficult to underestimate. "Each of the four parts of Derek Parfit's impressive and important book deserves detailed examination," writes Sydney Shoemaker of *Reasons and Persons*, "and nothing short of another book could give detailed examinations of them" (443). Parfit's reductionist contention, the proposition that psychological continuity and connectedness are more important than personal identity, "is widely and rightly held to be one of the finest pieces of work in contemporary philosophy" (Jonathan Glover 105). According to Alan Donagan, *Reasons and Persons*, "exhibiting strong sympathy with utilitarianism, although avoiding commitment to it, stands alone," with Parfit's volume deserving this encomium for "first show[ing] how serious are the moral difficulties raised by social policies" (772). Geoffrey McNicoll agrees. "One of Derek Parfit's several accomplishments in this fascinating and highly instructive book is to have made a substantial contribution to the development of population ethics" (545).[3]

Faulkner's intuitive morality effectively approved of Sidgwick's studied approach to personal conduct, and the utilitarian perspective on the rational theoretics of each–we dilemmas in *The Methods of Ethics* hints at one of Parfit's decisive conclusions in *Reasons and Persons*: self-interest "can be directly collectively self-defeating" (191). Faulkner's canon, so often inscribed with confrontational situations that implicate both personal morality and communal politics in their resolution, often delineates the consequences of this negative feedback. Moreover, Faulkner's embrace of the imperfect, his delineation of common instances where unmitigated self-interest becomes self-defeating, posits his literature as a domain of moral contemplation. "Given imperfect people and conditions," as Eileen John notes, "there needs to be a great deal of flexibility about what can count as a morally acceptable path through life." Embracing "the imperfect allows for a contrast between that kind of pragmatic morality and a morality of rigid expectations that appears unrealistic and insensitive by contrast" (294).

The resonances between Sidgwick's concept of and Faulkner's notion of morality help not only to evaluate the domain of moral contemplation but also to organize the current volume, sanctioning an interpretational matrix that offers not a study of Sidgwickian ethics but a prolegomenon to Faulknerian ethics, for which Sidgwick provides the principal theoretical foundation. While this introduction focuses on Faulkner's fiction, especially his novels, Faulkner's nonfictional realm demands some acknowledgment. To repeat, the duty of pursuing the general happiness includes all other virtues for Sidgwick, and in his public pronouncements, essays, speeches, open letters, and interviews, Faulkner often terms these subordinate qualities "the verities." Having first explicitly mentioned them via the character of Horace Benbow in *Flags in the Dust* (1929)—"they've just gone through with an experience that pretty well shook the verities and the humanities," the lawyer states of the veterans of World War I, "and whether they know it or not, they've got another one ahead of 'em that'll pretty well finish the business" (675)—Faulkner did not publically enumerate these verities until his "Address upon Receiving the Nobel Prize for Literature" (10 December 1950). They appear in this speech during Faulkner's advice to the aspiring author, who "must teach himself that the basest of all things is to be afraid; and, teaching himself that, forget it forever, leaving no room in his workshop for anything but the old verities and truths of the heart, the old universal truths lacking which any story is ephemeral and doomed—love and honor and pity and pride and compassion and sacrifice" (120).

Faulkner's inventory of virtues is short in comparison with Benjamin Franklin's seminal enumeration in *The Autobiography* (1791). Franklin's manifest comprises temperance, silence, order, resolution, frugality, industry, sincerity, justice, moderation, cleanliness, tranquility, chastity, and humility. The touchstone for Franklin is what Sidgwick would call "'Good' or 'Wellbeing.'" This ultimate standard "appears clearly when we consider any virtue in relation to the cognate vice—or at least *non-virtue*—into which it tends to pass over when pushed to an extreme, or exhibited under inappropriate conditions." For instance, "Common Sense may seem to regard Liberality, Frugality, Courage, Placability, as intrinsically desirable: but when we consider their relation respectively to Profusion, Meanness, Foolhardiness, Weakness, we find that Common Sense draws the line in each case not by immediate intuition, but by reference either to some definite maxim of duty, or to the general notion of 'Good' or Wellbeing: and similarly when we ask at what point Candour, Generosity, Humility cease to be virtues by becoming 'excessive'" (*Methods* 392; emphasis original).[4]

Franklin's determination to personify his manifest of virtues and the rigorousness of his daily self-testing in this matter hint at his own excessive and ultimately self-defeating, moral zeal. One cannot "ignore the fundamental importance of the restrictive and repressive virtues, or think that they are sufficiently developed in ordinary men at the present time, so that they may properly be excluded from moral admiration," concedes Sidgwick. Even so, in many instances, "they have been too prominent, to the neglect of other valuable qualities, in the common conception of moral Perfection." Franklin typified the quest for such perfection. In contrast, an enlightened moral theorist "is likely to lay less stress on the cultivation of those negative virtues, tendencies to restrict and refrain, which are prominent in the Common-Sense ideal of character," counsels Sidgwick, "and to set more value in comparison on those qualities of mind which are the direct source of positive pleasure to the agent or to others—some of which Common Sense scarcely recognises as excellences" (*Methods* 494). Faulkner's ethical perspective did not follow Franklin's self-avowed desire to "imitate Jesus and Socrates" (1385); rather, as the more frugal and moderate list of verities in his "Address upon Receiving the Nobel Prize for Literature" implies, Faulkner's felicific attitude was reasonably akin to Sidgwick's own.

Having set out his moral store, and having been asked and having accepted the role of American cultural ambassador after receiving his Nobel laureateship, Faulkner felt called on, and was occasionally explicitly asked, to reiterate his ethical stance. Shortly before embarking on his official tour of the Far East, he published an essay titled "On Privacy" (July 1955), which sets the loss of individual privacy in the context of the vanishing American Dream. That dream of "a sanctuary on the earth for individual man" (62) envisaged "liberty in which to have an equal start at equality with all other men, and freedom in which to defend and preserve that equality." The means of that defense were "individual courage," "honorable work," and "mutual responsibility" (65). Behavior had to square with conscience. "Each" person had to take account of the collective "we." Indeed, acts in accordance with conscience—and here Faulkner cites "self-discipline" (70), "gratitude for kindness, fidelity to friendship, chivalry toward women and the capacity to love" (71)—"alone" differentiate "us from animals" (71). The loss of individual privacy, however, as symptomatic of the failure to achieve the American Dream, indicts that unheralded and unidentifiable "moment in our history when we decided that the old simple moral verities over which taste and responsibility were the arbiters and controls, were obsolete and to be discarded" (71).

A month later, while Faulkner was in Japan, an interviewer enquired about "*pieta, gloria, virtus,* etc." in his novels. Were these human values of classical origin? "Have you studied Latin literature in your young years?" queried the interviewer. "I didn't," responded Faulkner, "because I doubt very much if the Latins invented glory and pity and integrity. I think that the Latins, like all the people, inherited a knowledge of glory and pity and integrity. I don't think they invented it, and I don't think that one has to have studied any literature to believe that glory and pity and integrity are important and valuable. I've seen ignorant people that didn't know the words, that acted on the belief that they were valuable and important" (134). Later, during the same tour, Faulkner visited the Philippines, where he talked at some length about freedom, conscience, and governance. One means employed by unreasonable authority in maintaining mastery, as Derrida argues in *The Gift of Death* (1995), relies on the inculcation of "responsibility as culpability" (56); Derrida draws on Søren Kierkegaard's *Fear and Trembling* (1843) and *The Sickness unto Death* (1849) to support this claim, and despite his reluctance to read philosophy, Faulkner's peroration in the Philippines echoes Kierkegaard too:

> The urgent question—truth—is freedom; that people—man—shall be free. And it seems to me that in the world today are not two ideologies facing one another that keep everybody else in fear and trembling. I would say that it is one everybody else in fear and trembling. I would say that it is one ideology against a simple natural desire of people to be free, and that I would choose to be free, and I don't believe that man can be free under a monolithic form of government. I think that he has got to have the liberty to make mistakes, to blunder, and to find his way, but primarily he must be free to say what he wants, to behave as he wants within the verities of universal truth which are that the weak shall be protected, that children shall be defended, that women shall be defended, that people shall not lie to each other, that no man shall be compelled to do what his conscience tells him is wrong to do, that he must have complete freedom within a government which allows him the right to be a check on that government, that when he does not like that government, he can say it: I don't like this and I will try to change it. ("Faulkner in Manila" 199–200)[5]

Faulkner insisted that truth was a responsibility of authorship. "What I mean by truth is the universal truth of compassion, honor, pride, courage, law." The responsible writer should not feel "inhibited from telling that truth" (205). Unreasonable authority should be resisted.

Kierkegaard emphasizes the same point in analyzing the biblical tale of Abraham and Isaac. Although God commands Abraham to sacrifice his son, Kierkegaard specifically "recalls," as Derrida notes, "Abraham's strange reply to Isaac when the latter asks him where the sacrificial lamb is to be found" (*Gift of Death* 58–59), because that response—"God will provide himself the lamb for a burnt offering" (Genesis 22.8)—prioritizes the father's compact with God. "He doesn't keep silent and he doesn't lie," remarks Derrida. "He doesn't speak nontruth." This covenant worries both Kierkegaard and Derrida. "According to Kierkegaard," expounds Derrida, "the highest expression of the ethical is in terms of what binds us to our own and to our fellows (that can be the family but also the actual community of friends or the nation)." Each individual must be active in protecting that individual's encompassing collective, but "by keeping the secret," as Derrida explains, "Abraham betrays ethics." Abraham's "silence, or at least the fact that he doesn't divulge the secret of the sacrifice he has been asked to make, is certainly not designed to save Isaac" (*Gift of Death* 59). This silence articulates Abraham's acquiescence to unreasonable authority, his willingness to perform an irresponsible sacrifice—and a similarly troubling compact informs Faulkner's understanding of extreme benevolence, with the virtue of self-sacrifice becoming a major aspect of both *Light in August* (1932) and *A Fable* (1954).

Faulkner explicitly returned to this theme in his "Interview with Jean Stein vanden Heuvel" (1956). "An artist can use Christianity simply as just another tool, like a carpenter would borrow a hammer?" queried Heuvel. "The carpenter we are speaking of never lacks that hammer," replied Faulkner.

> No one is without Christianity, if we agree on what we mean by the word. It is every individual's individual code of behavior, by means of which he makes himself a better human being than his nature wants to be, if he followed his nature only. Whatever its symbol—cross or crescent or whatever—that symbol is man's reminder of his duty inside the human race. Its various allegories are the charts against which he measures himself and learns to know what he is. It cannot teach man to be good as the text book teaches him mathematics. It shows him how to discover himself, evolve for himself a moral code and standard within his capacities and aspirations, by giving him a matchless example of suffering and sacrifice and the promise of hope. (246–47)

During his final public appearance, which took place at West Point in April 1962, Faulkner was again drawn back to the verities. "Sir, last night you stated that the basic goal of an author was to portray the conflict of the human heart. Now, just what do you feel today is the chief trouble with which people are concerned, or should be, and how much has this changed since, let's say in particular, the time of the Depression?" he was asked. "I don't think it has changed at all basically," he responded. "Only the ephemeral symptoms alter—they are not too important. But basically the drives of the heart are the same. It's the verities, for the verities have been the same ever since Socrates, which are courage and pride and honor—compassion." The basis of ethics does not change. "It's man's knowledge that at bottom he is not very brave, that he is not very compassionate, but he wants to be—his conscience—call it what you will, call it God, but he wants to be better than he is afraid that he might be—that he might fail, yet he still tries," and that striving necessarily involves "the verities which all the writing is about" (69).

To the same end, Sidgwick also defers in *The Methods of Ethics to* the Father of Western Philosophy, first recalling how "Socrates is said by Aristotle to have applied inductive reasoning to ethical questions" (98–99), and second remarking how Socrates's teachings on virtue emerged from this reasonable process. "Just as the generalisations of physical science rest on particular observations," maintains Sidgwick, "so in ethics general truths can only be reached by induction from judgments or perceptions relating to the rightness or wrongness of particular acts" (98). For the reasonable agent, the person who acknowledges collective demands, that process counsels the conscientious mitigation of self-interest. As he recalls in his "Preface to the Second Edition" (1877) of *The Methods of Ethics*, Sidgwick initially turned to Joseph Butler (1692–1752)—whose philosophical approach to duty at once challenged and helped to reform early utilitarianism—to support this conclusion. "Reasonable self-love and conscience are the chief or superior principles in the nature of man," states Butler in "Sermon III. Upon Human Nature" (1726),

> because an action may be suitable to this nature, though all other principles be violated, but becomes unsuitable if either of those are. Conscience and self-love, if we understand our true happiness, always lead us the same way. Duty and interest are perfectly coincident; for the most part in this world, but entirely and in every instance if we take in the future and the whole; this being implied in the notion of a good and perfect administration of things. Thus they who have been so wise in their generation as to regard only their own supposed interest, at the expense and to the injury of others, shall at last find, that he who has given up all the advantages of the present world, rather than violate his conscience and the relations of life, has infinitely better provided for himself, and secured his own interest and happiness. (52–53)

"I do not (I believe) differ materially from Butler in my view either of reasonable self-love, or—theology apart—of its relation to conscience," maintains Sidgwick. "Nor, again, do I differ from him in regarding conscience as essentially a function of the practical Reason." Sidgwick's "difference only begins when I ask myself, 'What among the precepts of our common conscience do we really see to be ultimately reasonable?' a question which Butler does not seem to have seriously put, and to which, at any rate, he has given no satisfactory answer" ("Preface to the Second Edition" xiii). Sidgwick found that acceptable response in Bentham's utilitarianism, which supplies the overarching ethical principle that establishes and directs the virtues that the present study places under the headings of *responsibility, benevolence, duty,* and *universalism.*

These precepts find expression in one of the rare occasions on which Derrida explicitly mentions Faulkner. Derrida's engagements with literature and literary figures tend to lie elsewhere, with Stéphane Mallarmé and Paul Celan in particular, but Derrida's relationship to modernism, especially to the work of James Joyce, reveals what Andrew J. Mitchell and Sam Slote call "a shaping hand in his own set of philosophical concerns" (1). A relatable conjunction (and possible molding) emerges between the Derridean and the Faulknerian, and that emergence concerns the ethical dimensions of writing and the responsible, dutiful, benevolent, and universalistic concerns of authorship. Even if writing is not explicitly "a moral or political duty," argues Derrida in "This Strange Institution Called Literature" (1989), "this experience of writing is 'subject' to an imperative: to give space for singular events, to invent something new in the form of acts of writing which no longer consist in a theoretical knowledge, in new constative statements, to give oneself to a poetico-literary performativity at least analogous to that of promises, orders, or acts of constitution or legislation which do not only change language, or which, in changing language, change more than language" (55).

The creative self-sacrifice in acquiescing to this imperative "is always more interesting" than the simple act of repetition. "In order for this singular performativity to be effective, for something new to be produced," maintains Derrida, "historical competence is not indispensable in a certain form (that of a certain academic kind of knowledge, for example, on the subject of literary history), but it increases the chances." Overtaken by the experience of writing, an author "cannot not be concerned, interested, anxious about the past, that of literature, history, or philosophy, of culture in general. S/he cannot not take account of it in some way and not consider her- or himself a responsible heir, inscribed in a genealogy, whatever the ruptures or denials on this subject may be. And the sharper the rupture is, the more vital the genealogical responsibility" ("This Strange Institution" 55). That *Absalom*, a novel to which Faulknerians and critics of literary modernism grant both supreme importance in the author's canon and great importance in twentieth-century literature, closes with a supplemental or an adjunctive "Genealogy" (314–15) is one small indication of Faulkner's commitment to this responsibility. Faulkner could not fail to credit the past. "Account cannot not be taken, whether one wish it or not, of the past," asserts Derrida. "Once again, this historicity or this historical responsibility is not necessarily linked to awareness, knowledge, or even the themes of history. What I have just suggested is as valid for Joyce, that immense allegory of historical memory, as for Faulkner, who doesn't write in such a way that he gathers together at every sentence, and in several languages at once, the whole of Western culture" ("This Strange Institution" 55).

In the present volume, the concepts of responsibility, benevolence, duty, and universalism subsume Faulkner's varying list of verities, with this strategy not only retaining the integrity of these organizing precepts but also prompting the chapter headings that structure the discussion that follows. That discussion is generally chronological, lightly sketching the trajectory of moral concerns in Faulkner's career, with *Absalom* as the apparent keystone to his canon. Six chapters flank the analysis of egoistic and universalistic hedonism undertaken in Chap. 4 that forms the architectonic and interpretative center of *Faulkner's Ethics*: the two outermost sections (Chaps. 1 and 7) consider responsibility with respective reference to "Barn Burning" (1939) and *A Fable* (1954); the two sections (Chaps. 2 and 6) within these discussions concern benevolence with respective reference to self-sacrifice in *Light in August* (1932) and the economics of the gift in *Intruder in the Dust* (1948); and the two sections closest to the interpretative center of the book (Chaps. 3 and 5) examine duty with respective reference to *Pylon* (1935) and *The Unvanquished* (1938). Concluding with a further examination of *A Fable*, titled "The Levine Shadow," *Faulkner's Ethics* dares to question the canonical status of *Absalom*, suggesting that Faulkner attempts to shift his keystone from the earlier to the later novel, doing so under the ethical demands of the Holocaust.

Thus, the chapters that follow answer Sidgwick's request in *The Methods of Ethics* to consider "the absolute and independent validity of common moral precepts." That deliberation must appeal "firstly to intuitive judgment after due consideration of the question when fairly placed before it:

and secondly to a comprehensive comparison of the ordinary judgments of mankind" (400). In turn, this procedure, as a means of promoting Sidgwick's overarching plea to practice the universal mitigation of self-interest, must pass the test of undecidability. "One often associates the theme of undecidability with deconstruction," observes Derrida in "Force of Law: The 'Mystical Foundation of Authority'" (1990). "Yet,"

> the undecidable is not merely the oscillation between two significations or two contradictory and very determinate rules, each equally imperative (for example, respect for equity and universal right, but also for the always heterogeneous and unique singularity of the unsubsumable example). The undecidable is not merely the oscillation or the tension between two decisions. Undecidable—this is the experience of that which, though foreign and heterogeneous to the order of the calculable and the rule, must [*doit*] nonetheless—it is of *duty* [*devoir*] that one must speak—deliver itself over to the impossible decision while taking account of law and rules. A decision that would not go through the test and ordeal of the undecidable would not be a free decision; it would only be the programmable application or the continuous unfolding of a calculable process. It might perhaps be legal; it would not be just. (252; emphasis original)

In effect, Sidgwick undertakes this justifiable process in *The Methods of Ethics*, and that undertaking confirms his assertion that "no quality has ever been praised as excellent by mankind generally which cannot be shown to have some marked felicific effect, and to be within proper limits obviously conducive to the general happiness" (493). Nevertheless, "it does not follow that such qualities are always fostered and encouraged by society in the proportion which a Utilitarian would desire: in fact, it is a common observation to make, in contemplating the morality of societies," as Sidgwick admits, "that some useful qualities are unduly neglected, while others are over-prized and even admired when they exist in such excess as to become, on the whole, infelicific" (493–94).

To promote felicific tendencies, the complementary perspectives of Sidgwick and Derrida encourage a rounded approach to the utilitarian contemplation of responsibility, benevolence, duty, and universalism; the present volume appeals to their authoritative but reasonable findings; and under this encouragement, Faulkner's canon reveals the ethical complexities of those human interconnections of which Judith Sutpen speaks in *Absalom*. "Faulkner's struggle is epic," writes Noel Polk in *Faulkner and Welty and the Southern Literary Tradition* (2008), "a heroic confrontation between cosmic forces—love and hate; justice and injustice; life and death—that are eternally antagonistic to each other and to human peace: one lives only under the terms of existential combat. It's an intensely moral struggle, that puts humanity—*man* he would say—in an irresolvable universal conflict whose antagonisms are permanently fixed in the nature of things" (11; emphasis original). *Faulkner's Ethics* offers the first extended analysis of this intense struggle.

Notes

1. Henceforth, unless stated otherwise, citations from *The Methods of Ethics* pertain to this edition.
2. The present volume also shares Frank Kermode's opinion in "Endings, Continued" (1989) of Derrida's approach to literature: "the presence of a stable 'crafted text' protected by constructive readings is hard to deny and is allowed even by Derrida" (86).
3. *On What Matters* (2011–17), Parfit's second and final major publication, appeared almost thirty years after *Reasons and Persons*. "*On What Matters*," in Husain Sarkar's judgment, "is a masterpiece. In this massive, profound, and powerful book—actually, says Parfit, it is several books rolled into one—Parfit offers in two large volumes innumerable fresh, deep, and systematic arguments, arguments that are as complex as they are lucid and learned, probing and meticulous, with hordes of intriguing examples and counterexamples, that constitute his moral theory; it is a veritable *tour de force*" (x).
4. In Faulkner's *If I Forget Thee, Jerusalem* (1939), the reluctant utilitarian Harry Wilbourne says something to similar yet sarcastic effect: "it was only recently I have clearly seen, followed out the logical conclusion, that it is one of what we call the prime virtues—thrift, industry, independence—that breeds all the vices—fanaticism, smugness, meddling, fear, and worst of all, respectability" (585). The utilitarian aspects of Wilbourne's thinking come to the fore most explicitly in his conversations with the newspaper reporter McCord. For, despite his anti-utilitarian credentials—McCord responds to Wilbourne's peroration on the deathly turn from autumn to winter with "for sweet Jesus Schopenhauer" (563)—Harry confronts the economically desperate situation he and Charlotte Rittenmeyer share with a calculating mind that forever fights that inborn will connoted by his surname.
5. Blotner's catalogue in *Faulkner's Library* and the deposits of her father's materials made by Jill Faulkner Summers to the University of Virginia Library suggest that Faulkner never owned any volumes by Kierkegaard.

CHAPTER 2

Responsibility (I): "Barn Burning"

In considering responsibility with reference to "the state of mind in which acts are done" (201), Henry Sidgwick (1838–1900) faces an immediate problem in *The Methods of Ethics* (1874), because "the distinction between 'motive' and 'intention' in ordinary language is not very precise." This imprecision arises because "we apply the term 'motive' to foreseen consequences of an act, so far as they are conceived to be objects of desire to the agent, or to the desire of such consequences: and when we speak of the intention of an act we usually, no doubt, have desired consequences in view." Nevertheless, undesired but predictable outcomes often arise, so "for purposes of exact moral or jural discussion, it is best to include under the term 'intention' all the consequences of an act that are foreseen as certain or probable." Sidgwick insists on these inclusions because "we cannot evade responsibility for any foreseen bad consequences of our acts by the plea that we felt no desire for them, either for their own sake or as means to ulterior ends: such undesired accompaniments of the desired results of our volitions are clearly chosen or willed by us" (202).

In also recognizing volition and concomitant outcomes, Jacques Derrida (1930–2004) suggests in *Given Time: I. Counterfeit Money* (1992) that actions make one "*responsible* for what one gives and what one receives" (63; emphasis original). This double bind cannot help but relate the economies of morality and language. "Language gives one to think," he explains, "but it also steals, spirits away from us, whispers to us [*elle nous souffle*], and withdraws the responsibility that it seems to inaugurate;

© The Author(s), under exclusive license to Springer Nature
Switzerland AG 2021
M. Wainwright, *Faulkner's Ethics*,
https://doi.org/10.1007/978-3-030-68872-1_2

it carries off the property of our own thoughts even before we have appropriated them." Derrida, who extends this necessary schema beyond the spoken idiom to all forms of textuality, furthers his argument in *On the Name* (1995). "By speaking of responsible discourse on responsibility," he notes, "we are *implying* already that discourse itself must submit to the norms or to the law of which it speaks. This implication would seem to be inescapable, but it remains disconcerting: what could be the responsibility, the quality or the virtue of responsibility, of a consistent discourse which claimed to show that no responsibility could ever be taken without equivocation and without contradiction? Or that the self-justification of a decision is impossible, and could not, a priori and for structural reasons, respond absolutely for itself?" (9; emphasis original). The willful submission to freedom of expression upholds at once the democratic rights of literature and the literary rights of freedom. This (ir)responsible acquiescence, which withholds no subject from the author, paradoxically and necessarily seeds lucidity with ambiguity. "This double function, this simultaneous proclamation and concealment, will be a principal theme of what follows," to appropriate Frank Kermode from *The Genesis of Secrecy: On the Interpretation of Narrative* (1979), "for I shall concern myself with the radiant obscurity of narratives" (47) in turning to Ernest Hemingway's "The Battler" (1925) and William Faulkner's "Barn Burning" (1939).

RESPONSIBILITY (I): "BARN BURNING"

> Now the general utilitarian reasons for leaving each rational adult free to seek happiness in his own way are obvious and striking: for, generally speaking, each is best qualified to provide for his own interests, since even when he does not know best what they are and how to attain them, he is at any rate most keenly concerned for them: and again, the consciousness of freedom and concomitant responsibility increases the average effective activity of men: and besides, the discomfort of constraint is directly an evil and *pro tanto* to be avoided. (Henry Sidgwick, *The Methods of Ethics*, 111–15)

Generally speaking, as interpolated from the debate concerning authorial influence and intertextuality, the terms "omission" and "inclusion" can be usefully applied to the respective compositional techniques of Ernest Hemingway (1899–1961) and William Faulkner (1897–1962). Three statements that span Hemingway's career establish, describe, and recapitulate his technique of omission. "You could omit anything," recalls

Hemingway in *A Moveable Feast* (1964) of his literary practice in the 1920s, "if you knew that you omitted and the omitted part would strengthen the story and make people feel something more than they understood" (75). The iceberg analogy from *Death in the Afternoon* (1932) expanded on this practical definition. "If a writer of prose knows enough about what he is writing about," states Hemingway, "he may omit things that he knows and the reader, if the writer is writing truly enough, will have a feeling of those things as strongly as though the writer had stated them. The dignity of movement of an ice-berg is due to only one-eighth of it being above water" (192). Hemingway's technical recapitulation appears in "The Art of the Short Story" (1959). "A few things I have found to be true," he avers. "If you leave out important things or events that you know about, the story is strengthened. If you leave or skip something because you do not know it, the story will be worthless. The test of any story is how very good the stuff is that you, not your editors, omit" (3).

Faulkner's technique of inclusion, which earns that description from juxtaposition with Hemingway's technique of omission, rather than from Faulkner himself, partially stems from his own advice. "Read, read, read," he asserted during his "Classroom Statements at the University of Mississippi" in 1947. "Read everything—trash, classics, good and bad, and see how they do it. Just like a carpenter who works as an apprentice and studies the master. Read! You'll absorb it. Then write. If it is good, you'll find out. If it's not, throw it out the window" (55). Faulkner was selective, as this quotation suggests, but inclusion rather than exclusion often prefigured his thoughts, and Hemingway certainly associated his contemporary with an unguardedly inclusive style. "My operatives tell me," he declares in *Death in the Afternoon*, "that through the fine work of Mr. William Faulkner publishers now will publish anything" (173). Often, as Joseph Fruscione documents, Hemingway's criticism of his coeval focused on Faulkner's "verbose, ornate style, and (over)productivity" (82). If Hemingway's technique produced the tip of the iceberg, with seven-eighths of his material a subliminal mass, then Faulkner's technique inverted the iceberg, with a supraliminal mass atop a submerged point.

Particularly speaking, however, as interpolated from the two authors' close but distinct reformulation of symbolist poetics, the economy of secrecy offers an alternative focus on their respective compositional techniques. This interpretive perspective, by heeding the thematic issues that the necessary debate concerning authorial influence and intertextuality has unfortunately overlooked, goes beyond the notion of semiotic secrecy, which forms the basis of so much poststructural debate. Gayatri Chakravorty Spivak summarizes that dominant notion in her "Translator's Preface" to Jacques Derrida's (1930–2004) *Of Grammatology* (1974). "Derrida suggests that what opens the possibility of thought is not merely the question of being, but also the never-annulled difference from 'the completely other.'" The "simple yet powerful insight" that enables this proposition understands "that the sign, phonic as well as graphic, is a structure of difference." Different and deferring, "the strange 'being' of the sign" is a matter of *différance*: "half of it always 'not there' and the other half always 'not that'" (xvii). The trace or track of that forever absent other, which is never present in its entirety, determines the structure of the sign; one sign leads to another sign; and this process is indefinite.

Going beyond the poststructuralism of semiotics in *Given Time: I. Counterfeit Money* (1992), however, Derrida retains his interest in secrecy while shifting the focus of that curiosity from the concept of *différance*. He not only discusses the socioeconomic prescience of Charles Baudelaire's (1821–67) "La fausse monnaie" ("Counterfeit Money") from the posthumously published *Le Spleen de Paris* (or *Petits poèmes en prose*) (1869), but also anticipates his own poststructuralist thoughts in *On the Name* (1995) concerning the relationship between the economy of secrecy and authorial (ir)responsibility. Retrospectively applying these contemplations to Baudelaire's prose poem—an exercise that Derrida does not undertake—at once invests in the speculation engendered by "La fausse monnaie" and recommends that analeptic application to texts with comparable *avant-la-lettre* tendencies, such as Hemingway's "The Battler," from *In Our Time* (1925), and Faulkner's "Barn Burning" (1939), which was originally published by *Harper's Magazine*.

Critics agree that Baudelaire's prose poetry influenced both Hemingway and Faulkner. Baudelaire, as James D. Brasch outlines, was among the "19th Century poets with whom Hemingway was most seriously involved" (29), and "Faulkner's reading of Baudelaire," as Scott G. Williams traces, "influenced his writing" (72). Baudelaire's renown stems in part from *Les Fleurs du mal* (*The Flowers of Evil*) (1857), with its foundation of literary symbolism, and Hemingway acquired his earliest edition of this work (Lévy's 1894 imprint) after he arrived in Paris on 22 December 1921. Three months later, on 25 March 1922, he published "American Bohemians in Paris," an editorial for the *Toronto Star* that decries how "the scum of Greenwich Village, New York, has been skimmed off and deposited in large ladles on that section of Paris adjacent to the Café

Rotonde." This "scummiest scum has come across the ocean, somehow, and with its afternoon and evening levees has made the Rotonde the leading Latin Quarter showplace for tourists in search of atmosphere" (148). Although this lament over the influx of irresponsible sightseers was the most accomplished of Hemingway's pieces for the newspaper, as Charles Fenton notes, "his final paragraph revolved around a name which must have mystified his Toronto readers" (124), that of Charles Baudelaire.

At once revered by his confrères for his poetic sensibility and notorious among the Parisian populace (in no small part for leading a leashed lobster through the Latin Quarter), this responsibly irresponsible artist was one of the phenomena of the Belle Époque. Eccentric, yet serious, as Hemingway establishes in his editorial, Baudelaire always stood out from the quarter's habitual denizens. "I suspect that Baudelaire parked the lobster with the concierge down on the first floor, put the chloroform bottle corked on the washstand and sweated and carved at the *Fleurs du Mal* alone with his ideas and his paper" (150). To Hemingway, explains Alex Shakespeare, "Baudelaire typified the artist who must park his bohemian habits (and crustaceous accessories) at the door if he was to purify" (237–38) his art, and Baudelaire's poetry would remain a source of inspiration for Hemingway, whose libraries would increasingly testify to this enduring reverence. By 1930, his Key West repository "contained three volumes of Baudelaire: *Les fleurs du mal et complement, Morceaux Choisies,* and *The Intimate Journals of Charles Baudelaire*," and by 1961, his Finca Vigia library contained "three additional copies of *Les Fleurs du Mal*" (238).[1]

"Source-hunting is at best," concedes Noel Polk in "William Faulkner's *Marionettes*" (1973), "a risky business, and with an author like Faulkner, who was so omnivorous and catholic a reader, the problems are multiplied many times" (250). In tracking down Faulkner's sources for his one-act play *The Marionettes* (1920), the conscientious Polk turns to "About the Sketches" (1958), Carvel Collins's introduction to Faulkner's *New Orleans Sketches* (1925), agreeing with Collins that "the most pervasive influence [...] seems to be that of the Symbolists" (250–51). This category includes "not only Verlaine and Mallarmé" but also "a whole host of other writers of late nineteenth-century Europe—Laforgue, Huysmans, Baudelaire, de Gourmont, Valéry, Gautier, and Flaubert" (251). In Collins's opinion, notes Polk, "Faulkner 'imported' the French Symbolists to the University of Mississippi campus" (251 n.12) at Oxford, where he briefly studied between 1919 and 1920, and where his family home was then located. In the immediate years that followed, as Jay Parini reports,

"Faulkner bounced back and forth between Oxford and New Orleans" (74) until, in 1925, he embarked on a literary sojourn in Europe. Faulkner arrived in Paris that August, and "he lived in the Latin Quarter," as François Pitavy records in "The Two Orders in *A Fable*" (2009), "for two-and-a-half months" (385).

Faulkner would also have witnessed the presence of Hemingway's transatlantic scum, but the moralities of the Latin Quarter cut both ways, with the local inhabitants willingly catering to the desires of American Bohemians. Postwar Paris was, as Polk relates in *Faulkner and Welty and the Southern Literary Tradition* (2008), "a loose, unstable confederation of French citizens with even looser morals, folks broken and resourceless after the war, who, at least as far as Americans were concerned, existed mostly to provide wine and food and other services" (33). Faulkner would have perceived the reciprocal nature of these irresponsibilities and, like Hemingway, would have regretted the passing of Baudelaire's influence on Parisian writers. Penned in September 1925, the notes on Faulkner's personal copy of Ludwig Lewisohn's *A Modern Book of Criticism* (1919)—"the only book he is known to have annotated extensively" (Bart Welling 583)—suggest as much, because this volume includes numerous references to Baudelaire. In "The Southern Myth and William Faulkner" (1951), Irving Howe explains how "Southern literature at its best—the work of Faulkner, Caldwell, Ransom, Tate, Warren—was conceived in an explosive mixture of provincialism and cosmopolitanism, tradition and modernity." Yet, "to burst into high flame it had to be stimulated, or irritated, by the pressures of European and Northern ideas and literary modes." The American predecessor who most readily elicited this conflagration was Edgar Allan Poe, but to appreciate Poe, Faulkner and his southern contemporaries "had first to understand what he had meant to Baudelaire"; to facilitate this understanding, "they had to possess a sophisticated awareness of the European literary past" (359), and Lewisohn possessed such knowledge.

For Lewisohn, ecstasy often furnishes the creative spirit. In "Faith and Knowledge: The Two Sources of 'Religion' at the Limits of Reason Alone" (1998), Derrida describes ecstasy as "*existence of the most extreme abstraction*" (55; emphasis original), which alights on and enlightens only a select few, artists who take responsibility for the potential irresponsibility arising from this alienation from conscious control. "In our age," opines Lewisohn, "Keats had it, and Shelley; Byron, despite his passion, missed it, and so did Wordsworth. We find it in Swinburne, he had it from the first;

but few French poets have it. Like the 'cold devils' of Félicien Rops, coiled in frozen ecstasy, the blasts of hell about them, Charles Baudelaire can boast the dangerous attribute. Poe and Heine knew ecstasy, and Liszt also; Wagner was the master adept of his century" (153–54). Such authoritative subservience is unsettling: it demands a responsible submission to an irresponsible impulse. In "The First Session" (1981), Derrida writes of the Pierrot in Stéphane Mallarmé's "Mimique" (1897), who murders his wife, miming his crime "all the way to the 'supreme spasm' the rising of ecstatic hilarity" (151). Yet such "pictures of love and death," as so often found in "Poe and Baudelaire, Wagner and Strauss," as Lewisohn advises, "must not be adjudged as a black crime" (154), and Derrida would agree because such artistic irresponsibility never enjoys complete abandon.

Baudelaire is more responsible than most both for this ecstatic provenance and for its influence on American modernists. "Possibly," as Lewisohn muses, "it was a relic of his early admiration and study of Baudelaire that set Wagner to extorting ecstasy from his orchestra by images of death and love" (154), and Wagner, as Stoddard Martin and Leon Surette respectively document, influenced T. S. Eliot and Ezra Pound. "Poetry (it is again Baudelaire who says it)," remarks Lewisohn, "'is akin to music through a prosody whose roots plunge deeper in the human soul than any classical theory has indicated'" (107), and "Faulkner," as Williams summarizes, "gorged himself on Baudelaire" (69), "absorb[ing]" (51), as Michel Gresset observes, an understanding of both Baudelaire's aesthetic code and his stylistic mannerisms.[2] In "Wealthy Jew," the short oration that opens his *New Orleans Sketches*, Faulkner draws on his Parisian inspiration. Faulkner's subject begins and closes his speech with the assertion that he "love[s] three things: gold; marble and purple; splendor, solidarity, color" (37, 38). The "semitic man" (285, 288, 474) in *Mosquitoes* (1927), whom A. Nicholas Fargnoli, Michael Golay, and Robert W. Hamblin describe as "an articulate if obsessive literary theorist" (195), utters the same phrase twice ("I love three things: gold, marble and purple" [532, 533]). Michael Millgate (300) identifies Faulkner's source as Théophile Gautier's *Mademoiselle de Maupin* (1835)—"Trois choses me plaisent: l'or, le marbre et la pourpre, éclat, solidité, couleur" (211)—a proposition with which Cleanth Brooks concurs (103) in *William Faulkner: Toward Yoknapatawpha and Beyond* (1978). "These three qualities," observes Lothar Hönnighausen, "recall the parnassian ideals of the three French forefathers of modernism, Théophile Gautier, Charles Baudelaire, and Gustave Flaubert" (565), and evoke not only the wholeness and harmony but also the radiance (or quid-dity) of the orthodox, responsible, yet inspirational aesthetics of Thomas Aquinas.

"Aquinas, the foremost thinker of the Dominican Order and the classi-cal theologian of the Latin church, is, among other things," explains Aidan Nichols, "a philosopher and theologian of the *sign.*" In *Quaestiones dispu-tatae de veritate* (1256–59), continues Nichols, Aquinas "affirms that natural knowledge of God in this life comes about *per speculum et aenigma sensibilium creaturarum*, 'through the mirror and enigma of sensory crea-tures'" (3; emphasis original). Baudelaire expresses a similar understand-ing in "Correspondances" from *Les Fleurs du mal*:

> La nature est un temple où de vivants piliers
> Laissent parfois sortir de confuses paroles;
> L'homme y passe à travers des forêts de symboles
> Qui l'observent avec des regards familiers. (193)

Against common expectation, Jean Moréas's *Le Symbolisme* (1886), which codified the creative guidelines developed from Baudelaire's groundwork into a manifesto, preferences expression for the sake of expression, evocation rather than description, social detachment instead of social involvement, and the efficacy of economy before the effects of sym-bolism. The resultant indeterminate complex, which promotes what Richard Rorty would have called a poststructural "lubriciousness of the tangled" (126) and which characterizes both *Les Fleurs du mal* and *Le Spleen de Paris* throughout, requires the intentional yet responsible sur-render of authorial control, and that submission necessarily partakes of the relationship between inviolable (or absolute) and revealable (or condi-tional) secrecy.

Derrida's analysis of this relationship, which effectively complements while outstripping Lewisohn's thoughts on the somewhat troubling beni-son of ecstasy, offers a means of gauging and interrogating the authorial surrender of control. The willful submission to freedom of expression upholds at once the democratic rights of literature and the literary rights of democracy. Hence, this intended irresponsibility withholds no subject from the author, but paradoxically and necessarily seeds lucidity with ambiguity—and this occlusion of transparency, this letting go before the reader is what guarantees Hemingway's works their place in (to appropri-ate Frank Kermode from *The Genesis of Secrecy: On the Interpretation of*

Narrative [1979]) "the secular canon." In other words, Hemingway's writing is "of such value that every effort of exegesis is justified without argument, as it is in the cases of, say, Joyce and Faulkner" (5). A Derridean approach to the economy of secrecy and authorial (ir)responsibility, therefore, recommends itself to an interpretation of the manner in which Hemingway and Faulkner surrender control, as each author considers his protagonist's rite of passage or movement toward the responsibility of self-authorship through the revelation of conditional secrets, in "The Battler" and "Barn Burning," respectively.

The inviolable secret connotes an open rather than a hidden truth and is, therefore, a paradoxical secret without secret. This obvious enigma, as Derrida expounds in *On the Name*, fills the reader with desire:

> When all hypotheses are permitted, groundless and *ad infinitum*, about the meaning of a text, or the final intentions of an author, whose person is no more represented than nonrepresented by a character or by a narrator, by a poetic or fictional sentence, which detaches itself from its presumed source and thus remains *locked away* [*au secret*], when there is no longer even any sense in making decisions about some secret behind the surface of a textual manifestation (and it is this situation which I would call text or trace), when it is the call [*appel*] of this secret, however, which points back to the other or to something else, when it is this itself which keeps our passion aroused, and holds us to the other, then the secret impassions us. (29; emphasis original)

The absolute secret, like an unbreakable code, encourages endless hypotheses of impassioned interpretation. Literary worth is the open secret of absolute secrecy against and allied to which the conditional secret inscribes a marked contrast. The condition of linguistic secrecy ensures that the revelation of a conditional secret cannot help but retain an inviolable level of secrecy: profit from exposure pointing toward privation from inviolability.

This curious relationship has political ramifications for Derrida. While absolute secrecy arises from a reserve of unfathomable information, conditional secrecy depends on a store of potential knowledge. Proprietorship of a revealable secret privileges its owner with a power over others, and this surplus potential can support interpersonal structures of an undemocratic nature. Inviolable secrecy, however, as its openness suggests, cannot fall foul of individual speculation. "Through its aporetic structure," writes

Alex Segal, absolute secrecy "displaces the use of (conditional) secrecy to attain power and is thereby tied to democracy" (190). This displacement makes literature a democratic form of expression: at one level, as explicitly promoted by *Le Symbolisme*, social detachment tends toward impersonality; at another level, as implicitly engaged with by all literature, the aporia of the inviolable secret, which connotes the gap between the actually communicated and the intended but inexpressible communication, separates a writer from his work. An author cannot decrypt the absolute mysteries of his texts anymore than a reader of those texts can. This absolute secrecy, as *On the Name* makes plain, is that "something *about*" literature that Derrida admires: "There is no passion without secret, this very secret, indeed no secret without this passion" (28; emphasis original). Breaking the power of mastery, breaking the obsession over personal identity, the inviolable secret offers literature as a form of gift, where gifting implies benevolence without return. Literature is an utterly secret donation, which thanks, or another form of payment, cannot repay.

Responsibly speaking, the essential affinity between the aporetic essences of literature and the gift both identifies a literary work with, and frees that work from, its author. In giving his name to a text, an author appears to feed his narcissism, but that appetite remains insatiable because that author is not his name. "Suppose that X, something or someone (a trace, a work, an institution, a child), bears your name, that is to say, your title," posits Derrida in *On the Name*. "The naive rendering or common illusion [*fantasme courant*] is that you have given your name to X, thus all that returns to X, in a direct or indirect way, in a straight or oblique line, *returns* to you, as a profit for your narcissism." Derrida explodes the fantasy generated by this irresponsible self-interest. "But as you *are* not your name, nor your title, and given that, as the name or the title, X does very well without you or your life, that is, without the place toward which something could *return*—just as that is the definition and the very possibility of every trace, and of all names and all titles," he explains, "so your narcissism is frustrated a priori by that from which it profits or hopes to profit" (12; emphasis original).

Both Hemingway and Faulkner experienced the narcissistic dilemma of authorship. Each man would win notable literary awards; each man would suffer mental privations. Summing up the psychological perspective, Christopher D. Martin posits Hemingway's probable "narcissistic personality traits" (351), while Michael Grimwood proffers Faulkner's life as "ample evidence of his narcissistic tendencies" (52). Faulkner would win the 1949 Nobel Prize for Literature. Hemingway would win the 1954 Nobel Prize for Literature. Both men would attempt to expunge, rather than simply secrete, however, certain aspects of the psychological states that had earned them their laureateships. Their expurgatorial use of alcohol is undoubted, and while Faulkner's recourse to electroconvulsive therapy (ECT) remains open to question, the evidence of Hemingway's recourse to this treatment is beyond doubt.[3]

Frighteningly for such psyches, which require yet fear reception and recognition, literature can survive without authorship. Indeed, the unattributed work of logographers (or ghostwriters) and the secrecy of anonymous authors (or "anons") instantiate the durability of autonomous texts. "The ability to disappear *in your name*," maintains Derrida, is what "returns to your name." The absolute secrecy that frees a text from its authorial seal is at the same time the condition that augments that authorial self. "In the two cases of this same divided passion," maintains Derrida, as if describing the creative struggles of either Hemingway or Faulkner, "it is impossible to dissociate the greatest profit and the greatest privation" (*On the Name* 13; emphasis original). Although the author can disappear into the inviolable privacy of literary ownership, the greater the autonomy of a text, the greater the possibility that intentionality lurks behind that supposed independence.

"For Derrida," as Segal stresses, "attention to authorial intention is a fundamental guardrail in the interpretation of texts" (191), with the relationship opened between text and author by absolute secrecy (in allying the aporias of literature and the gift) exhibiting paradoxical degrees of authorial responsibility. At one extreme, authorship is an irresponsible activity: the inviolable secrets of literature leave the field of expression unrestricted; secrecy hereby ties the destiny of literature, as Derrida argues in *On the Name*, "to a certain noncensure, to the space of democratic freedom (freedom of the press, freedom of speech, etc.)" (28). From this perspective, as Derrida contends in "Before the Law" (1982), the literary domain "is not only that of an instituted *fiction* but also a *fictive institution* which in principle allows one to say everything." To say all is "to totalize by formalizing, but to say everything is also to break out of [*franchir*] prohibitions"; that is, "to *affranchise* oneself [*s'affranchir*]—in every field where law can lay down the law" (36; emphasis original). At the other extreme, authorship is a responsible activity: the propositional nature of a work is an authorial duty. Unscrupulous literature, whether perfunctorily penned or knowingly produced, can spread unethical or politically fallacious messages through the accepted protocols of semiotics and the traditional meanings of (Saussurean) signs. Thus, the Derridean focus on authorial intention, as Segal insists, "no more consigns literary interpretation to unbridled subjectivism and pure arbitrariness than [it] severs literature from ethical or political accountability" (206 n.5).

Literature is at once the complete responsibility of an author and an appeal to impersonal democratism. Although usually a singular creation of an individual, which no one can gainsay, and so a secret matter of inviolable control, a literary work nonetheless leaves the propositional intent of that absolute accountability open to public scrutiny. "Responsibility must be infinite. That's why I always feel not responsible enough" (48–49), explains Derrida in "following theory" (2003), "because I'm finite and because there are an infinite number of others to whom or for whom or from whom I should be responsible. I'm always not responsible enough, and responsibility is infinite or it *is* not, but I cannot be responsible *to some extent* in the strict sense of 'responsibility.'" That is why, he concedes, "I always feel guilty" (49; emphasis original). The double bind of textual accountability, as pursued by Derrida in "Remarks on Deconstruction and Pragmatism" (1996), can thereby challenge the standard yet ironic concept of "politics and democracy as openness—where all are equal and where the public realm is open to all—which tends to deny, efface or prohibit the secret" (80). In another way, then, this double bind makes the responsible writer feel irresponsible, inscribing the impossible dissociation between authorial profit and privation more deeply into that author's psyche.

After this typically Derridean introduction, as though the boundaries of *Given Time* testify to the central relevance of the works of that author, works that lie just beyond its margins, the approach to Hemingway's "The Battler" and Faulkner's "Barn Burning" begins somewhat more earnestly with Derrida's typically elliptical approach to the textual accountability (or responsibility) of Baudelaire's "La fausse monnaie." "The referential structure of a title," states Derrida, "is always very tricky" (84)—and "La fausse monnaie" is no exception. This heading refers not only to the phenomenon of counterfeit money, "a sign without value, if not without meaning," but also to the subsequent narrative, "this text *here*, this story of counterfeit money" (85; emphasis original). "The title of a text," observes Segal, "would seem to be connected to its demarcation, its identity. Yet Derrida argues that in so far as counterfeit money is illegal, the title of 'Counterfeit Money' is without title" (194). Ordinarily, an introductory heading both identifies and begins a text; yet, according to

Derrida's thesis in "Before the Law," "the power and import of a title have an essential relationship with something like the law" (188–89); as such, the illegality of forged currency means that "La fausse monnaie" displays at once a valid and an invalid heading.

While "The Battler," as the title of an episode from Hemingway's *In Our Time*, engenders a similar sense of titular invalidity, seemingly announcing a particular individual's cognomen, but ultimately spilling over its definite article by referencing at least four agents, "Barn Burning," as the title of Faulkner's short story, engenders a stronger sense of dehiscence, referring not only to a transgressive activity that courts a break with lawful power but also to the narrative that follows. As with "La fausse monnaie," yet to differing degrees, "The Battler" and "Barn Burning" are invalid headings—or titles without title.

Opening from its titular framework to reveal two friends emerging from another frame, a Parisian shop doorway, Baudelaire's prose poem immediately arouses speculation concerning the responsibility of literary ownership. For, "in the civil code concerning ownership of literary works," as Derrida expounds in *Given Time*, "the fiction is attributed to its signatory, Baudelaire, and is entitled by him." Yet, "by reason and by virtue of the same right—what is called the *droit d'auteur* in French, that is, the right of the author—this fiction places the narrative not in the mouth, in the hand, or within the responsibility of the author but, of course, of the narrator" (93). This homodiegetic figure compounds the reader's interest with his commentary concerning the behavior of his colleague. "As we were walking from a tobacconist's," recalls the narrator, "my friend carefully sorted out his change: into the left pocket of his waistcoat he slipped the small gold coins, into the right, the small silver coins; into the left pocket of his breeches, a mass of large copper coins, and finally, into the right, a two-franc silver piece he had examined with noticeable attention" (48–49). The two men shortly encounter a beggar; each man hands over a coin; "my friend's offering," admits the narrator, "was much larger than mine" (49). The friend's donation, as responsible liberality that goes beyond, but does not (irresponsibly) traduce, common benevolence, appears to question the lack of generosity of the narrator, whose gift has remained within the boundaries of common duty. The responsible liberality of the narrator's colleague strikes at the bourgeois complacency of this automatic, but overly restrained, and therefore somewhat irresponsible benevolence.

"Considered as a Virtue," expounds Henry Sidgwick (1838–1900) in *The Methods of Ethics* (1874), "Liberality seems to be merely Benevolence, as exhibited in the particular service of giving money, beyond the limits of strict duty as commonly recognised" (324). The narrator, who has not matched his colleague in affording this "mere" extension, points out the discrepancy between their donations. He feels embarrassed at his own parsimony—"Meanness," according to Sidgwick, "being the vice antithetical to Liberality" (325)—and this feeling is acute. This intensity arises in part because parsimony "has a wider sphere than Liberality, and refers not merely to the taking or refusing of money, but to taking advantages generally: in this wider sense the opposite virtue is Generosity" (326). The narrator's friend, however, dismisses the issue nonchalantly: "the counterfeit coin" (49) constituted his supposedly generous gift. This rejoinder about the two-franc piece that had caught its possessor's attention only minutes earlier perplexes the narrator. "Liberality," writes Sidgwick, "appears to require an external abundance in the gift even more than a self-sacrificing disposition" (324), and the avowal of the narrator's colleague has exploded each of these requirements. Moreover, as Derrida explains in *Given Time*, "the narration is framed in such a way that, like the narrator, we are the friend's debtors, but to the paradoxical extent that we live on the very credit *we are obliged to extend to him*. Whether or not we take him at his word, we have only his word. We are at once his debtor and his creditor" (151; emphasis original). The reader partakes of the narrator's viewpoint and must ask, as the narrator does, why his colleague made his admission about the two-franc coin.

Notwithstanding this critical identification, the narrator remains "a fiction of the author," as Derrida maintains, and the responsible critic "must always suppose that Baudelaire does not by rights take" this figure's narrative, deliberations, and conclusions "at face value" (93). The narrative has entered a dubious cycle of economic exchange. "The moment the gift, however generous it be, is infected with the slightest hint of calculation, the moment it takes account of knowledge [*connaissance*] or recognition [*reconnaissance*]," as Derrida explains in *The Gift of Death* (1995), "it falls within the ambit of an economy: it exchanges, in short it gives counterfeit money, since it gives in exchange for payment" (112). Credence, as a matter of speculation, and credit, as the issue of accreditation, are suddenly at stake. Liberality seems "to be possible only to the rich," observes Sidgwick, and "in the admiration commonly accorded to it there seems to be mingled an element rather aesthetic than moral. For we are all apt to admire power, and we recognise the latent power of wealth gracefully exhibited in a certain degree of careless profusion when the object is to give happiness to others" (*Methods* 324). In the case of the narrator's colleague in "La Fausse monnaie," however, as Derrida explains of wanton immaturity, any grace attendant on this latent power has evaporated, because the extravagant donor is at once "*responsible* for his irresponsibility and for not yet being adult although he is or already can be adult" (168; emphasis original). Crucially, these two conjectures, the first concerning self-effacing altruism and the second concerning self-interested arrogance, exhibit a relationship that classical dialectics cannot resolve; "on the contrary," as Derrida expounds, "they superimpose themselves on each other, they accumulate like a capital of true or (perhaps) counterfeit money that may produce interest; they overdetermine each other in the ellipsis of the declaration." Each conjecture "is justifiable and each has a certain right to be credited, accredited. This is the phenomenon without phenomenality of counterfeit money" (*Given Time* 149).

In "The Battler," the unnamed, heterodiegetic, and inviolably secret narrator immediately arouses speculation by introducing both the protagonist Nick Adams, as he watches a "caboose" (97) disappear into the distance, and a series of short, puzzling details that concern Nick's physical and sartorial states. The reader, as Hemingway surely intends, must speculate; he must live on the credit he is obliged to extend to the narrator. This accreditation, which invests in the conditional secret of the narrator's disjunction between fabula and sjuzhet, immediately pays dividends. A form of lawful process has in fact been enacted on the train, as an analepsis reveals in expressing Nick's impotent rage at the dutiful brakeman who threw him off the caboose. The feigned sincerity of the man's interest in Nick—a ruse in which the brakeman, as a type of battler, whose responsibility lies with his employer, retained the conditional secret of his professional hostility toward freighthoppers—had disarmed the naïve Adams. "He had fallen for it," concedes Nick. "What a lousy kid thing to have done" (97). That concession signifies an early step on Nick's rite of passage. While the caboose, as a car attached to the rear of a freight train and dedicated to the occupancy of railroad workers (a group to which Nick does not belong), falls under the brakeman's authority on the tracks, the caboose, as a site in which the brakeman exercises that authority, represents a jail from which a chastised offender has been evicted.

In "Barn Burning," a similarly constituted narrator—unnamed, heterodiegetic, and inviolably secret—immediately arouses speculation by introducing both "the Justice of the Peace's court" and the seemingly inconsistent detail that this room "smelled of cheese" (3). The reader, as Faulkner surely intends, must speculate; he must live on the credit he is obliged to extend to the narrator. Again, this investment immediately pays dividends, with the revelation that due lawful process has in fact seconded a general store. Thus, Nick's rude awakening in "The Battler" to the excesses of seconding responsibility in a practically unlimited or undemocratic fashion finds a parallel in Colonel Sartoris (or Sarty) Snopes's growing awareness of the incongruity of a lawful hearing in an incommensurate setting. The differing potential of the two characters as bearers of conditional secrecy—their potential to fight undemocratic power with undemocratic power—lies within this parallel: Nick, who has already renounced his father, as textual interpolation from the other episodes of *In Our Time* suggests in positing the absolute secret of a silent paratext, should be capable of accepting the demands of conditional secrecy; Sarty, who attends his father Abner's appearance before the justice, and is both young enough and too young for the defendant to trust, is a potential revealer of conditional secrets. In each case, privileged knowledge slowly announces itself as a significant narratological detail within a peculiar ambiance of law, law enforcement, and the economics of exchange.

After his rough lesson at the hands of the brakeman, Nick's continued journey (or rite of passage) repeatedly promises a relatively easy prospect: the track "was well ballasted and made easy walking, sand and gravel packed between the ties, solid walking" (97). Nick spots a fire below the railway embankment, but he heeds the brakeman's lesson—his cautious approach retaining the secrecy of his presence: "Nick dropped carefully down the embankment and cut into the woods" and "waited behind the tree and watched" (98). Finally, he "walk[s] into the firelight" (98), approaching what (in effect) is another source of enlightenment, another (titular) battler, "a former champion fighter" (101), or no longer titled titleholder, Ad Francis

Ad and Nick appear to hit it off. Ad admits to being "crazy" (99), but the extent of his aberrancy is left as a conditional yet seemingly unimportant secret. In response, revealing his latent desire to shirk the demands of conditional secrecy, Nick recounts his treatment at the hands of the brakeman to this startlingly improbable imago. Nick's willingness to drop his guard reveals a cordiality that the unexpected appearance of Ad's companion, the African-American Bugs, seems to confirm. Ironically, however, the accustomed protocols of that geniality lull Bugs into a false sense of serenity; as a result, in forbidding Nick from lending Ad his knife, Bugs openly retains the conditional secret about Ad's craziness while accepting Nick's presence.

In the peculiar smelling courtroom of "Barn Burning," a local landowner, Mr. Harris, recalls the events that culminated in these proceedings against his tenant Abner Snopes. Snopes's "hog got into my corn," he tells the court. "I caught it up and sent it back to him. He had no fence that would hold it. I told him so, warned him. The next time I put the hog in my pen. When he came to get it," continues Harris, "I gave him enough wire to patch up his pen. The next time I put the hog up and kept it. I rode down to his house and saw the wire I gave him still rolled on to the spool in his yard," maintains Snopes's landlord. "I told him he could have the hog when he paid me a dollar pound fee" (3–4). That evening, relates Harris, "a strange nigger" came to collect Snopes's pig. Having paid the fine, and with the pig in tow, this intermediary then delivered a message: "He say to tell you wood and hay kin burn." Rather at a loss, Harris asked this strange African American, this secret agent, to repeat himself, but the tenor of the message remained the same: "that whut he say to tell you," the man replied: "wood and hay kin burn" (4). This message appeared irresponsible in seeming to break the criminal covenant of inviolable secrecy. "We do not commonly think that a crime is rendered less grave by being kept perfectly secret," remarks Sidgwick, "and yet a great part of the harm done by a crime is the 'secondary evil' (as [Jeremy] Bentham calls it) of the alarm and insecurity which it causes; and this part is cut off by complete secrecy" (*Methods* 291–92). The transitive relations that marked the communication between Snopes and Harris—the human links in its chain—simultaneously indict Abner for and absolve him from responsibility for the message. Harris being the origin of this evidence, rather than the unknown messenger, further weakens its legitimacy before the law. The justice's repeated call to produce the African American in person testifies to this flaw in Harris's suit against Snopes. Notwithstanding these legal considerations, complains Harris, "that night my barn burned. I got the stock out but I lost the barn" (4).

Harris's strange interlocutor has been the subject of much critical speculation. John N. Duvall, in particular, as "'A Strange Nigger': Faulkner and the Minstrel Performance of Whiteness" (2007) evinces, has invested himself in unmasking the (supposed) blackface of Abner Snopes. "As [Richard] Godden has pointed out," and as Duvall appreciates, "everything about Abner is associated with blackness—his black hat and frockcoat, but most particularly his relationship with fire. Faulkner's repeated use of the term 'niggard' to describe the fire that Abner burns for his family," notes Duvall, "serves as wordplay that both points toward, even as its etymological difference deflects attention away from, 'nigger.'" Duvall, however, takes Godden's argument further. "I wish to suggest that the story's 'strange nigger,' is actually in the store where the hearing takes place and is the very figure of the man in black, Abner Snopes. Since almost the only person Abner would trust with a dollar is himself (or close kin)," contends Duvall, "it seems plausible that Abner (or perhaps his eldest son) blackened up in order to collect his hog and deliver his warning in person without being recognized" (115).

Duvall immediately acknowledges "one logical and one textual" weakness to his proposal of a blacked-up Abner: "Harris would recognize such a ruse and would be immediately able to distinguish an artificial from an authentic black" (115). Nevertheless, and perhaps because the cultural mediation of race is his focus, Duvall misses the logical *and* textual objection to his thesis, the obvious reason why a blackened face would not have fooled Harris: that something other, that sign divorced from race, that Achilles' heel in terms of mimicry: Abner's "stiff and ruthless limp" (8). This alternative objection leaves Abner's secretive eldest son—presumably the Flem of Faulkner's subsequent fiction, but in "Barn Burning" the absolutely secret offspring who goes unnamed—as the sole candidate for the unknown African American (other than an unknown African American). What Faulkner no doubt intended, however, is the implantation of a fact that responsibly complicates racial issues by partaking of both conditional and absolute secrecy. From within the narrative, Abner inverts the structures of social power by withholding the truth behind this revealable secret. From outside the narrative, this retention becomes an absolute secret that displaces the use of conditional secrecy to attain such power—a displacement that reveals the reader's conditioning toward racial issues.

A tellingly empty communication, one that presages a dangerous change in attitudes, also comes into play in "The Battler." Bugs offers Ad some food, but "Ad did not answer. He was looking at Nick." Bugs repeats the offer—"I spoke to you, Mister Francis"—but "Ad kept on looking at Nick." Only now, within this insistent silence, does Nick feel "nervous." Ad now accuses Nick of abusing the economics of exchange. "Who the hell do you think you are?" he rails. "You're a snotty bastard. You come in here where nobody asks you and eat a man's food and when he asks to borrow a knife you get snotty" (101). In inviting Nick to join the camp,

Ad had gifted him an entrance to conviviality, yet the prizefighter, who spent his professional career in the so-called noble art of exchanging blows for money, cannot help but confuse gifting, or benevolence without return, with the redemption of extended credit. Self-interest has precipitously undercut altruism. "The commonly received view of special claims and duties arising out of special relations, though *prima facie* opposed to the impartial universality of the Utilitarian principle, is really maintained by a well-considered application of that principle," writes Sidgwick. "Morality is here in a manner protecting the normal channels and courses of natural benevolent affections; and the development of such affections is of the highest importance to human happiness, both as a direct source of pleasure, and as an indispensable preparation for a more enlarged 'altruism'" (*Methods* 439). "The Battler" illustrates how one genuine attitude can destabilize another. This confusing excess of motivational forces, which secrete as much as they reveal Ad's mental state, leaves Nick as dumbfounded as Faulkner's similarly shaken Harris.

Only after Bugs has revealed the conditional secret of "the cloth-wrapped blackjack" (102) in knocking out Ad without warning does he explain Ad's discreditable behavior. A conditional secret from Ad's past continues to influence his actions. Ad's supposed "sister" (102), who "looked enough like him to be twins" (103), had managed his career. During this period, however, the pair had married. Physical resemblance had supposedly precluded this alliance, and while the dubiousness of the relationship presumably contributed to the couple's eventual estrangement, Ad remains indebted to her financial management of his winnings. Bugs's revelation of this unresolved mystery complicates the economy of race that would normally have dominated his violent quieting of Ad. Bugs has revealed himself as not only the fourth battler in the story (after Nick, the brakeman, and Ad) but also Ad's partner in the economics of exchange. In benefitting from Ad's financial indebtedness, Bugs is his economic debtor, but in slaking Ad's annoyance, Bugs is his creditor—that credit prevents severer damage, either physical or lawful, to Ad than the future otherwise portends.

From Harris's point of view in "Barn Burning," Abner Snopes has slaked his annoyance through the impropriety of arson, an act of dissent Abner hopes to cloud in conditional secrecy, and without further personal evidence to offer the court, Harris must produce another witness. Harris hopes that Sarty is still innocent enough to respect the name of truth, and so reveal his father's conditional secret. When called to testify, Sarty wrestles with his conscience, but says nothing other than his whispered name. Faced with an otherwise silent, or secretive, minor in his court, the justice asks Harris incredulously, "Do you want me to question this boy?" (5). The moral definition of veracity seeds this question with complications. "For," as Sidgwick explains, "we may either require truth in the spoken words, or in the inferences which the speaker foresees will be drawn from them, or in both. Perfect Candour, no doubt, would require it in both." The unrealistic Harris invests his hopes in Sarty's candor. "The general utility of truth-speaking [is] so manifest as to need no proof," remarks Sidgwick, "but wherever this utility seems to be absent, or outweighed by particular bad consequences, we find that Common Sense at least hesitates to enforce the rule" (*Methods* 448), and Harris's conflict of responsibilities to the law, which he finally recognizes with a "violently, explosively" stated acquiescence to the justice's implicit expectation, falls in Abner's favor. Without an independent witness, the justice dismisses the case, but orders Abner to take his "wagon and get out of this country before dark" (5). The expectancy induced by the title of Faulkner's story is maintained, and the reader is free to speculate whether "Barn Burning" will reveal the currently inviolable secret about Harris's strange interlocutor, which the Snopeses hold in conditional secrecy. The tale immediately repays this speculation in kind. Displaced by the judge's sentence, Abner finds himself the tenant of Major de Spain, with whom he soon clashes.

"The moralist," notes Sidgwick, "is disposed to prescribe that indignation be directed always against acts, and not against persons; and if indignation so restricted would be efficient in repressing injuries, this would seem to be the state of mind most conducive to the general happiness" (*Methods* 449). Laws target actions, yet Abner Snopes believes that supposedly lawful judgments not only target individuals but indignantly do so in advance of any illegitimate acts. Nonetheless, while Abner certainly suffers under the warrantor–nonwarrantor dialectic, he remains a radically ambiguous participant in these relations. As Sarty's language acknowledges, his father is not insubstantial but substantially insubstantial: Abner exhibits "that impervious quality of something cut ruthlessly from tin, depthless, as though, sidewise to the sun, it would cast no shadow" (10); his presence is that of a "depthless" and "harsh silhouette" (14); he is both without depth and of a depth without bottom. From a capitalist perspective, Abner is a member of the lumpenproletariat; yet, this insubstantial component of that necessary lower order secretly speculates on speculation in a manner that costs his warrantors their ease. "It is doubtful whether average human nature is capable of maintaining [the] distinction" between act-directed and person-directed law enforcement, "and whether, if it could be maintained," as Sidgwick avers, "the more refined aversion would by itself be sufficiently efficacious." In consequence, "Common Sense hesitates to condemn personal ill-will against wrongdoers—even if it includes a desire of malevolent satisfaction" (*Methods* 449). That hesitation, as Abner's actions imply, can be exploited: unsatisfied by a judgment against him in favor of Major de Spain—a justice of the peace finds de Spain's tenant "responsible" (18) and "liable" (18) for the purposeful soiling of the major's one-hundred-dollar hall rug—Abner risks no gratuitous communication, whether in blackface or not, before taking his revenge. Worried about Sarty's conscience, Abner devises a safeguard against the boy's revelation of his father's plan to raze the major's barn, telling his wife to confine Sarty to their cabin. She tries to comply, but with his hopes for a settled life again disrupted, Sarty now accepts messenger responsibility: escaping his mother, he freely delivers (or gifts), in the name of "truth, justice" (8), a warning to the major.

Like "La fausse monnaie," therefore, a supposedly revealable secret empowers its holders in both "The Battler" and "Barn Burning," with each author's readers indebted to an equivocal sort of messenger. Unlike "La fausse monnaie," however, both Hemingway and Faulkner deepen this equivocation by investing their authorial gifts in the economics of alterity. Duvall argues that Faulkner's deployment of "figurative blackness is literally productive because it allows him a way to map imbricated relations between one form of otherness (racial) and other forms of otherness (gender/sexuality and class)." Figurative blackness, maintains Duvall, "allows Faulkner's readers to see that, whatever the residual racism of William Faulkner, his narratives negotiate racial struggle even when race seems absent from their field of vision; these narratives are, in other words, racialized in a way that enables a critical purchase on whiteness" ("Minstrel" 108). More fundamentally, however, the economy of secrecy rather than of race enables both Hemingway in "The Battler" and Faulkner in "Barn Burning" to map imbricated relations between multifarious forms of otherness.

Hemingway addresses this responsibility with Bugs's final openness, his responsible revelation of conditional secrets, blossoming into his temporary acceptance of the role of narrator: asking Nick questions and responding to Nick's unreported answers, Bugs temporarily erases not only Nick (in repeatedly referencing Hemingway's protagonist and assuming that character's unreported answers) but also the unnamed, heterodiegetic, and inviolably secret narrator:

> I can wake him up any time now, Mister Adams. If you don't mind I wish you'd sort of pull out. I don't like to not be hospitable, but it might disturb him back again to see you. I hate to have to thump him and it's the only thing to do when he gets started. I have to sort of keep him away from people. You don't mind, do you, Mister Adams? No, don't thank me, Mister Adams. I'd have warned you about him but he seemed to have taken such a liking to you and I thought things were going to be all right. You'll hit a town about two miles up the track. Mancelona they call it. Good-bye. I wish we could ask you to stay the night but it's just out of the question. Would you like to take some of that ham and some bread with you? No? You better take a sandwich. (103)

Faulkner addresses this responsibility with a combination of the permanently unrevealable secret of Harris's strange messenger and Sarty's revelation of the associated conditional secret. At once the strange man's debtor and creditor, was Harris (and, in turn, the reader) to have taken the relayed message as a warning or as an expression of inevitable intention? The secretive traces interwoven throughout the textual surface of "Barn Burning" pose this question and also imply that whatever the answer, the message from this stranger was a curious form of gift. Sarty's subsequent disclosure of a revealable secret, which structural and narratological analogies place alongside Bugs's rather than Nick's similar form of revelation, subtly intensifies the subtle differences between "The Battler" and "Barn Burning." Comparing the closing sentence of each story, sentences that bespeak the breaking of prohibitions through the responsible affranchisement of the self, confirms this slight but significant separation.

Nick, who "climbed the embankment and started up the track," cannot help "looking back from the mounting grade before the track curved into the hills," as he somewhat elliptically exits the narrative, to "see the fire light in the clearing" (104). Having seen the blaze of his father's revenge on de Spain burst against the night sky, with Abner's arson "blotting the stars," Sarty is "running again before he knew he had begun to run, stumbling, tripping over something and scrabbling up again without ceasing to run, looking backward over his shoulder at the glare as he got up, running on among the invisible trees" (24). His consternation spent, however, Sarty heads down into the enveloping prospect of "dark woods" (24) and

the stark conclusion to his story: "he did not look back" (25). Read pro-
leptically, two lines from Faulkner's "Carcassonne" (1926) effectively capture the figurative projection of Sarty as "a dying star upon the immensity
of darkness and of silence" (900) or as a perpetually moribund comet
heading "toward the blue precipice never gained" (895).[4] Sarty Snopes
faces (or looks forward to) ceaselessly approaching the inviolable secret of
revelation, an absolute mystery that forever keeps its distance through
imminence. The secret of this revelation, which is conditional to divine
responsibility, remains indict to humankind. In contrast, Hemingway's
Nick Adams prefers to go forward by looking backward, pursing his future
while avoiding the inviolable imminence of absolute revelation.

Firelight has enacted a double function in each tale—at once a beacon
of enlightenment for the protagonist and a radiant signal of obscurity for
the reader—but Hemingway supplements that enactment, so while the
futures for Nick and Sarty project beyond and through the frame of their
respective stories, these two projections diverge. On the one hand, "The
Battler" segues, significantly but almost without interruption, into the
vignette of Chapter VI from *In Our Time*. "This crossing unmistakably
signals the climax of *In Our Time*," as Philip Young observes: "X marks
the spot, as a short paragraph reveals that Nick is in the war, tells us that
he has been hit in the spine, and that he has made a 'separate peace' with
the enemy, [and] is no longer fighting the war for democracy" (14). Seen
in retrospect, "the firelight in the clearing" (104) at the end of "The
Battler" illuminates the narrative route into Nick's wartime experiences of
shooting (or firing), with the vignette revealing his physical trauma, his
psychological scarring, and the culminating enlightenment of his rite of
passage. Only thereafter, with his survival of adolescent death, can Nick
look "*straight ahead brilliantly*" (105; emphasis original). Nick's journey
in "The Battler," therefore, continues into Hemingway's canon. On the
other hand, Sarty's future after "Barn Burning" remains untold. Abner's
"niggard blaze[s]" during the American Civil War were "the living fruit of
nights passed during those four years in the woods hiding from all men,
blue or gray, with his strings of horses (captured horses, he called them)"
(7). The postbellum fires of the mercenary Abner offer no narrative illumination for his son, however, and Sarty appears nowhere else in Faulkner's
canon, because (presumably) Faulkner can learn nothing of that future.
The profit of "Barn Burning" and the privation of Sarty Snopes are indis-
soluble. This difference between potentially revealable and absolute

secrecy in the stories of Hemingway and Faulkner returns the critical focus to the inspiration provided by Baudelaire.

While the explicit narrative of Baudelaire's "La fausse monnaie" reveals a mendicant and the gifts of two benefactors, the implicit composition of his prose poem concerns receptive expectation and authorial (ir)responsibility. The reader is the author's other; textual expectancy inscribes that reader; and the author's gift confronts that expectation. Like Baudelaire's beggar, a credulous reader will accept any offering, but like Baudelaire's narrator, a scrupulous critic never dismisses all doubt. Alterity inscribes the downtrodden and the oppressed. Just as the imposition of alterity inscribed French beggars, so the enforcement of otherness inscribed African Americans, and while the prodigal gift presented in "La fausse monnaie" remains in doubt, the gifts of Baudelaire, Faulkner, and Hemingway remain no secret, with Baudelaire's American heirs assuming his bequest of a mystifying alterity. Faulkner and Hemingway "had to have, were made to have," as Kermode writes in *Pleasure and Change: The Aesthetics of Canon* (2004) of the process of aesthetic influence, surrender, and incorporation, "something of the exemplary modernity of Baudelaire, who said that the unique and supreme pleasure of love lies in the certainty of doing ill" (46–47). The ecstasy aroused by such antitheses, however, to repeat Lewisohn, "must not be adjudged as a black crime" (154). Taken together, then, these responsible authors, as their ethically accountable art attests, never took their readers for granted. What remains in doubt (or somewhat secretive) are the specifics that differentiate between these authors' perspectives on otherness, authorial (ir)responsibility, and revealable and absolute secrecy.

Derrida's thoughts concerning messianicism (or the messianism of theology) and the messianic proper (or the messianism of atheology) help to articulate these distinctions. Messianicism, as Derrida elucidates in "Faith and Knowledge," looks forward to the messiah's advent as a foreseeable occurrence. In contrast, remaining inviolably secret in its irreducibility to actual presence, the messianic proper is "*messianicity without messianism.*" This eschatological perspective envisions messianicity as "*the opening to the future or to the coming of the other as the advent of justice, but without horizon of expectation and without prophetic prefiguration*" (56; emphasis original). The secrets of Sarty (or Colonel Sartoris) Snopes, as absolute and conditional secrets that authorize and censure (as Nick Adam does with his "separate peace") a democracy to come, propel this figure beyond the frame of his particular tale and toward an infinitely unrealizable hope, a future (unlike Nick Adam's own) without horizon, as his canonical non-reappearance silently implies. "Breaking with the present," explains Segal, "the secret (and with it the gift and literature) testifies to such a radical future, as do the groundless and ad infinitum hypotheses to which the secret gives rise about the literary text, hypotheses never to be verified or falsified in any present" (193). Segal turns to John D. Caputo to corroborate this interpretation of Derridean thinking. "The 'messianic secret' is, there is no secret and the Messiah is never going to show up," states Caputo. "Derrida's secret is not some hyperousiological high he has had and that he now whispers in our ear. Far from it. To be 'in on the secret' does not mean you know anything, that you are 'in the know'—but rather in the 'no,' *non-savoir*" (102). In fine, as Derrida concludes, "*the messianic exposes itself to absolute surprise and, even if it always takes the phenomenal form of peace or of justice, it ought, exposing itself so abstractly, be prepared (waiting without awaiting itself) for the best as for the worst, the one never coming without opening the possibility of the other*" ("Faith and Knowledge" 56; emphasis original). What remains at issue, therefore, is the structure of experience.

The profound emanations of literature, which paradoxically lie on the surface of its texture, are depthless arrivals that at once speak of this general structure and gesture toward an unrealizable future. Baudelaire's "La fausse monnaie," which overtly considers secrecy and voluntary donation, is noticeably immanent, with the messianic proper, the ever-presently democratic, as a necessity of its own critical standing. "The Battler" and "Barn Burning" testify to comparable considerations of secrecy and voluntary donation by two of Baudelaire's keenest American admirers, but while the messianicism of the omissive Hemingway echoes that of the influential Baudelaire, the messianic proper of the inclusive Faulkner echoes that influence more secretively. In continuing Baudelaire's legacy, each author employs conditional secrets to fight the power of conditional secrecy, but the Faulkner of "Barn Burning" is more responsible (if only marginally) than the Hemingway of "The Battler" is in handling the irresponsibility of authorship. Faulkner's greater consciousness of freedom and concomitant responsibility increases the overall effectiveness of his tale, making his call on inviolable secrecy, his call to displace the use of revealable secrecy to command interpretation, the more democratic of the two stories.

Notes

1. "Besides these primary texts," as Shakespeare notes, "Hemingway also owned one biography (Edwin Morgan's *Flower of Evil: A Life of Charles Baudelaire*) and two books containing T. S. Eliot's essay 'Baudelaire'" (238).
2. Williams further argues that Faulkner readily reworked "La chambre double" from *Le Spleen de Paris* into "A Rose for Emily" (1930).
3. Joseph Blotner outlines both sides of the case concerning Faulkner and ECT. In November 1952, Faulkner "was admitted to the Westhill Sanitarium, a private hospital located on a well-cared-for estate at Riverdale in the Bronx." The psychoanalyst Eric P. Mosse was responsible for Faulkner's care. Mosse "specialized in the treatment of artists and he was particularly anxious to attend Faulkner because he admired his work. Diagnosing his illness as the result of drinking and depression, he advised electroshock therapy." Indeed, Mosse attested that he was responsible for "administer[ing] a series of these treatments—perhaps six in all." Nonetheless, Faulkner's daughter Jill maintained, as Blotner reports, "that she had never had any indication that her father had undergone electroshock and that she doubted that he had" (*A Biography. One-Volume Edition* 563). The answer to this contentious point remains an inviolable secret. In contrast, the revelation of Hemingway's recourse to ECT, as Edward Shorter and David Healy recount, occurred immediately after his death. "*Time* magazine exposed the story of his depression and his shock treatment at the Mayo Clinic in its obituary on July 14, 1961." This disclosure "debunked his wife's claim that the death was accidental" (155) instead of suicide.
4. Faulkner wrote "Carcassonne" not much earlier than 1926 and not much later than June 1931. "Blotner for one," notes Hans H. Skei in *Reading Faulkner's Best Short Stories* (1999), "assumes that 'Carcassonne' was written in the first months of 1926," and Skei thinks that Blotner's supposition (*Biography* 1:501–12), is "very reasonable" (69).

CHAPTER 3

Benevolence (I): *Light in August*

"Especially in modern times, since the revival of independent ethical speculation," observes Henry Sidgwick in *The Methods of Ethics*, "there have always been thinkers who have maintained, in some form, the view that Benevolence is a supreme and architectonic virtue, comprehending and summing up all the others, and fitted to regulate them and determine their proper limits and mutual relations" (238). Notwithstanding this insistence, "it might indeed be plausibly objected," as Sidgwick concedes, "that under the notions of Generosity, Self-sacrifice, etc., Common Sense praises (though it does not prescribe as obligatory) a suppression of egoism beyond what Utilitarianism approves: for we perhaps admire as virtuous a man who gives up his own happiness for another's sake, even when the happiness that he confers is clearly less than that which he resigns" (431–32). Yet, "even if there be a loss in the particular case, still our admiration of self-sacrifice will admit of a certain Utilitarian justification," as Sidgwick maintains, "because such conduct shows a disposition far above the average in its general tendency to promote happiness, and it is perhaps this disposition that we admire rather than the particular act" (432).

In "Faith and Knowledge: The Two Sources of 'Religion' at the Limits of Reason Alone," Derrida remarks how this dispositional excess conforms to "the ellipsis of sacrifice," with such benevolence invoking the double bind of "the law of the unscathed." Under this edict, "the humble respect of that which is sacrosanct (*heilig*, holy) *both requires and excludes* sacrifice, which is to say, the indemnification of the unscathed, the price of

© The Author(s), under exclusive license to Springer Nature Switzerland AG 2021
M. Wainwright, *Faulkner's Ethics*,
https://doi.org/10.1007/978-3-030-68872-1_3

immunity." When Immanuel Kant "speaks of the 'holiness' of the moral law," as Derrida notes, "it is while explicitly holding a discourse on 'sacrifice,' which is to say, on another instantiation of religion 'within the limits of reason *alone*': the Christian religion as the only 'moral' religion. Self-sacrifice thus sacrifices the most proper in the service of the most proper. As though *pure* reason, in a process of auto-immune indemnification, could only oppose religion as such to a religion or *pure* faith to this or that belief" (88; emphasis original). Sidgwick effectively identifies the source of this danger. "If one conceives the dictating Reason—whatever its dictates may be—as external to oneself, the cognition of rightness is accompanied by a sentiment of Reverence for Authority; which may by some be conceived impersonally, but is more commonly regarded as the authority of a supreme Person, so that the sentiment blends with the affections normally excited by persons in different relations, and becomes Religious" (*Methods* 39).

As philosophical successors to Kant, both Sidgwick and Derrida resisted the externalization of reasonableness, with each of them expressing a religious skepticism that nevertheless appreciated the relentless prospect of religion. "It is not necessary, if we are simply considering Ethics as a possible independent science, to throw the fundamental premiss of which we are now examining the validity into a Theistic form," avers Sidgwick. "Nor does it seem always to have taken that form in the support which Positive Religion has given to Morality" (*Methods* 507 n.1). The support of negative theology may be more to the point. Derrida would have agreed. Religious promise emerges from what he identifies in "Faith and Knowledge" as the bond between "the value of life" and "the theological machine" (87). The negative component of this machine provides discursive evidence of that alliance. In consequence, as Derrida writes in *On the Name*, "I trust no text that is not in some way contaminated with negative theology" (69). William Faulkner's *Light in August* (1932), with its fundamental relation of kenosis, in which the supremely benevolent Joe Christmas offers his body as living sacrifice, is one such trustworthy text. "Is there *one* negative theology, *the* negative theology?" (73; emphasis original) muses Derrida at the outset of "How to Avoid Speaking: Denials" (1981). His answer, which the following discussion of Faulkner's novel accepts in advance, is negative, and Derrida's further rhetorical question— "who has ever assumed the project of *the* negative theology *as such*, reclaiming it in the singular under this name, without subjugating and subordinating it, without at least pluralizing it?" (131 n.1)—is true of Faulkner's implicit assumption of negative theology in *Light in August.*

BENEVOLENCE (I): *LIGHT IN AUGUST*

No morality ever existed which did not consider ulterior consequences to some extent. Prudence or Forethought has commonly been reckoned a virtue: and all modern lists of Virtues have included Rational Benevolence, which aims at the happiness of other human beings generally, and therefore necessarily takes into consideration even remote effects of actions. (Henry Sidgwick, *The Methods of Ethics*, 96)

As the previous chapter illustrates, a consideration of William Faulkner's fiction under the spotlight of Jacques Derrida's philosophy is neither arbitrary nor illegitimate: related characteristics, common inclinations, and allied paths emerge from this process. Indeed, privileging the convergences between Faulkner's literature and Derrida's philosophy is a necessary task because these intersections inform and ultimately extend our understanding of what Derrida calls "a certain 'extremity'" ("Faith and Knowledge" 94). This particular limit concerns the developmental failure of the critique of violence, and the consequence of that failure, as Ihab Hassan argues in his Faulknerian meditations on "The Privations of Postmodernism" (2002), necessitates "the self-undoing of our knowledge" (5), a critical and exacting release from epistemological assumptions via the positive contaminations of negative theology.

"In negative theology," as John D. Caputo explains, "one can only make 'apophatic'—meaning negation or denial—assertions: one can only say what God is *not*. Apophatic is opposed to 'kataphatic' or affirmative discourse" (342 n.1; emphasis original). Although Derrida rarely cites Faulkner explicitly, preferring to discuss Faulkner's contemporary James Joyce, he brings the two modernists together on one occasion and in a discourse replete with apophatic constructs. "A writer cannot not be concerned, interested, anxious about the past, that of literature, history, or philosophy, of culture in general," he asserts in "This Strange Institution Called Literature: An Interview with Jacques Derrida" (1989). "S/he cannot not take account of it in some way and not consider her- or himself a responsible heir, inscribed in a genealogy." According to this stipulation, the accolade of conscientious inheritor "is as valid for Joyce, that immense allegory of historical memory, as for Faulkner, who doesn't write in such a way that he gathers together at every sentence, and in several languages at once, the whole of Western culture" (55).

Derrida would have appreciated the theological strands responsibly woven into *Light in August* (1932), but literary critics of a religious inclination have traditionally discussed this novel from a kataphatic perspective. They make specific reference to Faulkner's compositional template from the New Testament.[1] "Faulkner paralleled the twenty-one chapters of *Light in August*," states Virginia V. Hlavsa in "The Crucifixion in *Light in August*" (1991), "with the twenty-one chapters of the St. John Gospel" (127). This correspondence posits a double affirmation through open antithesis. On the one hand, the Word is metaphysical: "In the beginning was the Word, and the Word was with God, and the Word was God" (1.1). On the other hand, the Word is incarnate: "the Word became flesh and dwelt among us" (1.14). These Johannine contradictions support not only what Derrideans would describe as the "deconstructive tendencies" of Faulkner's novel but also the kataphatic aspects of its prolegomenon. In the first instance, as David R. Law notes in *Kierkegaard's Kenotic Christology* (2013), "the Logos has on entering human existence relinquished, divested, 'emptied' himself of his divine attributes" (22); simply put, that emptying has renounced the transcendence of the Word. In the second instance, a tireless positivity emanates from the figure of Lena Grove.

Pregnant, and approaching her term, Lena represents fullness, plenitude, the filling of that which was vacant, that which has environed her teenage years. Orphaned at the age of twelve, Lena had gone to live with her brother McKinley at Doane's Mill, Alabama, but this arrangement was no act of familial benevolence. "Twenty years her senior," McKinley "lived in a four room and unpainted house with his labor- and child-ridden wife," and during her time with them, "Lena did all the housework and took care of the other children." Doane's Mill was a site of arboreal denudation (or emptying). The mill had been "there seven years and in seven years more it would destroy all the timber within its reach," and the people conducting this denudation, as "hookwormridden" individuals, are themselves being emptied from within. Their settlement is officially nameless—"the hamlet which at its best day had borne no name listed on Postoffice Department annals"—and once all the timber has been removed, the site "would not [...] even be remembered" by its erstwhile occupants (402). Lena, as a "reserve of patient and steadfast fidelity," who lives in "unflagging and tranquil faith" (403), always stands out against this unnamed, unlisted, unremembered, and thus apophatic backdrop.

Falling pregnant in her early twenties, Lena leaves Doane's Mill in search of Lucas Burch (the father of her unborn child), doing so as a figure of positive plenitude. By the time she enters Jefferson, Yoknapatawpha County, Mississippi, some weeks later, carrying her "palm leaf fan" (403, 405), Lena has also acquired notable Christian associations: celebrants waved palm branches during Jesus's triumphal entry into Jerusalem, and the palm leaf of the victorious martyr soon graced Christian iconography. "Jesus performed two dramatic actions upon his final entry into Jerusalem," explains Mark E. Moore. "These are popularly named 'The Triumphal Entry' and 'The Cleansing of the Temple'" (45). In Lena's case, while entering Lucas's current hometown ensures a modest triumph, her practiced housekeeping promises a post-scriptum arrival, one that follows the moral emptying encapsulated by the main portion of the novel. As the prolegomenous standard bearer of kataphatic theology, whose figurative status finds structural support from the template of St. John's Gospel, however, the realization of this positive bookending has tended to obscure the apophatic strains that affirmatively infect the interstitial majority of Faulkner's novel.

Significantly, and in keeping with Johannine ambivalence, St. John's Gospel prefigures this positive contamination. "The Pharisees," on witnessing Jesus's arrival on Palm Sunday, "said to one another, 'You see that you can do nothing; look, the world has gone after him'" (12.19). With the phrase, *gone after him*, as R. C. H. Lenski explains in his seminal *The Interpretation of St. John's Gospel 11–21* (1942), "the Pharisees mean 'away from us,' and thus 'behind' or 'after him,' indicating the gulf between him and them." What Lenski calls "this dark background of hate," which foreshadows Jesus's crucifixion, "makes the whole spectacle on Palm Sunday dramatic in the highest degree: and this the more when we realize that all this murderous hate was perfectly known to Jesus, and that in the very face of it he followed his sure course" (858). That undoubted route was certain to end in benevolent self-sacrifice. "It would seem that, according to the common view of 'good,'" observes Henry Sidgwick in *The Methods of Ethics*, "there are occasions in which an individual's sacrifice of his own good on the whole, according to the most rational conception of it that he can form, would apparently realise greater good for others. Whether, indeed, such a sacrifice is ever really required, and whether, if so, it is truly reasonable for the individual to sacrifice his own good on the whole, are among the profoundest questions of ethics" (109 n.1).

The standard bearer of apophatic theology in *Light in August*, the figure who negotiates this ethical conundrum, is the character who shares Jesus Christ's initials and whose surname subsumes that of Christ: Joe Christmas. For Derrida, the relentless prospect of religion exists in what he identifies as the bond between "the value of life" and "the theological machine" ("Faith and Knowledge" 87), with negative theology providing discursive evidence of this alliance; consequently, he "trust[s] no text that is not in some way contaminated with negative theology" (*On the Name* 69). Faulkner's *Light in August*, with its fundamental relation of kenosis, in which the supremely benevolent Joe Christmas offers his body as living sacrifice, is one such trustworthy text. The negative theological strands that Christmas weaves, which draw on the unlimited reserve of impenetrable secrecy that envelops his racial origins as an absolute secret that Faulkner tells rather than reveals, create a powerful discourse on the sacrificial art of extreme benevolence.

"Whatever may have been the state of his soul," writes John Sykes of William Faulkner, "he was in no more than a token way a Christian 'insider'" (44). This supposed outsider was actually a layman of Presbyterian persuasion. "While generally alienated from religious institutions," as Robert L. Johnson chronicles, "Faulkner had a fairly intimate involvement with the churches of Oxford and the Presbyterians in particular" (68)—Johnson refers to the "two Presbyterian churches in Oxford" (68) of Faulkner's lifetime—and he spoke of that involvement during his spell as Writer in Residence at the University of Virginia (1957–58). "The Christian legend is part of any Christian's background, especially the background of a country boy, a Southern country boy," he remarked to "Visitors from Virginia Colleges" (15 April 1957). "My life was passed, my childhood, in a very small Mississippi town, and that was part of my background. I grew up with that. I assimilated that, took that in without even knowing it" (86).

Alfred Kazin describes Faulkner's "South as the most churchly region in the country, one historically obsessed with the elements of blood, pain, and sacrifice in the Christian story," a region standing in strong contrast to New England, which "turned everything into a cult of bland benevolence" (18). In agreement with this description, the Christian elements in the Faulknerian canon, including the benevolence of self-sacrifice, are rarely bland, unless by specific design, and Faulkner's preference for the Old Testament over the New supported his customary stance. On 11 March 1957, with students on the "Undergraduate Course in

Contemporary Literature," Faulkner was asked to list his favorite reading. "I read the Old Testament," he replied. "I read some of Dickens every year, and I've got a portable Shakespeare, one-volume Shakespeare, that I carry along with me" (50). On 16 May 1957, at a session with "Law School Wives," a member of the audience asked "why the New Testament didn't have as much to offer" as its precursor did? Faulkner stated that while the "New Testament is full of ideas," the "Old Testament is full of people, perfectly ordinary normal heroes and blackguards just like everybody else nowadays" (167). Faulkner reiterated the second part of this judgment before the "University and Community Public" (23 May 1958), in his final session at the University of Virginia, stating that he "like[d] all of it" (285), with its depiction of "scoundrels and blackguards," people "doing the best they could, just like people do now" (286).

As the introduction to the present volume relates, Faulkner was reluctant to read philosophy, but despite this disposition, his public pronouncements occasionally resonated with the writings of Søren Kierkegaard. The two men certainly shared a fondness for the Old Testament, as well as for Shakespeare, and Kierkegaard also declared an aversion toward blandness. "The pseudonymous author of the first volume of *Either/Or*," as George C. Bedell relates of Kierkegaard's inaugural publication, "tells in a memorable way what has happened to the modern world because of its tendency toward reflection" (16). It is for others to "complain that the age is wicked," expatiates this thinly veiled narrator, "my complaint is that it is wretched, for it lacks passion." In consequence, "my soul always turns back to the Old Testament and to Shakespeare." The characters "who speak there are at least human beings: they hate, they love, they murder their enemies, and curse their descendants throughout all generations, they sin" (1:22).

As a layman, Faulkner appreciated the gaps and vacancies in his own understanding of the numinous; "apophatic theology," as F. L. Cross and E. A. Livingstone explain, "can be seen as an assertion of the inadequacy of human understanding in matters Divine, and therefore a corrective within theology" (88), and Faulkner, unconsciously interweaving his regard for St. Augustine (354–430) with his interest in Jeremy Taylor (1613–67), was intuitively receptive to apophasis. "Faulkner would not have had to study the bishop of Hippo's works to have absorbed or understood the implications of his view," argues Seemee Ali, because "Augustine's vision is difficult to miss, whether one discovers it in the poetics of William Blake ('my senses discover'd the infinite in everything') or the intensely subjective encounter with being that marks the novel as a genre, from *Don Quixote* onwards" (297). Yet, Faulkner would eventually read R. H. Barrow's *Introduction to St Augustine:* The City of God (1950), and he would find much in Barrow's account that chimed with his own long-term reception of Taylor's *ars moriendi*. For, when convalescing from alcoholic poisoning in later life, as Joseph Blotner relates, Faulkner had "on the night table [...] his standard hospital reading," which included the Bible and Taylor's *Holy Living and Dying* (*Faulkner* 1:698). Indeed, as the Shakespeare of Divines, Taylor was particularly sobering. Taylor was "a lifelong favorite" (11), confirms Blotner in *William Faulkner's Library* (1964), and Faulkner would come to own three of Taylor's works: *The Rule and Exercises of Holy Living* (1650), *The Rule and Exercises of Holy Dying* (1651), and *Holy Living and Dying* (1656) (73–74).[2] If "Faulkner intuits the complexity that Augustine articulates" (298), as Ali believes, then his appreciation of Taylor's *ars moriendi* must not be overlooked.

Taylor is usually associated with a sacerdotal form of piety. "The primitive church in her discipline used to thrust their delinquent clergy *in laicam communionem*, even then when their faults were but small, and of less reproach than to deserve greater censures," observes Taylor in "Sermon X. The Minister's Duty in Life and Doctrine" (1672); "yet they lessened them by thrusting them 'into the lay communion,' as most fit for such ministers who refused to live at the height of sacerdotal piety" (517). Henry Trevor Hughes enumerates the advantages and disadvantages that attend this pietism. The strength of sacerdotal piety "lies in its historic appeal, its attraction for the sensuous imagination and its skill in enlisting all the arts in worship"—the Shakespeare of Divines hereby beguiled Faulkner's artistic sensibilities—and "it has, as its crowning act of worship, the Holy Eucharist." The weakness of this form of dutifulness "lies in its tendency to pride, exclusiveness and rigidity; it may become the champion of the reactionary and of effete authority, and the foe of spiritual progress, civil and religious freedom and political reform. Christ's yoke may be made difficult and His burden heavy" (155). This type of piety is a load to be carried, not a support on which to rely, and Faulkner undoubtedly relates something of this burden in *Light in August*.

Occasionally, however, Taylor also exhibits a mystical form of piety, and his exhortation to imitate Christ recalls that of Thomas à Kempis, the medieval Christian mystic whose writings remained influential throughout the seventeenth century. Although the calls from Taylor and Kempis are of different orders, Taylor's demand follows, at least in part, the mystic path set down by his antecedent. "Following the classical mystical stages of purgation, illumination, and union," as Timothy F. Sedgwick relates, "Kempis effects the interior life of holy intention through meditations and ejaculatory prayers" (213). The strength of mystical piety lies in "sav[ing] men from narrowness and sectarianism," explains Hughes; "it shows them the gleamings of the divine in what might be considered common and unclean" (156), but the "weakness" of this form of dutifulness, as R. H. Coats remarks, "is that it blurs the Christian outline and empties the historical revelation of its positive content" (248). In contrast, when Taylor "assumes the mystical way," as Sedgwick notes, "his meditations and prayers are given by way of the biblical narrative, from annunciation and baptism to crucifixion and resurrection" (213), ensuring that faith does not degenerate into religiosity.

In sum, *Light in August*, or, to put it the other way around, the Augustine light, lightly resonates with a mystical as well as a sacerdotal approach to apophasis. This double resonance helps to articulate the figure of Joe Christmas, who makes his narrative entrance in a "shed" (421), as Christ did, an introduction that Faulkner's heterodiegetic narrator fills with negative constructs: there is something about or without Joe: "there was something definitely rootless about him, as though *no* town *nor* city was his, *no* street, *no* walls, *no* square of earth his home" (421; emphasis added). As the Derrida of "Faith and Knowledge" might remark, and as various expressions of a particular pejorative throughout Faulkner's novel imply, Christmas manifests *"religion as phenomenology, enigma of the Orient, of the Levant and of the Mediterranean"* (46; emphasis original). For, while Lucas Burch's epithet for his coeval is "durn yellowbellied wop" (602), another of Christmas's acquaintances reveals that she too "thought maybe you were just another wop" (564). Christmas, then, as the leading figure of negative theology in the novel, figures a sort of apophatic boldness, an inconsistent insistence that goes beyond societal norms. "That is one of the essential traits of all negative theology," as Derrida notes: "passing to the limit, then crossing a frontier, including that of a community, thus of a sociopolitical, institutional, ecclesial reason or raison d'être" (*On the Name* 36), and "the language of adamantine resistance" (7) that Hassan's postmodern hermeneutic identifies in Faulkner's nonfiction—in collections such as the posthumously published *Essays, Speeches and Public Letters* (1965) and *Lion in the Garden* (1968)—reveals its hushed counterpart in *Light in August*, which speaks of God through the stentorious but practically voiceless voice, the Derridean *"voix blanche"* (*On the Name*

35), or benevolently self-sacrificing articulation, of the racially indeterminable Joe Christmas.

"*Light* (phos), *wherever this* (arché) *commands or begins discourse,*" as in the paratextual initiative taken by the title of Faulkner's novel, signals " *'the very notion of "god,"'*" as Derrida notes, *"'of which the "proper meaning" is "luminous" and "celestial"'*" ("Faith and Knowledge" 46; emphasis original). All the major characters in *Light in August* appear under the perplexing shadow thrown by this paratextual light, the numinous-luminous light of God, the troubling radiance that Joanna Burden's burning home will replicate, an impassioning symbol that cannot help but orient each and every figure, and none more so than Joe Christmas: the man who appears to flee its celestial radiance; a dissident, a heretic, a scapegoat—the sort of *pharmakos* Derrida discusses during his reading of "Plato's Pharmacy" in *Dissemination* (1981)—a man to be shunned, excluded, even sacrificed; a figure, like Jesus Christ, of ineradicable passion. Having read James George Frazer's *The Golden Bough* (1890, 1911–15), which dedicates chapters to the mystic origins of "Public Scapegoats" and to "Human Scapegoats in Classical Antiquity," Faulkner appreciated not only the cultural provenance of scapegoating but also how a society extirpates a pharmakos for rupturing social conventions or for somehow mooting such dehiscence.[3] Extirpation of a pharmakos appears to offer the community indemnification. Christmas's aversion to the culture that circumscribes, then expulses, and finally scapegoats him, a culture of depravity that his feelings do not exaggerate, is hardly surprising. At the same time, however, this rent, rip, or tear (whether actual or imagined) lets in light. This "dissident uprooting can claim to fulfill the vocation or the promise of Christianity in its most historic essence; thereby it responds," as Derrida argues, "to the call and to the gift of Christ, as it would resonate everywhere, in the ages of ages, rendering itself responsible for testifying before him, that is, before God" (*On the Name* 72). The pharmakos, perfectly aware of communal feelings yet personifying the benevolence of self-sacrifice, offers the luminousness of enlightenment.

Kenosis, as a major expression of this gift, concerns one side of the Johannine affirmation of the Word in particular. "What Christian thinkers from St. Paul to Kierkegaard have emphasized," explains Richard H. King in "World-Rejection in Faulkner's Fiction" (1991), is that "the doctrine of incarnation was a scandal to the Greeks, an offense to the Jews, and a paradox to believers" (67). In *The Gift of Death* (1995), as Deborah Madden and David Towsey aver, "Derrida is still following the contour of [this] difficulty" (398), which he first mapped in "Violence and Metaphysics" (1964). A term from Christian theology, kenosis actually derives from the New Testament, when St. Paul states in *Romans* that a Christian life, as spiritual endeavor, demands the ultimate act of benevolence: offering one's body as living sacrifice. As discussed in the introduction to the present volume, Kierkegaard and Derrida identify the troubling nature of the compact between Abraham and God, and that disturbing bond finds a parallel in the covenant between Jesus and the people of God. In his *Letter to the Philippians*, also from the New Testament, St. Paul elaborates on this sacrificial aspect of Christ: "Jesus, who, though he was in the form of God, did not count equality with God a thing to be grasped, but emptied himself, taking the form of a servant, being born in the likeness of men" (2.5–7).

Notwithstanding his biblical preference for the Old Testament, Faulkner's knowledge of the New Testament, as Hlavsa's essay on *Light in August* confirms, was thorough. Faulkner's full remark to the "Law School Wives"—"the New Testament is full of ideas and I don't know much about ideas" (167)—does not undercut this confirmation—knowing self-deprecation was one of the author's common tactics in public pronouncements. Indeed, he had recently returned to the New Testament in constructing *A Fable* (1954), usage that has drawn much critical fire. David L. Minter's complaint is typical: "*A Fable*'s basic affinity as well as much of its obtrusive framework lay with the New Testament," and this doubly unfortunate reliance signaled its author's loss of aesthetic power with "his move toward a fiction of ideas" (228). While the eighth chapter of *Faulkner's Ethics* reconsiders such complaints, present purposes contend that the New Testament framework of *Light in August* does not distend its kenotic contours.

As Madden and Towsey relate, the Pauline perspective on the mind of Christ posits "the contradiction of a power which is found in its own *kenotic* humbling" (407), a selfless act, which places Christ alongside members of the lowest earthly caste and which thereby indicts *superbia*. The "lust for domination," expatiates Barrow, "is a form of pride (*superbia*)—that sin from which St Augustine derives all others and which means the self-assertion of the individual." St. Augustine makes this "point quite clearly in the *de doctrina Christiana* [1.23] where he says that 'it is inherent in the sinful mind to crave for ever greater power over men and to claim as his right the obedience which is due to God alone in His right … When he strives after the domination of those who are by nature his equals, that is his fellow-men, he is guilty of insufferable pride'" (230). Augustine's interpretation of kenosis "is not strictly synonymous with a sin–grace model," as Matthew Drever emphasizes, but that understanding "is consistent with [his] wider contention that immutability–mutability constitutes the core difference between God and humanity" (76).

In *Holy Living and Dying*, Faulkner would have read Taylor's variation on St. Augustine's approach to kenosis—"he emptied himself of all his glories, took on him the form of a servant, in all things being made like unto us" (313)—and in *Light in August*, Christmas inherits the trait of humbling resemblance from his maternal grandparents. The "fanatical" Eupheus Hines and his placid wife are peripheral outcasts (or pharmakoi) who bear a resemblance to their neighbors: "the town looked upon them both as being a little touched—lonely, gray in color, a little smaller than most other men and women, *as if they belonged to a different race, species*" (651; emphasis added). In turn, their grandson will inhabit a pharmakonic mantle, but in his case, one akin to Christ's own: "though he was in the form of God" (2.6), to appropriate St. Paul from his *Letter to the Philippians*, "he humbled himself and became obedient to the point of death" (2.8). This obedience to unconditional benevolence—munificence that is unbidden—puts others before oneself. "For though doubtless a man may often best promote his own happiness by labouring and abstaining for the sake of others," as Sidgwick remarks, "it seems to be implied in our common notion of self-sacrifice that actions most conducive to the general happiness do not—in this world at least—always tend also to the greatest happiness of the agent" (*Methods* 9–10).

The kenotic act demands self-emptying, with the broader aspects of this imperative covering what Alex Dubilet calls "the rich and varied traditions of *imitatio Christi*" (27). Simply put, as Sedgwick affirms, "Christ is the great exemplar" (211), a divine presence that unreservedly discharges its divine quality. This disregard for preeminence, which "characterizes the nature of the transition between divinity and humanity" (11), served the practical and monastic forms of kenosis, which go "back to the exemplary lives of Anthony the Great and the Desert Fathers" (27). In *Outlines of the History of Ethics* (1886), Sidgwick traces these influences, starting with the example set by the Desert Fathers. "By strict seclusion and celibacy, severe simplicity of food and raiment, by fasting, prayer, and perpetual self-examination, by rigid regulation of all hours of work and leisure—sometimes by the wild extravagances of self-mortification of which Simeon Stylites is the popular example—the Eastern monk sought to strip off the soiled and clinging garment of carnal desires and worldly cares, and to fit himself for a purer and closer walk with God than the life of the world would allow" (128). Suppliants during this period dedicated themselves to self-examination, self-isolation, and self-emptying.

"Afterwards it became the accepted view that most of those who aspired after this more perfect way needed the support and control of an ordered community of persons with similar aspirations: thus when in the 4th century monasticism began to spread in Western Christendom," continues Sidgwick in *Outlines of the History of Ethics*, "the ideal of life which it generally commended was the life of the cloister" (128). Sidgwick identifies Augustine's "impressive ethical influence" as the developmental complement to this ideal. Augustine clarified "the relation between human and divine agency in Christian good conduct" (129). He reconciled "the freedom of the will" with "man's incapacity to obey God's law by his unaided moral energy" (131). This reconciliation resulted from a rational self-denial that promoted a love of God. "Faith and love are mutually involved and inseparable," explains Sidgwick; "faith springs from the divinely imparted germ of love, which in its turn is developed by faith to its full strength, while from both united springs hope, joyful yearning towards ultimate perfect fruition of the object of love. These three Augustine (after St. Paul) regards as the three essential elements of Christian virtue" (131). Augustine still recognizes "the old fourfold division of virtue into prudence, temperance, courage, and justice, according to their traditional interpretation; but he explains these virtues to be in their deepest and truest natures only the same love to God in different aspects or exercises" (131–32), and the ultimate expression of that devotion is kenosis.

This understanding of kenosis remained largely unaltered until the middle of the nineteenth century. "Throughout most of the Church's life," writes David Brown, "the 'self-emptying' or 'abasement' of God in Christ has been explained in terms of divine association with human lowliness rather than as entailing any real change to the divine nature itself" (1). Scholasticism dominated medieval ethics, but faded during the fourteenth and fifteenth centuries, when a quasi-legal treatment of morality came to the fore. This approach faded too, however, with Jeremy Taylor leading what Sidgwick calls in *Outlines of the History of Ethics* a renewed attempt "to find an independent philosophical basis for the moral code" (156). Only thereafter, as Brown observes, did the understanding of kenosis demonstrably shift, "partly thanks to the rise of biblical criticism, partly because of the new interest in human psychology, and partly because of explorations of new options in philosophy (principally Hegelianism)" (1). Owing to this conceptual transition, "the divine nature is now seen to be committed in the incarnation not merely to a symbolic drawing alongside humanity but also to an actual ontological entering into the human condition, with some real change in divinity itself" (1–2). In conclusion, therefore, "the problematic of self-emptying," as Dubilet emphasizes, "must not be interpreted as restricted exclusively to a theological or a philosophical domain, nor should it be seen as localizable exclusively within a premodern or a modern textual site" (12).

In his own small way, Faulkner contributed Joe Christmas to this evolving problematic. Christmas is a pharmakos who will be excluded and sacrificed, another kenotic figure of passion, another Christly imitation, and Faulkner's literature and Derrida's philosophy hereby meet in the spiritual sense that Hassan associates with Faulkner himself, whose "spiritual attitude" was "deeply acquainted with kenosis" (5).[4] This sort of acquaintance, to appropriate Dubilet, "is connected to the moral, spiritual, and theological need to reverse the human state of fallenness." For, "to rid oneself of the self is to attain once more a oneness with God." In this manner, "the more general movements of self-abnegation before God, of humility, and of spiritual poverty all contain what could be called a kenotic core" (27). The double nature of Christ centers on kenosis, and Christmas's miscegenate status in *Light in August*, a form of racial branding to which he is subjected and to which he sometimes acquiesces, is surely no coincidence: Joe the non-American American complements Christ the divine (or nonhuman) human. The ethics of kenosis anticipates the dismantling of subjectivity, the undoing of introjection, and this precedence helps to shed a critical light on Faulkner's novel. That acclaimed (or august) light reveals how the author problematizes the kenotic, with Christmas repeatedly manifesting the self-emptying effected by kenosis, as a call to detachment, to dispossession, and to nothingness, a call that denies interpellation and subjugation.

Residing in the decisive, but for literary critics largely underestimated, motif of kenosis, the impassioning potential of this denial simultaneously inhabits "all the other motifs that are inseparable from and dependent upon it," and specifically, to borrow Derrida's enumeration, those of *surnaming*, the *khōra*, and *immanence* ("Faith and Knowledge" 96). In *Light in August*—which affirms and reaffirms the primacy of the impersonal ("a body does get around" is Lena Grove's repeated refrain [420, 774])—the repetitive (but seemingly inexhaustible) violence of interpellation and subjugation come immediately to the fore in the deployment of sur-naming. This act concerns the attempt to enforce a name, whether first, intermediate, or final appellation: over-naming as overwriting and over-valuing, calling as repeatedly subjecting, calling—as with Jesus, Christ, Nazarene, Master, Son of God, Son of man, and Light of the World—in an attempt to pin down and to capture through signification. No such attempt has been made for the hamlet associated with Doane's Mill, whose itinerant workers are officially unworthy of topographical significance, but the siting of a pharmakos, as the story of Joe Christmas attests, is some-thing altogether different.

The silence on coming into the world that envelops the protagonist's *prénom* immediately testifies to significant (or signifying) violence. Milly Hines, the child's mother, reports her broken waters, but her voice, her words (in another apophatic denial) are left unreported. Meanwhile, the devilish Eupheus Hines, Milly's Father, Old Nick, the "Doc," or sur-named *pharmakeus* (Sykes describes him as a "backwoods prophet" [47]), who oversees the arrival of his daughter's pharmakos, "stood outside the hall door where he could" watch "until she died" (679). Parturition emp-ties Milly of both her child and her blood, so effective an emptying of life, in fact, that the narrative voids itself of hematological references in report-ing Milly's death.[5] Her son, as physical entrant into the symbolic realm, but with a *prénom* of an unknown value, like an algebraic "X," hereafter mediates between the possibilities of anonymity and polynymity. He mani-fests or sites the self-contradictions of over-naming: the freedom of detach-ment through self-identification remains restricted by naming from without via "the forced attachment (of the other)" (Dubilet 106).

Eupheus, as caretaker at the orphanage where, unbeknownst to the staff, he has offloaded his grandson, supplies the first iteration of sur-naming: "his name is Joseph" (683), he tells them; and X becomes Joseph X. Miss Atkins, the orphanage dietitian, immediately imposes the next iteration in accordance with the date of the infant's abandonment: "we'll name him Christmas" (683); the "X" becomes Xmas; Joseph X becomes Joseph Christmas. Sur-naming the infant with "Christmas" is a singular imposition, and the tension between the (ordinary) "Joe" and the (extraor-dinary) "Christmas" will constantly, repeatedly signify, promising him not only the greatest privation but also the greatest profit. As Thomas Dutoit explains in his preface to Derrida's *On the Name*, this sort of double impo-sition fills a lack, signifying a signified for a referent otherwise assumed to be empty or devoid of meaning, making a "proper name into a sort of sur-name, pseudonym, or cryptonym at once singular and singularly untranslatable" (xiv). For Eupheus, the cryptic of the cryptonym concerns the obverse of the obvious, with his grandson manifesting the devil's spawn.

"The 'surname' as 'nickname,'" to appropriate Dutoit, "supplement[s] a given name to the point of replacing it" (x). Yet, in naming God (or Joe Christmas), as Caputo makes plain, "we give the gift of what we do not have. For by naming we risk binding what is named, enslaving it, prescribing to it 'an assigned passion' […], which is why God himself 'slips away' […] from every name we give to Him" (43). This cryptonym displays an apophatic aspect: "a secret that is without content, without a content separable from its performative experience, from its performative tracing" (Derrida, *On the Name* 24). In *Light in August*, Christmas himself, as his comparable sur-naming suggests, will also slip away, as if in a form of glissement, in similar yet different manners than before, from every imposed appellation or attempt at enslavement. This evasiveness especially concerns the application from without of the "n" word, which occurs first when, "foist[ing] upon him […] the attributes of an adult" (489), Atkins repeatedly calls her charge a "little nigger bastard" (489, 491).

Simon McEachern, on to whom the orphanage (without revealing any racial concerns) eventually transfers their burden, applies a fourth iteration. "We force no one to take our children," boasts the matron, "nor do we force the children to go against their wishes, if their reasons are sound ones" (504), but the boy's silence throughout the adoption process allies subjective relocation with apophatic secrecy: "the child said nothing" (505); "still the child didn't answer" (505); "he said nothing at all" (505)—and "silence," to appropriate Derrida from "How to Avoid Speaking: Denials" (1981), "yet remains a modality of speech" (84–85). McEachern, as Sykes argues, "live[s] by a strict code of morality and duty" (46), but this strictness produces spiritual deafness. "Faulkner's Puritans," as Sykes maintains, "have a Christianity without Christ" (46); McEachern personifies this Faulknerian type; and deaf to the silent Christ before him, McEachern tries to neuter that nominal presence with a shift of signifier or sur-name. "'Christmas,'" he growls. "'A heathenish name. Sacrilege. I will change that.' 'That will be your'"—not the boy's, one notes—"'legal right,' the matron said" (505–6). And still their subject maintains his apophatic counsel: "the child was not listening. He was not bothered. He did not especially care, anymore than if the man had said the day was hot when it was not hot. He didn't even bother to say to himself *My name aint McEachern*" (506; emphasis original).

Nicknames applied during adolescence, of which "Romeo" is the most insistent, manifest a fifth iteration of sur-naming. At the restaurant-come-bordello that he frequents, Christmas self-contradictorily uses the name McEachern, not "*my name* […] *is Christmas*" (506; emphasis original), in the presence of the owner Max Confrey and Max's wife Mame. Max, however, maximizes the recourse to interpellation and subjugation, shifting the young man's name from McEachern to "Hiram" (534) to "the Beale Street Playboy" (556) to "Romeo" (541, 542, 556, 561). Nonetheless, the underlying essence of his subject fleeting reveals itself when Max inadvertently sur-names McEachern both Christmas ("sometimes Christmas lasts a good while. Hey, Romeo?" [541]) and Jesus ("for sweet Jesus" [540, 542]).

While the racist marker of "wop" (564, 602) manifests a sixth iteration of sur-naming, an intriguing seventh iteration, "Mr Christmas," comes from Lena Grove. Mrs. Hines, reports Lena, "keeps on talking about him [Lena's newborn] like his pa was that——the one in jail, that Mr Christmas" (701). The benevolent Lena is the only person to refer to Joe as "Mister." The next iteration of sur-naming is the "Xmas" of Gail Hightower's "Xmas cards." The premonitory advertising sign outside Hightower's house, even though the reverend "is no longer conscious of it as a sign" (441), reads: "REV. GAIL HIGHTOWER, D.D. / Art Lessons / Handpainted Xmas & Anniversary Cards / Photographs Developed"; this sign was "carpentered neatly by himself and by himself lettered, with bits of broken glass contrived cunningly into the paint, so that at night, when the corner street lamp shone upon it, the letters glittered with an effect as of Christmas" (440). Faulkner's masterful figurative anticipation here reveals a sign that points to the site of his protagonist's and Hightower's concluding acts in August, which come not long after a final use of the name Xmas, an iteration of the previous iteration, in Lucas Burch's note for the bounty for the capture of Joanna Burden's presumed murderer—"*Mr. Wat Kenedy Dear sir please give barer My reward Money for captain Murder Xmas*" (721).

Sur-naming, then, exemplifies Milly's son as the receptacle of others' signification, violent inscriptions that attempt to penetrate deeper than his "parchmentcolored" (487, 490) skin. In response, he attempts to empty himself by himself, through kenosis, of imposed signification. Ultimately, "Xmas" wishes to void himself of the "mas" of subjugation, and so return to the unknown value of an algebraic "X." This final algebraic shift, this mathematical move to the X, would both respect and protect Divinity. This transition would shift Christ "well beyond" what Caputo calls "the reach of the arrows of 'reference' that are aimed his way." In effect, Christmas's X would amount to "the beautiful cross that Jean-Luc Marion puts over the name of God, by means of which he would strike it out," but by which he keeps God safe. Marion's X invokes "crossed swords or arrows that defy anyone who would dare trespass. Only a god can save us, but only a god whom negative theology keeps safe. Outside the saving gestures of negative theology there is no salvation" (44).

Christmas's kenotic life acknowledges God as ultimate alterity. "In the love of God," explains Sedgwick of Jeremy Taylor's perspective on kenosis, "we are with humility drawn out in obedience to God's command to love of neighbor." This "journey of faith is the experience of holiness in the transformation of intent," a trajectory "fully realized and revealed in Jesus' passion, death, and resurrection." Although, "the shape of this life—its form or end—is *kenotic*," this end is multiple and thus seemingly endless (214; emphasis original). This journey is "not realized or completed in the act." The traveler "must act again and again, each time in a way that is similar to but different from before" (211), and Christmas's bouts of fasting, as acts of self-emptying and self-sufficiency, appear endlessly recurrent. He initially arrives in Jefferson with an empty stomach: "in all likelihood he had lived on cigarettes for two or three days now" (423). He then rejects the first means of filling that void. Byron Bunch "offer[s] his own pail" (423), but Christmas spurns Byron's generosity. "I aint hungry," he says. "Keep your muck" (424). Refusing food dates back to his adoption by McEachern, whose repeated attempts to feed Joe the Word elicited repeated periods of fasting.

The narrative details one occasion in particular. Just as Joe had refused to learn his catechism, so "he had had no breakfast," no lunch, no supper, so that by bedtime "he felt weak and peaceful." This calmness allowed him to imagine the ultimate emptiness he seeks: "it seemed to him that if he turned his head he would still see the two of them, himself and [McEachern], kneeling beside the bed, or anyway, in the rug the indentations of the twin pairs of knees without tangible substance" (512). This combination of corporeal and figurative hollowness testifies to McEachern's kataphatic efforts with his adopted son—the kataphatic prayer is often what Derrida calls merely "a preamble, an accessory mode of access" ("How to Avoid Speaking" 110). Even Simon's wife, who simply wished to satiate the boy's hunger, was unsuccessful. Joe simply refused her offering. With the same words of denial that Bunch will later hear—"I aint hungry" (512)—Joe "dump[ed] the dishes and food and all onto the floor" (513). He repeats this act of rejection in responding to the first meal Joanna Burden prepares for him; as a result, when "he went to work on Friday," "he had eaten nothing now since Wednesday night," and drawing no pay until Saturday, he will not eat until that evening (574).

Emesis, as an act thematically linked to, but distinct from, fasting, also expresses the kenotic life of Faulkner's protagonist. Indeed, synesthesia, as a symptom or sign of self-detachment, accompanied the vomiting induced by the sweet and cleansing toothpaste Christmas secretly swallowed at the orphanage. For, having taken his fill, the youngster "saw by feel alone now the ruined, once cylindrical tube" (488). As if in synesthetic sympathy, he then excreted the substance by another means, through perspiration. "He began to sweat. Then he found that he had been sweating for some time, that for some time now he had been doing nothing else but sweating." Self-detachment had enabled introspection. "He seemed to be turned in upon himself, watching himself sweating, watching himself smear another worm of paste into his mouth which his stomach did not want." The resultant vomiting not only defied digestion but also denied impregnation. For, hidden behind a curtain, his presence unknown to the female dietician and a male intern as they became sexually intimate, Christmas "wait[ed] with astonished fatalism for what was about to happen to him." Then he was sick, and "he said to himself with complete and passive surrender: 'Well, here I am'" (489). Christmas's vomiting provoked coitus interruptus beyond the curtain, and this interruption prevented the possibility of the dietician's empty womb, her khōra, being impregnated.

In "How to Avoid Speaking," Derrida introduces the subject of the khōra with reference to Plato's *Timaeus*, admitting to a double bind: "it is difficult to speak of this absolutely necessary place." Existentially inseparable from kenosis, the khōra is the "place 'in which' the mimemes of the eternal beings originate by impressing themselves (*typothenta*) there" (104). "Whether they concern the word *khōra* itself ('place,' 'location,' 'region,' 'country') or what tradition calls the figures—comparisons, images, and metaphors—proposed by Timaeus ('mother,' 'nurse,' 'receptable' [*sic*], 'imprint-bearer')," explains Derrida in *On the Name*, "the translations remain caught in networks of interpretation" (93). As an essential space for impregnation and imprint-bearing, this necessary matrix has an undeniably maternal aspect, being "the figure of figures, the place of the other figures" (120). This receptable receptacle cannot help being "associated, like passive and virgin matter, with the feminine element" (97). The khōra, to appropriate Frank Kermode from "Endings, Continued" (1989), "sounds like the *place*, and the *realm* we have it in us to desire, in so far as we are 'a certain species'" (92; emphasis original). In *If I Forget Thee, Jerusalem* (1939), the reluctant utilitarian Harry Wilbourne talks to his friend the "newspaper man" (555) McCord about "feel[ing] all your life rush out of you into the pervading immemorial blind receptive matrix" (589), and in *Light in August*, the dietician, Milly Hines, Christmas's erstwhile girlfriend Bobbie Allen, Joanna Burden, and Lena Grove are all variations of the imprint-bearer.

Parturition is an act of intense labor on Milly's part, a bloody birth that not only results in her death but also prefigures her son's subalternity: "the figure of the *Knecht*," writes Dubilet, "is produced through a foundational act of violence, which scars it in its very constitution, forcing it to apprehend life as something that can be lost and thereby producing a stubbornness of persistence that defines it as a subject" (106). In adolescence, Christmas meets Bobbie Allen, whom he understands to be virginal (or internally unsullied) and who appears to embody, therefore, a clean space for the unloading of Christmas's inner self. During their first sexual encounter, Bobbie's masturbatory hands move "like they were praying" (531), and she partakes of Christmas's "unworldly and innocent" quality, that quality "of something beyond flesh" (531). Her admittance of prophylactic self-emptying at their next meeting distresses him, however, and in consequence, he flees from the menstruating Bobbie, "fad[ing] on down the road" (538) until he is out of sight. The breathless Christmas, who has already killed a ewe, steeping "his hands in the yet warm blood" (535), now transfigures the arboreal space around him into a menstrual nightmare. Each tree "was cracked and from each crack there issued something liquid, deathcolored, and foul. He touched a tree, leaning his propped arms against it, seeing the ranked and moonlit urns," and he "vomited" (538). The adolescent Christmas, predisposed to the act of voiding, predisposed to fear the cyclical nature of menstruation, seeks permanent emptiness.

In one guise or another, however, the imposition of content keeps recurring. Simon McEachern's reappearance marks the first instance. McEachern, who had attempted to neuter Christmas's nominal presence with a shift of signifier, now tries to separate Christmas from Bobbie at a backwoods dance. Personifying the acts of interpellation and subjugation,

he silently rechristens Christmas as "Satan" (549), but pays for this imposition in being assaulted (possibly fatally) by his adopted son. Christmas's
subsequent wanderings eventually lead him to Joanna Burden. Already
post-menopausal, she surrenders her virginity to him, "a spiritual privacy
so long intact that its own instinct for preservation had immolated it"
(571). As an imprint-bearer who can bear no imprint, Joanna bears false
witness in announcing that she is to bear Christmas's child, but he soon
discovers the phantom nature of her condition: "you just got old" (603).
This revelation intensifies the aura of martyrdom that surrounds the laical
Joanna. She aspires, as her surname suggests, to a sacerdotal form of piety.
Joanna understands faith as a weight to be carried: she has learned to see
African Americans as "a shadow in which [she] lived, we lived, all white
people, all other people," as "the black shadow in the shape of a cross,"
and as martyrs in waiting (585). Indeed, the contemplation of subalternity
has left its imprint on her; it assumes khōric dominance and prefigures her
martyrdom too. "*Khōra* receives," as Derrida concludes, "so as to give
place to them, all the determinations, but she/it does not possess any of
them as her/its own. She possesses them, she has them, since she receives
them, but she does not possess them as properties, she does not possess
anything as her own" (*On the Name* 99).

    As his initial rejection of her food suggests, and despite their sexual
relations, Joanna will never fully possess Christmas. His response to her
calls to prayer affirms this contention. "When Faulkner lectured at West
Point shortly before his death," as Robert L. Johnson recounts, "he was
asked whether Joanna was not kin to some of Hawthorne's people and kin
to Kurtz in Conrad's *Heart of Darkness*. He nodded affirmatively, remind-
ing his questioner of Joanna's New England ancestry. This heritage is
borne out in Joanna's cumulative weight of wrath, guilt, and personal
responsibility" (76–77). The unlimited reserve of impenetrable secrecy
that envelops Christmas's racial origins increases that burden. As with
McEachern's repeated attempts, however, Joanna's spiritual efforts with
Christmas come to naught. To the apophatic mind, as Derrida explains,
"prayer is not a preamble, an accessory mode of access." Thus undertaken,
this act "constitutes an essential moment, it adjusts discursive asceticism,
the passage through the desert of discourse, the apparent referential vacu-
ity which will only avoid empty deliria and prattling, by addressing itself
from the start to the other" ("How to Avoid Speaking" 110). "Just
kneel," pleads Joanna. "Just make the first move." Christmas's "no" is

adamant (606). His resistance answers to a sacerdotal form of piety that pertains less to testimonial faith and more to confession.

"Taylor has no doubts about God's grace being necessary for our salvation," writes Hughes, "he is not one who feels confession to be without value" (77). In *The Rule and Exercises of Holy Living*, as Hughes maintains, Taylor "speaks of the blessing of confession as 'laying open our wounds for cure.' He adds that we may be very much helped if we take in the assistance of a spiritual guide" (91). Later, "in his preface to *Unum Necessarium* the value of confession is again stressed," but while "it is not to be exchanged for the tyranny of sin," the bondage of the Roman confessional must be avoided (90). Significantly, Joanna's interpretation of prayer, which binds her to the confessional, falls foul of this caveat. Her prayers, which exhibit an "abjectness of pride" (606), reveal a two-sided lust for domination. Her servitude demands Christmas's servitude too. She wishes Christmas to share her humility and pride in confessing their sexual relations, but his resistance admits to a God who knows everything. Derrida's analysis in *On the Name* of Augustine's *Confessions* supports this interpretation. "When he asks (himself), when he asks in truth of God and already of his readers why he confesses himself to God when He knows everything," as Derrida remarks, "the response makes it appear that what is essential to the avowal or the testimony does not consist in an experience of knowledge" (38–39). For, "confession does not consist in making known—and thereby it teaches that teaching as the transmission of positive knowledge is not essential." Genuine confession is apophatic. "Augustine speaks of 'doing the truth' (*veritatem facere*), which," as Derrida explains, "does not come down to revealing, unveiling, nor to informing in the order of cognitive reason." Instead, this act "comes down to *testifying*." Put succinctly, "I want 'to do the truth,' he says, in my heart, in front of *you*." Moreover, Augustine also wishes to testify, as Faulkner effectively does in *Light in August*, "'in my writing before many witnesses.'" Augustine sets down his testimony, as Derrida concludes, "because he wants to leave a trace for his brothers to come in charity in order to stir up also, at the same time as his, the love of readers" (39; emphasis original).

Christmas's sexual acts testify to his attempts at self-emptying into the khōric matrix. Supposed according to racial branding to be an outcast, Christmas seeks to dispossess himself of the impositions targeted at him as a pharmakos, "*receptive addressee*" (Derrida, *On the Name* 110; emphasis original), or "speculative kernel" (Dubilet 130). Indeed, the climax to the toothpaste scene at the orphanage will be echoed years later by the murderous climax in Hightower's house. For, on each occasion, sufficient unto himself, Christmas gives himself up in giving up himself: "that the path of self-sufficiency is, in fact, a violent path that leads to dissatisfaction," as Dubilet argues, "is demonstrated by the labyrinth of withdrawal, displacement, frustration, and performative self-contradiction that determine the subject in the textual forms that follow, as stoicism, skepticism, and ultimately the unhappy consciousness" (107). Christmas's behavior certainly becomes self-contradictory. Notably, having donned a pair of brogans that previously belonged to an African-American farmer—"the shoes, the black shoes smelling of negro" (650)—Christmas acts as if blackness suffuses his body—"that mark on his ankles the gauge definite and ineradicable of the black tide creeping up his legs" (650). This notable assumption of African-American heritage finds its contradictory counterpart in Christmas's stoicism as a hunted African American who acts as an assured majoritarian: "he went into a white barbershop like a white man, and because he looked like a white man they never suspected him" (657–58). The farmer's shoes now seem of little account. "Even when the bootblack saw how he had on a pair of second hand brogans that were too big for him, they never suspected" (658). On each side of this thwarted path to self-sufficiency, the freedom of self-detachment remains indelibly mediated, albeit in a disavowed way, by the forced attachment of the other.

The climactic event, which sums up the kenotic core immanent to this unhappy consciousness, is imminent. Faulkner scholar Doreen Fowler recognizes this mystic immanence in the Eleusinian Mysteries of which Frazer writes in *The Golden Bough*.[6] "The first gods were not transcendent, but immanent," notes Fowler; "they existed not above, but in the natural world" (140). In Faulkner's *The Sound and the Fury* (1929), Quentin Compson "longs for transcendence of periodic becoming," as Fowler maintains, "and he adamantly repudiates the immanence which his sister embodies" (151). Similarly, self-emptying through kenosis, as Dubilet explains, "affirm[s] an unrestrained immanence that precedes the difference between self and other" (13). Immanence is not an essence that can be realized "but something that is always already there, prior to and in excess of the formation of the subject or its positing in opposition to something other than it, a transcendence that can take the form of a norm, an ethical imperative, or a figuration of the divine" (16). Barrow discusses this ever presence in elucidating the Augustinian mysteries of *The City of God*. "For St Augustine," he writes, "the city in part exists here and now.

It therefore has no affinity with any city or Utopian or millennium which is imagined as starting at some date not yet reached, or as lying outside time." In Augustinian terms, continues Barrow, "the city already exists and men on earth are to become its citizens. The city exists, in so far as it exists, here and now, and in heaven and hereafter: for between the two times and the two places no line can be drawn" (140). Immanence illuminates what Dubilet describes as "the ways that various forms of transcendence collude in subjecting life, putting it to work, for their own ends" (16), and kenosis discloses the impersonal nature of this immanence, thereby "point[ing] to the collusive lie of the recurrent polemic staged between secular enclosures of subject and the theologically recuperated forms of transcendence that proclaim themselves as the only way to disappropriate that subject" (103).

Fittingly, as he approaches the culmination of his kenotic life in exposing the fallacies of racism, Joe Christmas is emptier than ever: "*I have not eaten since I have not eaten since* trying to remember how many days it had been" (644; emphasis original). Eventually, he eats, but it is, in effect, a self-emptying act: "he gathered and ate rotting and wormriddled fruit," and he consumed "enormous quantities of it, with resultant crises of bleeding flux." With this release, he exhibits "an expression of rapt bemusement," "thinking of nothing in an emptiness, a silence filled with flight" (646). Christmas follows this voiding with another, shaving at a spring in an act of self-laceration, cutting "himself three or four times" (647). He now senses the imminence of immanence: "when he thinks about time, it seems to him now that for thirty years he has lived inside an orderly parade of named and numbered days like fence pickets, and that one night he went to sleep and when he waked up he was outside of them" (644).

Yet, those thirty years of life remain a restricting construct, "a circle" that "he is still inside" (650). Accompanying repetitive (but never exhaustive) attempts at subjugation, the repeated kenotic acts of this unhappily beset consciousness climax in surrendering power over itself to Percy Grimm, the tarnished angel, whose grim appearance in the Derridean terms of "Faith and Knowledge" is "*at the same time hegemonic and finite, ultra-powerful and in the process of exhausting itself*" (52; emphasis original). Here, light (phos) signals Grimm's transcendence—"his face had that serene, unearthly luminousness of angels in church windows" (*Light in August* 741)—luminousness that comes from within, but luminousness that bespeaks his embodiment of "*the fanaticism or enthusiasm of the illuminated*" (Derrida, "Faith and Knowledge" 52; emphasis original). On the one hand, as Faulkner's heterodiegetic narrator notes of Grimm, "there was something about him irresistible and prophetlike" (734). On the other hand, reflecting, rather than displaying faith, the insufferable Grimm is a fallen angel of evil discredit, who displays what Derrida calls "illuminatism, *the frenzy of the initiates*" ("Faith and Knowledge" 52; emphasis original). As such, Grimm embodies majoritarian traits, and his influence over the *polis* is considerable: he and his state national guards "mov[ing] in a grave and slightly aweinspiring reflected light" (737), their faces "seem[ing] to glare with bodiless suspension as though from haloes" (741).

In facing these countenances, Joe Christmas effectively follows the tenets of St. Augustine, who (in Barrow's words) "urges Christian slaves to draw good out of evil if it is impossible for them to gain their freedom, until such time as human overlordship passes away" (231). Christmas elicits that extraction during his supposed flight from justice. Having been caught, he is first jailed in Jefferson, but must be transferred to another prison. Walking across the town square at the outset of this transfer and despite being handcuffed, he appears to make a break for freedom. During the ensuing chase, which Grimm heads, Christmas's manacles become another manifestation of the light in August: "as Grimm watched he saw the fugitive's hands glint once like the flash of a heliograph as the sun struck the handcuffs" (740); "his manacled hands high and now glinting as if they were on fire" (740). In effect, then, Christmas is not an escapee, but Grimm's guide. The heliographic handcuffs illuminate the fallen angel's path. Indeed, this episode ends in Hightower's house, that sanctuary of "cloistral dimness" (741), with "Christmas, running up the hall, his raised and armed and manacled hands full of glare and glitter like lightning bolts" (742). Heliography even directs Grimm's shots at his supposedly hiding quarry: "the table overturned and standing on its edge across the corner of the room, and the bright and glittering hands of the man who crouched behind it, resting upon the upper edge" (742).

The spectators of Grimm's subsequent castration of Christmas witness a grim spectacle:

> When the others reached the kitchen they saw the table flung aside now and Grimm stooping over the body. When they approached to see what he was about, they saw that the man was not dead yet, and when they saw what Grimm was doing one of the men gave a choked cry and stumbled back into

the wall and began to vomit. Then Grimm too sprang back, flinging behind him the bloody butcher knife. "Now you'll let white women alone, even in hell," he said. But the man on the floor had not moved. (742)

Like his victim, somewhat alienated, but unlike his victim, a generator of widespread support, Grimm is Faulkner's prototype of a "Nazi Storm Trooper" (41). Faulkner himself made this comparison while addressing the "Undergraduate Course in Contemporary Literature" at the University of Virginia on 9 March 1957; critics from Cleanth Brooks ("The Community and the Pariah" 1963) (240) to Grace Elizabeth Hale and Robert Jackson (2007) (34) to Stan Goff (2015) (321) have endorsed his comment, and Christmas sacrifices himself to this premonitory figure. "Christian preachers who have commended the religious life as really the happiest," as Sidgwick notes in *The Methods of Ethics*, "have not thought genuine religion irreconcilable with the conviction that each man's own happiness is his most near and intimate concern. Other persons, however, seem to carry the religious consciousness and the feeling of human affection to a higher stage of refinement, at which a stricter disinterestedness is exacted." Such unconditionally benevolent individuals practice "absolute self-renunciation and self-sacrifice" (138).

As if attempting to sympathize with unreserved benevolence, inculcated hyperbole now possesses the heterodiegetic narrator of *Light in August*, with the description of events almost overflowing that rendition: "the pent black blood seemed to rush like a released breath. It seemed to rush out of his pale body like the rush of sparks from a rising rocket; upon that black blast the man seemed to rise" (743). Notwithstanding that semblance, the dying subject, with his unconditional compassion for all others, has emptied himself for good. "He just lay there, with his eyes open and *empty of everything save consciousness*, and with something, *a shadow*, about his mouth" (742; emphasis added). Christmas's kenotic act, which eschews the claims of his body, offers a contemplative trace, a suggestion of food for thought. In *On the Prejudices, Predilections, and Firm Beliefs of William Faulkner* (1987), Brooks notes Faulkner's greatness, commending his fiction for supplying the "nourishment and remedies" needed by "the inner man." This interior essence "needs to be kept reminded," as Faulkner surely does with *Light in August*, "of the great virtues, such as honor, truth telling, courage, responsibility, and of Saint Paul's triad of faith, hope, and charity" (58).

Faulkner will offer another such reminder in *A Fable* in reemphasizing St. Paul's theological importance. "In the priest who attempts to persuade the corporal to repudiate his martyrdom Faulkner embodies several traits which connect a number of characters," observes Keen Butterworth. "The priest is the manifestation of institutionalized man. His faith is in the Church, not in Christ. For him Christ was only one of the many dreamers who 'had been bringing that same dream out of Asia Minor for three hundred years' [p. 363]. The only difference between Jesus and the others was that he had found 'a caesar foolish enough to crucify him' [p. 363]" (74–75). In counseling Stefan Demont, the Christ figure in the novel, to accept the Generalissimo's offer of a reprieve, notes Butterworth, "the priest tries to convince the corporal that it was Paul, not Christ, who was important—because he had been practical enough to found a church that would conquer Rome" (75). Faced with the unwavering rectitude of Demont, however, this man of God suddenly confronts his own failings. In consequence, the priest empties himself, committing suicide with the use of a body-piercing and blood-letting bayonet. "The proclamation of these virtues is ultimately, of course, the responsibility of the church," as Brooks maintains. "But philosophy has a role to play too, and so do literature and the humanistic disciplines generally. They are at the least extremely valuable ancillary forces. They do things which religion in its more theological and liturgical roles cannot do" (*On the Prejudices* 58). Demont's tuition of the priest in *A Fable* and Christmas's tuition of Grimm's spectators in *Light in August* are cases in point.

At one level, the shadow about the mouth of the mutilated Christmas mimics the accompanying emesis, attesting to an act of transference, to the vomiting witness's acceptance of the subject's task: "one might say that a gift that could be recognized as such in the light of day, a gift destined for recognition, would immediately annul itself" (29), to quote Derrida from *The Gift of Death*, but "what is moved only by something outside itself is neither alive nor said to be living" (85), as Dubilet asserts, while what is moved by something internally, as in the receptive witness of the grim kenosis in *Light in August*, is undeniably vital. In *The Rule and Exercises of Holy Dying*, as Sedgwick explains, and as Faulkner's reading of Taylor must have taught him, "purgation moves from meditations on the finite and temporal character of life to fasting as a bodily awareness of frailty and the opening of the heart to what endures." This developmental cleansing, which intends to turn the soul in its deepest intent, calls for illumination. "Scripture and specifically Christ reveals the truth of our lives, a truth which is known in worship and most fully in the Holy Eucharist. In this experience of letting go and of knowing the presence of God, there is reconciliation, peace, union with God" (215). In Sidgwick's view, self-sacrifice reveals "a disposition far above the average in its general tendency to promote" the utilitarian desire for benevolence, "and it is perhaps this disposition that we admire rather than the particular act" (*Methods* 432). Christmas's kenosis encourages such dispositional excess by putting Christian doctrine into action; Law writes that Kierkegaard understood "that people wish to accept Christianity as only a doctrine and not as a way of life demanding self-sacrifice and renunciation" (16); Faulkner effectively shared Kierkegaard's lament, and Christmas's kenosis challenges that common acceptance.

At another level, "while wanting to become nothing, it is necessary," as Caputo relates, "that the name of God remain something, an imprint left on the scarred body of language" (45). What persists of that necessary function is a remnant. "Some trace remains right in this corpus, becomes this corpus as *sur-vivance* of apophasis (more than life and more than death), survivance of an internal onto-logico-semantic auto-destruction," expounds Derrida: "there will have been absolute rarefaction, the desert will have taken place, nothing will have taken place but this place" (*On the Name* 55). In naming this site, explains Caputo, "negative theology becomes itself a desert, a desertification, a kenosis, or self-emptying, which empties itself of every predicate or attribute of God, every accusative category, and this because God is not whatever we say God 'is.' Praying God to rid us of God, apophatic theology empties itself of God, because God is the *Gottheit* beyond God, and then of the Godhead, because God is an *Über-Gottheit*" (44–45). The self-emptying prayers of apophatic theology are, therefore, the ascetic gestures that save the Godhead. "For God is safe in the bottomless abyss of nothingness, this desert place, leaving but His trace on language, burning and scarring language as He leaves the world, which is the event of language named negative theology" (45).

At a third level, only the shadow of unhappiness remains over Christmas's expiring consciousness, a shadow that intimates the insubstantial daydreams of grim mysticism. "How, then, could the finest promise of these mysteries—the murmur, probably, of the pitiful priests of Attis," as Louis Bouyer asks in discrediting pagan mythology, "how could this fail to appear derisory? For only the Christian Mystery, its content attested by the Word of the creative God coming down, not falling down, to our level to restore us, or rather to raise us up to his, only this could rescue us from the cosmic cycle of those rebirths, which only set travellers in motion again towards death, and open to us, once for all, the way to the only true immortality, that of the eternal God" (74).

One can summarize the contrast between Joe's shadowed silence and the narrator's hyperbole by quoting the passage from *The Mystical Theology* of Dionysius the Areopagite that Derrida turns to in "How to Avoid Speaking" in describing the apophatic journey "toward silent union with the ineffable" (80). Dionysius compares affirmative theology ("the former treatises") with negative theology ("the present treatise"):

> In the former treatises the course of the argument, as it came down from the highest to the lowest categories, embraced an ever-widening number of conceptions which increased at each stage of the descent, but in the present treatise it mounts upwards from below towards the category of transcendence, and in proportion to its ascent it contracts its terminology, and when the whole ascent is passed it will be totally dumb, being at last wholly united with Him Whom words cannot describe. (198)

The narrator's hyperbole reveals a kataphatic attitude that contrasts utterly with Christmas's shadowed silence.

The immortality of Christmas's actively passive suicide as kenotic act in *Light in August*—"though Common Sense would still deny the legitimacy of suicide, even under these conditions, it would also admit the necessity of finding reasons for the denial," an admission that implies "that the universal wrongness of suicide is at any rate not self-evident" (Sidgwick, *Methods* 356)—frees that consciousness, to appropriate Derrida, "from all authority, all narrative, all dogma, all belief—and at the limit from all faith" (*On the Name* 71). The enactment of negative theology empties itself of all inculcated hyperbole. This kenosis of discourse suggests that "despite analogies more disappointing even than they are striking," as Bouyer concludes, "it is from a source quite other than those of the pagan mysteries that the Pauline mystery derives, the Christian Mystery, the mystery of the one true God which alone contains in itself the mystery of man who was still God's creature even when he, along with the world itself, seemed to have escaped his hands" (74).

The world seems to have escaped Joe Christmas, but his handcuffs are deceptive manacles, which signpost his ultimate act. Christmas's kenosis, which prosecutes that final algebraic return to the originary X that both respects and protects Divinity, has successfully resisted the arrows of reference. "The name of God in negative theology," writes Caputo, "is like an arrow—like Husserl's intentional arrow—aimed at God, pointed toward God but never reaching its intentional object, never reaching fulfillment," and that arrow protects God from harm. A scar "would be inflicted if the name of God were actually to hit its mark and so to wrench God into manifestation, thus putting a violent end to God's absolute heterogeneity and holy height." To protect God's alterity requires "sav[ing] Him from the cutting tips and incisions of the accusing *kategoriai* of kataphatic theology, from ensnarement by some name. *Sauf le nom de Dieu*: safe the name of God is when it names everything save God. Safe God is when we know nothing of God, save the name" (44). Christmas's rigorous kenosis deprives him of Christ's name, the appellation around which his conscious life has coalesced, and thus respects the otherness of God in saving the name it excises. This undertaking manifests the dilemma of practical apophasis that negates both the name of God and everything except the name of God. This is "the double bind of a discourse that has been wounded by the logic of the impossible." In this economy of sacrifice, a gifted logic of the most severe asceticism, negative theology expires in order to survive. Apophasis "lives without altogether avoiding dying, deprives itself of what it most desires, empties itself of its richest treasure, losing, striking out, the name of God, but all this precisely in order to save it" (43).

The murderous scar inflicted by Grimm, in contrast to ingrained overstatement, speaks silently. This open wound encapsulates the textual majority (or interstitial narrative) that lies between the prolegomenon and the post-scriptum of *Light in August*, and in these structural and thematic terms, Faulkner's novel bears brief comparison with Plato's *Timeaus*. "If there is indeed a chasm in the middle of the book, a sort of abyss 'in' which there is an attempt to think or say this abyssal chasm which would be *khōra*, the opening of a place 'in' which everything would, at the same time, come to take *place* and *be reflected* (for these are images which are inscribed there), is it insignificant," wonders Derrida, "that a *mise en abyme* regulates a certain order of composition of the discourse?" (*On the Name* 104; emphasis original). The attempt at total reflection in *Light in August* encompasses both Joanna Burden and Gail Hightower. Joanna's lineage boasts a mixture of Protestantism and mysticism. Her grandfather, the erstwhile Catholic Calvin Burden, had married a Huguenot and had "formally den[ied] allegiance to the Catholic church" (576). That marriage had linked the appropriately named Calvin to the bloody history of

Protestantism. Calvin had then set about imbuing his son "with the religion of his New England forbears" (577). He "read to the child in Spanish from the book which he had brought with him from California, interspersing the fine, sonorous flowing of mysticism in a foreign tongue with harsh, extemporised dissertations composed half of the bleak and bloodless logic which he remembered from his father on interminable New England Sundays" (577).

Gail Hightower's mixture of Protestantism and mysticism echoes that of Joanna. Like Christmas, Hightower is another bearer of negative theology, and like Christmas, he manifests apophatic credentials. In effect, Byron Bunch wonders about these credentials during one of his visits to Hightower's house, when, "through the window, faint yet clear, the blended organ and voices come from the distant church, across the still evening. *I wonder if he hears it too* Byron thinks *Or maybe he has listened to it so much and so long that he dont even hear it anymore. Dont even need to not listen*" (457). For Dubilet, the kenotic process "remains tied to the presence of 'the middle term'"; a pharmakos, or "priestly figure," figures mediation; this figure is "the bearer and mediator" of that which "is divested" (113); and orthodox theology meets mysticism in Hightower. Hightower's sermons, which he conducts with "wild hands" and in a "wild rapt eager voice" (*Light in August* 446), combine what Sykes calls "biblical imagery" with "martial daring and divinely ordained glory" (47), leaving "the dogma he was supposed to preach all full of galloping cavalry and defeat and glory" (*Light in August* 443–44).

The apophatic theologian, as Derrida notes of the teachings of Dionysius, "must practice not a double language, but the double inscription of his knowledge." The transmission of this inscription evokes the "unspeakable, secret, prohibited, reserved, inaccessible (*aporreton*) or mystical (*mystiken*), 'symbolic and initiatory,'" on the one hand, and the "philosophic, demonstrative (*apodeiktiken*), capable of being shown" ("How to Avoid Speaking" 94), on the other. Indeed, one of Hightower's homilies turns into a self-emptying talk about another Mississippian light in August, which emanated from General A. J. Smith's razing of Oxford on 22 August 1864. To Hightower's congregation, this sermon is devoid of theological meaning, with their minister "talking about the Civil War and his grandfather, a cavalryman, who was killed, and about General Grant's stores burning in Jefferson until it did not make sense at all" (443). Interweaving the inexpressible with the expressible, his sermons initially interested, but ultimately baffled his congregation. "At the crossing point of these two languages, each of which bears the silence of the other," as Derrida relates, "a secret must and must not allow itself to be divulged" ("How to Avoid Speaking" 94).

As with the laical Joanna, an aura of martyrdom surrounds Hightower, who shares the aspiration to fulfill the sacerdotal form of piety that Hughes associates with Jeremy Taylor. "Christian preachers who have commended the religious life as really the happiest," to repeat Sidgwick, "have not thought genuine religion irreconcilable with the conviction that each man's own happiness is his most near and intimate concern" (*Methods* 138). Hightower's religious devotion and his own happiness do prove irreconcilable, however, and he turns to the kenotic benevolence of mortal self-sacrifice, as exemplified by Christmas. Alone at home after Christmas's murder, the "sweat begins to pour from" Hightower; "the sweat pours and pours," "springing out like blood, and pouring" (762). Under these emetic circumstances, the disgraced minister conjures up a roster of faces, including what appears to be that "of the man called Christmas," the man whom Grimm butchered in Hightower's own kitchen. Christmas's image, however, remains unclear. "It is confused more than any other, as though in the now peaceful throes of a more recent, a more inextricable, compositeness. Then he can see that it is two faces which seem to strive (but not of themselves striving or desiring it: he knows that, but because of the motion and desire of the wheel itself) in turn to free themselves one from the other, then fade and blend again." The two faces are those of Christmas and Grimm. They are complementary sides of the same enigma; they are all the virtues backed by all their cognate vices, and with this revelation, "it seems to [Hightower] that some ultimate dammed flood within him breaks and rushes away." This exodus "leav[es] his body empty" (763). Grace has expelled any disgrace.

From the Sidgwickian perspective of *The Methods of Ethics*, "such a sacrifice [...] shows a disposition far above the average in its general tendency to promote happiness" (432). This disposition figures the ethical hedonism that Sidgwick first encountered in the utilitarianism espoused by John Stuart Mill (1806–73), whose system of ethics offered "relief from the apparently external and arbitrary pressure of moral rules which I had been educated to obey," according to Sidgwick's recollection in his "Preface to the Sixth Edition" (1901) of *The Methods of Ethics*, "and which presented themselves to me as to some extent doubtful and confused; and sometimes, even when clear, as merely dogmatic, unreasoned, incoherent." Mill's own system, however, lacked clarity, with Sidgwick identifying an implicit divergence between psychological hedonism and ethical hedonism. "Both attracted me," he recalls, "and I did not at first perceive their incoherence." The first trajectory, which drew Sidgwick "by its frank naturalness," claims "that each man does seek his own Happiness." The second trajectory, which drew Sidgwick "by its dictate of readiness for absolute self-sacrifice," claims "that each man ought to seek the general Happiness" (xvii). These two approaches offer a practical means of negotiating between the demands made by self-interest, on the one hand, and individual duty to all others, on the other. Ultimately, however, "a sense grew upon [Sidgwick] that this method of dealing with the conflict between Interest and Duty, though perhaps proper for practice could not be final for philosophy" (xvii–xviii). For the practical purposes of people who do not philosophize, "the maxim of subordinating self-interest, as commonly conceived, to 'altruistic' impulses and sentiments which they feel to be higher and nobler is, I doubt not, a commendable maxim; but it is surely the business of Ethical Philosophy to find and make explicit the rational ground of such action" (xviii). What is more, as *Light in August* illustrates, that commendable maxim can demand unreasonable practice: the actions of Christmas in soliciting his murder at the hands of Grimm are rationally irrational, or unreasonably reasonable, in realizing a benevolence that cannot be reasonably expected of others.

Christmas's unbidden benevolence, as its unreasonably reasonable character suggests, is necessarily far-reaching. That extension suggests the existence of another cryptonymic X in Faulkner's novel. Lucas Burch, who impregnates Lena Grove, renames himself Brown in attempting to abandon her. Nonetheless, Lucas has a son by Lena, an X Burch or X Brown, whom Mrs. Hines names Joey after her daughter's son. This act of naming, which accompanies Lena's sur-naming of "Mr Christmas," confirms the suggestion of metempsychosis that the structural shift in the novel from interstitial majority to post-scriptum minority supports. In addition, the successive shifts from prolegomenon to interstice to post-scriptum reenact the dialectical movement from self-fulfillment to self-emptying to self-fulfillment that constitutes the radical and necessary plenitude of kenosis as *pleroma* (the fullness of Godhead that dwells in Christ). "The radicalism of the necessity must be stressed," as Dubilet insists, "God *must* come in, because under the condition of self-emptying and annihilation, the soul is no longer distinguishable from divine life. God must come in, because he is already there, not as united or unitable, but as already immanently one" (52; emphasis original). Between the prolegomenon and post-scriptum of Faulkner's novel, the figure of kenosis as pleroma traverses from an interiorization that is constitutive of a subject to a self-emptying in parturition: "a body does get around" (420, 774), muses Lena; a body does get a round, swelled, or prenatally full; but a body also gets a round, emptied, or a zero. The post-scriptum and prolegomenon, these "Parerga" to use Derrida's term, "*situate perhaps the fringe where we might be able, today, to inscribe our reflections*" ("Faith and Knowledge" 52; emphasis original), and consideration of this fringe in *Light in August* posits Lena's traversal from the opening to the closing pages of the novel as a generational movement, a movement for generation X, a movement from estrangement to familiarity.

The bodily accompaniment to the metempsychosis from Mr. Christmas to Lena's unchristened child is her baby's appetite: Lena, her baby boy, and Byron Bunch leave Jefferson by wagon, and the infant "hadn't never stopped eating, that had been eating breakfast now for about ten miles" (774). Kenosis has elicited pleroma. Coming into Jefferson, on another wagon, at the opening of the novel, the modestly triumphant Lena, as signaled by her palm leaf fan, had been "outside of, beyond all time" (419), and there she remains. Disembarking from that wagon had been an act of vacating that was and was not an act of emptying: "*when the wagon is empty of me again it will go on for a half mile with me still in it*" (404; emphasis original). Her peaceful expiration—"She expels her breath. It is not a sigh so much as a peaceful expiration" (407)—is premonitory of its violent, bloody counterpart from Mr. Christmas's throat. She empties herself to the extent that when she "tells her story again," she does so in "patient and transparent recapitulation" (417). Lena is inwardly and immanently enlightened. "Her face is calm as stone, but not hard. Its doggedness has a soft quality, an inwardlighted quality of tranquil and calm unreason and detachment" (412), and when facing the benevolence of others, as when Mrs. Armstid cooks her an unsolicited breakfast, Lena's "face [is] already fixed in an expression immanent with smiling" (415). "For St Augustine," to repeat Barrow on *The City of God*, and no matter whether one's environment is urban or rural, "the city in part exists here and now" (140).

Lena had been predictive of her child; she knew it to be a boy before its birth, but Lucas Burch always intended to leave her in the lurch. Surnaming cannot pin him down. On her journey from Doane's Mill to Jefferson, she had encountered "nameless faces and voices: *Lucas Burch? I dont know. I dont know of anybody by that name around here*" (403). Lena, however, persists. She will not give up, admits Armstid, "even when Jody Varner or some of them will tell her that that fellow in Jefferson at the planing mill is named Bunch and not Burch" (417), even when Jeffersonians keep naming him "Bunch instead of Burch" (435, 636). Lena "thought they had just got the name wrong and so it wouldn't make any difference" (435). Attested otherwise, this sur-naming makes both no difference and every difference: for Byron Bunch willingly accepts Lucas Burch's vacated place, and Lena Grove, whose arboreal surname literally relates to numerous trees and whose fecundity figuratively intimates reparation for the environing denudation of her teenage years at Doane's Mill, learns never to become impoverished, never to become a Burch or single birch.

Faulkner's post-scriptum, which closes on a nameless child, whom Lena may or may not allow Byron Bunch to adopt, blissfully intimates the open closure, or repeated self-emptying, of kenosis as pleroma. Privileging the intersections between Faulkner's literature and Derrida's philosophy, identifying some of their pertinent and inexhaustible resonances, reverberations in the positively negative space opened by apophatic theology, hereby concerns that certain extremity that Hassan reinvokes in closing his thoughts on "Fundamentalism and Literature" (2008). "This emptiness is what I want to offer my silent antagonist, the fundamentalist within," he writes. For, "without self-dispossession, without self-emptying—what theologians call kenosis—fear and craving persist," and grim "absolutism reigns" (29). The related line of Sidgwickian thought effectively agrees. "If we find that in our supposed knowledge of the world of nature propositions are commonly taken to be universally true, which yet seem to rest on no other grounds than that we have a strong disposition to accept them, and that they are indispensable to the systematic coherence of our beliefs," warns Sidgwick, "it will be more difficult to reject a similarly supported assumption in ethics, without opening the door to universal scepticism" (*Methods* 509).

In contemplating the apophatic, as Derrida does in "How to Avoid Speaking," "one passes—in a completely necessary and as if intrinsic fashion—to the question, which can always become the heading for an injunction: how not to speak, and which speech to avoid, in order to speak *well?*" (85; emphasis original). With this contemplation, one risks being branded among "those who have nothing to say or don't want to know anything." Yet, "if the risk is inevitable, the accusation it incurs need not be limited to the apophatic moment of negative theology. It may be extended," as Derrida warns, "to all language, and even to all manifestation in general."

This danger "is inscribed in the structure of the mark" (75). Ethics must accept this risk, and Faulkner takes such a gamble with the theological tenor of *Light in August*, which is at once an audacious, a liberating, yet a questioning reformulation of certain strains of apophasis. "In the long run, the identifiable traditions and discourses of Christian apophatic theology are loyal to the thing itself and its Truth," concludes Caputo. "Apophatic theology in the long run is not mad. Its self-emptying kenosis is a witness and a martyr" (46), which simultaneously testifies to and yields to "referential transcendence" (Derrida, *On the Name* 68), to what Caputo deems "the truth at any price" (46). *Light in August* does not restate mundane negation, but recuperates essential negativity, and in Faulkner's novel, as in Caputo's interpretation of Derrida's considerations of apophasis, "the several voices of negative theology are brought back into monological unison, encircling the expenditure of negations in a higher affirmation" (45) of unconditional benevolence.

NOTES

1. The only extended study of Faulkner and kenosis appears to be Lylas Dayton Rommel's PhD on "A Poetics of Shame and the Literary Meaning of Kenosis" (2004). Rommel compares the use Feodor Dostoevsky and Faulkner make of kenosis as an organizing principle. Rommel's overall approach, however, takes a kataphatic route.

2. In *The Unvanquished*, Rosa Millard calls John Sartoris's office "the library because there was one bookcase in it" (329), and the encased contents are eclectic: "a Coke upon Littleton, a Josephus, a Koran, a volume of Mississippi Reports dated 1848, a Jeremy Taylor, a Napoleon's Maxims, a thousand and ninety-eight page treatise on astrology, a History of Werewolf Men in England, Ireland and Scotland and Including Wales by the Reverend Ptolemy Thorndyke, M.A. (Edinburgh), F.R.S.S., a complete Walter Scott, a complete Fenimore Cooper, a paper-bound Dumas complete, too, save for the volume which Father lost from his pocket at Manassas (retreating, he said)" (329–30).

3. "Faulkner evidently found Frazer fascinating," reports Hlavsa in "*The Golden Bough*" (1999). "Rowan Oak, the name he gave his Oxford home, is actually one type of the sacred golden bough." Moreover, "when Faulkner stayed with Sherwood Anderson in New Orleans in 1925, much of their talk was of Freud, Eliot, and Frazer, with an abridged *Golden Bough* on Anderson's coffee table. Later, Faulkner would be observed reading Frazer at the time he was writing *Light in August*" (153).

4. Concentrating on "The Bear" from Faulkner's *Go Down, Moses* (1942) in "The Privations of Postmodernism," Hassan notes that there "are some aspects of kenosis, the exigencies of spirit, in Faulkner's fiction" (15), but mentions *Light in August*, with its "explicit Christian references" (11), only in passing.

5. In *Reading for the Body* (2012), Jay Watson similarly remarks "the murder of Joanna Burden, the birth of Lena Grove's son, and Gail Hightower's unsuccessful attempt to deliver a Negro baby," scenes that must "involve significant amounts of blood," but (self-emptying) scenes in which "blood is almost completely absent from the narrative" (154).

6. "In the great mysteries solemnised at Eleusis," relates Frazer, "the union of the sky-god Zeus with the corn-goddess Demeter appears to have been represented by the union of the hierophant with the priestess of Demeter, who acted the parts of god and goddess" (2:138).

CHAPTER 4

Duty (I): *Pylon*

The rational estimate of consequences, argues Henry Sidgwick in *The Methods of Ethics*, "not only supports the generally received view of the relative importance of different duties, but is also naturally called in as arbiter, where rules commonly regarded as co-ordinate come into conflict" (425–26). On the one hand, this consideration reveals "how certain acts—such as kind services—are likely to be more felicific when performed without effort, and from other motives than regard for duty." On the other hand, this consideration reveals how an individual, "who in doing similar acts achieves a triumph of duty over strong seductive inclinations, exhibits thereby a character which we recognise as felicific in a more general way, as tending to a general performance of duty in all departments" (429). According to nineteenth-century mental hygienists, the best time for instilling devotion to duty was childhood, and this inculcation would ensure adult mental health. Who ought to undertake this task? For mental hygienists, the answer was simply: dutiful parents, but especially mothers, were best placed.

Fundamentally, what was and what remains "at issue," to appropriate Derrida in *On the Name*, "is the concept of duty, and of knowing whether or up to what point one can rely on it, on what it structures in the order of culture, of morality, of politics, of law, and even of economy" (9). Indeed, by the interwar years of the twentieth century, as a number of prominent psychologist argued, a rise in delinquency pointed to negligent parenting. The seminal figure in the ensuing theoretical debate and

© The Author(s), under exclusive license to Springer Nature Switzerland AG 2021
M. Wainwright, *Faulkner's Ethics*,
https://doi.org/10.1007/978-3-030-68872-1_4

resultant clinical practice was John Bowlby (1907–90). His work on *attachment* focused on an infant's need for a reliably protective presence; many infants were being deprived of the natural and necessary attachments of childhood; the responsibility for this deprivation lay with their undutiful parents. Society must take responsibility for remedying this unwarranted dismantlement of family life; an infant's reliance on attachment is an inherent predisposition that requires adequate parental accommodation; and the appropriate social medicine includes the promotion of the dutiful fulfillment of that demand. William Faulkner effectively enters this debate in *Pylon* (1935).

DUTY (I): *PYLON*

> Some, however, would go further, and say that it ought to be treated as a distinctly social virtue: for the propagation and rearing of children is one of the most important of social interests. (Henry Sidgwick, *The Methods of Ethics*, 331)

William Cuthbert Faulkner, whom A. Nicholas Fargnoli, Michael Golay, and Robert W. Hamblin describe as "one of the most important literary figures in American literature" (ix), was born on 25 September 1897 in New Albany, Mississippi, America. The annual Faulkner and Yoknapatawpha Conference, which the University of Mississippi, Oxford, established in 1974, celebrates and promotes this importance. Edward John Mostyn Bowlby, whom "American historians have identified," as Marga Vicedo adduces, "as the most important figure in post-Second World War debates about maternal deprivation" (402), was born on 26 February 1907 in Bournemouth, Dorset, England.[1] The annual John Bowlby Memorial Conference, which the Centre for Attachment-Based Psychoanalytic Psychotherapy, London, established in 1994, celebrates and promotes this importance. The American Faulkner and the English Bowlby, whose births were separated by almost ten years and over four thousand miles, might seem dissimilar (even unrelated) figures, but their family backgrounds nurtured similar (even relatable) thoughts on twentieth-century familial relations.

Maud Falkner (née Butler) was the reserved mother of four sons in what Cheryl Lester calls a "bourgeois family" (276). "There is a suggestion of ambivalence about mothering on her part," as Jay Martin relates in "Faulkner's 'Male Commedia'" (1994), "a commitment to the duty of meeting the infant's needs, rather than softness or tenderness." Maud "apparently fulfilled her obligations," but she offered "little of the mutuality in feeding and playing necessary to nourish [an] infant's psyche" (144).[2] Her eldest son, William, suffered from colic during his neonatal months, and Maud's third son, John, later recounted how their mother could ease William's condition only by "rock[ing] him in a straight chair, the kind you have in the kitchen." In consequence, "the neighbors said the Falkners were the queerest people they ever knew; they spent all night in the kitchen chopping kindling on the floor" (11). In "'The Whole Burden of Man's History of His Impossible Heart's Desire'" (1982), Martin cites this testimony, adding that all of Maud's children "had persistent feeding problems" and how "the suggestive details in [John Faulkner's] account revolve around the means of solace chosen by Maud: a straight wooden chair used as if it were a rocker, thrust like an ax into the floor." This image, which emphasizes the hardness of Maud's succor, points to maternal behavior that was "troubled in its affective relations" (612).

Maud's commitment to the duty of mothering relied on a succession of substitutes. These replacements somewhat compensated the Falkner boys for their mother's emotional ambivalence. Sallie Falkner, William's paternal grandmother, was the first of these substitutes. "In 1901," as Martin notes, "she made a special trip from Ripley, Mississippi, to Oxford," where the Falkners now lived. She nursed William through a bout of scarlet fever. The next maternal substitute was Maud's mother: Leila Butler "came specifically to help take care of John, but in her spare time she played with Willie" ("Faulkner's 'Male Commedia'" 146). Finally, later in the year of Leila's arrival, Maud engaged an African-American servant, Caroline Barr. While each of these women offered a counterbalance to Maud's maternal deficiencies, her eldest son, as Jay Parini reports, "lavished [particular] affections on Mammy Callie" (125). Put succinctly, William reciprocated what Judith L. Sensibar calls Caroline's "emotional warmth" (30); he singled this "mammy" out with affection; and two years after her death, he would formally acknowledge their erstwhile bond in dedicating *Go Down, Moses* (1942) to her memory.[3]

Maud Falkner's preoccupation with her husband Murry accounted in large part for her maternal reticence; her duty of care focused on him; she had to mother Murry and count on her children's self-reliance. Murry had suffered a series of disappointments: his bid for the family railroad company auctioned by his paternal grandfather had been too late, while his successive business interests in an oil mill, an ice plant, a livery business, and a hardware store had realized no profit. Notwithstanding Maud's efforts, and despite (or because of) his family obligations, Murry turned to alcohol for support. "The indulgence of a bodily appetite is manifestly imprudent, if it involves the loss of any greater gratification of whatever kind," counsels Henry Sidgwick in *The Methods of Ethics*, "and otherwise wrong if it interferes with the performance of duties" (328). Maud would be periodically obliged to admit her husband to the Keeley Institute, near Memphis, for treatment, and William and his brothers accompanied their parents on several occasions. The family depended on Maud's fortitude; that endurance demanded stoicism; William soon "learned from Maud not to express any emotion that indicated need or weakness" (Sensibar 183); and affectional reservations soon pertained between William and his mother, on the one hand, and William and his father, on the other hand.

Maria Bowlby (née Lloyd-Mostyn) practiced a "style of mothering," as Judith Issroff describes in "Winnicott and Bowlby: Personal Reminiscences" (2005), which was "cold, remote, formal and distant, [and] essentially absent" (60).[4] She delegated the majority of her maternal duties—like Maud Falkner, Maria Bowlby had four children, but unlike Maud, she had three sons and one daughter—to a professional nursemaid. "An intelligent disciplinarian," according to Mario Marrone, "Nanna Friend" (8) provided the childcare in a family that typified what Jeremy Holmes calls "the English *haute bourgeoisie*" (13). Edward singled this "nanny" out with affection because parental preoccupations deprived him of firsthand solicitude: on the one hand, while his mother favored her youngest son, Jim, she also played the uxorious wife; on the other hand, his father, Anthony Alfred Bowlby, as a major-general in the British Army and a renowned surgeon, remained a dutiful professional. Edward, whose parents sent him to boarding school in 1914, saw little of his father, especially after the outbreak of European hostilities; and Maria underwrote this paternal absence by withholding her husband's wartime correspondence from their children.

"It is sometimes given as a distinction between Justice and Benevolence," remarks Sidgwick, "that the services which Justice prescribes can be claimed as a right by their recipient, while Benevolence is essentially unconstrained" (*Methods* 242–43). In certain cases, argues Sidgwick, this view is certainly true: "parents," for instance, "have a right to filial affection and to the services that naturally spring from it" (*Methods* 243). In citing this example, however, Sidgwick unconsciously assumes that children have previously and unquestioningly benefitted from parental affection. Neither Edward Bowlby nor William Faulkner enjoyed this automatic benefaction. Hence, Bowlby's early experiences, like those of Faulkner, fostered emotional inhibitions. Each boy turned to a non-biological relative (a nanny and a mammy, respectively) for affectional reciprocity. "It is indeed culture or cultivation that must supplement a deficient nature," writes Jacques Derrida in "That Dangerous Supplement" from *Of Grammatology* (1974) of Jean-Jacques Rousseau's description in *Émile, or On Education* (1763), of the "petted," spoiled, or otherwise undutiful mother, "a deficiency that cannot by definition be anything but an accident and a deviation from Nature" (146). The familial bourgeois environments of Faulkner and Bowlby were psychosocially alike in their "accidental" deficiencies. Indeed, later acts of self-naming would confirm the emotional distance between each son and his parents: William reinserted a "u" into his surname, at once distancing himself from the paternal epigone and forging a bond with his father's distant forebears; Edward, though retaining half of his mother's maiden appellation, dropped his Christian name, becoming John. Hence, each entered adulthood, with its necessary distancing (if not separation) from parental absence, as well as its potential for the redirection of stifled cathexis through higher education, personally rebranded.[5]

Faulkner had not finished high school, but thanks to the vocational training program for war veterans, he enrolled at the University of Mississippi in 1919. His academic disinclination, however, soon showed. "He seemed quite interested the first few weeks," as Robert Coughlan records, "but then he began cutting classes" (52–53). No one was surprised when Faulkner withdrew from his degree. The date was 5 November 1920. He required a different sort of emotional outlet. Faulkner wanted to write, and looking for inspiration during the years that immediately followed, he "bounced back and forth between Oxford and New Orleans" (Parini 74). Then, "on 7 July 1925," as Lisa Paddock chronicles, "Faulkner embarked from New Orleans with his friend, the artist and architect William Spratling, on the steamer *West Ivis*, bound for Europe" (413). His luggage included introductory letters to literary figures—figures whom Faulkner would never approach owing to his affective reticence.[6]

Unlike Faulkner, Bowlby was academically inclined, and he enrolled at Trinity College Cambridge, where he became "profoundly interested in and bonded 'almost worshipfully' with Darwin" (Issroff, "Personal Reminiscences" 17), who had gone up to Christ's College Cambridge almost a century before. In 1928, Bowlby "gained a first class degree in pre-clinical sciences and psychology" (Holmes 18), and the following year, he moved to London. Here, he not only began clinical medical studies at University College Hospital but also started psychoanalytic training under Joan Riviere at the Institute of Psycho-Analysis. Having gained his medical qualification in 1933, Bowlby stayed in London, joining the Maudsley Hospital, where his studies included psychiatry.

By the time of Bowlby's certification, Faulkner had long since abandoned formal education in favor of authorship and had already published seven novels. The 1930s would also witness Bowlby's beginnings as an author. Self-expression through writing compensated both men for a latent absence that resounded to the vestiges of parental failure. In answer to their parents' abstention from affective duties, Faulkner and Bowlby substituted the supplement of language, and this substitution related to each man's desire to propagate their own names. "The argument," as Gayatri Chakravorty Spivak explains of Derrida's exposition of this relational economy, "points [...] to the theme of the play of desire around the proper name: The narcissistic desire to make one's own 'proper' name 'common,' to make it enter and be at one with the body of the mother-tongue; and, at the same time, the oedipal desire to preserve one's proper name, to see it as the analogon of the *name* of the father" (lxxxiv; emphasis original).

By February 1934, as Michael Zeitlin chronicles in "*Pylon* and the Rise of European Fascism" (2012), Faulkner found himself in New Orleans, where he "witnessed [...] the opening of the $4,000,000 Shushan Airport" (97). That experience would provide the groundplot for his novel *Pylon* (1935), with Faulkner translating Shushan Airport, New Orleans, and Louisiana, into Feinman Airport, New Valois, and Franciana, respectively. In a letter to his mother from Paris, dated 18 August 1925, Faulkner had attested to his almost worshipful bonding with the "very very modernist"— "futurist and vorticist"—as well as with the "more-or-less moderns, like Degas and Manet and Chavannes" (13); and in *Pylon*, he combines his familiarity with New Orleans with his recollections of both Paris and its Exposition Internationale des Arts Décoratifs et Industriels Modernes. New Valois manifests "an uncanny metropolitan labyrinth akin in so many respects to the surrealists' Paris" (Zeitlin, "Fascism" 97), and the modernist airport's patron, "the powerful capitalist" (Zeitlin, "Fascism" 106) Colonel H. I. Feinman, resembles the unscrupulous Abraham Lazar

Shushan, who presided over the New Orleans Levee Board when the new facility was built in his name between 1929 and 1933.

In a psychoanalytical sense, Faulkner's letter detailing the Parisian exposition bears witness to his dependence on, yet separation, from his mother—and a wider familial sense of the uncannily familiar would soon envelop Faulkner's novel. On 25 March 1935, *Pylon*, a tale of mechanics, parachutists, and pilots that seemingly climaxes in the fatal accident of the barnstorming Roger Shumann, appeared in print. On 10 November, as Hamblin chronicles in *Myself and the World: A Biography of William Faulkner* (2016), "during an air show in Pontotoc, thirty miles east of Oxford, Dean Faulkner" crashed the plane his brother William "had provided him"; he died on impact; Shumann's "fictional fate proved tragically prophetic," the figurative katabasis to a meteoric year (62). The dutiful Faulkner, who had been nominal patriarch since the death of the ineffectual Murry in 1932, took immediate responsibility for the relational wreckage: Louise, Dean's wife, was pregnant at the time of her husband's death, and Faulkner pledged to become (in effect) the child's surrogate father. This promise complicated William's current familial entanglements. He had married six years earlier, and his wife, divorcée Estelle Franklin (née Oldham), already had two children (Melvina Victoria ["Cho Cho"] [b. 1919] and Malcolm ["Mac"] Argyle [b. 1923]) from her previous marriage.[7]

In addition to these related personal machinations, the general duty of rearing children appeared ever more challenging. "Raising a child was surely difficult in the nineteenth century," writes Kathleen W. Jones, "but for many families in the 1920s and 1930s, parenting seemed to offer new sets of trials," with "the slow accumulation of lifestyle changes, apparent as early as the 1890s, reach[ing] a climax after World War I" (121). The postwar world was "defiantly 'modern' and self-consciously 'different,' and commentators from the contemporary journalist Frederick Lewis Allen to the historians Peter Stearns and Ann Douglas have reaffirmed this transformation of culture" (121–22). In particular, Daniel Horowitz emphasizes the emergence in America of what might "appropriately be labeled *modern moralism*" (162; emphasis original). For modern moralists, who "assumed the nobility of folk who lived in natural communities" (162), the recent evolution of familial relations had been particularly and painfully marked.

The year 1935 proved transformative for Bowlby too. While Faulkner had been proofreading *Pylon*, Bowlby had been studying another of that year's publications, the Scottish psychiatrist Ian D. Suttie's *The Origins of Love and Hate*. This prescient investigation of infantile relations resonated with Bowlby's Darwinism. "The child is born with a mind and instincts *adapted to infancy*," reasons Suttie, "a simple attachment-to-mother who is the sole source of food and protection" (15; emphasis original). Retention of the mother dominates the infant, "a need which, if thwarted, must produce the utmost extreme of terror and rage, since the loss of mother is, under natural conditions, but the precursor of death itself" (15–16). Infanthood prioritizes survival; Darwin had emphasized the environmental aspects of this precedence; the family, especially the mother, manifested this environment; and Suttie believed that "Darwin[ism] would change psychoanalytic thinking" (Susan Budd 65).

In agreeing with Suttie, Bowlby simultaneously distanced himself from the prevalent view among their British contemporaries, in which childhood neurosis was a matter of heredity. "While Bowlby believed that heredity could play a role in emotional disturbance," as Robert Karen observes, "he doubted that hereditary difficulties would lead to neurosis unless the environment had somehow exacerbated them" (28). For Bowlby, the familial environment influenced the infant's psychological development more profoundly than biological heredity did, lifestyle changes precipitated by World War I were now influencing family relations, and societies must counter these detrimental pressures by supporting and promoting dutiful parenting. In the modern environment, the symmetry of inherent bonding requires asymmetrical support: parental attachment to their infants, as a moral and cultural duty, must bolster that biological predisposition.

Darwinism appealed to Faulkner too. Accepting some parental responsibility for his stepson, Faulkner was occasionally instructing Malcolm, and this tuition drew on Faulkner's engagement with evolutionary thought. "[W]ill you get me a good Darwin?" Faulkner would ask a New York friend in 1938, "I want it for my fifteen year old boy who is messing with anthropology. *Origin of the Species*, I mean" (Joseph Blotner 2:1008). "In my synonymity," Faulkner would later write to Albert Erskine (c. 7 May 1959) concerning *The Mansion* (1959), "'living' equals 'motion, change, constant alteration,' equals 'evolution'" (429). One can cursorily gauge Faulkner's own epistemological development in the shift from his delineation of biological heredity in *Sanctuary* (1931), in which congenital syphilis predestines Popeye Vitelli's delinquency ("he had no hair at all until he was five years old, by which time he was already a kind of day pupil at an institution: an undersized, weak child with a stomach so delicate that the slightest deviation from a strict regime fixed for him by the doctor would throw him into convulsions" [392]), to his discussion with Simon Claxton (1962) of "Man in his dilemma—facing his environment" (277).

The Darwinian appeal to the author of *Pylon* is, of course, immediately apparent in the evolutionary aspects of Faulkner's attachment to his mother tongue. This bond, which stands in stark and telling contrast to the practical silence that pertains between Laverne and her six-year-old son Jack Shumann, is evident on two levels. In terms of linguistic evolution, while Faulkner's neologistic portmanteaus, with their encasement of new meanings, populate the novel (e.g., on a single page, "neartweed," "neat-gleamed," "dullsilver," and "gearwhine" [833]), sedimentary over-determinations of signification are also apparent (e.g., the synonyms for "aeroplane," which include "machine" [786], "ship" [803, 891, 989], "crate" [804, 806, 925], and "job" [989]). In terms of intertextual evolution, the novel reverences and references several authors, including T. S. Eliot, William Shakespeare, and Arthur Rimbaud. Faulkner's detached attachments to these authors, to appropriate Eliot on the aesthetics of Thomas Middleton and Cyril Tourneur, "exhibit that perpetual slight alteration of language, words perpetually juxtaposed in new and sudden combinations, meanings perpetually *eingeschachtelt* into meanings, which evidences a very high development of the senses" ("Philip Massinger" 185).

Detached attachment to familial touchstones in literature provides an intertextual springboard for Faulkner's evolutionary originality in *Pylon*, with the conflation of biological evolution and cultural modernity in the novel evincing his increasing unease at humankind's impingement on the natural environment and the ramifications of that encroachment for familial environing. The highway to the Feinman airfield, which has appeared from the primeval depths ("the road [...] ran out of the swamp" [785]), heads toward "something low, unnatural," which exudes "a chimaera quality which for the moment prevented one from comprehending that it had been built by man and for a purpose" (785–86). The provenance of that "something" is also oddly evolutionary—"the oyster-and-shrimpfossil bed notched into the ceaseless surface of the outraged lake and upon which the immaculate concrete runways lay" (794) has been culturally conceived from the biological—and the aerodrome itself is an ambiguously "modernistic" creature from the Pleistocene Epoch: "a mammoth terminal" designed and raised by humankind "for some species of machine of a yet unvisioned tomorrow" (786). Even the dredge on Lake Rambaud, as the heterodiegetic, and therefore somewhat alien, narrator relates, "looked like something antediluvian crawled for the first time into light" (938). The entire Feinman edifice and its environs comprise, then, according to an apt malapropism from the mechanic Jiggs, an "organization or organasm" (840) that is at once biological and synthetic.

The mechanisms and machinery of modernity are expropriating the natural world. While airplanes are stinging organisms ("mosquitoes" [803]; "gnat[s]" [806]; "waspwaisted, wasplight" [787]), their mechanics and pilots "aint human" (804, 805, 813). Fittingly, the annoyingly interruptive voice on the Tannoy, which is a "disembodied noise" that blares "brazen, metallic, and loud" (790), catalogues the mechanistic attributes of this archetypal species: "cut him and it's cylinder oil; dissect him and it aint bones: it's little rockerarms and connecting rods" (933–34). This mechanistic takeover complements what Zeitlin calls in "*Pylon*, Joyce, and Faulkner's Imagination" (1996) the "appropriately 'alienated' narrative voice[s]" of *Pylon*—voices divorced from the human family, voices "now determined by the imperatives of a mechanized culture" (200). What is worse, this alienation of expression threatens to prosecute an inner disarticulation, with modernity voiding speech, "as if the [metallic] voice actually were that natural phenomenon against which all manmade sounds and noises blew and vanished like leaves" (792).

The alienation propagated by modernity underscores the novel's central theme of familial contamination, a theme that Faulkner had recently explored in "Golden Land" (May 1935). The protagonist of this short story is Ira Ewing, Jr. He fled his home in agrarian Nebraska, has become a wealthy realtor in Beverly Hills, California, but has suffered as a result: Ira's marriage is a failure, his son Voyd is vacant and cynical, and his daughter, who rechristened herself April Lalear on becoming an actress, is embroiled in a widely publicized sex trial. The ultimate victim of the Californian urban-industrial milieu appears to be the Ewing family unit. As H. R. Stoneback concludes, the "only positive character is [Ira's] mother" (155), but his maternal needs mean that she suffers too. On his father's death twenty years earlier, Ira "had returned to Nebraska, for the first time, and fetched his mother back with him, and she was now established in a home of her own" (703). Ira is thoroughly attached to his mother, "not once in the nineteen years had he failed to stop [...] on his way to the office (twenty miles out of his way to the office) and spend ten minutes with her" (703–4), and his mother is thoroughly attached to Ira, but her abiding wish is to return to Nebraska, where she bore and raised him.

The cityscape of New Valois and the new Feinman Airport, with its "façade faintly Moorish or Californian" (786), describe a relatedly insalubrious land of gold ("corrupt at its inception like the city," writes Susie Paul Johnson, "the airport is dedicated with an airshow," which affords Colonel Feinman the "opportunity for exploiting the flyers and the crowd with its craving for thrills" [291]), and they set the backdrop for an extended delineation of similarly disrupted familial relations in which, as John N. Duvall notes in *Faulkner's Marginal Couple* (1990), three of the major characters are "refugees from agrarian communities" (82): Roger Shumann originates from Myron, Ohio; Laverne comes from Iowa; and Jiggs avoids his home state of Kansas. With a novel instead of a short story under his command, Faulkner explores the familial reasons for, and probable consequences of, the relational complexities of these "refugees" in significant depth.

That significance effectively orbits the two schools of psychoanalysis then most prominent: the approaches of Sigmund Freud and Melanie Klein. Holmes elucidates why and how Bowlby dutifully skirted these schools too. Although "the Oedipus complex with its emphasis on castration anxiety reflected the patriarchy of its day" (9), and although Freud, the author of *The Interpretation of Dreams* (1899), was gradually relinquishing the intellectual foreground in the 1930s, his daughter Anna was emerging as "defender of the true Freudian faith" (3). That faith worried Bowlby. He felt that its followers, "burrowing in the obscure texts of the psychoanalytic testament" (131), fostered both "an atmosphere of dogmatism" and "an outmoded metapsychology" (128). More importantly, Bowlby questioned, as he would later emphasize in *Attachment*, the first of his three volumes on *Attachment and Loss* (1969, 1973, and 1980), the "closed system" (20) of Freudian preformationism. "Preformationism," as defined by Derrida in "Force and Signification" (1967), is "the well-known biological doctrine, opposed to epigenesis, according to which the totality of hereditary characteristics is enveloped in the germ, and is already in action in reduced dimensions that nevertheless respect the forms and proportions of the future adult" (23). According to preformationism, nascent sexuality alone drives psychological development through a succession of distinct, predetermined phases.

Suttie and Bowlby developed similar alternatives to preformationism. The main difference between their innovations concerned the motivational need for infant–mother bonding: for Suttie, this need focused on companionship; for Bowlby, this need focused on protection and posited a distinction between secure and anxious attachment, understanding the latter as the precursor of developmental difficulties and adult psychoses. Riviere was reluctant to accept, let alone encourage, Bowlby's interest in familial environing. In consequence, Bowlby turned to Klein, under whom he started studying in 1937. As Bowlby testifies in his first published paper, "The Abnormally Aggressive Child" (1938), Klein not only taught him the "technique of play-analysis" (233), but more especially seeded his interest in the subjective "object" (230). He had already learned from Riviere how a complex synthesis accounts for personality: "that self, that life of one's own, which is in fact so precious though so casually taken for granted," as Riviere would later summarize in "The Unconscious Phantasy of an Inner World Reflected in Examples from Literature" (1952), "is a composite structure which has been and is being formed [...] out of countless never-ending influences and exchanges between ourselves and others" (317). Klein took these psychological subjects and their interactions as *object relations*. Bowlby approved of this open (or environmental) rather than closed (or intrapsychic) perspective. Like Riviere, however, Klein continued to view the newborn subject as, according to Riviere in "On the Genesis of Psychical Conflict in Earliest Infancy" (1936), "entirely autistic, not only lacking in objectivity, but at first without objects" (276), and Bowlby rejected the resultant theoretical reliance on the autonomy of neonatal phantasy. Neither the Freudian nor the Kleinian school shared his belief in infant–mother attachment as a psychological bond *sui generis*.

Instead, Bowlby posited *attachment theory* as a Darwinian variation on Kleinian object relations, with the conditioning issue being security, not sexuality. Attachment describes how an individual forms emotional ties with people whom that individual perceives to be kind, considerate, and protective. The related theory "emphasizes," as Bowlby stresses in *A Secure Base* (1988), "the primary status and biological function of intimate emotional bonds between individuals" (135). Bowlby couples the infant to the family in uncoupling the infant from preformationism. Dutiful parenting is important because the familial environing of the infant determines several simultaneous lines of psychic development, and "whilst attachment behaviour is at its most obvious in early childhood," as Bowlby insists, "it can be observed throughout the life cycle, especially in emergencies" (26). Imagined geometrically, as prompted by Bowlby's relationship to the schools of Klein and Freud, attachment theory traces a hyperbolic trajectory: the foregrounded focal point is Kleinian; the background focal point is Freudian; for, as Issroff notes in "Bowlby and

Winnicott: Differences, Ideas, Influences" (2005), "as a trained psycho-analyst, Bowlby never altogether ignored the inner world" (131).

Faulkner also distanced himself from Freud. "What little of psychology I know," he would claim before the "Department of Psychiatry" (7 May 1958) at the University of Virginia, "the characters I have invented and playing poker have taught me. Freud I'm not familiar with" (268). Yet, while in Paris in 1925, as Parini relates, "Faulkner applied himself with a strange intensity to 'Elmer,'" a barely unmediated work of "naked autobi-ography" (87–88). That intensity and that paucity of mediation cast *Elmer* as a personal duty on Faulkner's part, and a gauge of the psychological issues with which Faulkner wrestled is the never finished state of this work. "Critics have repeatedly drawn attention to its Freudian aspects," observes Parini, "as if Faulkner sat with the work of the great Viennese doctor on his lap while he scribbled" (88). As Faulkner would admit in his interview with Jean Stein vanden Heuvel in 1956, "everybody talked about Freud when I lived in New Orleans" (251), and two years after "Elmer," in *Mosquitoes* (1927), Julius Kauffman and Dawson Fairchild discuss the poetry of Julius's sister Eva (and by association Eva herself) in terms of "Dr Ellis" and "emotional bisexuality" (461). If he lacked firsthand knowledge of Freud's work, then Faulkner was aware of Freudian notions secondhand, as *Mosquitoes* intimates, with Havelock Ellis supplying the intervening link. Hence, as if returning to an unfulfilled duty, Faulkner returns in *Pylon* to the familiar ground of these formative experiences, and "the very fact that Faulkner had never read Freud," as John T. Irwin main-tains, "would mean that in those conversations in New Orleans he could have absorbed many ideas whose ultimate derivations from Freud he would not have been aware of" (5). Like Bowlby, Faulkner did not ignore the unconscious mind (he might not have read Freud, but, as he joked in his "Interview with Betty Beale" [1957], "neither did Shakespeare" [268]), and while Bowlby's attachment theory reformulated the social sci-ence of familial relations, Faulkner's *Pylon* performed a relatable (if minor) form of reassessment.

In verifying his nascent thoughts about attachment, Bowlby turned to likeminded psychiatrists, psychoanalysts, and psychologists, those profes-sionals in America who were conducting inductive tests. These confrères included David Levy, René Árpád Spitz, Margaret Ribble, and Therese Benedek. Whereas both Freud and Klein failed to painstakingly verify their theories, the Bowlbian theorist must, as Bowlby himself would later aver in "Commentary: Where Science and Humanism Meet" (1988), "examine the idea, consider its implications, match it against other observations, use a variety of other methods of observation to view it from other perspectives, compare its explanatory powers with those of other hypotheses, and so on" (81). Sidgwick notes a similar responsibility concerning what he calls "the duties of the Affections, the rules that prescribe either love itself in some degree, or the services that naturally spring from it in those relations where it is expected and desired" (*Methods* 345); the moral philosopher "cannot decide *a priori* which of these alternatives is preferable; we have to refer to psychological and sociological generalisations, obtained by empirical study of human nature in actual societies" (*Methods* 346).

In 1927, when the Institute for Child Guidance opened in New York, "its director Lawson Lowrey agreed to the creation of a special research unit, headed by Levy" (Jones 289 n.13). The purpose of Levy's team was to identify and treat childhood neuroses owing to *maternal privation* (the total absence of the mother or mother substitute); such "grave privations" ("The Abnormally Aggressive Child" 232) were of early and abiding concern to Bowlby; and the undertakings of Levy's unit verified Bowlby's interwar findings: the continuity and quality of maternal solicitude is vital to the psychological development of infants. Attributing Bowlby's formative thoughts to the years immediately preceding his seminal monograph for the World Health Organization (WHO), *Maternal Care and Mental Health* (1951), as Vicedo tends to do, is a mistake, therefore, because Bowlby conducted much of the groundwork for this volume before World War II, with many of his notable concepts appearing in embryo in a number of publications during the late 1930s.

For example, in collaborating with E. P. M. Durbin, Bowlby would develop his formative ideas into a shared examination of *Personal Aggressiveness and War* (1939). "To permit children to express their *feelings* of aggression, whilst preventing *acts* of irremediable destruction," counsel Durbin and Bowlby, is "one of the greatest gifts that parents can give to their children" (42; emphasis original). An imbalance between permission and prevention can seriously damage a child's mental health. Adolf Hitler exemplifies such impairment. His father was too strict and his mother was too lenient. "Hitler felt intense guilt over his mother's death," note Durbin and Bowlby, and "the defeat of Germany in 1918 was regarded by him as a repetition of her death." *Mein Kampf* supports their diagnosis. "In his book," observe Durbin and Bowlby, "he describes how, when he learnt of the defeat and the proclamation of the Republic, he wept for the first time since he had stood by the grave of his mother" (135 n.1). Hitler's reticence in *Mein Kampf* concerning his father manifests a stark contrast. This near silence speaks of paternal privation. In effect, as Durbin and Bowlby conclude, the demagogue who was fomenting European turmoil came from an emotionally divided home, and one ought to understand this conclusion, which appears simplistic at first sight, as an anticipatory contribution to recent scholarly debates concerning Hitler and Nazism. The relevant discussions question why Hitler took exception to the comprehensive mobilization of women, where to position him on the scale of weak to undisputed dictator, and how he reacted to institutional and judicial misgivings.[8] Nazi Germany, attached to the alienating voice of the strangely detached yet charismatic dictating machine Adolf Hitler, would direct that alienation toward a scapegoat, and that detachment would end in the Holocaust.[9] In *Pylon*, Faulkner's novel of alienated voices, "such murderous echoes are felt," as Zeitlin argues, "on the level of presentiment and premonition" ("Fascism" 110).

Underlying Bowlby's speculation on the dysfunctional nurturing of psychological extremes was his interest in the *everyday child* of *maternal deprivation* (the excessive absence of the mother or mother substitute). In these less marked but more widespread cases, as Bowlby relates in *Maternal Care and Mental Health*, the concept of the broken home was "scientifically unsatisfactory." In its place, he "put the concept of the disturbed parent-child relationship" (12). Everyday children, who exhibit neither psychopathy nor delinquency, but whose misbehavior often presages social maladjustment, come from all social classes. Fortunately, child guidance can circumvent this danger, as long as clinicians concentrate not only on adaptable infants but also on maladapted parents. In America during the 1930s, the related opinions of Levy, Spitz, Ribble, and Benedek "were well known among child analysts, but with Bowlby's [WHO] report they gained greater visibility in psychoanalytic and psychiatric circles" (Vicedo 409). Hence, the familial perspective foregrounded in Faulkner's *Pylon*, which complements the Bowlbian perspective of the 1930s, but which significantly predates Bowlby's *Maternal Care and Mental Health*, reveals the novelist's prescience.[10]

This emotional intelligence and spiritual-aesthetic appreciation of postwar infant–parent attachment emerged from the less-than-secure attachments of Faulkner's childhood. To appropriate Issroff of Bowlby, "at a time when the psychoanalytic emphasis was on intra-psychic imputed structures and their functioning as perceived in the analytic situation"

("Differences, Ideas, Influences" 119), Faulkner interrogated the familiar from a perspective nurtured by an emotionally reticent childhood, with his scrutiny reaching beyond the premonitory orbit of Dean Falkner's demise. In particular, to malign or dismiss maternal importance was to court disaster, as the inability to retrieve Roger Shumann's lifeless body in *Pylon* intimates: what matters, where the psychosocial effort should be trained, where "the beacon's beam [...] with its illusion of powerful and slow acceleration" (944) should be focused, is on the maternal (not the paternal): for, "the dredge squatted inactive now, attached as though by one steel umbilical cord not to one disaster but to the prime oblivious mother of all living and derelict too" (949–50). At the biological level, maternal sustenance is an unthought and unconditional necessity, but social evolution must not mimic this detached form of attachment: societies must be dutiful in not divorcing the sentient mother from her sentient child.

Bowlbian principles aid the exploration of Faulkner's psychosocial insights concerning this overarching duty in *Pylon*, and the novel reciprocates in shedding light on those principles, but some literary critics might question the legitimacy of this reciprocity. Bowlby, however, had "a rare facility with the English language" (18), as Victoria Hamilton argues, and "Commentary: Where Science and Humanism Meet," one of Bowlby's final papers, testifies to his lifelong belief in consilience, welcoming "efforts to build bridges" in a culture "still plagued by inbred schools of thought which fail to communicate with each other" (82). Whether concerning its terminology (such as "attachment" and "detachment") or its figures, analogies, images, and metaphors, a Bowlbian inflected hermeneutic elicits networks of psychological insight from the concordance its interpretive application forges with its methodological subject. Notwithstanding this defense, Bowlby's objections to, and adaptations of, interwar psychoanalysis might seem overstated to a twenty-first-century observer, so their sociohistorical context needs emphasizing, and Faulkner's *Pylon* can play a useful role in that contextualization. "There is indeed a real problem about how social and historical factors are *related* to the unconscious," states Terry Eagleton, "but one point of Freud's work is that it makes it possible for us to think of the development of the human individual in social and historical terms" (141; emphasis original). Bowlby thought in this manner; Holmes makes a related point: "psychoanalysis, perhaps more than it would care to admit, is influenced by the prevailing cultural climate" (9), and the emergence of maternal deprivation as a social issue during the 1930s informed both Bowlby and Faulkner.[11]

That Bowlby proffered an inclusive theory, one that does not strictly confine its concepts and terminology to the discursive contours of social science, cannot be doubted. Above all, by avoiding an esoteric discourse, Bowlby wished to inform habitual thoughts and customary practices; so the repeated references in Faulkner's novel to a contemporary case of familial relations are all the more appropriate when taking Bowlbian notions into account. This attachment to the theme of deprivation comes boldly to the fore in the newspaper headlines concerning the Dionne **"QUINTUPLETS"** (826, 850; emphasis original). Born in Canada on 28 May 1934, these girls became the first quintuplets to survive infancy, but their parents, Elzire and Oliva-Édouard, were pilloried as undutiful. Allan Roy Dafoe, the obstetrician in the case, "had no faith in the Dionnes' ability to understand the simplest principles of preventive medicine" (Pierre Berton 76), so the Canadian government took "legal guardianship of the girls away from their parents" (Elizabeth A. Reedy 77). Although allowed access, the parents were excluded from fundamental decisions concerning their daughters, and they were "reduced to very undignified battles with the Dafoe-appointed nurses for control over the daily details of [the] nursery, from prayers to hair styles" (Mariana Valverde 59). Nonetheless, the **"QUINTUPLETS GAIN"** (826, 850; emphasis original) headlines in *Pylon*, if a reference to the girls' weight, appear to support the authorities' decision.

From a philosophical perspective, this case fell into what Sidgwick identifies in *The Elements of Politics* (1891) as the perennial ethical debate over "whether Government may properly prohibit acts merely because they involve a *risk* of mischief to others" (xiv; emphasis original). Parental states seem disinclined to interfere with parents. "Since the burden of rearing and training children should be, as far as possible, thrown on their parents, it seems desirable, so far as this burden is fairly taken up, that the parents discretion in the training of the child should be left as unfettered as possible" (140). Nevertheless, state interference is clearly expedient when "the child's interests are manifestly being sacrificed, either through the greed or passion of the parents, or through gross neglect or ignorance" (140–41). At the time of the Dionne case, clinical fears over undutiful parenting were still linked, as Dafoe's judgment intimated, to the concept of *mental hygiene*. The related regimen dated back to the late-nineteenth century. In 1881, the physician, mental hygienist, and suffragist Mary Putnam Jacobi counseled that "no ideas can enter the forming mind except from without, from communication with its fellows, or from the transformation of sense impressions. It is therefore largely in our power to determine the nature of the ideas of any child who is *thoroughly* guarded from his cradle" (122; emphasis original). The power to instill the hygienic habits of calmness, self-control, emotional unresponsiveness, and self-reliance was invested primarily in the mother. "Fears of going too far, having too much or too little, and losing control were not unique to this generation," avers Barbara Sicherman, "but they have rarely been elevated into a rationale for designing a way of life" (899). Mental hygienists would have approved of the detached self-reliance of Maud Butler and Maria Bowlby, on the one hand, and disapproved of the attached dependence of Elzire Dionne, on the other, but each judgment would have been flawed from a Bowlbian perspective.

In effect, mental hygiene pointed up the contradictory nature of female self-reliance, which depended on the environment in which women lived and worked. To physicians trained during this generation, such as Roger Shumann's father Carl in *Pylon*, mental hygiene remained a pressing issue, especially after the mobilization of a female industrial workforce during World War I. The postwar dutifulness and vocational "cleanliness" of women came under scrutiny. What ought to be the role of women now that the hostilities were over? This query, to appropriate Sidgwick from *The Methods of Ethics*, "expresse[d] a part of the meaning with which the words 'ought' and 'duty' are used in ordinary thought and discourse." For "when we say that a [wo]man 'ought' to do anything, or that it is [her] 'duty' to do it, we mean that [s]he is bound under penalties to do it; the particular penalty considered being the pain that will accrue to [her] directly or indirectly from the dislike of [her] fellow-creatures" (29). As soon as Laverne appears in Faulkner's novel, "looking almost like a man in the greasy coverall" (790), questions as to the dutifulness and vocational "cleanliness" of women arise. Concerning the mental domain, Laverne is trusted when she works on her husband's airplane as a member of a male-directed team (or family)—"the woman passed them the tools as needed; they did not even have to speak to her, to name the tool" (863)—but Laverne's solo attempt to service the machine fails: "she had put the supercharger back on with the engine head still off and the valves still out" (880). Carl Shumann would have decried Laverne's overconfident self-reliance and misplaced sense of duty in this instance. "While physicians sometimes noted the harm caused by women's 'limited sphere of physical and mental occupation, as compared with that of the male sex,'" notes Sicherman in quoting from the physician and surgeon Henry Putnam

Stearns's *Insanity: Its Causes and Prevention* (1883), "they were more apt to stress the dangers of 'undertaking, with perhaps insufficient equipment, a career just a little beyond her real mental strength'" (898).

In *Pylon*, concerning the physical domain, the taint of prostitution alights on Laverne. In *Maternal Care and Mental Health*, with reference to Tage Kemp's work for the League of Nations on *Prostitutes: Their Early Lives* (1938), Bowlby notes the link between "prostitutes" and their "love deprivation" (35) as children, and in Faulkner's novel, the reporter's "archadultress" (811) Laverne is seemingly available for a low price. In borrowing five dollars from the reporter, Jiggs tells him, "let her underwrite you" (875). "Underwrite me?" queries the reporter. "Sure," he replies. "Then you wouldn't even have to bother to put anything back into your pocket. All you would have to do would be to button up your pants" (876). According to a fellow journalist, pilots like Roger Shumann fly "because they have got to do it, like some women have got to be whores" (975). By structural implication, Laverne is one such volitionless woman, and Roger's parents will ascribe prostitution to her in explaining the money they find secreted in Jack's toy: "where would she get a hundred and seventy-five dollars," asks Carl's wife, "that she would have to hide [...] in a child's toy?" (990). They are wrong on both counts: Laverne is no whore; the reporter hid the money. She does not exemplify Kemp's report.

Faced with the intolerance that prompts such assumptions, however, Laverne insists on avowing a heredity taint. She tells Carl Shumann that she was "born bad." Roger's father is less critical in this instance: "nobody is born anything," he replies, "bad or good" (986). Carl's opinion is effectively Bowlbian, and biographical details suggest that familial relations, rather than biological heredity, account for Laverne's self-misconstrual. One period of deprivation ("her older sister that was married sent for her to come live with them when her folks died" [965]) reiterated another ("she hadn't had much fun at home with a couple of old people like her father and mother" [965]). Bowlby would have cited this double deprivation as the preclusive factor in the formation of a robust conscience. "Seemingly doing away with the idea that the superego has its origin in the resolution of the Oedipus complex," explains Inge Bretherton with specific reference to *Maternal Care and Mental Health*, "Bowlby claims that during the early years, while the child acquires the capacity for self-regulation, the mother is a child's ego and superego" (761). Bowlby's contention reveals his lingering attachment to "mother" Klein. "To Klein, there is no real distinction between the ego and the superego," observes Eli Zaretsky. "The ego takes shape in relation to internal representations of the mother and is the centre of 'moral' or, more precisely, 'ethical' relations" (37). Even though Klein did not believe in infant–mother attachment as a psychological bond *sui generis*, she effectively agreed with Bowlby: the infant–mother dynamic, rather than the Oedipus complex, accounts for the emergence of conscience.

Laverne's present situation (with Roger Shumann, Jack Holmes, and her son) bears similarities to Lena Grove's predicament (with Lucas Burch, Byron Bunch, and her son) in *Light in August* (1932). When the orphaned Lena falls pregnant, her brother McKinley, for whom she housekeeps, "call[s] her whore" (403), and she leaves in search of Lucas Burch, the baby's father. Laverne's double deprivation, however, ushers in depravation. "The sister was about twenty years older than Laverne and the sister's husband was about six or eight years younger than the sister and Laverne was about fourteen or fifteen." Grooming by Laverne's brother-in-law soon becomes abuse. "The husband started teaching Laverne how to slip out and meet him [...] and he would buy her a glass of soda water." Laverne probably "thought that was all the fun there was in the world and that since he would tell her it was all right to twotime the sister that way, that it was all right for her to do the rest of it he wanted" (965). Laverne's tainted upbringing, not her biological heredity, promoted *insecure-disorganized* attachment.

In adults, as Bowlby explains in *Maternal Care and Mental Health*, insecure-disorganized attachment "make[s] for promiscuity," and a vicious circle results "whereby one generation of deprived children provides the parents of the next generation of deprived children" (95).[12] Laverne and Roger are, according to their marriage certificate, Jack's everyday parents. "For the parent, being the cause of the child's existing in a helpless condition," as Sidgwick notes in *The Methods of Ethics*, "would be indirectly the cause of the suffering and death that would result to it if neglected." Even so, "this does not seem an adequate explanation of parental duty, as recognised by Common Sense"; rather, parents owe their children "affection (as far as this can be said to be a duty) and the tender and watchful care that naturally springs from affection: and, if [they] can afford it, somewhat more than the necessary minimum of food, clothing, and education." The question of "how far beyond this" a parent "is bound to go," he concedes, "does not seem clear" (249). Sidgwick would raise this concern again—"a question to which political economists generally have given rather vague answers: viz. what general assumption may legitimately be made as to the limits of parents' willingness to sacrifice their own present comforts and satisfactions to the future well-being of their children"—in *The Principles of Political Economy* (1883). On reflection, he concludes, "it will correspond fairly to the facts as they exist in England at the present time if we assume that average parents in all classes are willing to make considerable sacrifices in order to give their children the training required to enable them to remain in the same grade of society as the parents themselves: but are not usually willing to make the greater sacrifices required to raise them above their own class" (323).

From the Bowlbian perspective of fifty years later, the social factors of insecurity and disorganization that animate Laverne and Roger threaten to foster the social maladjustment of an everyday child (or tarnished angel) in Jack.[13] Bowlby identifies the main dangers, factors that in his fearful estimation were becoming increasingly commonplace in Western cultures during the 1930s, as illegitimacy (Jack was conceived out of wedlock), an unnatural home group (dice determined who became Laverne's husband; Laverne remains mutually attached to Roger and to Holmes; her son seemingly retains two father figures; Laverne is pregnant with Holmes's child), and distended kindred relations (Laverne's parents are dead; Roger's parents live in rural Ohio; Holmes's parents rate no mention). "It is, no doubt, usually thought that Morality, as well as law prescribes certain conditions for all connubial contracts," notes Sidgwick in *The Methods of Ethics*, "and in our own age and country it is held that they should be (1) monogamic and (2) permanent." All things considered, however, "it seems clear that neither of these opinions would be maintained to be a primary intuition" (347). Yet, while "permanent marriage-unions now cause some unhappiness, because conjugal affection is not always permanent," connubial permanence is still "thought to be necessary, partly to protect men and women from vagaries of passion pernicious to themselves, but chiefly in order to the better rearing of children" (21). In this matter, "it would seem that there can be no fundamental distinction drawn, in the determination of duty, between the actual state of society and an ideal state" (20). "It is probably only in communities in which the greater family group has ceased to exist," supposes Bowlby in *Maternal Care and Mental Health*, "that the problem of deprived children is found on a serious scale." In contrast, where family groups comprise three or four generations, close relatives are "always at hand" to ensure continuity of childcare (72).

Maud Falkner had turned to three older women—two of whom were family members—for help in fulfilling her maternal duties. Sallie Falkner, Leila Butler, and Caroline Barr had provided some continuity of care for the Falkner boys, but each woman's role as mother substitute, rather than occasional maternal support, had emphasized Maud's emotional detachment from her children. Murry had remained the focus of her self-reliance. Maternal replacements had cast a psychological shadow over the Falkner boys. In the substitute as supplement, to appropriate Derrida from *Of Grammatology*, "everything is brought together: progress as the possibility of perversion, regression toward an evil that is not natural and that adheres to the power of substitution that permits us to absent ourselves and act by proxy, through representation, through the hands of others" (147). A generation later in the Fa(u)lkner dynasty, when there remained many rural pockets of what Bowlby calls "close-knit and much intermarried village groups" (*Maternal Care* 72) in America as well as in Britain, Estelle Faulkner would make a related supplementary appeal. In an interview with Louis Daniel Brodsky, Estelle's eldest grandchild Victoria Fielden Johnson recalled that "both Mama [Melvina Victoria] and Malcolm stayed at the Oldhams' until Pappy bought Rowan Oak. Then my mother moved down there and sort of 'became' a Faulkner. But Malcolm, who was quite frail and very young, stayed on at the Oldhams'" (136). Physical distance hereby emphasized prolonged parental detachment, with Malcolm separated from his mother, father, and stepfather; and this long-term aloofness facilitated his maladjustment: "'he had [psychological] problems for the rest of his life'" (152).

In "What Is a City?" (1937), Lewis Mumford argues that urban life is replacing "family and neighborhood" with "primary groups and purposive associations" (184); a familial sort of defamiliarization results; but Mumford does not share the qualms of modern moralists. In contrast, as *Maternal Care and Mental Health* makes plain, Bowlby highlights the peripatetic demands on "many communities of Western industrialized culture" (72), demands that exacerbate the dangers of such defamiliarization, dangers that kindred distention intensify. Young adults "migrate far from their birthplaces and, not infrequently, [have] to move many times in the course of their married lives" (72–73). These "families have such loose ties with their local societies that for whole communities it has ceased to be a tradition to help a neighbour in distress" (73). Three quarters of a century earlier, Sidgwick had referred to this tradition, relating it via a decreasing scale of relatedness to the duty of general benevolence: "we should all agree that each of us is bound to show kindness to his parents and spouse and children, and to other kinsmen in a less degree: and to those who have rendered services to him, and any others whom he may have admitted to his intimacy and called friends: and to neighbours and to fellow-countrymen more than others" (*Methods* 246). Turning again in *Maternal Care and Mental Health* to an America contemporary for confirmation—and one with a coincidental link to Faulkner—Bowlby cites the "social fragmentation, of which Mumford and others have written" (73).[14] In *Pylon*, having traveled not only "across the United States four times" but also across "Canada and Mexico" (793), six-year-old Jack is understandably disoriented, and in the wake of Bowlby's findings, the Hungarian psychiatrist Léopold Szondi would identify an *uprooting syndrome* in which the constantly relocated child, like the child of maternal deprivation (and like William Faulkner, Malcolm Franklin, and John Bowlby themselves), represses the need for solace.

Thereafter, as an outlet for this repressed desire and as Jack exhibits—and as Maud Falkner and Maria Bowlby might have termed their children's respective affections for Mammy Callie and Nanna Friend—the deprived infant fixates on the *indiscriminate attachments* that Bowlby identifies with the (normally) transient first stage of forming healthy infant–adult bonds. When Jack first appears in the novel, Jiggs spots him in the aircraft hangar, not alongside Roger's airplane with his legal parents, but as if doubly detached, "in another clump of dungarees beside another aeroplane" (787). Later, when the Shumanns break for lunch, Jack is again detached, joining them from "a group across the hangar" (865). The reporter is another of Jack's indiscriminate attachments, and while being minded at the Amboise Street whorehouse, the boy becomes the center of a grotesque parody on secure attachment, with "the madam and a little young whore and the whore's fat guy in his shirtsleeves and his galluses down, playing with the kid" (822–23).

In *Maternal Care and Mental Health*, Bowlby issues "a special note of warning [...] regarding the children who respond [...] by a cheerful undiscriminating friendliness, since people ignorant of the principles of mental health are habitually deceived by them" (25). Outward happiness can mask deep-seated psychological problems. Jack's description as "spoiled" (787) summarizes this ambivalence. On the one hand, despite Laverne's attempts at the kind of strictness of which Durbin and Bowlby would have approved—"I bet you a dime you haven't spent that nickel," asks the reporter. "Naw," replies Jack of the reporter's earlier gift. "I aint had a chance to. She wouldn't let me" (932)—Jack is spoiled with sweets and ice creams from the ill-directed generosity of the reporter.[15] On the other hand, Roger's desire for detachment, a life of "no ties; no place where you were born and have to go back to" (805), has spoiled Jack: the boy, who was born in the nondescript and practically untraceable birthplace of "a hangar in California" (806), and whose mother's adult loyalties to Roger and Holmes often override her maternal reliability, has no firm attachments, no object relations untarnished by deprivation, and struggles to accept his detachment. Indeed, indiscriminate attachment, according to Bowlby, is a symptom of *insecure avoidance.* "These children show few overt signs of distress on separation, and ignore their mother on reunion," as Jeremy Holmes relates, but "they remain watchful of her" (105). In psychoanalytical terms, the Jack of Freudian preformationism—"a small towheaded boy in khaki miniature of the men" (787)—must make way for the Jack of Bowlbian insecure-avoidance.

Another outlet for the repression fostered by uprooting, as Bowlby notes in *Maternal Care and Mental Health* of Szondi's findings, is an "increase of aggression" (44). Jack's pent-up hostility is released when anyone questions his paternity. "Who's your old man today, kid?" asks Jiggs. "Now the boy," as if in response to a Pavlovian trigger, "rushed at Jiggs, his fists flailing" (787). A Bowlbian would read this aggression as an attempt to overcome the feelings of helplessness caused by paternal deprivation: Jack's biological father, as an attachment figure, and as announced by "the mixedup name, Jack Shumann" (977), is forever missing; two father figures (Roger Shumann and Jack Holmes) equate to no father at all. Laverne appears to understand this dilemma; she was the first to ask "Who's your old man?" (807); she instigated the release of her son's otherwise inexpressible anger. "As early as the 1930s," writes Jeremy Holmes, "Bowlby saw loss and separation as key issues for psychotherapy and psychiatry. It was the men—the fathers, sons, brothers, husbands, lovers—who died: it was a men's world that went to war." Bowlby's attachment theory, however, concentrates on maternal deprivation. "Bowlby's strong identification with his much-absent father comes through in his medical imagery, but he does not emerge as a live figure in the family drama as depicted by Bowlby" (36). In contrast, the much-absent father emerges, alive and kicking against familial duties, in the family drama that Faulkner depicts in *Pylon.*

Jiggs's complete detachment from his family is foregrounded by Faulkner. "The place I'm staying away from right now is Kansas," admits

Jiggs. "I got two kids there; I guess I still got the wife too." For Bowlby, the father is the absent and unseen breadwinner, but Jiggs openly shirks the role of economic provider. He avoids Kansas because his family requires maintenance. "Jesus, I couldn't even keep back enough to have my shoes halfsoled." Ironically, the onetime parachutist has jettisoned his children, detaching their paternal bond, as if it were an umbilical cord from an oblivious father: "I would make a parachute jump and one of them would have the jack and be on the way back to town before I even pulled the ripcord" (785). Beyond Jiggs, and with Bowlby's conspicuously absent fathers in mind, the temporary headquarters of the American Aeronautical Association during the Feinman Airport inauguration, the Hotel Terrebonne in New Valois, cannot help but carry an appellative irony. "Parents, especially mothers, are much-maligned people" (122), Bowlby would insist in "The Roots of Human Personality" (1959), but Roger Shumann and Jack Holmes, rather than Laverne, detach themselves from the supposedly good earth (or terre bonne) in *Pylon*. Flying offers the two men a temporary transcendence, or "quiet detachment" (845), that is unavailable to Laverne (who no longer performs parachute jumps), and that separation enables them to overlook down-to-earth duties such as parenthood.

Both Bowlby and Faulkner stress the ramifications of illegitimacy, an "unnatural" home group, and distended kindred relations. To use a term coined by the American attachment theorist Mary D. S. Ainsworth, these factors—which preclude Laverne's main desire: "all I want," she tells Roger, "is just a house, a room; a cabin will do, a coalshed" (887)—deny the establishment of a *secure base*. Ainsworth's concept, explains Germán Posada, "captures well Bowlby's notion that while attachment ties the child to his mother, it also allows him to explore his surroundings" (32). A secure base, agrees Jeremy Holmes, "provides a springboard for curiosity and exploration. When danger threatens we cling to our attachment figures. Once danger passes, their presence enables us to work, relax and play—but only if we are sure that the attachment figures will be there if we need them again. We can endure rough seas if we are sure of a safe haven" (70). Yet, while theory, practice, and effect most interested Bowlby, practice, effect, and symbolism most interested Faulkner—and much of the psychologically intense symbolism in *Pylon* concerns phallic insecurity. For Zeitlin, "Faulkner's stunningly overdetermined figure for modernity" comprises "the phallic pylons, the revolving airplanes, the inevitable smashing of machines, the burning of the pilot's corpse, the crowd's mesmeric fascination, the front-page, boldface publicity" ("Fascism" 100), and the Hotel Terrebonne, with "the nameless faience womanface behind the phallic ranks of cigars" (815), foregrounds the male member to the supposed detriment of its female counterpart.

All glimpses of such dominance, however, are undermined by the deconstructive tendencies of the text. Gender demarcations, in particular, are blurred, transposed, or canceled. "Jack [Holmes], like Laverne," remarks Duvall, "is marked androgynously" (*Couple* 83). Holmes's face bespeaks femininity ("he wore a narrow moustache above a mouth much more delicate and even feminine than that of the woman" [797]) and looks as though he resorts to cosmetics ("under his eyes the faint smudges of dissipation appeared to have been put there by a makeup expert" [797]). Laverne's face bespeaks masculinity ("that hard boy's face" [807]), her attire is utilitarian ("a pair of stockings rolled in turn into a man's clean white shirt" [791]), the workshop overalls she dons are anything but feminine ("looking almost like a man in the greasy coverall" [790]), and the trench coat she occasionally wears is unisex ("will fit anybody" [816]; "sexless" [828]). In sympathy with this disregard for gender, the group share duties concerning the airplane, but not in sympathy with this disregard, this sharing rarely extends to the tasks of parental duty that attachment demands: the men remain in the familial background.

Just as Bowlby pushed Freud to the background, so he pushed fatherly deprivation to the background. In contrast, Faulkner performs the counteractive operation, pushing the deflated, defeated, conquered, or mis(s) appropriated phallus to the background, where it subsequently resides. "Faulkner significantly chose *a* pylon, not pylons, as the initial image for his novel," as Joseph R. McElrath argues, "and close reading reveals that, indeed, there is a singular focal object, Laverne Shumann" (277). Put succinctly, Faulkner reevaluates the pillars (or pylons) of family relations, in effect, offering a figurative representation of Bowlby's hyperbolic model. Laverne is the field pylon around whom the rest of the family, her son and four men, circulate; their attachment to this reference point seems psychologically vital; and the airfield "apron," as a stereotypical referent and sign of motherhood, underscores her familial preeminence. "The architectural layout of Feinman Airport," as Zeitlin explains, "controls and inhibits the movement of the crowd" ("Fascism" 103), but despite these hindrances, Roger, Holmes, Jiggs, and the reporter repeatedly return to this referential sign: Roger and Holmes "had to go around to reach the apron" (931); Jiggs "had no ticket and so though he could pass from the apron into the rotundra as often as he pleased, he could not pass from the rotundra to the apron save by going around through the hangar" (800); the reporter "saw the five aeroplanes dart upward, diminishing, as he reached the apron" (884). To repeat: like Bowlby, Faulkner does not abandon the unconscious mind; rather, the apron in *Pylon* emerges as a constituent of a male nightmare. "As in an anxiety dream," writes Zeitlin, "Jiggs and the reporter, finding themselves caught up short by sudden barriers to their progress, must double back along an elaborate and 'tedious' succession of pathways" ("Fascism" 103).

Jiggs's most ambivalent description of Roger expresses an unrelievable male stress, a need for the apron, a wish for maternal comfort and attachment. Having dubiously requisitioned a monococque for the $2000 Vaughn Trophy race, Roger is both "a kidnapper" (925) and Charles "Lindbergh" (925), whose baby had been kidnapped and murdered in 1932. A figurative masturbation accompanies the doomed attempts to relieve such anxiety, with the singular cock, Roger's phallus, his pylon, "the perennially undefeated" (909) member that once rode Laverne in a cockpit, ultimately revealing its impotence, or lack of inner strength. For, as Jiggs explains of the monococque (or singular cock) that the desperate Roger will dare to fly: "it aint got any crossbracing" (924). In reality, rather than Roger's phallus riding Laverne, the female organ engirths the twin towers of double penetration: Roger Shumann and Jack Holmes, a pair of farmers' boys, are "two buried pylons in the one lowadrowsing womandrowsing pylondrowsing" furrow (849). That the reporter cannot bring himself to say the word "monococque"—"it's mon—mon—" (924)—comes as little surprise. Caught between female enclosure and male abandon, trying to remain close to the lake pylon while trying to maintain maximum speed, as Roger is and does during the Vaughn Trophy race, centrifugal effect overcomes centripetal force: the reporter seeing "something like a light scattering of burnt paper or feathers floating in the air above the pylontip" (935). The phallus, which has flattered to deceive, is fatally hoisted with its own petard.

After Roger's crash, the airplane's "wings had reappeared on the surface [of the lake] almost immediately" (937), yet the pilot's body remains submerged. At this juncture, Laverne's seemingly detached (or inhuman) voice—"she did not scream nor faint (she was standing, quite near the microphone, near enough for it to have caught the scream) but instead she just stood there and watched the fuselage break in two and said, 'Oh damn you, Roger! Oh damn you! damn you!'" (936)—takes over the utterly detached (or inhuman) Tannoy, and the futurism of chapter 5 ("And Tomorrow") slips into the awakening of chapter 6 ("Lovesong of J. A. Prufrock"). In effect, in Eliotian response to Roger's deathly submergence beneath the maternal lake, the "human voices"—which include that of the amplified Laverne—"wake us, and we drown" ("The Love Song of J. Alfred Prufrock" 16). The narrative's attachment to neologistic portmanteaus, which Derrideans would identify as symptomatic of textual phallogocentrism, now breaks down into linguistic detachment. The reporter, who must telephone in his story, is forced to disarticulate: "yes," he shouts of Roger's airplane, "f-u-s-e-l-a-g-e" (940). Nor can Holmes utter the homophone of his own surname—"if the seventy-five wont ship him ho—" (953)—when talking of Roger's anticipated (but never to be realized: **"AVIATOR'S BODY RESIGNED TO LAKE GRAVE"** [980; emphasis original]) burial in Myron.

Winning the Vaughn Trophy would have allowed Roger to follow Matt Ord's example, whose healthy familial attachments contrast starkly with those of the Shumanns. Tellingly, this prime case of a secure base remains offstage: "from somewhere toward the rear they could hear a dinnertable being set, and a woman's voice singing obviously to a small child" (889–90). Attachment exerts "an invisible but powerful pull on the child, just as heavenly bodies are connected by gravitational forces," notes Jeremy Holmes. "But unlike gravity, attachment makes its presence known by a *negative* inverse square law: the further the attached person is from their secure base, the greater the pull of attachment" (70; emphasis original). In *Pylon*, that attraction was strong enough for Matt to put his family (almost) first: the dutiful father has semi-retired from racing, with (presumed) legitimacy, a "natural" family group, and a settled life providing the Ords's child with an (unobtrusively obtrusive) secure base.

Similarly, and in the wake of Roger's death, Laverne supposes that her son's adoption offers both him and his unborn sibling the best prospects. Roger's parents, as Jack's possible grandparents, are his closest kin. Unfortunately, Roger's mother seems detached from life ("a faded woman with faded eyes and a quiet faded face" [989]), and more alarmingly, Roger's father exhibits *insecure resistance*. This Bowlbian behavior pertains to infants who are extremely distressed by separation from their mother and who are not easily pacified on her return. "They seek contact," explains Jeremy Holmes, "but then resist by kicking, turning away, squirming or batting away offered toys. They continue to alternate between anger and clinging to the mother" (105). Carl Shumann, who seems to be entering a second childhood, bemoaning the fact that he and his wife "are old"

(985), behaves in this manner. Roger's death has triggered his psychological reversion. Having adopted Jack, and with Laverne having left, Carl wants to wake the sleeping child, but his wife demurs. "Let me alone," he rages, "pushing with his hand at the empty air now since she stood back now" (988). Renaming his "grandson" as his son—"'Roger,' he said, 'wake up. Wake up, Roger'" (989)—Carl inadvertently supports the diagnosis of his own maladjustment. To repeat Bowlby's insistence in *A Secure Base*, "attachment behaviour [...] can be observed throughout the life cycle, especially in emergencies" (26).

Carl's father "had settled" in Ohio "when he come into the country"; he had farmed the land; and Carl continued to live in the property after his father's death. Although "nobody tried to farm much" (964), Carl only lost this agrarian groundplot after Roger started flying. "The old man wanted Roger to be a doctor too," relates Jiggs, "hammering that at Roger all the time Roger was a kid and watching Roger's grades in school." In response, falsifying school reports rather than preparing to be a physician, Roger would "doctor up his report cards for the old man" (243). Then, on discovering Roger's absenteeism, Carl became indulgent. "He mortgaged the place to buy his son a flying machine" (985), and after Roger crashed this airplane, the doctor borrowed money for its repair. Where Roger is concerned, Carl is the sort of "almsgiver" who "convince[s] himself that his gift," to quote Sidgwick, "is not likely to entail any material encouragement to improvidence." From this perspective, Carl is an anachronism, remaining tied to the past. "The general sense that care and knowledge are required even to minimize the danger has caused almsgiving to be now regarded as a difficult art," opines Sidgwick, "instead of the facile and applauded indulgence of the pleasurable impulses of benevolence that it once seemed to be" (*Political Economy* 594). Roger's debts plunge his parents into a downward economic spiral, and by the time of his death, they live in "a kind of cenotaph, penurious and without majesty." This flimsy bungalow, with *Pylon* again invoking Faulkner's insalubrious "Golden Land," is "built in that colored mud-and-chickenwire tradition which California moving picture films have scattered across North America as if the celluloid carried germs" (984). The fruit of Carl's misplaced parental duty is infected. A tainted product of modern culture (for which Hollywood is a synonym), his bungalow has the metaphorical status of a fetid but empty tomb, a mausoleum filled with a loved son's permanent absence.

Carl's repressed anger at the paternal–filial detachment effected by Roger's death fully erupts when Jack awakes. Disoriented by his new relational environment, feeling the full strength of his bonding needs, the boy asks for his familiar attachments: "'Laverne,' he said. 'Jack. Where's Laverne? Where'm I at?'" Deprived of his accustomed family, the boy then asks not for his grandparents, but for his airplane, the toy the reporter bought him. "Where's my new job? Where's my ship." Beyond exemplifying how the motivation behind infant–mother bonding focuses on the child's desire for either companionship (as in Suttie's belief) or protection (as in Bowlby's belief), Jack's relational disorientation signals his unspoken but genuine need for affection. "Like Nature's love," as Derrida notes in quoting Rousseau's *Émile*, "'there is no substitute for a mother's love.'" This love "is irreplaceable; what one would substitute for it would not equal it, would be only a mediocre makeshift" ("That Dangerous Supplement" 145). Spurned, and so performing an act of irremediable destruction, Carl "stamp[s] upon [the toy] with blind maniac fury" (989), and the scene closes with the insecurely resistant doctor collapsed next to his seated wife, "his head in her lap, crying" (990).

All these pieces of evidence point to the unlikeness of Jack escaping generational contamination. "It seems clear," agrees Duvall, "that the old man will psychically damage the child who will now reside in the bosom of an Ohio agrarian community" (*Couple* 93). The prospect of Jack's teenage delinquency is high. In "Forty-Four Juvenile Thieves: Their Characters and Home Life" (1944), which remains a "classic study" (Angela Dixon 278), Bowlby identified two factors of etiological significance. The first factor is separation from parents, especially from the mother, during infancy: "the child is suddenly removed and placed with strangers; he is snatched away from the people and places which are familiar and whom he loves and placed with people and in surroundings which are unknown and alarming" (39). The second factor is "inhibition of love by rage and the phantasies resulting from rage" (55), with the separated child responding to parental, especially maternal, absence with feelings of fury and acts of destructiveness. That Laverne has relinquished her parental duties in abandoning Jack to his putative grandparents only exacerbates these factors, an abandonment that exposes the boy to the deep-seated psychological problems of Carl Shumann, which themselves appear to stem from anxieties of paternal–filial detachment. The vicious airborne maneuver that caused Roger's death finds its analogue in the vicious circle of unreliable attachment that firmly ensnares Jack. Carl's insecure resistance makes a tragic sacrifice of Laverne's detachment from her son, and Bowlby recalls the generic tragedy: "a warning that the decision to remove a child from his own home is one of great gravity was given [over] 20 years ago by a distinguished quartet of American psychiatrists and social workers" (*Maternal Care* 70) in *Reconstructing Behavior in Youth: A Study of Problem Children in Foster Families* (1929), an American publication, whose authors (W. Healy, A. F. Bronner, E. M. H. Baylor, and J. P. Murphy) actually boasted a transatlantic pedigree.[16]

Sidgwick's consideration in *The Methods of Ethics* of "the duties of the Affections" (345) touches on the topic fostering. "If we confine ourselves to the special relations where Common Sense admits no doubt as to the broad moral obligation of at least rendering such services as affection naturally prompts," he muses, "still the recognised rules of external duty in these relations are, in the first place, wanting in definiteness and precision: and secondly, they do not, when rigorously examined, appear to be, or to be referable to, independent intuitions so far as the *particularity* of the duties is concerned." Sidgwick takes for his example "the duty of parents to children" (346; emphasis original). In this instance,

> we have no doubt about this duty as a part of the present order of society, by which the due growth and training of the rising generation is distributed among the adults. But when we reflect on this arrangement itself, we cannot see *intuitively* that it is the best possible. It may be plausibly maintained that children would be better trained, physically and mentally, if they were brought up under the supervision of physicians and philosophers, in large institutions maintained out of the general taxes. We cannot decide *a priori* which of these alternatives is preferable; we have to refer to psychological and sociological generalisations, obtained by empirical study of human nature in actual societies. (346; emphasis original)

Bowlby supplies such a reference in *Maternal Care and Mental Health*, and his conclusion is stark: "children thrive better in bad homes than in good institutions" (68), and "any mother," as Carl Shumann's inability to finish one of his statements to Laverne in *Pylon* adumbrates, "is better— better than" *none* (987). The Dionne case corroborates this Bowlbian perspective. For, despite the constant visits of Elzire and Oliva-Édouard proving their parental devotion, the quintuplets spent the nine years following their state adoption in a purpose built hospital, where "they were exhibited daily to tourists who paid a fee to see them" (Reedy 78). The

"QUINTUPLETS GAIN" (826, 850; emphasis original) headlines in *Pylon* were physiologically correct, but psychologically incorrect: only in 1998, when "the Canadian government paid the three surviving Dionne women approximately $2.8 million dollars" was their "emotional damage" officially acknowledged (Reedy 78). Government agencies had deprived not only the family of a sui generis right but also the parents' right to discharge their moral duties.

Bowlby believed that children "should be involved in any decisions about their welfare" (Holmes 43). This progressive attitude was rarely in evidence in industrialized societies during the 1930s. *Light in August* suggests as much when Joe Christmas's orphanage (to revisit an argument from Chap. 3 of the present volume) offloads him onto Simon McEachern. "We force no one to take our children," claims the matron, "nor do we force the children to go against their wishes, if their reasons are sound ones," but Joe is silent throughout the adoption process: "the child said nothing"; "still the child didn't answer"; "he said nothing at all" (505). In *Pylon*, Jack is asleep when Laverne and Carl come to their understanding, and most "of the problems which arise as a result of moving an older child to a foster-home are caused," as Bowlby insists, "by the failure to recognize the deep attachment which a child has for his parents." This depth is profound even if his parents "have given him little affection" (*Maternal Care* 58). The reporter in *Pylon*, whose inculcated intuition directs his indiscriminate attachments—"it was as though some sixth sense, some economy out of profound inattention guided him, on through the blank door and the tool room and into the hangar itself [...] where Jiggs sat" (943)—can appreciate this depth: his familial complexities, which include an unidentified father and a mother who carries the taint of prostitution, are comparable to those of Jack Shumann.[17]

Each in tune with his own sixth sense, Bowlby and Faulkner appreciated attachment, yet neither man bonded easily with his own children. Using Bowlby's own system of classification, the familial environments of childhood had fostered each man's *avoidant attachment*. That behavior aimed at forestalling parental rejection by attempting to minimize parental need. In *Loss: Sadness and Depression*, the final volume of *Attachment and Loss*, Bowlby terms this mechanism "defensive exclusion" (44). Both Bowlby and Faulkner had to play the role of father, but neither man was comfortable in doing so: simulation counterfeited (or defensively excluded) his purported acceptance of reality. However tacitly, Bowlby blamed his parents for this difficulty, as his chapter on "Boarding-Homes" (or should that be "Boarding Schools"?) in *Maternal Care and Mental Health* implies: "parents," he counsels, "need to be encouraged to realize that because of the nature of children's feelings for them they have a tremendous power over their happiness," a felicific gift that "they cannot abdicate try as they will" (125). Only after another generational step, did Bowlby, who "found fatherhood a difficult role," accede to this power: "he was, by contrast, in his daughter Mary's words, a 'brilliant grandfather'" (Holmes 25). In this personal way, Bowlby maintained his fascination with, yet distanced himself from, the strained attachments of modern familial relations. Filial detachment from his own parents, however, markedly survived his own death. Bowlby was cremated, as his parents had been, but unlike his parents' ashes, Bowlby's remains were buried at Trumpan Church on the Isle of Skye, Scotland, not interred alongside theirs at Brookwood Cemetery in Surrey, England.

When Dean Faulkner abdicated his paternal power by misadventure, his brother William, feeling a measure of dutiful guilt, took over the responsibility for Dean's family. Even so, and as *Pylon* intimates, Faulkner experienced related (Bowlbian) difficulties. Laverne's unborn child, whose father (Jack Holmes) is purportedly known, and Jack Shumann, whose father (Roger Shumann or Jack Holmes) is purportedly unknown, could be figurative substitutes for Jill Faulkner, William's daughter with Estelle, and Malcolm Franklin, Estelle's son with Cornell. When Faulkner married Estelle, Malcolm was of Jack Shumann's age, and as with Jack, Malcolm's paternity raised doubts. Parini discusses these reservations. After the birth of Melvina Victoria, Estelle soon fell pregnant again, despite her growing estrangement from Cornell. "Franklin grew highly suspicious and in due course sued her for divorce on grounds of adultery." Most of Faulkner's biographers, including Frederick R. Karl (269) and Judith L. Sensibar (566 n.40), discount the possibility that Malcolm was Faulkner's son; yet, Faulkner "maintained a close, even possessive, friendship with Estelle throughout her unhappy marriage to Franklin," as Parini maintains, and "seems to have hinted" that he was Malcolm's father (97). The married Faulkner's familial absences, however, were common knowledge. "Mac admired his stepfather," state Fargnoli, Golay, and Hamblin, "but Faulkner often neglected him for his work as he neglected other family relationships" (396). According to Sidgwick, "practical conflict, in ordinary human minds, is mainly between Self-interest and Social Duty however determined" (*Methods* 87). The extraordinariness of Faulkner's mind simply compounded this common antagonism. His negligence sometimes knew no bounds. "Malcolm had been bereft of both his fathers, hadn't he?" asks Brodsky. "Yes," replies Victoria Fielden Johnson, "and this created terrible, terrible insecurity, horrible insecurity." Just as Jack Shumann in *Pylon* does not know the identity of his father, so Malcolm "didn't know where he belonged, which father was really his." Deprivation bordered on privation. "At a certain point," reiterates Victoria Fielden Johnson, Malcolm "became quite mentally unstable" (152).

Faulkner understood the need to negotiate actively the strains of familial attachment. He might have welcomed a return to the *juste milieu* (or golden mean) of the so-called "less-developed communities" (*Maternal Care* 72, 90) for which Bowlby appeared to yearn. Indeed, that other writer, the reporter in *Pylon*, seems to be "in actual sight of the other side of Styx: of the saloons which have never sounded with cashregister or till; of that golden District where gleam with frankincense and scented oils the celestial anonymous bosoms of eternal and subsidised delight" (803). This vision is a mirage, however, as Faulkner appreciated, and feminists would decry the biological standards behind Bowlby's demarcations. This criticism prompted some of Bowlby's colleagues, including Ainsworth and Donald Winnicott, to distance the concept of attachment from that of gender. In the process, Bowlby's name became detached from his own theory. In contrast, Faulkner realized the unrealizable nature of such a return, the irretrievable breast of idealized maternity, but like his father before him, another retreat into the unrealizable past, another retreat from the "Golden Land" toward the golden mean, was alcohol. For Maud's eldest son, as David L. Minter argues, "the conflicts epitomized by the journeys to the Keeley Institute almost certainly aroused anxiety that ran deep. In years to come he avoided referring to these scenes yet persisted in repeating them" (15). Nonetheless, an inability to rewrite his personal past, and periodic bouts of alcoholic detachment did not preclude the honest insightfulness of his literature, and the obelisk in Oxford Memorial Cemetery that bears John Wesley Thompson Falkner's roundel on its northern side but Sallie Falkner's (his wife's) roundel on its southern side—a paternally *and* maternally marked pylon encircled by markers to numerous deceased relations, including to their epigonic son Murry, to his maternally reserved wife Maud, and to John and Sallie's fatally meteoric grandson Dean, but not to William Faulkner—testifies in retrospective anticipation to their eldest grandson's fascination with, yet distancing from, the strained attachments of modern familial relations.

As the reporter in *Pylon* muses, "it's like there was a kind of cosmic rule for poverty like there is for waterlevel, like there has to be a certain weight of bums on park benches or in railroad waitingrooms waiting for morning to come," like there has to be for dutiful parenting (as today's Bowlbians might add), "or the world will tilt up and spill all of us wild and shrieking and grabbing like so many shooting stars, off into nothing" (847). In fine, the mutual resonances between William Faulkner's *Pylon* and John Bowlby's attachment theory bring their authors together in a summary lesson for the related non-zero rule, which this chapter offers in closing: children single out their parents with attachment, and parents must reciprocate.

NOTES

1. The American historians whom Vicedo cites include Maxine L. Margolis (1984), Julia Grant (1998), and Ann Hulbert (2003). In 1991, the British child psychiatrist John Byng-Hall provided an overall summation of Bowlby's importance, which remains valid. "Bowlby, as with all prophets, was not honoured as much in his own country (or clinic) as he was abroad. This was manifest in the steady flow of international figures that would visit him." Bowlby's "influence was much more pervasive abroad—*especially in the U.S.A.* where attachment theory is all the rage in child development research—than in the [Tavistock] Clinic," London, where he was "certainly the most illustrious member of the staff," or in "the U.K." (13; emphasis added).

2. Martin, who fleetingly mentions Bowlby in "Faulkner's 'Male Commedia'" (158), comes closer than any other Faulkner scholar to identifying Bowlby's hermeneutical importance. In effect, however, and in keeping with the overriding approach of current analysts and clinicians, Martin detaches Bowlby's name from Bowlbian theory.

3. "She reared all of us from childhood," stated Faulkner in his "Funeral Sermon for Mammy Caroline Barr" (5 February 1940). "She stood as a fount not only of authority and information, but of affection, respect and security" (275).

4. Donald Winnicott was an English pediatrician and psychoanalyst.

5. Maud's third and fourth sons, John and Dean, followed William's example and adopted the surname Faulkner, but her second son, Murry, retained the surname Falkner.

6. Faulkner's friend Phil Stone penned these letters. The intended recipients included Arnold Bennett, T. S. Eliot, James Joyce, and Ezra Pound.

7. Estelle had married Cornell Franklin on 18 April 1918; they had separated in 1926; and had divorced on 29 April 1929.

8. To some extent, Durbin and Bowlby's findings also anticipate Rudolph Binion's psychological study in *Hitler among the Germans* (1976), which focuses on the death of Hitler's mother, the "misapplication" of the pungent disinfectant iodoform by a suspect father figure in the form of her Jewish doctor Eduard Bloch, and the mustard gas that poisoned Hitler during World War I.

9. Uta Gerhardt (1998) provided one of the first detailed discussions of Hitler's alien and sinister charisma. Durbin and Bowlby prophesied that "force will not cure Hitler or Mussolini of the desire to kill" (48).

10. *If I Forget Thee, Jerusalem* (1939) confirms Faulkner's foresight. The leading characters in *The Wild Palms* section, Harry Wilbourne and Charlotte Rittenmeyer, respectively suffer and inflict familial detachment, with motherhood appearing to be an unwanted condition. Harry, who "was the youngest of three children, born to his father's second wife in his father's old age," found himself orphaned "at the age of two" (515). That status came with his father's death, but the demise of his mother—did she die in childbirth?—remains unspoken. Harry's maternal detachment finds its complement in Charlotte, who abandons not only her husband, but more worryingly her daughters (aged two and four) to live with Harry. When Charlotte falls pregnant with Harry's child, she persuades him, against his better judgment as a medical intern, to perform an abortion. For Charlotte, the emotional cost of children is overwhelming: they extract a price she is unwilling to pay. "They hurt too much," she tells Harry. "Too damned much" (642). Despite Harry's care, the abortion goes badly, with Charlotte dying from "*toxemia, septicemia*" (647; emphasis original). Nemesis seems to have visited a mother for overriding her maternal instincts—and Harry's fifty-year prison term of hard labor for manslaughter endorses that visitation.

11. After *Personal Aggressiveness and War*, Bowlby's interest in the childhood genesis of mental illness resulted in his next significant publication, "The Influence of Early Environment in the Development of Neuroses and Neurotic Character" (1940), which approaches its subject via the statistical findings from "about 150 cases" (154). Bowlby's broad hypothesis alights on the causative effects of familial factors during infancy. He notes that adolescent neuroses often manifest themselves in delinquent behavior, "but concentration on the so-called criminal to the exclusion of the people with whom he lives," as he later writes in "Research into the Origins of Delinquent Behaviour" (1950), "is to study only half the problem." In fact, "it takes two to make a delinquent" (571), and government agencies generally overlook this reciprocity, despite the cultural emergence during

the interwar years of the leitmotif of youthful aberrance. In America, Warner Brothers released *The Public Enemy* (1931), which featured James Cagney's breakthrough role as Tom Powers. Cagney's portrayal of Powers was deemed captivating enough to threaten social mores. Powers found a literary counterpart that same year in Popeye Vitelli from Faulkner's *Sanctuary*. In Britain too, delinquency became a subject for the serious novelist, with Graham Greene's *Brighton Rock* (1938) offering a protagonist, the gang leader Pinkie Brown, who harbors what Trevor L. Williams calls an "extreme distaste for marriage" (73). Interwar Western society seemed to elicit, and sometimes almost celebrate, the delinquent.

12. Holmes argues that personal experience had informed Bowlby of this lineal danger. While Bowlby's maternal grandfather "had abandoned" his wife "for a younger woman" (25), each of Bowlby's parents "had had a special relationship with one parent" (15).

13. Universal-International released a film version of *Pylon* with the title of *The Tarnished Angels* in 1957.

14. Mumford was coeditor of *American Caravan* when the magazine published Faulkner's "Ad Astra" (1931).

15. The most "substantial" meal that Jack is seen eating ("a sandwich" [822]) is provided by the Amboise Street madam, and the theme of growing up versus maturing, which *The Reivers* (1962) will explore in depth, appears during the same scene, when "the fat guy want[s] to buy the kid a beer" (823).

16. Healy was born in England. His coauthors were born in America.

17. Yet, the reporter can avow to having a "conscience" (814), the only character in the novel to do so. Moreover, as François Pitavy argues in "Le Reporter: Tentation et derision de l'ecriture" (1976), the reporter's "luxation télépathique" (95) or telepathic dislocation, what a Bowlbian would call his "detached attachment" to Laverne, her son, and Jiggs, implies that the reporter, not the heterodiegetic narrator, recounts the boy's adoption.

CHAPTER 5

Universalism: *Absalom, Absalom!*

Henry Sidgwick opens his "Preface to the First Edition" of *The Methods of Ethics* with "the simple assumption (which seems to be made implicitly in all ethical reasoning) that there is something under any given circumstances which it is right or reasonable to do, and that this may be known" (vii). Sidgwick expounds on this supposition in his "Preface to the Sixth Edition." Immanuel Kant's tenet—"*act from a principle or maxim that you can will to be a universal law*"—impresses him as indubitable. "The Rational Egoist," explains Sidgwick, "might accept [this] Kantian principle and remain an Egoist. He might say, 'I quite admit that when the painful necessity comes for another man to choose between his own happiness and the general happiness, he must as a reasonable being prefer his own, *i.e.* it is right for him to do this on my principle'" (xix; emphasis original). Like as not, "'as I probably do not sympathise with him in particular any more than with other persons, I as a disengaged spectator should like him to sacrifice himself to the general good: but I do not expect him to do it, any more than I should do it myself in his place'" (xix–xx). Sidgwick accepts both sides of this argument. "No doubt it was, from the point of view of the universe, reasonable to prefer the greater good to the lesser, even though the lesser good was the private happiness of the agent. Still, it seemed to me also undeniably reasonable for the individual to prefer his own" (xx). In consequence, he understands that two approaches take happiness as an ultimate end; namely, egoistic hedonism and universalistic hedonism. Sidgwick often terms the former simply egoism; he often terms

M. Wainwright, *Faulkner's Ethics*,
https://doi.org/10.1007/978-3-030-68872-1_5

the latter simply utilitarianism. While egoism pursues self-interest, utilitarianism mitigates that pursuit. "The practical blending of the two systems is sure to go beyond their theoretical coincidence," avers Sidgwick. "It is much easier for a man to move in a sort of diagonal between Egoistic and Universalistic Hedonism, than to be practically a consistent adherent of either." One might assume that "only in an ideal polity that 'self-interest well understood' leads to the perfect discharge of all social duties, still, in a tolerably well-ordered community it prompts to the fulfilment of most of them, unless under very exceptional circumstances." On the one hand, "few men are so completely selfish, whatever their theory of morals may be, as not occasionally to promote the happiness of others from natural sympathetic impulse." On the other hand, "a Universalistic Hedonist may reasonably hold that his own happiness is that portion of the universal happiness which it is most in his power to promote, and which therefore is most especially entrusted to his charge" (84).

Jacques Derrida has been accused of promoting a form of undiluted egoism. This accusation stems from the misconstrual of poststructuralist theory by his overenthusiastic followers at Yale University during the 1970s. They equated *différance* with unlimited interpretation. This misunderstanding, which Derrida had anticipated in "Structure, Sign, and Play in the Discourse of the Human Sciences" (1966), amounts to "the Nietzschean *affirmation*, that is the joyous affirmation of the play of the world and of the innocence of becoming, the affirmation of a world of signs without fault, without truth, and without origin which is offered to an active interpretation." The contrasting reaction, which Derrida had simultaneously anticipated, amounts to "the saddened, *negative*, nostalgic, guilty, Rousseauistic side of the thinking of play" (292; emphasis original). Derrida's preemption of these responses was characteristically balanced. "Although these two interpretations must acknowledge and accentuate their difference and define their irreducibility," he states, "I do not believe that today there is any question of *choosing*—in the first place because here we are in a region (let us say, provisionally, a region of historicity) where the category of choice seems particularly trivial; and in the second, because we must first try to conceive of the common ground, and the *différance* of this irreducible difference" (293; emphasis original). As Frank Lentricchia concludes, "the fundamental aspects of Derrida's writing plainly do not sanction" what his Yale University followers might reasonably be accused of enjoying; namely, "a new hedonism" (169). For Derrida, as for Sidgwick, while questions of self-love and hedonism remain multifaceted, unmitigated dedication to self-interest is unreasonable. A consummate literary figuration of this unreasonableness is Thomas Sutpen from William Faulkner's *Absalom, Absalom!* (1936).

Universalism: *Absalom, Absalom!*

I have avoided the inquiry into the Origin of the Moral Faculty—which has perhaps occupied a disproportionate amount of the attention of modern moralists—by the simple assumption (which seems to be made implicitly in all ethical reasoning) that there is something under any given circumstances which it is right or reasonable to do, and that this may be known. (Henry Sidgwick, "Preface to the First Edition," *The Methods of Ethics*, vii)

In a much quoted episode, William Faulkner handed the newly completed manuscript of *Absalom, Absalom!* (1936) to his friend and fellow Hollywood screenwriter Dave Hempstead with the words, "I think it's the best novel yet written by an American" (Joseph Blotner, *A Biography. One-Volume Edition* 364). In the opinion of most Faulkner scholars, as adduced by Joseph R. Urgo and Noel Polk in *Reading Faulkner: Absalom, Absalom!* (2010), Faulkner's own "assessment remains valid" (xi).[1] *Absalom*, to appropriate Jacques Derrida from "That Dangerous Supplement," is "a decisive articulation of [its] logocentric epoch" (162), and personally considered, that importance supported Faulkner's further understanding, as summarized in his "Interview with Cynthia Grenier" (1955), that the novel was the "keystone" (223) to his evolving canon (or "world" [223]). Thomas Sutpen is the principal constituent of this keystone, and an ethical reading of *Absalom* cannot overlook this character, whose narrative presence even survives his death. Nevertheless, the following interpretation of Faulkner's novel remains provisional, desiring neither to prejudge nor preclude the findings of future ethical analyses. Indeed, the moral tenor of Faulkner's text predicts the likelihood of prospective ethical readings, because no other Faulkner novel emphasizes morality and conscience, or links rationality and morality, more openly than *Absalom* does in tracing Sutpen's ever presence.

This trace initially emerges from the opening accounts of Rosa Coldfield and Mr. Compson, two responsibly irresponsible narrators, whom many traditional Faulknerians, including Olga W. Vickery in *The Novels of William Faulkner: A Critical Interpretation* (1959), Cleanth Brooks in *William Faulkner: The Yoknapatawpha Country* (1963), Melvin Backman in *Faulkner: The Major Years* (1966), and Michael Millgate in *The Achievement of William Faulkner* (1966), have simply overlooked. "The first two tellings of Sutpen's story," confirms John T. Matthews in "The Marriage of Speaking and Hearing in *Absalom, Absalom!*" (1980), "are usually dismissed by critics as varieties of irrelevance" (575). That seeming insignificance emerges from their responsible irresponsibility. Rosa Coldfield, as the first of these unheralded narrators, reveals her contradictory status in at once implicitly acknowledging the aporias inherent to narration and actively embracing her narratorial role: "*(Or try to tell you, because there are some things for which three words are three too many, and three thousand words that many words too less, and this is one of them)*" (138; emphasis original). Rosa makes this pronouncement to her sounding board in Quentin, Mr. Compson's son, but by separating these words from her surrounding narration with ellipses, Faulkner typographically reiterates the aporetic absences that necessarily leave that account open to endless conjecture.

In a related manner, as the second unheralded narrator, the responsibly irresponsible Mr. Compson hedges his comments. The rhetoric he employs, as Matthews remarks, "caution[s] us that any recovery of immediacy and intelligibility will be the product of a fiction which acknowledges itself as such" ("Marriage of Speaking" 582–83). Mr. Compson, often deferring to the account given by his father General Compson of Sutpen's life, prefaces narrative details with numerous qualifications, as if accommodating the transmission errors (of mishearing, misinterpretation, and misunderstanding) that inevitably occur during casual conversation. These qualifications echo the circumspection of a utilitarian tract of the same period—both Rosa Coldfield and Mr. Compson give their biographical testimonies in the narratorial present of 1910—a time when "Millian and Kantian theories of morality were in their ascendency," as Richard Kenneth Atkins chronicles, "and Henry Sidgwick's highly theoretical approach to ethics framed discussions of the subject matter" (194).

In his homespun way, Mr. Compson cannot help but admit the conundrum of interhuman coordination, a philosophical concession at once in accordance with and in distinction from his counsel to Quentin in *The Sound and the Fury*. "Because no battle is ever won," he cautions his son. "They are not even fought. The field only reveals to man his own folly and despair, and victory is an illusion of philosophers and fools" (935). In carefully surveying this scene, however, Sidgwick claims no such victory, with *The Methods of Ethics* emphasizing the "Fundamental Paradox of

Egoistic Hedonism" (136). For, in defining egoistic hedonism (or egoism) as "the widely accepted proposition that the rational end of conduct
for each individual is the Maximum of his own Happiness or Pleasure"
(xxviii), and in accepting the common perception that "the ruling motive
in such a system is [...] 'self-love'" (89), Sidgwick foregrounds the attendant paradox, which admits "that the impulse towards pleasure, if too
predominant, defeats its own aim" (48). Rosa Coldfield's and Mr.
Compson's narratives, compelling accounts that not only appreciate both
their limitations and their imperfections, but also chart Sutpen's self-
interest and its culmination in self-defeat, hereby fall within the orbit of
utilitarianism.

These biographies agree in positing a lack of solicitude as the root cause
of Sutpen's ultimate failure. "His mother was a mountain woman, a
Scottish woman" (199), who died, probably during parturition, while
Sutpen (b. 1807) was yet a child. Her widower moved his family east from
the mountains of Virginia to the coast. That relocation only served, however, to separate Sutpen from the context of his mother's fleeting presence. General Compson recalled how Sutpen "said something [...] about
his mother dying" (184), and one can read Sutpen's "something," as
Matthews does, as deliberate understatement: his offhand comment
"suppress[es] the fact that everything he remembers about a simpler,
purer time is already contaminated with an aura of loss" ("Marriage of
Speaking" 589). That feeling prescribes Sutpen's behavior, and as the
analysis of *Pylon* in the preceding chapter of this volume confirms, this
form of absence spoke profoundly to Faulkner. "If, premeditating the
theme of writing," one begins by speaking of the irreplaceable mother and
the substitution of mothers, as Rousseau does in *Émile, or On Education*,
as Derrida does in "That Dangerous Supplement" in analyzing Rousseau's
text, and as Faulkner does in *Pylon* and *Absalom*, this is because "more
depends on this" topic "than is thought" (12). A mother's love is inimi-
table; any substitute is unworthy; indeed, any replacement "would be only
a mediocre makeshift" (145; emphasis original).

A critic of poststructuralism might condemn Derrida as a mediocre
makeshift in this argument, a disingenuous link in a disingenuous argument, but one can refute this objection in turning to Faulkner's knowledge of Rousseau. Evidence of this philosophical acquaintanceship appears
as early as *Soldiers' Pay*. "Faulkner's experiments in *Soldiers' Pay*," as David
A. Davis remarks, "demonstrate the growth of an immature but ambitious
writer exploring new forms" (40), and Joe Gilligan, who "swam through

the tedious charm of Rousseau's 'Confessions'" to his own "hushed child-ish delight" (228), figures those authorial attributes. Faulkner's philo-sophically maturing works of the 1930s also resonate with Rousseauan philosophy. "Golden Land" offers fleeting evidence of this reverberation. At one level, as the preceding chapter of *Faulkner's Ethics* argues, Faulkner's short story concerns Ira Ewing's barely repressed maternal needs. At another level, as Robert W. Hamblin and Charles A. Peek relate, "'Golden Land' is primarily an evocation of place and mood, a set of thematic varia-tions on California as a place of corruption" (155). An underlying aspect of this decay, which concerns not just Californian ecology, but Western morality in general, is a widespread cultural ignorance that spans the con-temporary, as personified by Albert Einstein, to the ancient, as personified by Esculapius. Faulkner's narrator connects these two figures through his evocation of Rousseau. The "names and faces and even voices" of the wealthy owners of Californian properties—on the one hand, the nouveau riche; on the other hand, the descendants of the Gilded Age—"were glib and familiar in back corners of the United States and of America and of the world where those of Einstein and Rousseau and Esculapius had never sounded" (702).

Faulkner's knowledge of Rousseau, as this cursory summation of his authorial journey from stifled infantile pleasure in *Soldiers' Pay* to stifled adult dependency in "Golden Land" implies, is undoubted. Cleanth Brooks recognizes this philosophical familiarity too, but his statement in *William Faulkner: The Yoknapatawpha Country* that Faulkner "is certainly no simple follower of Rousseau" (32) is problematic. Brooks correctly suggests that Rousseau does not influence Faulkner in a naïve manner, but Brooks incorrectly suggests that Rousseau's philosophy is simple. More accurately adduced, Faulkner's intellectual links to Rousseau are complex; the maternal void figures in these connections; and that contribution is evident in *Absalom*. This manifestation helps to set Faulkner's self-avowed keystone apart from his other novels. "Throughout Faulkner's work there are significant mothers," as Michel Gresset and Noel Polk note, "mothers who dominate and oppress" (29), but those of *Absalom* feature by their absence. "Born into her parents' old age at the price of her mother's life," observes Matthews, "Rosa guiltily tries to deny her own presence by living in an imagined world, what she calls a 'might-have-been which is more than truth'" ("Marriage of Speaking" 576). Rosa's life appears to have demanded her mother's death. Gresset and Polk cite Quentin Compson's mother in *The Sound and the Fury* as their prime example of maternal significance; yet, the treatment of her in *Absalom* is markedly different: as if necessitating her death alongside those of Sutpen's and Rosa's mothers, she goes completely unremarked.

Sutpen's widowed father does not remarry; no maternal substitute appears; and culture is left to compensate for Thomas's irretrievable loss. "It is indeed culture or cultivation," as Derrida explains, "that must supplement [...] a deficiency that cannot by definition be anything but an accident and a deviation from Nature" ("That Dangerous Supplement" 146). In Thomas's young eyes, this supplement amounts to the conspicuous consumption enjoyed by the owner of the Tidewater plantation where his father now works. In responding to his mother's irreplaceable absence, Thomas weans himself vicariously on this man's outlandish wealth, remarking how his father's employer not only owns shoes, but also enjoys the freedom of not having to wear them:

> And the man who owned all the land and the niggers and apparently the white men who superintended the work, lived in the biggest house he had ever seen and spent most of the afternoon (he told how he would creep up among the tangled shrubbery of the lawn and lie hidden and watch the man) in a barrel stave hammock between two trees, with his shoes off and a nigger who wore every day better clothes than he or his father and sisters had ever owned and ever expected to, who did nothing else but fan him and bring him drinks. (188)

Most interpretations of *Absalom* identify the turning point in Thomas's life as the insult he subsequently receives at this plantation owner's residence. "Sutpen, as a boy, was turned away from the front door of a Tidewater mansion by a Negro servant and made to go to the back door," relates Peter L. Hays, "a humiliating slight he never forgot" (72). "It was enough of an insult that Sutpen was brashly denied entry through the front," writes Dorette Sobolewski: "over and beyond that, though, it was complete humiliation for a white person like Thomas Sutpen to be turned away from the front entrance by a Black person" (70). "The incident of the young Sutpen himself before the door of the Tidewater mansion, sent by a Negro servant around to the back before he can even state his business," confirms Donald M. Kartiganer, "has been frequently noted by critics as being a turning point in his career" (44).

Beneath the ostensible racial overtures of this event, however, lies the inescapable void of maternal loss, as Sutpen's recourse to understatement again reveals: "it was like that," he told General Compson of the Tidewater incident, "like an explosion—a bright glare that vanished and left nothing, no ashes nor refuse: just a limitless flat plain with the severe shape of his intact innocence rising from it like a monument" (197). Something of lasting moment had occurred, therefore, and whatever the critical majority believes, that occurrence concerned maternal absence rather than racial presence. For, conditioning his immediate response to rejection, that void demanded Sutpen's escape into the natural, originary space of ontogenesis: he fled the mansion; he entered the nearby woods; he headed for a canebrake where "an oak tree had fallen across it and made a kind of cave" (192); and "he crawled back into the cave and sat with his back against the uptorn roots" (192–93). Birth, with the severing of the umbilical cord, deracinates; the death of Sutpen's mother had compounded that deracination; and the inescapable void of maternal loss, triggered by relegation bordering on rejection at the Tidewater mansion, grounded him in natural self-sufficiency. Sutpen was born of mother but was reborn of Mother. Driven back into the space from which parturition had expelled him, Sutpen emerged from this supplementary birth with a reinforced trust in the ruling motive of self-love; as a result, the natural conspired with the cultural, and self-interest began to dominate Sutpen's behavior.

"His trouble," according to General Compson's asseveration about Sutpen, "was innocence" (182). This purity amounted to the biological inherence of self-interest. This innocence, culturally confirmed by the plantation owner's conspicuous consumption at Tidewater, "instructing him as calm as […] others had ever spoken" (197), promoted the egoistic hedonism that General Compson called Sutpen's "code of logic and morality" (227). This amoral strategy was a compulsion—"not what he wanted to do but what he just had to do" (182)—and that compulsion turned him into a self-interested hawk. In the sense advanced by evolutionary biologists, a hawk intensifies interrelational offensiveness until an opponent retreats or retaliates, and "the ruthless Sutpen code of taking what it wanted provided it were strong enough" (99) manifested such hawkishness. Indeed, as the unalloyed embodiment of his selfish genes, and thus motivated by self-love, Sutpen started to become both the personality and the presence of egoistic hedonism. The plantation system appeared to serve this development, and having left his father's household to pursue his intentions, the Caribbean appeared to suit Sutpen's mission in life: on the one hand, because "money was to be had quick if you were courageous   and   shrewd"   (206–7),   where   shrewdness   meant "unscrupulousness" (207); on the other hand, because "high mortality was concomitant with the money and the sheen on the dollars was not from gold but from blood" (207). Sutpen's country of choice was Haiti, which "might have been created and set aside by Heaven itself," according to General Compson, "as a theatre for violence and injustice and bloodshed and all the Satanic lusts of human greed and cruelty" (207). Here, as Sutpen immediately appreciated, the "self-reliance of mountains and solitude" (199), as embodied by his father, had to make way for the actualization of self-interest: "he would not only need courage and skill, he would have to learn to speak a new language, else that design to which he had dedicated himself would die still-born" (205). The codes and articulations of that language must serve his desire for self-actualization in perpetuity.

Sutpen's first wife initially appeared to fit this design. She was the daughter of the plantation owner for whom he deputized. Sutpen "had got at last that wife who would be adjunctive to the forwarding of that design he had in mind" (209). Treated as a supplement, however, she posed a conundrum, being both sufficient and insufficient for Sutpen's needs. This contradiction, as Derrida explains of such dangerously maternal supplements, is essential. In terms of sufficiency, "presence, always natural, which for Rousseau more than for others means maternal, *ought to be* self-sufficient," and "its *essence*, another name for presence, may be read through the grid of this ought to be" ("That Dangerous Supplement" 145; emphasis original). In terms of insufficiency, "the supplement adds itself, it is a surplus, a plenitude enriching another plenitude" ("That Dangerous Supplement" 144). As Sutpen had already experienced in weaning himself on conspicuous consumption, a supplement is both compensatory and vicarious, "an adjunct, a subaltern instance which *takes-(the)-place*," but he never fully awakens to this compensatory failure. Substitutive, a supplement "is not simply added to the positivity of a presence, it produces no relief, its place is assigned in the structure by the mark of an emptiness" ("That Dangerous Supplement" 145; emphasis original); an adjunct remains never more than a surrogate; original presence never rematerializes.

Sutpen's design, his conception of consummated self-love, fell into this adjunctive trap: he aimed for self-perpetuation through reproduction; and when his first wife bore him a son, she seemingly enabled him to meet this end. Charles Sutpen, "who was *the* Sutpen with the ruthless Sutpen code" (99; emphasis added), promised much, and this potential had a felicific effect on his father. This supplemental adjunct to Thomas's biological male line ostensibly secured his design. Thomas's wife, as a maternal substitute, had apparently supplied his worthy successor. Thomas Sutpen's egoistic hedonism appeared to have attained its end. As the narratological penumbra that envelops his wife suggests, however, the supposed nature of this attainment soon came to the fore. "For any distinct image," as Julian Murphet observes, "we must depend principally upon Sutpen's own account, mediated in turn by Colonel Compson, Mr. Compson, and his son, Quentin," and "in that narrative echo chamber, we are thrown back almost entirely upon the grammatical and syntactic resources of *negation* to sense her at all." Even the name Eulalia, which sometimes accompanies the narratorial recollections of Thomas's first wife, boasts "no reliable authority" (253; emphasis original). Absence marks her textual presence.

Indeed, she could never be more than a maternal substitute, an adjunct that leaves Sutpen's egoism less than satisfied, and he could not help but discover a reason—one from beyond the economy of supplementary—to account for this dissatisfaction. Haiti had fooled him; the country was unsuited to his design; it was the land of the miscegene: "a little island […] halfway between the dark inscrutable continent from which the black blood, the black bones and flesh and thinking and remembering and hopes and desires, was ravished by violence, and the cold known land to which it was doomed" (207). Ironically, while Eulalia had always been an adjunct in accordance with Sutpen's maternal needs, Sutpen "found that" his wife "was not and could never be, through no fault of her own, adjunctive or incremental to the design which [he] had in mind" (199). From the plantation owner and his family, "there had been not only reservation but actual misrepresentation," misrepresentation that had "voided and frustrated without his knowing it the central motivation of his entire design" (217). A cultural contingency that could not be indefinitely deferred made its ever-presence felt in explaining her insufficiency: Thomas Sutpen "*found out that* [*Charles's*] *mother was part negro*" (292; emphasis original).

The pangenetic fallacy cast Eulalia as fatal to Sutpen's scheme, so he "put his first wife aside like eleventh and twelfth century kings did" (199). Moreover, while Sutpen understood the male bequests of procreation as accumulation, their son apparently manifested procreation as attenuation: Charles's blood was inferior to the pure blood of his father. Charles Sutpen was, but the person hereafter known as Charles Bon was not, an adjunct. Instead, as a miscegene, or mule-like end to potency and fertility, Bon was a tainted supplement. He broke the rules of nature. Bon's separation from the natural overwrote his perpetuation of the generations. In so reasoning, Sutpen was faithful to an inculcated fallacy, or to what Sidgwick in *The Methods of Ethics* calls an idol of the tribe ("we avoid the 'idols of the cave' by trusting Common Sense, but what is to guard us against the 'idols of the tribe'?" [152]), and thus he put his son aside too.

General Compson "said there was no conscience about that, that Sutpen sat in the office that afternoon after thirty years and told him how his conscience had bothered him somewhat at first but that he had argued calmly and logically with his conscience." Sutpen, as a purely self-interested logician, eschewed moral reasonableness, and considered this issue, as if it were an economic problem, "until it was settled" (216). This settlement confirmed Sutpen as both the personality and the presence of egoistic hedonism; he now manifested the culturally informed expression of his selfish genes; and the central qualification to his apophatic materialization in Jefferson adumbrated the immanence of his self-interest. For, he emerged out of nowhere ("He was already halfway across the square when they saw him, on a big hard-ridden roan horse, man and beast looking as though they had been created out of thin air and set down in the bright summer sabbath sunshine in the middle of a tired foxtrot—face and horse that none of them had ever seen before, name that none of them had ever heard, and origin and purpose which some of them were never to learn" [25]), into the communal center of Yoknapatawpha County, Mississippi. Sutpen's culturally informed self-interest "would not seem like an obvious locus of moral significance, so it has a quality of coming out of nowhere, of not being part of a recognized moral activity," to appropriate Eileen John, and so it presents, nevertheless, a "moral challenge" (291).

A casual glance at *The Methods of Ethics* would appear to discount this challenge. "It is sometimes thought," notes Sidgwick, "that there is an important class of refined and elevated impulses with which the supremacy of self-love is in a peculiar way incompatible, such as the love of virtue, or personal affection, or the religious impulse to love and obey God" (137). In the normal understanding of these impulses, however, this difficulty is overlooked. No modern school of moralists "has noted any inherent incompatibility between the existence of these affections and the supremacy of rational self-love." What is more, "Christian preachers who have commended the religious life as really the happiest, have not thought genuine religion irreconcilable with the conviction that each man's own happiness is his most near and intimate concern" (138). As a more rigorous reading of *The Methods of Ethics* confirms, however, rational mediation is the significant factor in this reconciliation, because "all morality rests ultimately on the basis of 'reasonable self-love.'" In other words, ethical precepts "are ultimately binding on any individual only so far as it is his interest on the whole to observe them" (7), an obligation that puts the moral onus on the individual's reasonableness. In *Absalom*, Thomas Sutpen's irrationally rational tactic of "singleminded unflagging effort" (59) served his hawkishness; that duty was the strategic expression of his egoistic hedonism; and that self-love put reasonableness aside.

The young Sutpen's socioeconomic environing confirmed and hardened his embodiment of unreasonable egoism. Alexis de Tocqueville (1805–59)—the French historian and political scientist whose life and observations the young Sidgwick would cursorily review for *Macmillan's Magazine* (November 1861)—contemplated such environmental conditioning in *Journey to America* (1831–32). "The principle of the republics of antiquity was to sacrifice private interests to the general good," he remarks. "In that sense one could say that they were *virtuous*" (210; emphasis original). In subtle contrast, the American principle "*seems to be* to make private interests harmonize with the general interest," so that "a sort of refined and intelligent selfishness *seems to be* the pivot on which the whole machine turns" (210–11; emphasis added). The principles of individual and general well-being appear to merge. The result is American democracy. "The doctrine of self-interest well understood, by imperceptibly inculcating certain habits, brings many people closer to real virtue," expounds Alan S. Kahan in *Tocqueville, Democracy, and Religion: Checks and Balances for Democratic Souls* (2015), and Tocqueville "finds in the self-interest well understood of the Americans a democratic substitute for virtue" (60), but he ultimately deems this substitute, this near virtue, unreasonable owing to its ingrained selfishness.

Sidgwick at once censures and commends Tocqueville. "He was destitute of one power, necessary in the pursuit of the highest truth," argues Sidgwick in his *Macmillan's Magazine* article; "he could not endure to doubt." This failing undermined Tocqueville's "earnest [...] search after truth." In fine, "'shallow' and 'superficial' are the last epithets that could be applied; and yet we cannot call him profound, either in character or intellect" (41). Despite these reservations, Tocqueville's criticism of the American doctrine of self-interest well understood dovetails with the mature Sidgwick's reasoning in *The Methods of Ethics*. "It has been widely held by even orthodox moralists," observes Sidgwick, "that all morality rests ultimately on the basis of 'reasonable self-love'" (7). Sidgwick defers in this instance to Joseph Butler (1692–1752). "Reasonable self-love and conscience are the chief or superior principles in the nature of man," asserts Butler in *Analogy of Religion, Natural and Revealed* (1736): "because an action may be suitable to this nature, though all other principles be violated; but becomes unsuitable, if either of those are" (414). In referencing this passage in his "Preface to the Second Edition" (1877) of *The Methods of Ethics*, Sidgwick "do[es] not (I believe) differ materially from Butler in my view either of reasonable self-love, or—theology apart—of its relation to conscience" (xiii), and this shared perspective allows him to tacitly indict the America of Tocqueville's time. "We are continually becoming convinced that old laws are unjust (*e.g.* laws establishing slavery): indeed, this continually recurring conviction seems to be one of the great sources of change in the laws of a progressive society." For Tocqueville, as for Sidgwick, antebellum America was intolerably well-ordered, a community based on exploitation, with the plantation economy satisfying the self-interest of one section of the population at the expense of another. These were exceptional circumstances in an intolerably well-ordered community. They prompted the imperfect discharge of social duties. "The conviction that slavery is unjust can hardly be traced to anything in the established order of the slave-holding society," notes Sidgwick, "but seems to arise in a different way" (*Methods* 272).

Sutpen's less than reasonable self-love diverged even further from Sidgwick's ideal polity than the ersatz virtue identified by Tocqueville did. Sutpen could never perfectly discharge his social duties nor could he ever attain to socially accepted grandeur. Cumulative and accumulative supplementation would always prove both insufficient and unsatisfying. Sutpen's unreasonable self-love would never fill the maternal void that impelled his unreasonableness. As in Derrida's concept of supplementarity, Sutpen embodied two significations whose cohabitation was as strange as it was necessary: in terms of sufficiency, he was self-regarding; in terms of insufficiency, he was extra-regarding. In the opening three chapters of *The Methods of Ethics*, as Sidgwick summarizes in chapter four, "I have been concerned to insist on the felt incompatibility of 'self-regarding' and 'extra-regarding' impulses only as a means of proving their essential distinctness." In truth, Sidgwick "do[es] not wish to overstate this incompatibility: I believe that most commonly it is very transient, and often only momentary, and that our greatest happiness—if that be our deliberate aim—is generally attained by means of a sort of alternating rhythm of the two kinds of impulse in consciousness" (51). Sutpen's associated rhythm, however, was essentially self-regarding. Initially, on his arrival in Yoknapatawpha, an impatience that was both introverted and self-stoking served this impulse: "it was General Compson who first realised that at this time Sutpen lacked not only the money to spend for drink and conviviality, but the time and inclination as well: that he was at this time completely the slave of his secret and furious impatience" (27).

Sutpen's self-regard demanded a self-sufficiency that refused economic indebtedness: "it was General Compson who knew first about the Spanish coin being his last one, as it was Compson (so the town learned later) who offered to lend Sutpen the money to finish and furnish his house, and was refused" (33). Sutpen returned from his subsequent absence from Yoknapatawpha with a French architect and numerous Haitian slaves; Sutpen returned from his second absence from Yoknapatawpha with the furnishings for his mansion. On each occasion, the payment for these chattels and goods was cloaked in a secrecy that provided Jefferson's "vigilance committee" (36, 47) with a moral challenge. They embedded him in, and accounted for his newfound wealth from, the morally dubious world of gambling. Sutpen disregarded this evaluation—Mr. Compson describes the vigilance committee as expressing "public opinion in an acute state of indigestion" (37)—and this disregard restated Sutpen's amorality. Because the word "amoral" is explicitly associated in *Absalom* (63, 114) with women and black blood, but with no one or nothing else, common evaluation hereby ranked Sutpen alongside the female sex and African Americans. Rather ironically, then, public opinion classed Sutpen with those elements who had first facilitated but then undermined the realization of his design. Nonetheless, by 1860, Sutpen's strategic rationale had made him "the biggest single landowner and cotton-planter in the county," a position he had "attained by the same tactics with which he had built his house—the same singleminded unflagging effort and utter disregard of how his actions which the town could see might look and how the indicated ones which the town could not see must appear to it" (58–59). His plantation, "Sutpen's Hundred," covered one hundred square miles. Sutpen certainly lived, worked, and played on a grand scale, but to the townspeople of Jefferson he remained a parvenu.

"We must allow," opines Sidgwick, "for the intermingling of moral with purely hedonistic preferences in the estimate of common sense" (*Methods* 153). This allowance need not apply to Sutpen. The practical blending of egoistic and universalistic hedonism "is sure to go beyond their theoretical coincidence," believes Sidgwick. "It is much easier for a man to move in a sort of diagonal between Egoistic and Universalistic Hedonism, than to be practically a consistent adherent of either" (*Methods* 84). Yet, whatever the demands of his lifestyle, and however taxing they became, Sutpen abjured utilitarianism. "He couldn't even realise," according to General Compson, "that his trouble, his impediment, was innocence" (193). Unalloyed self-interest at once promoted and impeded the achievement of his design, but "because of that innocence which he had never lost" (198), Sutpen failed to recognize let alone acknowledge this double bind. He never appreciated, however implicitly, the fundamental paradox of egoistic hedonism. On the one hand, his selfish efforts were indirectly individually self-defeating. On the other hand, his selfish efforts were directly collectively self-defeating. Sutpen's "naive use of language" (Matthews, "Marriage of Speaking" 588), as impeded articulation, captured his self-confounding position. Simple utterances expressed the simplicity of his ruling code. For, beyond the impulse of self-interest, Sutpen possessed no evolutionary potential. In fact, his strategic attitude was regressive. Matthews notes how "Sutpen slavishly copies the rhetoric and vocabulary of his design from accounts of how things were done in the past" ("Marriage of Speaking" 593); and the astute General Compson implies Sutpen's evolutionary regression in remarking an "attitude that nobody ever knew exactly" from whom "he had *aped* it" (198; emphasis added).

Thus, historical extrapolation from Adam Smith (1723–90), the man whom Sidgwick identifies as the founding plutologist, does not lead to the egoistic hedonist whom Faulkner figures in Thomas Sutpen. "It is striking to find the author of the *Wealth of Nations*, the founder of a long line of plutologists who are commonly believed to exalt the material means of happiness above all other," observes Sidgwick, "declaring that 'wealth and greatness are mere trinkets of frivolous utility,' and that 'in ease of body and peace of mind, all the different ranks of life are nearly upon a level, and the beggar who suns himself by the side of the highway possesses that security which kings are fighting for'" (*Methods* 155 n.1).[2] Even for Smith, "that wealth, in the pursuit of which most men agree in concentrating their efforts, and on the attainment of which all congratulate each other—wealth, for which so many risk their health, shorten their lives, reduce their enjoyments of domestic life, and sacrifice the more refined pleasures of curiosity and art—is really a very doubtful gain, in the majority of cases," as Sidgwick explains, "because the cares and anxieties which it entails balance, for most men, the slight advantage of the luxuries which it purchases" (155). In contrast, entertaining no such philosophical doubts, Sutpen strove unremittingly to satisfy himself. Unlike the majority of people—"for even when men definitely expect greater happiness from the course of conduct which they choose than from any other," as Sidgwick maintains, "it is often because they think it the right, or more excellent, or more noble course; making, more or less unconsciously, the assumption […] that the morally best action will prove to be also the most conducive to the agent's happiness" (*Methods* 153)—Sutpen abided by the unconscious axiom that an individual's purely self-interested actions best conduce to that individual's utmost happiness.

The legacy of a supposedly untainted biological male line consumed Sutpen's self-interest. He desired, above all else, a Thomas Sutpen, Jr. "This kind of supplementarity," as Derrida notes in analyzing Rousseau's *Émile*, "determines in a certain way all the conceptual oppositions within which Rousseau inscribes the notion of Nature to the extent that it *should* be self-sufficient" ("That Dangerous Supplement" 146; emphasis original). This imperative drove Thomas Sutpen: he should have been autotelic; he should have begotten Thomas Sutpen ad infinitum. Sutpen's misguided self-love necessitated a fitting adjunct, and his search for that accumulative fit alighted on the virgin (or unfarmed) acreage of Yoknapatawpha. As forever an outsider, and so an unreserved supplement, however, Sutpen strained to fulfill his natural self-sufficiency. His supplementation of nature always compensated for that which ought to have lacked nothing in itself, and both the community and its natural settings of Jefferson and Yoknapatawpha were ostensibly lacking. Indeed, as Derrida warns, "*blindness to the supplement is* the law"; and, in a sense, the less than exploitative residents of their economically virgin territory had drawn Sutpen to them. The perspective, insight, or vision of Yoknapatawphans, as nascent capitalists, was clouded by this attraction. The resultant opacity facilitated an acknowledgement that saw, but failed to recognize, Thomas Sutpen. "It does not suffice to locate [the] functioning [of supplementarity] in order to *see* its meaning," explains Derrida. "The supplement has no sense and is given to no intuition." Although the locals of Yoknapatawpha effectively summoned the supplement, they could not "make it emerge out of its strange penumbra" ("That Dangerous Supplement" 149; emphasis original). Yoknapatawphans were doves—evolutionary biologists explain dovishness as an altruistic strategy in which individuals retreat when faced with an unpleasant escalation in interrelational behavior—to Sutpen's hawk. Only the "Cassandralike" (17, 49) Rosa Coldfield managed to draw Sutpen's character from its peculiar darkness, but as "Cassandra" (50, 147), no one deferred to her: they heard, but failed to listen to, her testimony.

The unconscious and unrequitable essence of Sutpen's supplementarity dominated his behavior in Yoknapatawpha, and the multiplicity of narratorial agents in *Absalom* speaks for, and from, this illimitable reserve, with the principal narrator shifting from Sutpen's contemporary (Rosa Coldfield), to someone separated from him by a single generation (Quentin Compson's father), to two people separated from him by two generations (Quentin Compson and Quentin's university roommate Shreve [or Shrevlin] McCannon). While these narrators mine the limitless resource that was Sutpen's presence and is Sutpen's history, their figuration of him as self-love personified fosters a strange yet necessary cohabitation, which reveals itself both in unmediated significations and through narratorial negotiations that become progressively more strategic. "The negativity of evil will always have the form of supplementarity," as Derrida explains in "That Dangerous Supplement," because "evil is exterior to nature, to what is by nature innocent and good," and "supervenes upon nature" (145). Sutpen, who materialized in Jefferson as if out of nowhere, exhibited an exteriority. Indeed, as Rosa's unmediated epithets ("ogreshape" [10] and "fiend blackguard and devil" [12] of his "ogreworld" [17] in an "ogre-tale" [17]) indicate, she initially thought him unnatural. From her perspective, Sutpen was what Derrida would call "contingent evil coming from without to affect the integrity of the subject" ("That Dangerous Supplement" 153). This sort of supplement is potentially lethal, it has a "fatal advantage" in being "properly *seductive*; it leads desire away from the good path, makes it err far from natural ways, guides it toward its loss or fall and therefore it is a sort of lapse or scandal" ("That Dangerous Supplement" 151; emphasis original).

As such, Sutpen even managed to beguile Goodhue Coldfield, the father of Rosa and her elder sister Ellen, from the path of righteousness. Whereas Thomas was both the personality and the presence of egoistic hedonism, Goodhue attempted (but failed) to be both the personality and the presence of universalistic hedonism. For Sidgwick, "a Universalistic Hedonist may reasonably hold that his own happiness is that portion of the universal happiness which it is most in his power to promote, and which therefore is most especially entrusted to his charge" (*Methods* 84). Sidgwick hereby preempts objections that the assumption of universalistic hedonism would produce the total abandonment of self-interest.[3] Eileen John, in effect, agrees. "The embrace of the imperfect allows for a contrast between [a] kind of pragmatic morality and a morality of rigid expectations that appears unrealistic and insensitive by contrast" (294). Goodhue Coldfield appeared to embody an unrealistically rigid morality. "Philosophers in recent decades, following out some of Nietzsche's concerns," as John relates, "have taken an interest in what might be called the 'personality' and presence of morality, as in questions of how stern and pure it is, how encompassing and relentless its demands" (286). The supposedly "unimpeachable" (41) Goodhue, as the tenor of his respectable Christian name and his role as a "Methodist steward" (16, 34) imply, projected a relentless morality: he was "a man with a name for absolute and undeviating and even puritan uprightness in a country and time of lawless opportunity, who neither drank nor gambled nor even hunted" (34).

In effect, Goodhue outwardly conformed to Tocqueville's understanding of Christianity, as spelled out in the third volume of *Democracy in America* (1840). "Christianity at one end touches the doctrine of interest well understood and at the other the doctrine [...] that I could call with Christianity itself, the doctrine of the love of God. In sum, a religion very superior in terms of loftiness to the doctrine of interest well understood because it places interest in the other world and draws us out of this cesspool of human and material interests" (3:925). Tocqueville "does acknowledge the role that self-interest itself plays in religious belief," as Kahan relates in "Checks and Balances for Democratic Souls" (2015). "Indeed, he says that all 'positive religions' mix self-interest with duty in order to facilitate practice," but "Tocqueville clearly prefers the love of God to the bribe of Paradise" (108). In contrast, Goodhue preferred the bribe of Paradise to the love of God, with the related self-accreditation thoroughly informing his behavior. "His religion," as John Sykes notes, "amounts to a chilly, accountant's kind of legalism" (44–45). Goodhue did not offer his uprightness as a gift; rather, he banked his altruism for future requital. "He seems to have intended to use the church into which he had invested a certain amount of sacrifice and doubtless self-denial and certainly actual labor and money for the sake of what might be called a demand balance of spiritual solvency," Mr. Compson tells Quentin, "exactly as he would have used a cotton gin in which he considered himself to have incurred either interest or responsibility" (40). Goodhue's unreasonable self-interest left Rosa "to wonder what our father or his father could have done before he married our mother that Ellen and I would have to expiate and neither of us alone be sufficient" (17). Her contrasting perspective amounts to what Sidgwick identifies as "an ethical view widely held by persons whose moral consciousness is highly developed: viz. that an act, to be in the highest sense virtuous, must not be done solely for the sake of the attendant pleasure, even if that be the pleasure of the moral sense; so that if I do an act from the sole desire of obtaining the glow of moral self-approbation which I believe will attend its performance, the act will not be truly virtuous" (*Methods* 42).

Although Goodhue's Methodism prompted a limited enlightenment— he freed two female slaves "as he came into possession of them (through a debt, by the way, not purchase), writing out their papers of freedom which they could not read," but put them "on a weekly wage which he held back in full against the discharge of the current market value" (69)—that inspiration failed to enlighten him concerning the purely self-interested Sutpen.[4] Goodhue had amassed some equity before settling in Yoknapatawpha, and while Goodhue's "conscience [...] wouldn't let him" use his economic reserves fraudulently, Sutpen "persuaded" him to do so. Goodhue thought the scheme would fail. He would then "insist on taking his share of the blame as penance and expiation for having sinned in his mind" (214). Yet, when Goodhue "saw that it had worked it was his conscience he hated, not Sutpen;—his conscience and the land, the country which had created his conscience and then offered the opportunity to have made all that money to the conscience which it had created" (215).

This scheme amounted to a tactic in Sutpen's overall design; the inward-looking Goodhue was left to curse his conscience; and Sutpen was free to seduce Ellen through the legalized rites of marriage. She became the next explicit manifestation in Sutpen's life of the necessary yet adjunctive side of supplementarity. The apparently extra-regarding act of marriage again served his design of self-actualization in perpetuity. He made no conscientious effort to restrict the ruling motive of self-love. Indeed, according to the interpretation of Shreve McCannon, Sutpen wanted to emulate the dying Abraham, wishing in effect that "I might rest mine eyes upon my goods and chattels, upon the generations of them and of my descendants increased an hundred fold as my soul goeth out from me" (268). Sutpen's Hundred would be the topographical embodiment of that "an hundred fold." This plantation would "remind him (if he ever forgot it) that he was the biggest thing in [the] sight [of Yoknapatawphans] and in his own too" (298). Sutpen, as Thadious M. Davis argues, "presumes the necessity of dynasty, that he must produce both a legal heir, one who is white and male, and an estate or cultivated land with a house such as his Supten's Hundred, in order to authenticate himself within Mississippi society" (154), and that presumption, which Davis does not dwell on, emerges from Sutpen's all-consuming love of self.

In Ellen, as a woman of pure blood, Sutpen seemingly found his fitting adjunct. She gave birth to a son, Henry, in 1839, and to a daughter, Judith, in 1841. Henry did not embody, however, Sutpen's desired descendant. This son, "with the Coldfield cluttering of morality and rules of right and wrong" (99), took after his maternal grandfather: he exhibited that "puritan heritage—that heritage peculiarly Anglo-Saxon—of fierce proud mysticism and that ability to be ashamed of ignorance and inexperience" (90). In fact, Henry was less of a Sutpen than his sister was, as their differing responses to their father's barn fights testified. Still unable to satisfy his self-interest, "the ritualistic fighting of his slaves," as Urgo and Polk explain, "marks his insistence that he must perform his superiority rather than base it on his property" (118), and "while Henry screamed and vomited" (*Absalom* 99) during these rituals, Judith appreciated them. She displayed "the same cold and attentive interest with which Sutpen would have watched Henry fighting with a negro boy of his own age and weight" (*Absalom* 99). Yet, while Judith sported more of her father's egoistic hedonism than Henry did, she remained a daughter. The amorality, which ranked Thomas Sutpen alongside the female sex and African Americans, refused to recognize either the female Judith or the miscegenate Charles as a true genealogical supplement.

In turn, Ellen proved herself incapable of fulfilling, arresting, domesticating, or taming her husband's virulent needs. She could never fill Sutpen's unassuageable void of maternal loss; her children could not meet his lineal demands; and these failures were decisive for their marriage. Realizing a procreative end in Ellen, Sutpen increasingly absented himself from home, determined in his singular pursuit of self-satisfaction. "Between auto-eroticism and hetero-eroticism," as Derrida explains in "That Dangerous Supplement," "there is not a frontier but an economic distribution" (155). Sutpen's barn fights, which partook of this economy, expressed the corrupt nature of his love of self. Onanism, with its unconscious recall of the infantile fort-da, boasts a certain behavioral privilege; masturbation enacts a dubious form of maternal remembrance; and this dangerous supplement retains a certain privilege. "For it is not the question of diverting total enjoyment toward a particular substitute," as Sutpen's homosocial combat did, "but now," to appropriate Derrida, "of experiencing it or miming it *directly and in its totality*" (152; emphasis original). Restitution by the onanistic, as with the linguistic, supplement affords an immediacy of experience, restitution "as consciousness or conscience" that "*dispenses with passage through the world.* What is touching is touched, auto-affection gives itself as pure autarchy" (153–54; emphasis original).

Henry's birth had initially stifled Sutpen's sense of deferred pleasure. "But what is no longer deferred is also absolutely deferred," as Derrida cautions in "That Dangerous Supplement." "The presence that is thus delivered to us in the present is a chimera. Auto-affection is a pure speculation. The sign, the image, the representation, which come to supplement the absent presence are the illusions that sidetrack us. To culpability, to the anguish of death and castration, is added or rather is assimilated the experience of frustration." Auto-affection, as pure speculation, discounts the alterity of the genealogical adjunct, the supplement that is supposed to guarantee the future satisfaction of that auto-affection: enjoyment and abstinence, wisdom and happiness escape in equal measure. "The enjoyment of the *thing itself is* thus undermined, in its act and in its essence, by frustration," as Derrida maintains. "One cannot therefore say that it has an essence or an act (*eidos, ousia, energeia*, etc.). Something promises itself as it escapes, gives itself as it moves away, and strictly speaking it cannot even be called presence" (154; emphasis original). Thomas Sutpen's egoistic hedonism evidenced the rule of pleasure pursued but forever postponed, and the incomplete nature of self-satisfaction began to haunt him.

Although he had put Charles Bon aside, assuming the permanent sidelining of this earlier "mistake," his firstborn son now reappeared. One of the perilous aspects of the dangerous supplement is what Derrida calls its "power of *procuring* an absent presence through its image" (155; emphasis original); and Sutpen unwittingly but effectively summoned to Yoknapatawpha a presence that he had refused to formally acknowledge. Like his father before him, Charles first materialized in Yoknapatawpha as if from nowhere, "almost phoenix-like, fullsprung from no childhood." In an irony that gainsaid Sutpen's attitude toward him, this son appeared to exceed his father, being not only "*the* Sutpen with the ruthless Sutpen code" (99; emphasis added), but also *the* Sutpen "with an ease of manner and swaggering gallant air in comparison with which [his father's] pompous arrogance was clumsy bluff" (61). Charles's arrival at Sutpen's Hundred ought to have betrayed Sutpen's self-deception that "after more than thirty years, more than thirty years after my conscience had finally assured me that if I had done an injustice, I had done what I could to rectify it" (219). To Sutpen's mind, having balanced his moral books for the (at worst) amoral act of rejecting a miscegene, he deserved no censure, so Charles now attempted to force the issue: he plighted his troth to his unsuspecting half sister. Sutpen did not, however, change his stance. Even during the extra-regarding hiatus of the civil war, and despite his service as a confederate colonel, he remained essentially self-regarding, as the neglected Ellen's death in 1863 confirmed, and his aim on surviving the conflict remained the propagation of an untainted male line. Thus, when hostilities permanently ceased, and when Henry subsequently murdered Charles and then disappeared, these losses barely counted with Sutpen: Charles bore tainted blood; Henry was more Coldfield than Sutpen.

Effectively without a male heir, the widowed Sutpen returned to the devastated landscape of Yoknapatawpha, where he found himself divested of most of his "*ten-mile square*" (135; emphasis original). Nevertheless, when he "felt and heard the design—house, position, posterity and all—come down like it had been built out of smoke," he interpreted this disaster, according to Quentin, "not" as "moral retribution," but as the repercussions from an "old mistake." Furthermore, as "a man of courage and shrewdness," Sutpen believed he "could still combat" these consequences (221). The reaction of General Compson, who at the time repeatedly questioned Sutpen about his misguided concept of "Conscience? Conscience?" (219), made no impression on him. In ethical terms, Sutpen's shrewdness was always unscrupulousness, and Sutpen did not know, and would never realize, that his unswerving loyalty to egoistic hedonism was at fault. He simply held to "his conviction that [his current situation] had all come from a mistake and until he discovered what that mistake had been he did not intend to risk making another one" (221). Thus, he pinned his self-interested hopes on Rosa Coldfield, and immediately erred again. Sutpen remained to her the epitome of vice and perversion. Rosa considered him a contingent evil that threatened her personal integrity. She could not help, however, but mirror her nemesis. Rosa understood that Sutpen could not relinquish what promised to restore the desired presence of the other, and just as the maternal supplement meant everything to him, so the supplement of language will mean everything to her.

As this complementarity foretold, Rosa was, as her sister had been, seduced to Sutpen's Hundred. For, on Henry's death, she took up residence at the plantation in Sutpen's absence, and slowly but inextricably fell under Sutpen's dangerously supplemental spell. This epitome of vice and perversion was the only man for her, and though she ultimately rejected the subaltern role of deferred wife by returning to Jefferson— "one must conclude," writes Deborah Clarke, "that Sutpen's blunt statement that she is wanted only to bear sons is what enrages her, not the suggestion of premarital sex" (130)—Rosa never awakens from mental seduction. Her experience constructed a particular supplement, what Derrida might call "an edifice of significations" ("That Dangerous Supplement" 153), and this construction has remained Rosa's obsession, an ever presence that she will constantly revivify in retelling and reliving the Sutpen history. Rosa's longing for, but permanent separation from, Thomas Sutpen encapsulates the pleasure and the guilt of that dangerous supplement: onanism that recalls not so much her permanent virginity, but her *pucelage*. Derrida uses this term to describe Rousseau's admission in his *Confessions* concerning Thérèse's maidenhood. "*Pucelage*," as Derrida's translator Gayatri Chakravorty Spivak explains, "is the more earthy French word for the actual physical fact of sexual intactness, in the female the membrane itself" ("That Dangerous Supplement" 150 n). Sexual frustration and the frisson of autoeroticism—what the heterodiegetic narrator in *Absalom* calls "the rank smell of female old flesh long embattled in virginity" (5)—charge the atmosphere of Rosa's house. "Despite her incontestable virginity," as Matthews notes, "she recalls an adolescence that had awakened the 'root bloom and urge' of passion" ("Marriage of Speaking" 578).

Rosa's linguistic onanism ensures what Murphet calls "the cancellation and sublation of narrative time itself" (275). Her past enthralls her present. For, as Quentin, her virtually silent interlocutor, will silently complain, "*I have had to listen too long*" (161; emphasis original), "*I have heard too much, I have been told too much; I have had to listen to too much, too long*" (171–72; emphasis original). Rosa's repeated recourse to the Sutpen story cannot help but express a dangerous supplement. "The experience of auto-eroticism is lived in anguish," as Derrida notes. "Masturbation reassures [...] only through that culpability traditionally attached to the practice, obliging children to assume the fault and to interiorize the threat of [punishment] that always accompanies it" ("That Dangerous Supplement" 150–51). In the present of 1910, just as in the past with Sutpen's unconscious enthrallment to maternal remembrance, Rosa cannot relinquish what immediately restores to her a semblance of the needed other. Almost complete silence accompanied Sutpen's obsession; almost anything but silence accompanies Rosa's obsession; petrified in immaturity, she cannot give his memory up, any more than she can relinquish her use of language.

"To the end of his life," quotes Derrida of the self-avowal in Rousseau's *Dialogues* (Pléiade, I, 800), "he will remain an aged child" ("That Dangerous Supplement" 153). Rosa remains an aged child to the end of her life too, and her confessions to Quentin signal that life's forthcoming closure. "The Quentin Compson preparing for Harvard," the Quentin Compson of "the South, the deep South dead since 1865 and peopled with garrulous outraged baffled ghosts," must listen "to one of the ghosts which had refused to lie still even longer than most had, telling him about old ghost-times" (6). For Quentin, Rosa's restitution of Sutpen's presence through language is at once immediate and symbolic. This sort of linguistic contradiction cannot easily be dismissed. Her restitution of Sutpen's presence by language has the force to affect both the rhetorical construction and the narrative architecture of Faulkner's novel. "The abrupt insinuations of opposition, reality, even what Freud calls 'unpleasure' into the lives and stories of Rosa, Sutpen, Henry, and Quentin all take place as failed reversals," observes James A. Snead, "whose 'fractured' chiasmus may be seen as the rhetorical keystone of *Absalom, Absalom!*'s narrative architecture. The attempted, or the broken 'A:B :: B:A' structure repeats in the novel on the sentence, paragraph, and chapter levels." Beyond the self-destructiveness of Sutpen's design, this rhetorical device suggests that "the figure upon which he bases that design is, fatally for him, self-deconstructive" (22).

This tragedy emerged from Sutpen's complete denial of universalism: his self-interest was certain to be directly collectively self-defeating. General Compson recalled that Sutpen "had never learned how to ask anybody for help or anything else and so he would not have known what to do with the help if Grandfather could have given it to him." Even after Charles's murder by Henry, and Henry's disappearance without trace, Sutpen "still knew that he had courage, and though he may have come to doubt lately that he had acquired that shrewdness which at one time he believed he had, he still believed that it existed somewhere in the world to be learned and that if it could be learned he would yet learn it" (225). Notwithstanding this belief, all Sutpen's logic and calculation remained blindly self-interested, unappreciative of the coordination demanded by interpersonal dilemmas. Sutpen "struggled to hold clear and free above a maelstrom of unpredictable and unreasoning human beings, not his head for breath and not so much his fifty years of effort and striving to establish a posterity," according to General Compson, "but his code of logic and morality, his formula and recipe of fact and deduction whose balanced sum and product declined, refused to swim or even float" (227). In fine, Sutpen's codification of life failed to appreciate the ramifications—both self- and extra-regarding—of interhuman coordination.

John von Neumann (1903–57) investigated these ramifications in defining modern game theory in "Zur Theorie der Gesellschaftsspiele" (1928).[5] *Game theory*, as John Davis Williams expounds, is shorthand for "the theory of games of strategy" (3). The word strategy, "as used in its everyday sense, carries the connotation of a particularly skillful or adroit plan, whereas in Game Theory it designates any *complete* plan." Put succinctly, "*a strategy is a plan so complete that it cannot be upset by enemy action or Nature*; for everything that the enemy or Nature may choose to do, together with a set of possible actions for yourself, is just part of the description of the strategy" (16; emphasis original). Each participant is a rational *player*, the response of each player is strategically coordinated, and silence conditions the situation.[6] In *coordination problems*, each player in a self-interested situation has to anticipate the other players' choices and pick a strategy according to the prospects of preference-satisfaction. "Coordination games," as Michael S. Alvard and David A. Nolin emphasize, "are characterized by common interest among players" (534). As Paisley Livingston relates, "in some models a single 'player' is comprised of a number of 'agents'" (69), and most game-theoretic modeling deals with two-player dilemmas, as John Davis Williams observes, because "many situations which are not strictly two-person games may be treated as if they were" (13).

Von Neumann expresses the fundamental conundrum of coordination with mathematical and linguistic precision:

> The present paper is concerned with the following question: n players S_1, S_2, ... , S_n are playing a given game of strategy, Φ. How must one of the participants, S_m, play in order to achieve a most advantageous result? The problem is well known, and there is hardly a situation in daily life into which this problem does not enter. Yet, the meaning of this question is not unambiguous. For, as soon as n > 1 (i.e., Φ is a game of strategy in the proper sense), the fate of each player depends not only on his actions but also on those of the others, and their behavior is motivated by the same selfish interests as the behavior of the first player. (13)

To repeat the thoughts of Faulkner's Mr. Compson from *The Sound and the Fury*, the field of human endeavor "only reveals to man his own folly and despair, and victory is an illusion of philosophers and fools" (935), but like Sidgwick before them, neither John von Neumann nor his colleague Oskar Morgenstern was fooled. "We feel that the situation is inherently circular" (13), concludes von Neumann of interhuman coordination; for "there is exhibited," confirms Morgenstern, "an endless chain of reciprocally conjectural reactions and counter-reactions" (174). Each of von Neumann's n players, S_1, S_2, ... , S_n, is an egoist; the sum of the egoistic, $\sum_{i=1}^{N} Si$, gives the overall outcome; and that result, which involves a conflict that answers to both individual and communal demands, is inescapably moral.

In 1933, von Neumann became one of the first mathematicians appointed to the Institute of Advanced Study (IAS), an independent postdoctoral research center at Princeton, New Jersey. Among von Neumann's contemporaries, the institute would recruit Albert Einstein and J. Robert Oppenheimer as well as Oskar Morgenstern, and in the aftermath of winning the 1949 Nobel Prize for Literature, while spending two brief periods at Princeton University (November 1952 and March 1958), Faulkner would briefly gravitate toward these luminaries. Fittingly coincidental to this gravitation is the fundamental conundrum intuitively outlined by Judith Sutpen in Faulkner's *Absalom*:

> You get born and you try this and you dont know why only you keep on trying it and you are born at the same time with a lot of other people, all mixed up with them, like trying to, having to, move your arms and legs with strings only the same strings are hitched to all the other arms and legs and the others all trying and they dont know why either except that the strings are all in one another's way like five or six people all trying to make a rug on the same loom only each one wants to weave his own pattern into the rug. (105)

This interconnectedness amounts to the problematics of coordination; players choose either cooperation or defection in these daily situations; many games present a wider range of behavioral choices, but the theory of games of strategy separates these options into a series of paired decisions. "Whether the outcome of a game is comic or tragic, fun or serious, fair or unfair," as Steven J. Brams states, "it depends on individual *choices*" (6; emphasis original).

Judith Sutpen's philosophical intuition appreciated this dependency. This appreciation set her apart from her father. His postwar reliance on egoistic hedonism—"*the old logic, the old morality which had never yet failed to fail him*" (231; emphasis original)—confirmed this difference. His self-love still pursued self-perpetuation through reproduction, the legacy of a supposedly untainted biological male line, but untempered by ethical concerns, fostered by conspicuous consumption, and founded on maternal absence, Sutpen's "*problem contained some super-distillation of this lack: that he was now past sixty and that possibly he could get but one more son, had at best but one more son in his loins*" (230; emphasis original). That purified absence manifested itself in Sutpen's final child, and this last (and fleeting) cast toward posterity—his *daughter* with Milly Jones—confirmed the self-defeating nature of his egoism. Sutpen set aside the child and her mother as no better than animals. "Well, Milly," he told her, "too bad you're not a mare too. Then I could give you a decent stall in the stable" (236). This rejection not only connoted the termination of Sutpen's design, but also provoked an unseen corollary, "that morality" of Milly's grandfather Wash Jones "that was a good deal like Sutpen's" (237). The methods of ethics suggest that this likeness, expressing one of the "abrupt insinuations of opposition" (22) of which Snead writes, was in point of fact complementary: the egoistic Thomas had triggered a response from the universalistic Wash.

In *As I Lay Dying* (1930), Cash Bundren prepares his dying mother's coffin within her hearing, but his supposed insensitivity has a sensitively utilitarian aim: his mother wishes to inspect the finished article. A similar necessity in *Absalom* displays Wash Jones's utilitarian credentials. He and a friend had to prepare Charles Bon's coffin. "*They hammered and sawed right under the back parlor window—the slow, maddening rasp. rasp. rasp. of the saw, the flat deliberate hammer blows that seemed as though each would be the last but was not, repeated and resumed just when the dulled attenuation of the wearied nerves, stretched beyond all resiliency, relaxed to silence and then had to scream again.*" When the exasperated Rosa questioned them, "*why there? why must it be just there?*," Jones proffered a wholly utilitarian reason: "*Because hit wouldn't be so fur to tote the box*" (125; emphasis original). Jones's tutoring of Sutpen ("*I'm going to tech you, Kernel*" [154; emphasis original]) turned out to be just as utilitarian; that moral attitude "told him he was right in the face of all fact and usage and everything else" (237); and so two hawks faced each other. Neither man backed down. Jones murdered Sutpen. This act effectively began the dismantling of

Sutpen's already terminal design. Jones then died in defying the authorities who came to arrest him for Sutpen's murder.

Sutpen had failed to register what amounts to a utilitarian necessity: "the hedonistic calculations of youth," counsels Sidgwick, "require modification as we advance in years" (*Methods* 147). One should not "infer from this that the pursuit of pleasure is necessarily self-defeating and futile," he adds; "but merely that the principle of Egoistic Hedonism, when applied with a due knowledge of the laws of human nature, is practically self-limiting; *i.e.* that a rational method of attaining the end at which it aims requires that we should to some extent put it out of sight and not directly aim at it" (*Methods* 136). Without self-limitation, "a dubious guidance to an ignoble end appears to be all that the calculus of Egoistic Hedonism has to offer" (*Methods* 200); Thomas Sutpen's history supports Sidgwick's stark conclusion; and the strange yet necessary cohabitation of narratorial negotiations in *Absalom* structurally confirm that support in undercutting the egoism of singular narration.

At the outset of the novel, with Rosa Coldfield telling Thomas Sutpen's history to Quentin Compson, the young man's listening becomes a form of negotiation between *Absalom* and the earlier *The Sound and the Fury*, on the one hand, and the later "Appendix: The Compsons" (1946), on the other. "The coincidence of Rosa's story and Quentin's," as Matthews recognizes, "confirms that the truth of a narrative arises from how it is created and shared, and not strictly from its content" ("Marriage of Speaking" 586–87). When Sutpen offers her the subaltern role of deferred wife, "Rosa gathers up her morality" ("Marriage of Speaking" 580) and returns to town, withdrawing behind the "presbyterian effluvium" of her "puritan righteousness" (49). This episode must resonate with Quentin, whose sister Caddy, as *The Sound and the Fury* recounts, had offered herself to him sexually. Quentin's reaction had matched that of Rosa. For, as "Appendix: The Compsons" relates, "lov[ing] not the idea of the incest which he would not commit, but some presbyterian concept of its eternal punishment: he, not God, could by that means cast himself and his sister both into hell, where he could guard her forever and keep her forevermore intact amid the eternal fires" (710).

As if collapsing these intertextual gaps, Quentin's listening in *Absalom* becomes a strategic negotiation not so much with Rosa's account—he is resigned to being her sounding board—as within himself: "then hearing would reconcile and he would seem to listen to two separate Quentins now." On the one hand, there is the Quentin preparing for Harvard, but who must listen to his father, and especially Rosa, "telling him about old ghost-times." On the other hand, there is the Quentin "who was still too young to deserve yet to be a ghost, but nevertheless having to be one for all that, since he was born and bred in the deep South" (6). These two separate Quentins echo the bygone "strophe and antistrophe" (26) of the negotiations between the communal voices of Thomas Sutpen's contemporaries in Yoknapatawpha. Against the background silence imposed by history and by death, Quentin cannot interrogate any player in that history other than Rosa (and, to a lesser extent, his father); he cannot hear other firsthand renditions of that history; as a result, he manifests "two separate Quentins now talking to one another in the long silence of not-people in notlanguage" (6). Memories are being passed on from Rosa Coldfield (and to an attenuated extent from Mr. Compson) to Quentin, but they become split, debated, negotiated, and (ir)reconciled between Quentin's two personas (the one readying himself to learn; the other previously inculcated). In sum, the three of them—Rosa and the two Quentins—begin to turn the remorse that other interested parties do not seem to have felt—"*(Only they destroyed him or something or he destroyed them or something. And died)—and died. Without regret. Miss Rosa Coldfield says, (Save by her) Yes, save by her. (And by Quentin Compson) Yes. And by Quentin Compson*" (7; emphasis original)—to ethical account.

Hence, when Shreve McCannon enters narratorial negotiations with Quentin, he must do so as a moral strategist. On the one hand, there is the southern Quentin who cannot help but invoke his antebellum heritage. On the one hand, there is the northern (born in "Alberta" [213, 315]) Shreve. As a negotiating tactic, Shreve niggles away at Quentin, suggesting that southerners are inbred. Talking of Rosa Coldfield, whose name he usually prefixes with the word "aunt," Shreve archly queries, "you mean she was no kin to you, no kin to you at all, that there was actually one Southern Bayard or Guinevere who was no kin to you?" (144–45). Shreve's rhetoric also serves his strategy. In one tactic, he piles insults on Thomas Sutpen, whom he calls "this Faustus, this demon, this Beelzebub" (148). In another tactic, Shreve incessantly reiterates an assumption of truthfulness concerning his interpretation. "'So [Sutpen] just wanted a grandson,' he said. 'That was all he was after. Jesus, the South is fine, isn't it. It's better than the theatre, isn't it. It's better than Ben Hur, isn't it. No wonder you have to come away now and then, isn't it'" (180). Shreve "teases Quentin" (312), opines Brooks in *William Faulkner: The Yoknapatawpha Country*, but goading better describes Shreve's approach.

Quentin counters Shreve by remaining silent: "Quentin did not answer" (180); "Quentin did not answer him" (180); "Quentin did not answer this either" (181). Nonetheless, in discussing the locket in which Charles Bon finally substituted his morganatic wife's picture for that of Judith, Shreve maintains the tactic of incessant reiteration. "Dont you know?" he asks Quentin. "It was because he said to himself, 'If [I live ...], it will be all right; I can take it out and destroy it. But if [I die ...], it will be the only way I will have to say to [Judith], *I was no good; do not grieve for me.*'" "Aint that right?" insists Shreve, "Aint it? By God, aint it?" In a third tactic, Shreve questions the reliability of Quentin's father as a narrator. "And your old man wouldn't know about that," insists Shreve. "Why the black son a of bitch should have taken her picture out and put the octoroon's picture in, so he invented a reason for it. But I know. And you know too. Dont you? Dont you, huh?" (295; emphasis original). The dialogic monologue of Quentin–Shreve has broken down by this point into an interrogation of Quentin by Shreve. That McCannon's Christian name echoes the verb *shrieve* (or *shrive*), as in *to free from guilt* or *to administer the sacrament of reconciliation*, suggests that the Canadian is trying to inform Quentin's conscience. Nevertheless, Quentin's "yes" (295) to Shreve's insistent assumption of the truth, "Aint that right? Aint it? By God, aint it?" (295), is no expiation of southern guilt, but a means of stopping the interrogation.

Thus, as presaged by the "two separate Quentins" (6), and as realized in the penultimate chapter of *Absalom*, interpersonal negotiation becomes intrapersonal, with a heterodiegetic voice having to intervene. "It was Shreve speaking," relates this narrator, "though save for the slight difference which the intervening degrees of latitude had inculcated in them (differences not in tone or pitch but of turns of phrase and usage of words), it might have been either of them and was in a sense both: both thinking as one" (250). This intrapersonal negotiation leads to a conjectural and counter-conjectural circle, as in the type that Morgenstern identifies, in which Quentin and Shreve produce "some happy marriage of speaking and hearing wherein each before the demand, the requirement, forgave condoned and forgot the faulting of the other—faultings both in the creating of this shade whom they discussed (rather, existed in) and in the hearing and sifting and discarding the false and conserving what seemed true, or fit the preconceived—in order to overpass to love, where there might be paradox and inconsistency but nothing fault nor false" (261). From this coordinative circling emerges the conception of two Charles

Bons in connection with Henry Sutpen. On the one hand, there was the Charles who thought *"what could I not mold of this malleable and eager clay which* [...] *father himself could not."* On the other hand, there was the Charles who thought of *"that young clodhopper bastard,"* and who wondered, *"How shall I get rid of him"* (262; emphasis original).

Neither Quentin nor Shreve is conscious of any interpersonal distinction, and the resultant intrapersonal condition becomes further complicated, as the heterodiegetic narrator reveals, when Quentin represents "Quentin-Henry" (275) and Shreve represents "Charles-Shreve" (275). From this structural viewpoint emerges the classic coordination problem of Henry's wartime impasse with Charles. By the outbreak of the hostilities, Henry has learned that Sutpen fathered Charles, thus realizing the incestuous nature of Bon's intentions toward the unsuspecting Judith. Charles acknowledged the indeterminate outcome to the conjectures and counter-conjectures of the resultant coordination problem: *"It's because I dont know myself what I am going to do and so he is aware that I am undecided without knowing that he is aware. Perhaps if I told him now that I am going to do it, he would know his own mind and tell me, You shall not"* (282; emphasis original). Eventually, as if the goading Shreve and the goaded Quentin have retrospectively taken over the respective roles of Charles and Henry, Charles offered the solution of passive suicide, inciting Henry to shoot him: "'I am out in front of you a lot now; going into battle, charging, I will be out in front of you——' and Henry panting, 'Stop! Stop!'" (283). When Thomas Sutpen, as both the personality and the presence of self-interest, eventually discussed the problem of Charles and Judith with Henry, he could not help but know of each son's solution to their dilemma, just as Henry showed no surprise in his father's knowledge: *"To [Henry] it is logical and natural that their father should know of his and Bon's decision"* (291; emphasis original). In game-theoretic terms, Sutpen knew that Henry was going to cooperate with Charles's defection—*"You are going to let him marry Judith, Henry"* (291; emphasis original)—and tried to dissuade him: *"He cannot marry her, Henry"*; *"He must not marry her, Henry"*; *"He must not marry her, Henry"* (292; emphasis original).

"Nothing, in effect, can be grounded on chance—the calculation of chances, strategies—that does not involve at the outset a limited structuring of the situation," complains Jacques Lacan in *The Four Fundamental Concepts of Psycho-Analysis* (1977). "When modern games [*sic*] theory elaborates the strategy of the two partners, each meets the other with the maximum chances of winning on condition that each reasons in the same way as the other. What is the value of an operation of this kind," remarks Lacan, "if not that one's bearings are already laid down, the signifying reference-points of the problem are already marked in it and the solution will never go beyond them?" (40). The value of this kind of operation in the case of Henry Sutpen and Charles Bon reveals itself in their father's assumption of the role of game-theoretic *banker*. A banker—who is either extrinsic or intrinsic to the play, and who comprises an agency, authority, or a combination of the players themselves—ranks the possible outcomes of the game. In the role of game-theoretic banker, Thomas Sutpen made a *strategic move* that allowed him to *alter* the options and payoffs for his sons' game, with the racist "morality" of pangenesis, as one of Sidgwick's "idols of the tribe" (*Methods* 152), trumping the moral prohibition on incest. Sutpen told Henry that Charles's "*mother was part negro*" (292; emphasis original). This discovery changed the payoffs in Henry's coordination problem with Charles. In consequence, Henry altered his stance from cooperation to defection. The game-theoretic banker had successfully changed the signifying reference-points of the problem: "*it now depended on what Bon would do*" (292; emphasis original), because Henry now shared his father's delusion. "Henry appears more amenable to incest," as Christy A. Cannariato notes, "but draws the line at miscegenation" (118). That delusion shows through in the description of Henry's agonizing over his forthcoming murder of Charles: a racist trope attaches itself to the racist Henry: Bon sees "*the whites of* [*Henry's*] *inrolled eyes*" (294; emphasis original).

   Thomas Sutpen's alternative option as interventionist banker would have been to change the game from Charles's perspective. If Sutpen had acknowledged Charles as his son, then Charles would have changed his game-theoretic choice from cooperation to defection: as his substitution of locket pictures adumbrated, he would not have married Judith. Nevertheless, Charles's father could not countenance this option, which would have left a branch of the Sutpen line open to miscegenate perpetuation. In effect, the overwhelming coordinative dilemma had always been between Sutpen and his eldest son. "*I have*," as Charles told Henry, "*been giving him the choice for four years*" (294; emphasis original). In the wider context of the American Civil War, the North (represented in the linguistic negotiation of the compound narrator by Charles–Shreve) had been giving the South (represented in the linguistic negotiation of the compound narrator by Thomas–Quentin) the chance to cooperate for four years, but the fear of miscegenation had prevented Southern cooperation.

What is worse, that idol of the tribe has extended its grip to 1910 and the darkened room that Quentin and Shreve occupy in New England. The fallacy of miscegenation still casts its invisible shadow: Harvard is clad in "snowborn darkness" (299).

To requote Derrida, "the supplement has no sense and is given to no intuition." On the one hand, "reason is incapable of thinking this double infringement upon Nature: that there is *lack* in Nature and that *because of that very fact* something *is added* to it." On the other hand, "one should not say that Reason is *powerless to think this*; it is constituted by that lack of power." In fine, reason cannot "determine the supplement as its other, as the irrational and the non-natural, for the supplement comes *naturally* to put itself in Nature's place" ("That Dangerous Supplement" 149; emphasis original). Talking of, thinking about, and negotiating over Thomas Sutpen—a supplemental figure predetermined by maternal lack—constitute *Absalom*. "What unites the word 'supplement' to its concept was not invented by Rousseau" ("That Dangerous Supplement" 149–50). The originality of the functioning of the supplemental concept, as *Absalom* admirably demonstrates, "is neither fully mastered by Rousseau nor simply imposed by history." For, "to speak of the writing of Rousseau is to try to recognize what escapes these categories of passivity and activity, blindness and responsibility." Texts such as *Absalom* are important in pursuing that escapee. If they "*mean* something, it is the engagement and the appurtenance that encompass existence and writing in the same *tissue*, the same *text*. The same is here called supplement, another name for differance" ("That Dangerous Supplement" 150; emphasis original).

Thomas Sutpen, as a Derridean "a terrifying menace," expresses Faulkner's *avant-la-lettre* awareness of *différance*. Sutpen induced consternation because "the supplement is also the first and surest protection against that very menace" ("That Dangerous Supplement" 154). The residents of Jefferson both desired and feared Sutpen's presence. On the one hand, they showed their approval in attending his house parties and his barn fights. On the other hand, they showed their disapproval in throwing mud at Sutpen and Ellen after their wedding. Sutpen's contradictory essence helps to explain why the novel obsesses most Faulknerians. *Absalom* at once encapsulates and passes on the dangerous supplement. "This is why," to appropriate Derrida, "it cannot be given up. And sexual auto-affection, that is auto-affection in general, neither begins nor ends with what one thinks can be circumscribed by the name of masturbation" ("That Dangerous Supplement" 154–55). The issue of the supplement is not only of Faulkner's writing, but also of Faulkner's readers. "We should begin by taking rigorous account of this *being held within* [*prise*] or this *surprise:* the writer writes *in a* language and *in* a logic whose proper system, laws, and life his discourse by definition cannot dominate absolutely." While the writer uses "them only by letting himself, after a fashion and up to a point, be governed by the system," the reading process "must always aim at a certain relationship, unperceived by the writer, between what he commands and what he does not command of the patterns of the language [and logic] that he uses." Furthermore, the reader must respect "the conscious, voluntary, intentional relationship that the writer institutes in his exchanges with the history to which he belongs thanks to the element of language." Such respect is vital. "This indispensable guardrail has always only *protected*, it has never *opened*, a reading," but criticism "would risk developing in any direction at all and authorize itself to say almost anything" without this safeguard ("That Dangerous Supplement" 158; emphasis original).

Sutpen's self-love was a perverted self-interest, one that protected him from moral expenditure while operating within the wider ethical framework demanded by universalism. "This apparently egotistical economy," as Derrida remarks in "That Dangerous Supplement," "functions within an entire system of moral representation. Egotism is redeemed by a culpability, which determines auto-eroticism as a fatal waste and a wounding of the self by the self" (156). In Derrida's opinion, "this perversion," this self-indulgence to the point of self-consumption, "is not truly condemnable" (155), because the individual inflicts only self-harm. Derek Parfit (1942–2017) would have tightened Derrida's argument. The agential context is all important. "As conditions change," he writes of the social milieu, "we may need to make some changes in the way we think about morality." *Absalom* makes the same distinction. "Common-Sense Morality," as Parfit observes, "works best in small communities." That moral attitude suited the majoritarian perspective in the antebellum South. "When there are few of us, if we give to or impose on others great total benefits or harms, we must be affecting other people in significant ways, that would be grounds either for gratitude, or resentment," as Parfit notes in *Reasons and Persons* (1984). "In small communities, it is a plausible claim that we cannot have harmed others if there is no one with an obvious complaint, or ground for resenting what we have done" (85–86).

Although postbellum changes occurred slowly, alterations did occur, and these changes presaged the great migration, technical and industrial innovations, and the rise of the metropolis. In turn, America became the driving force behind the interconnectedness of worldwide economics. Under these global conditions, observes Parfit, "each of us can now, in countless ways, affect countless other people." As such, "we can have real though small effects on thousands or millions of people. When these effects are widely dispersed, they may be either trivial, or imperceptible." In consequence, "for the sake of small benefits to ourselves, or our families, each of us may deny others much greater total benefits, or impose on others much greater total harms. We may think this permissible because the effects on each of the others will be either trivial or imperceptible. If this is what we think, what we do will often be much worse for all of us." Alternatively, "if we cared sufficiently about effects on others, and changed our moral view, we would solve such problems." Asking whether a personal act will harm other people is not enough. "Even if the answer is No, my act may still be wrong, because of its effects. The effects that it will have when it is considered on its own may not be its only relevant effects." Instead, if one ascertains that a personal act will be one of a set of such acts, one should ask whether these collective acts will harm other people. Otherwise, "if each of us rather than none of us does what will be better for himself—or for his family, or those he loves—this will be worse, and often *much* worse, for everyone" (*Reasons* 86; emphasis original).

The shouts in the postbellum night that haunt the close of *Absalom* effectively express this Parfitian dilemma. The traces of Thomas Sutpen's legacy amount to flesh and blood in addition to testamentary evidence. Rosa confirms her suspicions that Henry is secretly housed in his father's mansion. Added to this discovery is the revelation that Henry is dying. In response to Rosa's recourse to an ambulance, Henry's protectors, rather than hand him over to an official agency, raze the house. Yet, even with Henry's death, another Sutpen remains. Wash Jones's murderously utilitarian tuition had initiated the dismantling of the would-be patriarch's design. The remaining trace of Thomas Sutpen finishes that process. Charles had fathered a son; that son, Charles Etienne de Saint Valery Bon, had fathered his own son; that Sutpen goes by the generic name of Jim Bond; and no one can silence Bond's presence. Whereas Thomas Sutpen would have deemed Bond a miscegene, Bond deconstructs the binaries of race in de-constructing Thomas Sutpen's design. "Do you want to know what I think?" asks Shreve. "No," answers Quentin. "Then I'll tell you," retorts Shreve. "I think that in time the Jim Bonds are going to conquer the western hemisphere" (311). This prospect haunts the orthodox south.

"There was nothing left now, nothing out there now but that idiot boy to lurk around those ashes and those four gutted chimneys and howl until someone came and drove him away. They couldn't catch him and nobody ever seemed to make him go very far away, he just stopped howling for a little while. Then after a while they would begin to hear him again" (309). On the one hand, Bond's howling is a cry of victory, because unalloyed self-interest, as personified by Thomas Sutpen, has been defeated. On the other hand, Bond's howling is a cry of despair, because the correctness of that defeat has failed to convince unvanquished southerners. The irresolution between Quentin and Shreve confirms this despair. Although their dialogue remains an interrogation of Quentin by Shreve, Quentin's "yes" to Shreve's "aint it?" was only a temporary and an expedient capitulation, as his seven-time refusal of Shreve's insistence that he, Quentin, "hate[s]" the south reveals at the close of the novel: "'I dont hate it,' Quentin said, quickly, at once, immediately; 'I dont hate it,' he said. *I dont hate it* he thought, panting in the cold air, the iron New England dark: *I dont. I dont! I dont hate it! I dont hate it!*" (311; emphasis original). The narrative ends here, but the novel itself closes with a supplemental, or adjunctive, "Genealogy" (314–15). This biographical list, with its entry of "whereabouts unknown" (315) for Jim Bond, reconfirms the irresolution attending the ethical hope of egoism mitigated by universalism. That hope is abroad. Overtaken by the experience of writing, to requote Derrida from "This Strange Institution Called Literature," "a writer cannot not be concerned, interested, anxious about the past, that of literature, history, or philosophy, of culture in general." The writer "cannot not take account of it in some way and not consider her- or himself a responsible heir, inscribed in a genealogy" (55); Faulkner recognized his responsibility to literary inheritance in penning the best novel until then written by an American; and that bequest interrogates the negatives and positives that attend self-interest.

NOTES

1. "*Absalom, Absalom!*," avers David L. Minter in *William Faulkner: His Life and Work* (1980), "stands as the supreme expression of his longstanding concern with the relation between poet and poem, teller and tale, experience and imaginative construct, history and art" (158). For Frederick R. Karl, as he states in *William Faulkner: American Writer* (1989), "*Absalom* is the peak of Faulkner's fictional achievement," and "is unquestionably the

greatest American novel since the turn-of-the-century publication of Henry James's *The Ambassadors, The Wings of the Dove,* and *The Golden Bowl*" (582). In *Creating Yoknapatawpha: Readers and Writers in Faulkner's Fiction* (2006), Owen Robinson traces how "the intensity of the reader-writer relations explored in *Absalom, Absalom!* is never matched in the rest of Faulkner's work," and concludes that the novel "represents the finest single achievement of Faulkner's career" (121). In his contribution to *The New Encyclopedia of Southern Culture* (2014), Carl E. Rollyson is a little more circumspect, but ranks the novel highly in Faulkner's canon: "*Absalom, Absalom!* (1936), perhaps Faulkner's greatest achievement, explicitly conjoins his southernness and his universality in the partnership of the southerner, Quentin Compson, and the Canadian, Shreve McCannon, Harvard roommates, whose exploration of the southern past provokes questions about the meaning of history itself" (258).

2. The inner quotations come from Adam Smith's *The Theory of Moral Sentiments* (1759) (261, 265).

3. Faulkner's English contemporary Aldous Huxley, according to Mitchell Green's reading, offers this objection in *Brave New World* (1932). "Huxley's *Brave New World* asks what would be the case were a society to exist based on principles associated with hedonic [*sic*] utilitarianism." Under these circumstances, submits Green, "the state would support an orgiastic religion and drug-induced anaesthetization of its citizens, it would suppress all independent inquiry, and so forth" (360).

4. From a religious perspective, Faulkner "puts the story of the Sutpens in the context of the Biblical account of David and Absalom," as John T. Irwin notes, "in order to question the moral significance of that account, for what is at issue is nothing less than a questioning of that Judaeo-Christian morality, based on the Bible, that in Sutpen's world not only tolerated the enslavement of blacks but even justified it" (150–51).

5. Sonya Bargmann translated von Neumann's paper into English as "On the Theory of Games of Strategy" (1959).

6. Talking does not break this lack of communication, because the conversations of self-interested players are *cheap*: their verbal interactions never amount to more than phatic chatter. "When players' preferences are perfectly opposed," explains Vincent Crawford, "such a message cannot convey any useful information," and "the only equilibria are 'babbling' equilibria, in which the Sender's message is uninformative and is ignored by the Receiver" (287).

CHAPTER 6

Duty (II): *The Unvanquished*

F. H. Bradley in "My Station and Its Duties" (1876) first posited the connection between an agent's duty and that agent's social position. Bernard
Williams takes that connection as his philosophical starting point. "In a
case such as the duties of a job, the job may have been acquired voluntarily, but in general duties, and most obligations other than those of
promises, are not acquired voluntarily" (7). Obligatory duties concern
morality, but they do not necessarily demand virtuousness. "We should
scarcely say," avers Henry Sidgwick in *The Methods of Ethics*, "that it was
virtuous—under ordinary circumstances—to pay one's debts, or give
one's children a decent education, or keep one's aged parents from starv-
ing, these being duties which most men perform, and only bad men
neglect" (219). Williams adds that duties "look backwards, or at least
sideways. The acts they require, supposing that one is deliberating about
what to do, lie in the future, but the reasons for those acts lie in the fact
that I have already promised, the job I have undertaken, the position I am
already in" (8). For Jacques Derrida, in *On the Name*, a duty connotes a
rule, one that "is recurrent, structural, general, that is to say, each time
singular and exemplary." Exemplarity arises because that duty "commands
action of such a sort that one not act simply by conformity to the norma-
tive rule but not even, by virtue of the said rule, out of respect for it." Of
vital importance to the notion of duty is, therefore, "knowing whether or
up to what point one can rely on it, on what it structures in the order of
culture, of morality, of politics, of law, and even of economy (especially as

© The Author(s), under exclusive license to Springer Nature
Switzerland AG 2021
M. Wainwright, *Faulkner's Ethics*,
https://doi.org/10.1007/978-3-030-68872-1_6

to the relation between debt and duty)." In other words, "whether and up to what point one can trust what the concept of duty lays down for all responsible discourse about responsible decisions, for all discourse, all logic, all rhetoric *of* responsibility" (9; emphasis original).

The responsibilities of duty may require acts of reconciliation. Derrida considers this demand in "Force of Law: The 'Mystical Foundation of Authority'" (1990). "How to reconcile the act of justice that must always concern singularity, individuals, groups, irreplaceable existences, the other or myself *as* other, in a unique situation, with rule, norm, value, or the imperative of justice that necessarily have a general form," he wonders, "even if this generality prescribes a singular application in each case? If I were content to apply a just rule, without a spirit of justice and without in some way and each time inventing the rule and the example, I might be sheltered from criticism, under the protection of law, my action conforming to objective law, but I would not be just." Derrida further notes how people act *"in conformity* with duty but not *through* duty or *out of respect* for the law [*loi*]. Is it ever possible to say that an action is not only legal, but just? A person is not only within his rights [*dans son droit*] but within justice? That such a person is just, a decision is just? Is it ever possible to say, 'I know that I am just'?" (245; emphasis original). "In the ordinary thought of unreflective persons," as Sidgwick notes, "the duties imposed by social opinion are often undistinguished from moral duties: and indeed this indistinctness is almost inherent in the common meaning of many terms. For instance, if we say that a man has been 'dishonoured' by a cowardly act, it is not quite clear whether we mean that he has incurred contempt, or that he has deserved it, or both: as becomes evident when we take a case in which the Code of Honour comes into conflict with Morality" (*Methods* 30–31). Derrida's questions and Sidgwick's musings capture the implicit, underlying concerns of the maturing Bayard Sartoris in the aftermath of the American Civil War as depicted in William Faulkner's *The Unvanquished* (1938).

DUTY (II): *THE UNVANQUISHED*

The perplexity which we seemed to find in the Morality of Common Sense, as to the relation of moral excellence to moral effort, is satisfactorily explained and removed when we adopt a Utilitarian point of view: for on the one hand it is easy to see how certain acts—such as kind services—are likely to be more felicific when performed without effort, and from other motives than regard for duty: while on the other hand a person who in doing similar acts achieves a triumph of duty over strong seductive inclinations, exhibits thereby a character which we recognise as felicific in a more general way, as tending to a general performance of duty in all departments. (Henry Sidgwick, *The Methods of Ethics*, 429[1])

The prolongation of the American Civil War has long taxed both military historians and social commentators. "The Civil War was the first major protracted conflict of the industrial age," as Paul David Nelson chronicles in "Cost of the Civil War" (2013), "and proved to be enormously costly in terms of government expenditures, lost production, Southern devastation, and casualties" (1:442). During the conflict, the abolitionist Frederick Douglass had articulated what amounts to a related summation in "The Mission of the War" (1863), a speech he first delivered in Philadelphia. "In common with the American people generally," he lamented, "I feel this prolongation of the war to be a heavy calamity" (266). Within months of Douglass's avowal, as Bruce Catton reports in *This Hallowed Ground: The Story of the Union Side of the Civil War* (1956), "the Confederate armies were coming to the end of the tether." Hostilities would not cease, however, until General Stand Watie surrendered on 23 June 1865. In the interim, Confederate forces "could do little more than play out the string," ensuring a great deal more suffering: "deaths on battlefield and in hospital, men slain in meaningless little crossroads skirmishes, typhoid and dysentery and scurvy doing their stealthy work behind the lines" (363).

William Faulkner, who owned a copy of *This Hallowed Ground*, had expressed similar concerns over this bloody prolongation in *The Unvanquished* (1938), a story of the Confederate side of the civil war.[2] Set three years into the conflict, "Raid," the third of the seven sections that comprise Faulkner's novel, at once describes the stalemate that preceded the expiration of the Confederacy and questions "the reason for it [...]— what point of strategy, what desperate gamble not for preservation, since hope of that was gone, but at least for prolongation, which it served" (384). Douglass had effectively identified that reason in broad terms in "The Mission of the War." "A radical change was needed in the morals and manners of the people," he averred. "Nothing is better calculated to make this change than the slow and steady progress of the war" (266). In emphasizing the excruciatingly drawn out conclusion of this stagnation, the conventional codes and duties imposed by social opinion that contributed to that protraction, and the radical alterations that ought to have succeeded those impositions, *The Unvanquished* encourages the use of an interpretive tool that is appropriate to, but surprisingly underused in, this ethical context; namely, game theory. *The Unvanquished* emerges from this application as a war work dedicated to the moral ramifications of strategic games. The novel illustrates how the coordinative frameworks that underpin disputes predicated on political, racial, generational, or other duties also offer the structural routes by which to negotiate and settle those disputes. This illustration not only promotes *The Unvanquished* as an important successor to Faulkner's previous novel, *Absalom, Absalom!*, but does so by favoring the structural significance of human interrelations over the formal and narratological experiments that had heretofore characterized the author's canon.

The most common coordination problems—the Prisoner's Dilemma, Deadlock, Chicken, and the Assurance Game—constitute the set known as *social dilemmas*. These logically intractable dilemmas arise from the structural inherence of disputed coordination: the choices on offer provoke reciprocal conjecture and counter-conjecture; and the self-interested act of selection faces an unsatisfactory choice between the solutions on offer. Game theory classes the stalemate reported in Faulkner's "Raid" as a coordination problem of asymmetric form; this form comprises a combination of Deadlock and Chicken; and game theorists name this combined situation Bully. Deadlock, which characterized the Northern perspective, promotes defection. The temptation for unilateral defection betters the punishment for bilateral defection, which surpasses the reward for bilateral cooperation, which betters the sucker outcome for unilateral cooperation.[3] Bilateral defection produces a chaffing equilibrium. The "two parties fail to cooperate," as William Poundstone notes, "because neither really wants to—they just want the other guy to cooperate." Each side tries to coerce the other, through either physical force or moral persuasion, and an impasse develops. "Deadlock," maintains Poundstone, "is not properly a dilemma at all" (218). In theoretic terms, Glen H. Snyder and Paul Diesing support this contention, but they attribute more significance to its practical effects than Poundstone does. "Empirically," they maintain, "the story is not that simple" (124). Complexities arise because each player lacks the willingness either to think reflexively or to bargain. The resultant combination of complementary deficiencies marks the dispute as a bilateral "duty or absolute constraint" (128). Ruling *hard-liners*, as irreflexive thinkers unwilling to negotiate, veto any concessions mooted by *soft-liners*, as reflexive thinkers willing to negotiate; as a result, breaking the equilibrium in Deadlock often requires third-party intervention.

Chicken characterized the Southern perspective. Bertrand Russell defined this social dilemma in *Common Sense and Nuclear Warfare* (1959). Russell's example "is played by choosing a long straight road with a white line down the middle and starting two very fast cars towards each other from opposite ends. Each car is expected to keep the wheels of one side on the white line." Bilateral destruction becomes imminent as the cars approach one another. "If one of them swerves from the white line before the other, the other, as he passes, shouts 'Chicken!,' and the one who has swerved becomes an object of contempt" (19). "In a Chicken game," explains Barry O'Neill, "one person or the other must compromise to avoid a mutual disaster. Each player wants to convince the other that he or she will not back down." Defection is a duty imposed by social opinion: the person who compromises "is 'chicken'" (264). The temptation of uni-lateral defection betters the reward for bilateral cooperation, which sur-passes the sucker outcome for unilateral cooperation, which betters the punishment for bilateral defection. "As played by irresponsible boys," remarks Russell, "this game is considered decadent and immoral, though only the lives of the players are risked," but when "played by eminent statesmen," this game is "reprehensible." The Cold War, as the title of Russell's study suggests, had spawned a geopolitical manifestation of Chicken: "since the nuclear stalemate became apparent, the Governments of East and West have adopted the policy which Mr. Dulles calls 'brink-manship'" (19). Calling someone a chicken for supposed cowardice, how-ever, goes back to at least the fourteenth century. "The word was applied in a disparaging sense in Middle English as early as 1330," relates the *Chambers Dictionary of Etymology*, "and had the meaning of cowardly per-son in the phrase *cherles chekyn* probably before 1400, in *Morte Arthur*" (165). The concept of Chicken is not limited, therefore, to the postnu-clear world.

The strategic picture takes precedence over historical detail in the the-ory of games of strategy. "The signifying reference-points of the problem are already marked in it," to requote Jacques Lacan from the previous chapter, "and the solution will never go beyond them" (40). The signifi-cance of game theory thus lies in its ability to tease out the behavioral subtleties that structural impositions demand. After three years of hostili-ties, as Faulkner's "Raid" attests, each side in the American Civil War con-tinued to defect; this was their strategic duty; in consequence, the second-best outcome from Deadlock attended the Northern alliance, while the worst outcome from Chicken attended the Southern Confederacy. The continued defection of the South seemed irrational, but while cooperation would have ensured the Confederacy a slightly better outcome, that option would have guaranteed the defecting alliance the best possible result. Similarly, the Northern alliance refused to cooperate (or stop bullying), because cooperation would have guaranteed not only the worst outcome to the North, but also the best outcome to the defecting South. These game-theoretic preliminaries set the foundations for both the emphasis on and the analysis of the moral formulations of *The Unvanquished*, codes of conscience that relate in particular to the members of one family, the Sartorises, whose contesting attitudes toward duty dominate Faulkner's novel.

On analyzing the patriarch John Sartoris, the stubbornness of the South in the face of inevitable defeat becomes clear: hard-line Southerners acknowledge that loss, not with immediate concession, but with continued resistance. John Sartoris breaks the mold of the "astute statesman" sketched by William Lecky in his *History of European Morals from Augustus to Charlemagne* (1869), which was among not only Mark Twain's favorite books, but also Henry Sidgwick's reference books for *The Methods of Ethics*. "In periods of great convulsions when passions are fiercely roused," writes Lecky in a passage that Sidgwick quotes in full (427), "it is neither the man of delicate scrupulosity and sincere impartiality, nor yet the single-minded religious enthusiast, incapable of dissimulation or procrastination, who confers most benefit upon the world. It is much rather the astute statesman, earnest about his ends but unscrupulous about his means, equally free from the trammels of conscience and from the blindness of zeal, who governs because he partly yields to the passions and the prejudices of his time" (1:42).[4] Almost blinded by zeal, John Sartoris fully yields to the passions and the prejudices of his time, thereby swelling the mold of Lecky's astute statesman beyond breaking point. On analyzing Bayard Sartoris, the zealous patriarch's son, however, *The Unvanquished* reveals a philosophical form of retrospective anticipation, a forward-looking morality that teaches the maturing Bayard to question social duties in instituting and respecting the restrictions and impediments of an informed conscience. Tracing this revelation helps to account for the critical neglect, or textual–critical impasse, that has forestalled a basic discussion of *what matters* in the novel. "Most critics have found it a minor work," complains John Lowe, "and virtually all of them view its treatment of the Civil War as a cop-out, a lapse on Faulkner's part into an easy defense of the Old Order, popularized in an earlier time by romantic and racist Plantation School writers like Thomas Nelson Page" (407).[5]

The sociological move from *each* to *we*, a shift that encourages a game-theoretic investigation, helps to unlock this critical stalemate. Philosophical engagement with game theory, especially Derek Parfit's championing of the resultant moral mathematics, informs this shift. For Parfit, a rational player is neither a derivative of nor a natural substitute for anyone else; that player's practical considerations are first-personal deliberations; and that player's deliberate actions are that player's responsibility. Morality enters the equation because environmental considerations mean that that responsibility, as Faulkner's comparable understanding suggests in the light of Judith Sutpen's concept of hitched strings in *Absalom*, includes all the players in the game. To what extent players consider the morality of their strategic actions depends on the development of their consciences. Sidgwick understood "Ethics as the science or study of what is right or what ought to be, so far as this depends upon the voluntary action of individuals" (4). The philosophical progress of which Parfit writes in *On What Matters* (2011–17)—"unlike later poets or playwrights, who have no advantages over Homer or Shakespeare, later philosophers do have advantages, since philosophy makes progress" (1:xxxiii)—extends that science. "Those who hold that the edifice of physical science is really constructed of conclusions logically inferred from self-evident premises," concedes Sidgwick, "may reasonably demand that any practical judgments claiming philosophic certainty should be based on an equally firm foundation" (509), and the extension of ethics aims to meet this concession. The science or study of what is morally correct could then transform the everyday thoughts of unreflective people.

For game theorists, the moral mathematics of Bully and Chicken involve both dovishness and hawkishness. In a game of Bully, the bully threatens, hoping to force the other player to cooperate. Bully and Chicken, as Parfit argues in *Reasons and Persons* of strategic games in general, concern both warnings and threats. "When I say that I shall do X unless you do Y, call this a *warning* if my doing X would be worse for you but not for me, and a *threat* if my doing X would be worse for both of us. Call me a *threat-fulfiller* if I would always fulfil my threats" (20). If a bully's opponent is not a dove, the bully backs down, tending to fulfill the initial threat in a redirected form, so that the consequences of an unmet warning usually transpire. The tragic fate of the Sutpens in *Absalom* lies in that (previously quoted) "ruthless Sutpen code of taking what it wanted provided it were strong enough" (99). This unalloyed embodiment of hawkishness offers little room for the negotiation, compromise, or cooperation that would enable the players in Judith's allegory to interweave rather than cross-thread their rug.

"We are often," explains Parfit in *On What Matters*, "members of some group of whom it is true that if *each* rather than none of us does what would be in a certain way *better*, *we* would be doing what would be, in this same way, *worse*" (1:302). Hence, to repeat Parfit's counsel from *Reasons and Persons*, one should not ask, "'Will my act harm other people?' Even if the answer is No, my act may still be wrong, because of its effects." Instead, "I should ask, 'Will my act be one of a set of acts that will *together* harm other people?' The answer may be Yes" (86). The each–we differences that precipitated the American Civil War created a moral space concerning who belongs to which groups. On the one hand, Southern statism denied the expansion from states to nation. On the other hand, Northern demands for racial equality widened the individual self-interest of Southern majoritarians to encompass kith as well as kin. Philosophically speaking, as Parfit relates, the self-interest theory (or S for short) implies that each individual "is disposed to do what will be better for himself, or his family, or those he loves" (62); racism and statism adopt this economy of inter-relatedness and exchange; and social accretions soon harden such adoptions into rigid duties. Racial prejudice, as a misinformed strain of biological essentialism, draws an arbitrary line that denies the expansive nature of human union. To circumscribe in this manner is at once irrational, illiberal, and immoral; as a result, the divide between the two sides in the American Civil War became particularly entrenched. "Though not considered among his greatest literary achievements," as Don H. Doyle concedes, "*The Unvanquished* may stand," as Doyle argues, "as one of his more discerning interpretations of history" (216). Much of that insight concerns the problem of coordinating codes of conduct. In effect, Faulkner recognized the strategic situation, Bully, that soon crystallized around the divided wartime response to the expansive nature of human union. Moreover, he traces the development of a conscience in Bayard Sartoris that comes to occupy the moral space concerning group membership.

Coordination problems are universal, but spatially and temporally specific. In compositional terms, Faulkner's sociohistorical environment was conducive to his composition of *The Unvanquished*, because prescient correspondences articulated not only his present circumstances, but also the setting of his novel. As with any new publication from a critically notable writer, the compositional background of *The Unvanquished* preceded the authorial-critical encounter, with Faulkner fearing a Deadlock that would forestall positive recognition of his abilities. Two years before *The Unvanquished* appeared in print, Faulkner had published *Absalom*, which would widely be considered his greatest work. Yet, as Faulkner lamented in October 1938, acknowledging the controversy surrounding *Sanctuary* (1931), that exemplar of "the sensational, risqué, and immoral fiction that he was often identified with" (David M. Earle 231), "I'll always been known as the corncob man" (qtd. in Joseph Blotner, *Faulkner: A Biography. One-Volume Edition* 400).[6]

Concerning the impersonal compositional background of *The Unvanquished*, the separate parts of which Faulkner composed between 1934 and 1938, European politics established an especially pertinent correspondence.[7] "Though Faulkner lived long after the [civil] war was over," as Wade Newhouse notes, "he recognized that his own lifetime was filled with incredible historical events, changes, and potential revolutions that were as emotionally and culturally significant as his inherited memory of the Civil War had been" (153). Faulkner's European odyssey of 1925 suggests as much. When he disembarked at Genoa, having sailed the Atlantic, Faulkner stepped into Benito Mussolini's Italy, and he would translate "a key episode from that experience," as Michael Zeitlin relates in "*Pylon* and the Rise of European Fascism," "into both 'Divorce in Naples' and *Elmer*" (105). That episode involved his fellow traveler William Spratling's arrest for what Spratling calls "a crime against the royal family of Italy" in which he "placed a coin on the floor and stamped on the king's face" ("Chronicle of a Friendship" 15). Spratling becomes George in Faulkner's "Divorce in Naples" (1931). In this tale, as Massimo Bacigalupo argues, "Faulkner's insistence on the 'political' nature of George's arrest is significant if we remember that this was Mussolini's Italy, in which the police forces played a large role and 'disrespectful' foreigners would be easily suspect" (323–24). The king supported Mussolini, backing which Il Duce still valued, and punishment could result from publicly disrespecting the monarch. Appropriating Spratling's experience for *Elmer*, "two gendarmes in swallow-tail coats and broad short hats" (423) detain the eponymous protagonist, with the detailed description of the gendarmes' uniforms—outfits, as Zeitlin observes, "worn by the Carabinieri, Mussolini's fascist police force" ("Fascism" 105)—indicating Faulkner's acute eye for his political surroundings.

Faulkner held fascism in contempt; moral duty elicited artistic insistence; "I most sincerely wish to go on record," he would later write "To the President of the League of American Writers" (1938), "as being unalterably opposed to Franco and fascism" (198). Faulkner's attitude toward Nazism was no different. Adolf Hitler—whom *Time* magazine featured on its cover three times in the interwar years (21 December 1931, 13 March 1933, and 13 April 1936), but whom Isaac McCaslin in Faulkner's *Go Down, Moses* (1942) would deride as an "Austrian paper-hanger" (249–50)—had been destabilizing Europe since 1933. In that year, Paul von Hindenburg had lost his game of Chicken with the Nazi party leader; the German president's reluctant cooperation had been undutiful; in consequence, he had had to appoint Hitler chancellor. The Danzig Crisis, which effectively preceded the outbreak of World War II, would also result from a game of Chicken. On 31 March 1939, British Prime Minister Neville Chamberlain would address the House of Commons concerning Hitler's insistence that Danzig rejoin the German state, and the implications of that demand for Polish sovereignty. "Consultations, he said, were in progress with other Governments on the questions and disputes of the moment," as Donald Cameron Watt documents. "While these were in progress, if any action clearly threatened Polish independence and if the Poles felt it vital to resist such action by force, Britain would come to their aid; as would France." A parliamentary majority supported Chamberlain, but the prime minister's "declaration bore many similarities," as Watt relates, to the "ultimate manoeuvre" in a "game of Chicken" (185). The British tactic "left no option whatever for the British Government. If the Poles took up arms, then Britain fought too. The decision, war or peace, had been voluntarily surrendered by Chamberlain" (185–86). Nevertheless, Chamberlain's dutiful defection did not ignore Germany's subsequent invasion of Poland, and military intervention (somewhat tardily) ensued.

The corresponding strategic background in *The Unvanquished* comprises the American Civil War and its immediate aftermath. "The men" of the South, reports Bayard Sartoris, "have gone on with the War for two years after they knew they were whipped" (465). They remained loyal, as did their opponents, to dutiful defection. Personal relations play out against this background of stalemated Bully. Hence, while focusing on the Southern aspect of these relations, *The Unvanquished* (in effect) traces the related and foregrounded expressions of Chicken, Deadlock, and Bully. The novel promotes this compositional strategy from the start, in an opening episode, "Ambuscade," that relates an attempt by Bayard and his African-American companion Ringo to shoot a mounted Union officer. The temptation to ambush this colonel is overwhelming, but their ambuscade kills the soldier's horse rather than the soldier himself; and, as soon as the boys discover this outcome, they chicken out, hiding under the skirts of "their" maternal grandmother, Rosa Millard.[8] In stark contrast, Rosa is openly courageous in passively yet successfully confronting the knowing colonel, who "look[s] at her skirt for a whole minute," "then go[es] back to her face," with "Granny g[iving] him look for look" (340).

"Retreat," episode two of *The Unvanquished*, demonstrates how Chicken governs the relationship between Rosa and the elderly Joby, the senior slave in John Sartoris's household. With John away at the front, Joby, who is male but black, wants to dominate Rosa, who is female but white. Concerning many tasks, he initially disobeys her instructions, but eventually kowtows. Rosa's insistence that they take a musket with them on their planned relocation to Memphis is a prime example. "'We wont need hit,' he said. 'Put it in the wagon,' Granny said. 'Nome. We wont need nothing like that. We be in Memphis so quick wont nobody even have time to hear we on the road'" (348). Rosa "didn't say anything at all. She just stood there holding out the musket until after a while Joby took it and put it into the wagon" (348–49). The preteen Bayard Sartoris, displaying his strategic precociousness, sums up this game: "that's how Joby and Granny were and Granny always beat him, not bad: just exactly enough" (349). Rosa knows not only how to warn, but also how to threaten, and her "willfulness" (Bertram Wyatt-Brown 86) is apparently willing enough to shift from warning to threatening—and Joby is unwilling to test this apparent readiness.

Joby repeatedly tries to bully Rosa, but she repeatedly refuses to be a dove; each of their disputes, while foregrounded on a combination of gender and race, must negotiate its underlying coordinative structure. These situations of repeated conflict, with their resolution in Rosa's favor, offer the reader some of the comic leavening so typical of Faulkner's oeuvre. An incident involving John Sartoris's cousin by marriage, Drusilla, her horse Bobolink, and a group of Union soldiers in "Raid," then provides an explicit manifestation of hawkishness. The soldiers demand Drusilla's horse; they expect her, as a woman, and as a woman whom they outnumber, to be dovish; and her hawkish defiance surprises them. "The lot was full of Them," recalls Drusilla's cousin Denny, "and Dru stopped Bobolink and jumped down [...] and put the pistol to Bobolink's ear and said I cant shoot you all because I haven't enough bullets [...] but I wont need but one shot for the horse," so "which shall it be?" In game theory, Hawk–Dove is an escalating variant of Chicken, so this supposed dove is true (or dutiful) to her maiden name, which is Hawk. The Union soldiers chicken out; they cooperate in leaving Drusilla and Bobolink unmolested; but they fulfill their threat in a redirected act, one of moral turpitude: "They burned the house and went away" (380).

Drusilla's hawkish defiance of the soldiers presages a further escalation in resistance. On learning of her fiancé Gavin Breckbridge's death at the Battle of Shiloh, she joins the military irregulars led by her cousin John. Drusilla's seemingly irregular behavior actually fits the patriarchal Southern code, which demands coordinative defection in the face of sociopolitical opposition. Such defiance, which characterizes John Sartoris, Rosa Millard, and Drusilla Hawk, appears to be a Southern duty that cuts across gender demarcations; and while Drusilla blends for a period into the strategic background, and out of the foreground narrative, that narrative continues to emphasize examples of Chicken and Bully. All of the strategic games delineated in *The Unvanquished*, as François Pitavy notes, "mark marginal incidents" ("Two Orders" 387). Nonetheless, structures of coordination provide their signifying reference-points, and this structural grid is an essential part of that "truth of historical events" with which Pitavy privileges the connotations of "the fiction writer" over the denotations of "the historian" ("Two Orders" 387 n.10).

"Raid" presents the background impasse as greater proof of the war than the fighting itself is. For, there occurs in the midst of the conflict an episode "in which [...] the sorry business which had dragged on for three years [...] congealed into an irrevocable instant" (384), in which background Bully spawns a specific foreground game, the Chicken of "an irrevocable gambit." This time, the contest is "not by two regiments or two batteries or even two generals, but by two locomotives": one Southern, the other Northern. The Southern representative dares to ride the line from Atlanta to Chattanooga, its driver showing courage in "slip[ping] into the roundhouse in the dark" (384); and the ultimate payoff for the bilateral defection that dutifully follows, as its Southern participant and commentators know in advance, is "annihilation" (385). Notwithstanding this presentiment, which Southerner "would not pay that price" (385) for continuing to defy a bully? The morals of the people, as Douglass insisted from his racially freighted viewpoint in "The Mission of the War," required radical alteration. What he failed to appreciate from that perspective,

however, was that Southern cooperation necessitated Northern cooperation too—an ethical bind that *The Unvanquished* responds to with that
(aforementioned) concern over "what point of *strategy*, what *desperate
gamble* not for preservation, since hope of that was gone, but *at least for
prolongation*," this game "served" (384; emphasis added).

The Southern locomotive bears a "Saint Andrew's cross nailed to the
cab" (385). The saltire traditionally symbolizes Christian power, a representation that appeals to the Southern mindset, and a power seemingly
emphasized when the Northern locomotive fails to catch its daring counterpart. "The other [locomotive], the Yankee one, was right behind it,"
relates Drusilla. "But they never caught it." The North then reverts to
supposed type, fulfilling its threat in the redirected form of a scorched
earth policy that denies each party access to the railroad: "the next day,"
as Drusilla recalls, "they came and tore the track up" (386). This story of
a race, so free of racial significance, so mythic in its telling, transforms both
Bayard's and Ringo's understanding of their wartime standing. "In fact,"
as Newhouse argues, "it changes their very notion of what 'participating'
in such an event might mean. Bayard notes that 'Ringo and I had seen
Yankees; we had shot at one,' but such a moment becomes meaningless
beside the sense of history and moral destiny symbolized in the feuding
trains" (155).

The next foregrounded game in the novel brings the strategic focus
back to the familial. This gambit concerns the numerous and (after the
first instance) felonious requisitions of previously purloined goods (the
chests of household valuables, and, more especially, the mules) by which
Rosa Millard, with the aid of Bayard, Ringo, and Ab Snopes, seals a pact
between foreground and background strategies.[9] "Even if it is part of the
War effort, it is still immoral to lie and steal," as Noel Polk maintains in
Faulkner and Welty and the Southern Literary Tradition, but Rosa manages to acquire "a somewhat cleaner conscience" (84) by sharing these
requisitions among the members of Brother Fortinbride's church. This
game escalates, as the fourth section of *The Unvanquished* relates, into the
gamble of "Riposte in Tertio," which reveals the naïveté of Rosa's business
dealings with the obviously dishonest Grumby gang. The very irregular
Grumby is an ally of the chicken stealing Ab Snopes: "it wont be a house
or a cabin they will ever pass as long as Ab Snopes is with them that he
wont leave a indelible signature, even if it aint nothing to capture but a
chicken or a kitchen clock" (428). True to his game-theoretic disposition,
Grumby is a bully, and he eventually defects. Grumby, whose cowardice is

signaled by the song of a particular bird ("there was a bird somewhere—a *yellow*hammer—[Bayard] had been hearing it all the time" [442; emphasis added]), shoots Rosa dead. Thus, in "Vendée," which comprises part five of the novel, Ringo and Bayard track Grumby down. True to strategic type, he defects again: two poorly aimed shots from him go unanswered by Bayard, who then, with Ringo's help, kills Grumby in hand-to-hand combat.

The vengeance meted out to Grumby by the dutiful Bayard and Ringo coincides with the war's end. "Through four desperate years," writes Catton, "Abraham Lincoln had been groping his way toward a full understanding of the values that lay beneath the war. He had seen a profound moral issue at stake, and more than any other man he had worked to make that issue dominant" (393–94). Strategically speaking, Lincoln had eventually cooperated, he had broken the bloody impasse in breaking a duty or supposed constraint; as a result, "die-hard Republicans [were] bitter" (379), and they "denounced him as being a weak compromiser" (380). In his own small way, Bayard has groped toward the same moral issue, and the concurrence of Bayard's revenge on Grumby with the armistice closes his dedication to patriarchal Southern duty. Hereafter, as a hard-liner dedicated to a soft-line, he refuses to defect aggressively when faced with strategic opposition. The difference in beliefs behind the American Civil War had been so entrenched that the conflict had lasted two years beyond the Southern realization of defeat. Hence, while the maturing Bayard is a rarity in both acknowledging this bloody prolongation and learning to accept (rather than resist) its outcome, the strategic background for most Southerners remains Bully. Southern majoritarians still consider themselves unvanquished, and they maintain this resolve whatever Northern politicians intend and enact. Legislative changes following President Andrew Johnson's peace proclamation of 20 August 1866 sought to lower legal barriers between peoples by widening political power in the South to include the small farmers and tradesmen the president termed "plebeians." The North attempted, in terms of strategic morality, to forego bullying. The psychological counterpart to democratization, however, remained largely unmet in the South. Supremacists continued to draw arbitrary racial lines that denied the expansive nature of human union, and Johnson's laissez-faire attitude toward African-American suffrage emboldened these hard-liners.

Democratic progress required treatment of the residual psychological impasse. In *The Unvanquished*, Bayard's practical philosophy, his moral engagement with strategic games and his implicit awareness of each–we differences, responds to this demand. Faulkner invests the postbellum university graduand with a philosophical form of retrospective anticipation, which acknowledges but goes beyond the promising, yet ultimately unavailing, prospect of American Pragmatism. That acknowledgement tacitly approves of the approach to dutiful conduct outlined by the Father of American psychology, and leading Pragmatist, William James (1842–1910). He championed pragmatic acts as ethical acts. Behavior must square with conscience. "Each" person must take account of the collective "we." James made three connected assertions concerning the philosophical theories behind such conduct: they must influence individual behavior directly; the result would produce an evolutionary struggle for survival between the enacted hypotheses; this contest would select a pragmatic rationalism that had rigorously proven its ethical (and religious) fitness.

Like William James, whom he explicitly references in *On What Matters*, Parfit championed pragmatic acts as ethical acts.[10] Unlike James, Parfit refuted philosophical deference to evolutionary fitness, with self-interest being a case in point. "The Self-interest Theory has long been dominant," he argues in *Reasons and Persons*, "it has been assumed, for more than two millennia, that it is irrational for anyone to do what he knows will be worse for himself. Christians have assumed this since, if Christianity is true, morality and self-interest coincide. If wrongdoers know that they will go to Hell, each will know that, in acting wrongly, he is doing what will be worse for himself" (130).[11] The longtime dominance of the self-interest theory seems to speak for its evolutionary fitness. That appearance is deceptive. "We should reject the Self-interest Theory about rationality," insists Parfit. "S is the theory that gives most importance to the difference between people, or the *separateness of persons*. S tells *me* to do whatever will be best for *me*. For S, the fundamental units are *different lives*. My supreme concern should be that my whole life goes as well as possible. Each person is rationally required to give to himself, and to his own life, absolute priority" (444; emphasis original). This overriding concern precipitates the *practical problem* that "unless something changes, the actual outcome will be worse for everyone" (62). The each–we dilemmas of Southern Confederacy manifested this hazard during the American Civil War—"S," warns Parfit, "can be directly collectively self-defeating" (*Reasons* 191); and Faulkner delineates the human consequences of this manifestation—basic problems that concern "both politics and morality" (Parfit, *Reasons* 62)—in *The Unvanquished*.

Bayard Sartoris's practical philosophy, which effectively accepts this twofold demand, also effectively defers to the overriding contention of Charles Sanders Peirce (1839–1914), the Father of American Pragmatism. The period when Faulkner published the various episodes that would ultimately comprise *The Unvanquished*, 1934–38, partially overlapped the publication dates of the early volumes of Peirce's collected papers, 1931–35, and Faulkner was pragmatic in preparing his novel.[12] "When Faulkner revised the stories to make them into a novel," explain James C. Hinkle and Robert McCoy, "he made an attempt to make his fictional timetable consistent from chapter to chapter and with events of the War which have known dates, but he was not especially conscientious in doing this. The result is that it is now impossible to construct an internally consistent chronology for *The Unvanquished* which matches all details of Faulkner's text and all dates of real historical events, but we can come very close—close enough so that the few inconsistencies are hardly troublesome" (211). The ethical imperative behind the novel, however, was more demanding; in dutifully answering that insistence, Faulkner appended a concluding episode, "An Odor of Verbena," which ties the novel together around contesting peacetime manifestations of traditional and progressive morality.[13]

Fundamental to Peirce's mindset, as he makes clear in *Principles of Philosophy*, is "the present infantile condition of philosophy" (342). One of his "vitally important truths" counsels "not trusting to reasonings about questions of vital importance but rather to hereditary instincts and traditional sentiments" (357). Like James, therefore, Peirce takes an evolutionary stance, with the sentiments and instincts to which he so often defers, as Richard Kenneth Atkins traces, being "the outcome of human evolution" (24). Although they are theoretically fallible, as Peirce admits, sentiments and instincts are, he insists, "practically infallible for the individual" (346). Hence, accepting that morality "is not a bad thing, taking it in the true evolutionary sense" (*Reviews, Correspondence, and Bibliography* 245), Peirce falls into the same trap that catches James: he fails to appreciate that a moral theory "cannot be justified simply by an appeal to the intuitions that its teaching may have produced" (Parfit, *Reasons and Persons* 130).

In "An Odor of Verbena," Professor Wilkins, who teaches Bayard law at the University of Oxford, certainly acts according to sentiments and instincts. Learning of John Sartoris's murder by Ben Redmond, the professor's rational side, his reasoning faculty, cannot cope. In breaking the news to Bayard, Wilkins cannot rationalize a response, but reverts to Southern type: "He was trying to find the words," recounts Bayard, "with which to offer me his pistol." Like Peirce, Bayard recognizes the infantile condition of (American) philosophical tendencies, as embodied by the professor, who appears throughout this scene to be "somewhere beside or *behind*" his supposed student (465, 466; emphasis added). Bayard, with the retrospective anticipation of the philosophical order with which Faulkner invests him, and with Wilkins as his sorry exemplar, rejects a Peircean reliance on sentiments and instincts. Rather, in their own small way, Bayard's thoughts prefigure those of Parfit: self-interest is often directly collectively self-defeating; preferable is a moral duty that appreciates the individual's membership of a collective.

Nevertheless, the European philosophical tradition accommodates Peirce the philosopher more easily than it does James the psychologist, and that heritage, as bequeathed by (among others) John Stuart Mill, Immanuel Kant, Henry Sidgwick, and Derek Parfit, concerns the rational theoretics of each–we dilemmas to which Peirce pointed. For Parfit, as he states in *On What Matters*, "Kant is the greatest moral philosopher since the ancient Greeks." Even so, "Sidgwick's *Methods* is," believes Parfit, "the best book on ethics ever written." Certainly, "there are some books that are greater achievements, such as Plato's *Republic* and Aristotle's *Ethics*," but "Sidgwick's book contains the largest number of true and important claims." One ought not to be surprised "that, though a less great philosopher than Plato, Aristotle, Hume, and Kant, Sidgwick could write a better book. Sidgwick lived later" (1:xxxiii). Parfit headed the thoroughly modern vanguard that flourished in Peirce's wake by emphasizing the collective danger of blindly following self-interest. A theory, which Parfit designates as T, is "*directly collectively self-defeating* when it is true that, if *all* of us successfully follow T, we will thereby cause our T-given aims to be worse achieved than they would have been if *none* of us had successfully followed T" (*Reasons* 53). The practical importance of collective self-defeat of a direct nature is significant. "The simplest cases may occur when (a) Theory T is agent-relative, giving to different agents different aims, (b) the achievement of each person's T-given aims partly depends on what others do, and (c) what each does will not affect what these others do." This set of conditions holds for the self-interest theory (*Reasons* 56).

Parfit counsels that meliorizing, rather than optimizing or satisficing, must govern moral behavior. Self-interest to the point of selfishness aims for the biggest payoff. Satisficing involves doing just enough to succeed. Meliorizing is the intermediate attitude of unselfish advancement that goes beyond mere satisfaction. Morality meets rationality in the outcomes to social dilemmas that are better than satisfactory, on the one hand, and better than selfish self-defeat, on the other. In accepting this conclusion, the philosophical discourse of the each–we dilemma meets the game-theoretic discourse of the coordination problem. Pragmaticism hereby finds its epistemological heir in the moral mathematics of a reductionist approach to utilitarianism. This meeting charts the altruistic and egoistic responses to coordination problems. Parfit outlines these possible outcomes in *Reasons and Persons*. A player shows altruism either because egoism becomes impossible (outcome 1) or because that player becomes altruistically disposed. A player might become altruistically disposed because altruism has become the better choice. Altruism might now be the better option because of a change in that player's situation (outcome 2) or attitude (outcome 3). Alternatively, whether or not a player becomes altruistically disposed, it may now be true that altruism would not be worse (outcome 4). Otherwise, despite being a worse option, a player may still become altruistic (outcome 5). Outcomes (1) and (2) are political solutions that change the situation; outcomes (3) to (5) are psychological solutions that require a change of mindset.

Outcomes (1) and (2) are usually more achievable than outcomes (3) to (5) are. "Much clinical evidence from psychoanalysis suggests that, on balance," as John Bowlby notes in "A Psycho-Analytic Approach to Conflict and its Regulation" (1958), "modes which attempt the suppression of conflict are unsatisfactory and that modes which give it full recognition are better" (169). "For the cases of Custom and Law are not similar," explains Sidgwick, "as in every progressive community there is a regular and settled mode of abrogating laws that are found bad. but customs cannot be thus formally abolished, and we only get rid of them through the refusal of private individuals to obey them." Hence, "it must be sometimes right to do this, if some customs," such as those biased against peoples on the grounds of race, "are vexatious and pernicious." Progressive minds "frequently judge" the customs of "antique and alien communities to be" inequitable (247). Applied to *The Unvanquished*, this judgment casts John Sartoris and his followers, rather than African Americans, as antique and alien. Sidgwick's conclusion does not preclude the difficulties in achieving such progress. "It is dangerous in legislation to advance beyond Positive Morality, by prohibiting actions (or inactions) that are generally approved or tolerated," he concedes. Nonetheless, "up to the point at which this danger becomes serious, legislation is a most effective instrument for modifying or intensifying public opinion, in the direction in which it is desirable that it should progress" (458). This issue of social dynamics is usually less problematic "in a well-organised society," where "the most important and indispensable rules of social behaviour will be legally enforced and the less important left to be maintained by Positive Morality." Law hereby constitutes "the skeleton of social order, clothed upon by the flesh and blood of Morality" (459).

In the immediacy of the postbellum South, however, social organization remained open to exploitation, and as the closing two parts of *The Unvanquished* illustrate, achieving an equitable resolution between postbellum politics and postbellum morals was fraught with intense and bloody difficulties. The penultimate episode, "Skirmish at Sartoris," follows John Sartoris's reaction to the proposed election of the former slave Cassius Q. Benbow as local marshal. In effect, Bruce Catton's "little" but fatal "skirmishes" in *This Hallowed Ground* have found a postbellum echo: John Sartoris shoots Benbow's Missourian canvassers (the Burdens) dead; he then rigs the election, thereby securing his denial of African-American suffrage. "No reflective person," remarks Sidgwick, "is prepared to lay down 'conformity to custom' as a fundamental moral principle: the problem, then, is to find in the rights and obligations established by custom in a particular society at a particular time an element that has a binding force beyond what mere custom can give" (82–83). John Sartoris remains unreflective, however, on the issue of African-American suffrage, and overrides legal practice because he, who "was anything and everything except a lawyer" (476), cannot overwrite the law. Indeed, jurisprudence is a domain in which the only Sartoris who "can hold [his] own" is Bayard, the student "trained in the law" (477).

Bayard's acceptance of the South's vanquishment and his subsequent immersion in academia constitute what Bowlby would call "a major change" in his "psycho-social environment." In effect, Bayard accepts the Bowlbian prospect that "he is faced with the task of developing a completely new set of plans for dealing with his situation," and the essential Bowlbian step in reorganizing his psychosocial outlook "is to relinquish an outdated model of his world and the plans based on it." That abandonment will enable him "to develop a new model" ("Conflict and its

Regulation" 178). Fortunately, Bayard's time at university affords him contemplation. For, as Bowlby avows, "only when time allows is it possible to take a model out of long-term store, to reflect on it and to modify it in greater or lesser degree in the light of new information." This sort of reflection, despite the conservative influence of Wilkins, facilitates Bayard's task of modifying his moral outlook. In contrast, Drusilla's ethical perspective remains more conservative, in large part because of her more intimate wartime experiences. "Internal models are built up from past experience," avers Bowlby, and "they inevitably reflect the past, not the present." This essential conservatism contains an inertial drag that resists change. "Whereas internal models are extraordinarily efficient in helping us deal with a stable environment," concludes Bowlby, "they are at their worst when the individual is confronted with major change" ("Conflict and its Regulation" 179).

In closing the novel, "An Odor of Verbena" extrapolates from the conservative patriarch's unlawful, but doomed, alternative to superscription. This narratological extension points to a barely present, or textually obscured, activity: the background strategy enacted by John Sartoris, the hard-line strategy that his son links to the "strange times" (451, 453). "Father and the other men," recalls Bayard, "organised the night riders," supremacists who "ke[pt] the carpet baggers from organising the negroes into an insurrection" (470). One can surmise the provisos enforced by these postbellum reincarnations of John Sartoris's wartime irregulars. Disconnecting himself from lawful impositions of a unionist nature, relying on his sentiments and instincts as duties or absolute constraints, John Sartoris believes that he holds the moral high ground. From this position, he castigates both Thomas Sutpen and Ben Redmond; but while Sutpen's military service (as related in *Absalom* and accepted in *The Unvanquished*) is undoubted, "Redmond had not been a soldier, he had had something to do with cotton for the Government" (472), and John Sartoris casts him as a chicken

Redmond "could have made money himself out of it but he had not and everybody knew he had not, Father knew it," as Bayard appreciates, "yet Father would even taunt him with not having smelled powder" (472). The implication of Redmond's surname—that he favors neither white nor black; that his views on race are progressive—was borne out by his wartime status as a noncombatant. Redmond's moral disposition anticipated the philosophical standards promoted by William James, who enlisted for war service, but whose health invalidated his application. "William James, public-minded, ebullient, and credulously optimistic, and William Faulkner, intensely private, reserved, and skeptically ironic," observes David H. Evans, "seem in many ways distant souls," but they "share something fundamental": their "pragmatic standpoint" (236); and while Redmond's ethos anticipated the philosophical standards promoted by James, that ethos also anticipated the rejection of Peirce's philosophical example.

Although Peirce was another noncombatant supporter of the Union, "even late in his life," as Atkins emphasizes, "he did not find the cases for or against slavery particularly persuasive." Worse, "those prejudices that Peirce had inculcated from his aristocratic Cambridge upbringing are precisely those sentiments that are antiquated, now misfitting, now incongruous, now unworkable" (35). Atkins can offer little in Peirce's defense: "Peirce's sentimental conservatism is not an ethical theory—much less is it a political theory—but a bit of advice about how we should conduct our lives while we *wait* for our philosophical investigations to reach their conclusions in a properly scientific manner" (36; emphasis added). Peirce's practical philosophy anticipates "contemporary debates in ethics, the philosophy of religion, and the philosophy of action." For Peirce, as Atkins states, "philosophy, including ethics and the philosophy of religion, should be strictly scientific. As such, its inquiries must be conducted rigorously and its present conclusions regarded as provisional" (1)—demands that Sidgwick and Parfit would condone—but Peirce's readiness to wait revealed his loyalty to conservative notions. In his "Interview with Russell Howe," which would appear in the *Sunday Times* (4 March 1956), Faulkner the man, rather than Faulkner the artist, would reveal a similar dogmatism. In the opinion of the abolitionist Frederick Douglass, the protracted nature of the American Civil War had facilitated a change in moral attitudes, but according to the racial commentator William Faulkner, a "Go slow" (258) in African-American suffrage should accompany the indefinite Cold War.

"Within its domain," complains Jacques Derrida in "Cogito and the History of Madness" (1963), "Reason leaves us only the recourse to stratagems and strategies" (36), but if one remains inside that domain, as Peirce's call for methodological rigor demands, then the reasonable Parfit emerges as a suitable respondent to Peirce. Stemming from this acceptance, the Parfitian discourse of each–we dilemmas meets the game-theoretic discourse of coordination problems in classing John Sartoris, with his "violent and ruthless dictatorialness and will to dominate" (472), as a bully. Yet, while this strategic attitude echoes the patriarch's interpretation of the Northern stance toward the South both during and after the civil war, the present is beginning to overwrite the living past. This moral progress comes home to the Sartorises with that most intimate of Chickens: the Drusilla–Bayard kiss in which Drusilla dares Bayard, Bayard calls her bluff, and Drusilla accepts his audacity:

> "Kiss me, Bayard."
> "No."
> "Kiss me, Bayard." So I leaned my face down to her. But she didn't move, standing so, bent lightly back from me from the waist, looking at me; now it was she who said, "No." So I put my arms around her. Then she came to me. (474)

This embrace at once lowers the physical boundaries between lives and breaches the social boundaries of marriage. Neither participant backs down; each is, in essence, a threat-fulfilling hawk. Marriage to John Sartoris has not expunged the attitude implied by Drusilla's maiden name.

The most destructive outcome in Chicken occurs when, as in this case, both participants suffer punishment for bilateral defection; and the Drusilla–Bayard kiss, as with Bertrand Russell's two motorists, surely foreshadows destruction. The ethical features of this outcome site *The Unvanquished* beyond the Plantation School; rather, as John T. Matthews observes in his Introduction to *William Faulkner in Context* (2015), "Faulkner engages self-consciously with the plantation romance tradition" (5). The Plantation School, "in refighting the moral issues of the war in popular fiction," as Lowe explains, "sought 'justice' for the South, a justice the region failed to achieve in battle" (407–8), but Faulkner's self-conscious reanimation of these issues offers an equitable perspective. For, immediately after learning of the Drusilla–Bayard kiss from Bayard himself, John Sartoris finally recognizes, albeit to a limited degree, his own failings: the patriarch announces his determination to "do a little moral housecleaning" (477). Viewing Faulkner's canon chronologically, the razing of Thomas Sutpen's mansion at the end of *Absalom*, the clearing of a monument to a "fiend blackguard and devil" (12) and his amoral duty to self-interest, prefigures this prospective ethical cleansing. A game-theoretic approach to authorial matters confirms this contention: Faulkner was playing an intertextual strategy between the two novels, with these texts meeting (or cooperating) in moral figurations that lower the boundaries between them.

When Shreve [or Shrevlin] McCannon explicitly enters the narration in *Absalom*, he does so as a game-theoretic player, and Harvard roommate Quentin Compson is his opponent. "Let me play a while now" (231), he interjects; and Thomas Sutpen's hawkish game of self-interest becomes the narratorial plaything between two players of games of strategy. Quentin and Shreve, "whether they knew it or not, in the cold room," were "dedicated to that best of ratiocination which after all was a good deal like Sutpen's morality and Miss Coldfield's demonising." Moreover, their Harvard room was "not only dedicated to it but set aside for it and suitably so since it would be here above any other place that it (the logic and the morality) could do the least amount of harm" (231). Shreve's bullying of Quentin while they negotiate the Sutpen history turns their plaything into a ruthless coordination problem. As the Mississippian Quentin's refusal of the Canadian Shreve's accusation about hating the south reveals, however, the coordination problem between them remains unresolved, much as the situation between the Confederacy and the Union remained during the bloody prolongation of the American Civil War. This analogy provided Faulkner with a strategic bridge from *Absalom* to *The Unvanquished*. While the razing of Thomas Sutpen's mansion plays on a different ethical register to Bayard Sartoris's refusal to shoot Redmond, the later novel undoubtedly inherits a broad moral directive from its distinguished predecessor, and suggests Faulkner's anticipation (even at this stage in his career) of a canonical keystone other than *Absalom*.

John Sartoris's patriarchal commitment to moral cleansing is neither an admission of guilt nor a plea of innocence concerning any suffering that results from Southern actions, but does evince his demotion from privileged master to unprivileged man. When denoting John as a father, the narrative always employs a capital "F," as if the senior Sartoris masters the process of signification. This capitalization is a symptom of the paterfamilias's lifetime of capitalizing on racial exploitation. A slippage from "F" to "f" would acknowledge an estrangement of the Father, and more especially of the Word of the Father, from the Word of the Law. That slippage never occurs. John Sartoris is no longer a master of signification, yet he retains his Fatherly status in finally accepting not only that his sociopolitical desires and those of the United States are irreconcilable, but also that this irredeemable estrangement makes him an anachronism—and the truly anachronistic is a dead presence.

That John Sartoris's statement of his moral objective immediately follows both his stated deference to Bayard's legalistic mastery and Bayard's revelation concerning his embrace with Drusilla signals, moreover, a form of generational bequest. In continuing to defect against Redmond—and "Redmond aint no coward" (473, 477)—until Redmond's cooperative determination eventually breaks, John Sartoris confirms the paradoxical sense of this bequest. Redmond had that "quality [...] which permitted him to stand as much as he did from Father, to bear and bear and bear until something (not his will nor his courage) broke in him" (472). Their strategic game—John Sartoris "knew that Redmond would have to oppose him *to save his face* even though he (Redmond) must have known that" (473; emphasis added)—is bound to end in bloodshed: Redmond shoots Sartoris dead. John Sartoris's commitment to defection, however, was a sham: he was unarmed when triggering Redmond's violent response. "I have now accomplished the active portion of my aims" (477), John Sartoris had told his son during their final conversation, with the patriarch's moral commitment ending in a passive suicide by which the Father, who expects loyalty to the codes of his suzerainty, transfers responsibility for the South to his son.

Charles Sanders Peirce, like Colonel John Sartoris, was the Father of his particular domain. Where Sartoris's capital "F" was symptomatic of his dedication to racial separation, Peirce's capital "F" was symptomatic of his dedication to epistemological separation. Peirce's unwillingness to compromise, his determination to be a philosopher, almost led to insolvency. He avoided this state of affairs only thanks to William James's intervention. Peirce accepted the teaching position proffered by James, but this impediment to cleaning his personal "publishing" house of unpublished material effectively banished his works from widespread recognition until after his death. Along a relatable trajectory, Sartoris's moral housecleaning, as passive suicide, banishes him entirely from his own home. "Ever since Charles Peirce," writes Marc Elliott Bobro, "it has been commonplace for personal identity theorists to ask the question of meaningful survival" (100). This query "comes in several guises" (100)—such as John Sartoris's in William Faulkner's *The Unvanquished*—but all of these forms interrogate each–we coordination.

One of the most promising psychological approaches to these relations, as Parfit argues in *On What Matters*, is the moral solution offered by a particular construal of Kantian consent. "Kant's claims about consent," according to Parfit, "can be interpreted in two ways. On the *Choice-Giving*

Principle, it is wrong to treat people in any way to which these people *cannot actually* give or refuse consent, because we have failed to give these people the power to choose how we treat them." This interpretation "is clearly false." The alternative interpretation is more promising. "On the *Consent Principle*, it is wrong to treat people in any way to which they *could not rationally* consent, if we gave them the power to choose how we treat them" (1:8). This contention "gives us an inspiring ideal of how, as rational beings, we ought to be related to each other. We might be able to treat everyone only in ways to which they could rationally consent; and this might be how everyone ought always to act" (1:9). John Sartoris's passive suicide, as a moral lesson, is *not* Kantian. He could not reasonably expect others to follow his example. This unreasonable bequest leaves Bayard, on the one hand, to forge his own moral course, and Drusilla, on the other hand, to rely on the new while wedded to the old.

In accordance with the past, the moral duty of fierce resistance to sociopolitical opposition, the hard-line Drusilla is "the Greek amphora priestess of a succinct and formal violence" (468), the supplicant who hands Bayard a pair of dueling pistols in the expectation that he will forcefully avenge his father's death. In accordance with the future, the pistols symbolize the potency and fertility of male youth, but not the moral duty espoused and practiced by the Oxford graduand. Hence, Drusilla's personal political-and-moral crisis reaches its apotheosis when, despite the attendant signals, Bayard clearly refuses to play the game according to the hard-line code that motivates her. Bayard is determined on a different and softer play: he rejects Drusilla's offering: he "crossed to the *piano* and laid the pistols *carefully* on it" (483; emphasis added). He has profoundly reassessed inherited moral formulations, and whatever the social ramifications, Bayard is more conscientiously astute than he was. He now figures the sort of reasonableness of which Sidgwick writes, in explicitly drawing on Lecky, "prefer[ing] the mental state of apprehending truth to the state of half-reliance on generally accredited fictions, while recognising that the former state may be more painful than the latter" (399; Lecky 52ff). "Bayard Sartoris in *The Unvanquished* does manage to transform the code of violence that his father and the war have bequeathed to him" (151), as Gary Lee Stonum remarks, but the manner and nature of that transformation need deeper examination than Stonum's simple statement of the fact. Bayard is in possession of those previous formulations, he understands those duties, but they no longer possess him.

The attendant signals, which include the aural, visual, and olfactory, are crucial to this interpretation of "An Odor of Verbena." Appropriately, the olfactory holds the greatest significance. While a member of Sartoris's wartime irregulars, "Drusilla would no more have bothered with flowers than Father himself would have," but postbellum she keenly "gather[s] sprigs of verbena." She wears them "in her hair because she [says] verbena [is] the only scent you [can] smell above the smell of horses and courage" (469). That conjunction extracts and distils the background relevance of verbena, with its odor environing the narrative foreground, as its intitulation for the final part of *The Unvanquished* confirms.[14] "The verbena or vervain," note Ernst and Johanna Lehner, "was sacred to Mars, the Roman god of war" (49); as such, Drusilla has invested verbena with a significance that simultaneously carries notorious postbellum connotations: the Knights of the White Camellia, the K.K.K., the Silver Shirts, *and* Drusilla's Knights of the Purple Verbena.[15] "Because of the conservative nature of models," as Bowlby observes, "we must expect that, before undertaking the task of modifying models, every effort will be made, first, to demonstrate that no major environmental change has taken place and, when that fails, to try in every way possible to reverse the change" ("Conflict and its Regulation" 179). Drusilla meets this expectation.

After handing Bayard the dueling pistols, Drusilla removes the verbena sprigs she wears: "one I give to you to wear tomorrow (it will not fade), the other I cast away," she tells him, "now let me look at you" (481). That gaze, in the presence of Aunt Jenny Du Pre (John Sartoris's widowed younger sister) and Louvinia (the family cook), sees through Bayard. His moral stance is clear. Drusilla stood "staring at me," recounts Bayard, "with intolerable and amazed incredulity which occupied her face alone for a whole minute while her eyes were completely empty; it seemed to me that I stood there for a full minute while Aunt Jenny and Louvinia watched us, waiting for her eyes to fill" (481–82). That wait ended with an ocular expression "of bitter and passionate betrayal" (482). Bayard's postbellum ethos is transparent, and "the answer to threat-fulfillers, if we are all transparent," as Parfit argues in *Reasons and Persons*, "is to become a *threat-ignorer*" (20). Transparent threat-ignorers "avoid becoming the slaves of threat-fulfillers" (21).

For Richard H. King in "*A Fable*: Faulkner's Political Novel?" (1985), "only with *Go Down, Moses* did Faulkner succeed in creating a fictional setting in which two characters—Lucas Beauchamp and Ike McCaslin—appear as moral agents" (7), but Bayard's appearance as such in *The*

Unvanquished is obvious. Bayard has matured into a transparent (or trust-worthy) threat-ignorer: once, when threatened, he had hidden under his grandmother's skirts; by the time he faced Grumby, however, he had acquired the courage to force his opponent's defection. In contrast, Bayard's father, despite his moral vow, could not change his disposition enough to become a transparent (or trustworthy) threat-ignorer. In the two years before his death, John Sartoris's eyes had acquired a "transparent film," but this lucidity reminded Bayard of "the eyes of men who have killed too much" (476), and his father had counted on this transparency in dying at Redmond's hands. Bayard, as a transparent threat-ignorer, denies the old equivalence between cooperation and chickening out. "If a man has given no pledge to maintain a custom or habit," to appropriate Sidgwick, "it seems hard that he should be bound by the unwarranted expectations of others" (270). The son will face his father's murderer, but whatever the expectations of others, and whatever the strategic behavior of Redmond, Bayard will cooperate. "Bayard rejects his father's dueling pistols, having decided," as John T. Irwin notes, "that he will face his father's killer unarmed and either be killed or drive Redmond out of town by the sheer moral force of his presence" (57). If Redmond defects, then Bayard will receive the sucker outcome for unilateral cooperation, which is death.

Bayard's prospective denial of patriarchal ethics, or warranted expectations, removes Drusilla's transcendental keystone; in consequence, hysteria emerges from the crumbling edifice of her formerly reliable psyche. Drusilla's ("Peircean") sentiments and instincts hereby escape Bayard's behavioral code. His fresh approach has revealed the demise of John Sartoris's authority as the demise of moral bankruptcy (what Newhouse calls "Faulkner's careful critical evaluation of the hollowness and deceptive fragility of [...] Lost Cause narrative mythology" [163]). Drusilla evades, but cannot dispel, this revelation. In abjuring Drusilla as his wife, Bayard has replaced her husband, with a wiser, but more detached (and less overtly masculine) authority. He overwrites the time-honored Southern code with his notion of duty. "The notion 'ought'—as expressing the relation of rational judgment to non-rational impulses—will find a place in the practical rules of any egoistic system," as Sidgwick counsels, "no less than in the rules of ordinary morality, understood as prescribing duty without reference to the agent's interest" (36). To Drusilla, an inferior, impaired authority has usurped omnipotence; and abjection characterizes her reaction: she is fearful yet fascinated.

Failure to relinquish an outdated worldview, as Bowlby warns, "can result in psychiatric illness" ("Conflict and its Regulation" 178). Drusilla's horrified laughter displays an ecstasy of sexual frisson, which the old code had satisfied with its violent acts, but which fully discloses its current lack of satisfaction: "the unconscious, the repressed, suppressed pleasure," to appropriate Julia Kristeva, "gushing forth" (206) from Drusilla, despite her efforts at restraint:

> "I kissed his hand," she said in an aghast whisper; "*I kissed his hand!*" beginning to laugh, the laughter, rising, becoming a scream yet still remaining laughter, screaming with laughter, trying herself to deaden the sound by putting her hand over her mouth, the laughter spilling between her fingers like vomit, the incredulous betrayed eyes still watching me across the hand.
>
> "Louvinia!" Aunt Jenny said. They both came to her. Louvinia touched and held her and Drusilla turned her face to Louvinia.
>
> "I kissed his hand, Louvinia!" she cried. "Did you see it? *I kissed his hand!*" the laughter rising again, becoming the scream again yet still remaining laughter, she still trying to hold it back with her hand like a small child who has filled its mouth too full. (482; emphasis original)

Repelled, but fascinated, Drusilla must be removed from Bayard's presence. Aunt Jenny orders her to be taken upstairs. The name Drusilla is of late-Latin origin, derived from "the old Roman family name *Dr(a)usus*," as *A Dictionary of First Names* (2006) relates, and is later "borne in the Bible by a Jewish woman [...] who was converted to Christianity by St Paul" (88). Drusilla is a woman who, despite the intervention of a St. Paul in the guise of Bayard, cannot cooperate with, let alone convert to, his saintly code. Drusilla is as morally unreflective as her husband had been. "In the ordinary thought of unreflective persons," writes Sidgwick, "the duties imposed by social opinion are often undistinguished from moral duties: and indeed this indistinctness is almost inherent in the common meaning of many terms" (30). Sidgwick then illustrates his argument: "if we say that a man has been 'dishonoured' by a cowardly act, it is not quite clear whether we mean that he has incurred contempt, or that he has deserved it, or both: as becomes evident when we take a case in which the Code of Honour comes into conflict with Morality" (30–31).

The sainted Bayard—as if the Saint Andrew's cross of the Southern mindset has come to denote a chiasmus via the Drusilla–Bayard kiss—has reassigned the significances associated with Chicken, Deadlock, and Bully.

The equivalences that once pertained—defection with duty and bravery, cooperation with disloyalty and cowardice—have been overturned, and this alteration, in effectively unhinging Drusilla's system of signification, foregrounds the unadulterated yet "very wise instead of intolerant" (480) attitude of Aunt Jenny. Whereas Drusilla is associated with verbena, Aunt Jenny is associated with jasmine: the two cuttings, which she brought from her home in Charleston, are "bushes in the garden now" (479); and "jasmine" is usually connotative of "amiability and cheerfulness" (Lehner and Lehner 119). Aunt Jenny, who "know[s]" that Bayard is "not afraid" (483), talks of the bravery of those who find another way (at least at an individual level) to defy strategic impasses: "I used to see a lot of blockade runners in Charleston. They were heroes in a way, you see—not heroes because they were helping to prolong the Confederacy but heroes in the sense that David Crockett or John Sevier [were]" (485–86); these alternative heroes were not wedded to the orthodox expectations that were protracting the bloody Deadlock.

"Two of the conditions that facilitate relinquishing and replacing models," relates Bowlby, "are (a) opportunity to discuss the position with an informed and congenial friend (b) support and encouragement in tackling the task from a trusted companion (attachment figure)" ("Conflict and its Regulation" 180), and Bayard's moral stance receives Aunt Jenny's informed backing. "In distributing our praise of human qualities, on utilitarian principles," expounds Sidgwick, "we have to consider primarily not the usefulness of the quality, but the usefulness of the praise: and it is obviously not expedient to encourage by praise qualities which are likely to be found in excess rather than in defect." Thus, for example, "however necessary self-love or resentment may be to society, it is quite in harmony with Utilitarianism that they should not be recognised as virtues by Common Sense, in so far as it is reasonably thought that they will always be found operating with at least sufficient intensity." Nevertheless, as in Drusilla's judgment of Bayard, "when a man seems clearly deficient in resentment, he is censured for tameness," while "when self-love comes into conflict with impulses seen to be on the whole pernicious," as in Aunt Jenny's judgment of Bayard, "it is praised as Prudence" (428).

In conformation of Aunt Jenny's wisdom, and like his father before him, Bayard meets Redmond unarmed. Moreover, in emphasizing his wish to defuse the present situation, Bayard does not go to town on his father's stallion (that "stood for me too" [484]), but on his own mare ("Betsy" [484]). William James championed pragmatic acts as ethical acts;

behavior must square with conscience. Bayard, in effect, agrees. "I must," he had explained to Aunt Jenny, "live with myself" (483). He must test his own methods of ethics in meeting Redmond: "*At least this will be my chance to find out if I am what I think I am or if I just hope; if I am going to do what I have taught myself is right or if I am just going to wish I were*" (466; emphasis original). The coordination condition of silence dominates this test in Redmond's office. "We didn't speak," recounts Bayard. "It was as if we both knew what the passage of words would be and the futility of it; how he might have said, 'Go out, Bayard. Go away, boy' and then, 'Draw then. I will allow you to draw' and it would have been the same as if he had never said it" (488). Yet, as he did against John Sartoris, Redmond defects—and, like Grumby, he fires twice before his opponent's response—although in this instance, Redmond's actions merely gesture toward the old code. "Faulkner has given us the ethical forensics," as Peter Sharpe observes, to read this scene (95). Redmond gestures rather than enacts, partly because he retains some progressiveness in the form of tolerance, and partly because he is spent:

> Maybe I didn't even hear the explosion though I remember the sudden orange bloom and smoke as they appeared against his white shirt as they had appeared against Grumby's greasy Confederate coat; I still watched that foreshortened slant of barrel which I knew was not aimed at me and saw the second orange flash and smoke and heard no bullet that time either. Then I stopped; it was done then. I watched the pistol descend to the desk in short jerks; I saw him release it and sit back, both hands on the desk. (489)

"Having payed [*sic*] obeisance to the *form* of the duel," notes Sharpe, "this Sartoris had subverted its *content*" (96; emphasis original). From a Sidgwickian perspective, what Sharpe calls "Bayard's unorthodox 'triumph'" (85) casts the young Sartoris as no ordinary man, but one of a certain moral persuasion. "To retain a genuine kindly feeling towards a man, while we are gratifying a strong impulse of aversion to his acts by inflicting pain on him," avers Sidgwick, "requires a subtle complexity of emotion too far out of the reach of ordinary men to be prescribed as a duty." Ordinarily, "we must allow as right and proper a temporary suspension of benevolence towards wrong-doers until they have been punished" (323). Beyond the prescription of duty, yet punishing his father's murderer in a judicious manner, Bayard manages to retain his benevolence toward Redmond.

When he had entered Redmond's office, Bayard smelled "nothing except the verbena in my coat" (487), "walk[ing] steadily on enclosed in the now fierce odor of the verbena sprig" (488), but after Redmond's shots, "the smell of powder smoke," rather than the odor of verbena, "linger[s]" (490) on the air. Vanquished, as his gesture ultimately indicates, Redmond leaves Mississippi for good. Bayard has outdone the old courage, the old duty. Reasonableness, as Bayard's "individual code of behavior" (246–47), to quote Faulkner's interview with Jean Stein vanden Heuvel, has shown him "how to discover himself, evolve for himself a moral code and standard within his capacities and aspirations" (247). That evolution is in truth (Parfitian) philosophical development; ratiocination (to use a term from Faulkner's lexicon) has triumphed over inculcation (or Peircean sentiments and instincts); the irenic has vanquished the antagonistic. Bayard can now calm his own thoughts, lying down in the backwoods: "I went to sleep almost before I had stopped thinking" (491); he has fulfilled, to quote again from Faulkner's interview with vanden Heuvel, "his duty inside the human race" (247), his commitment to each–we coordination.

"Though many of Faulkner's characters and critics make the mistake of idealizing the past so strongly as to resist change," avers Polk, "Faulkner himself never does. He constantly argues that the capacity to cope with change is the test of maturity in an individual; but even these terms—cope and test—point to the intensity of the moral struggle that change entails for a people who invest their individual and communal lives, their places in time and space, in the values of the past, those 'old' verities" (*Faulkner and Welty* 21). Bayard does not make that mistaken investment, but Drusilla does. On returning home, he discovers that she has left a single sprig of verbena on his pillow, which "fill[s] the room, the dusk, the evening with that odor" (492). When asked about Drusilla's offering, Faulkner explained to students of an "Undergraduate Course in Contemporary Literature" (9 March 1957), "the sprig of verbena meant that she realized that that took courage too and maybe more moral courage than to have drawn blood, or to have taken another step in a[n] endless feud of an eye for an eye." Faced with perpetuating the cycle of violence, Drusilla now feels obligated to make a decisive, terminating move. This gambit goes beyond the Lacanian: Drusilla simply quits the game. She leaves Yoknapatawpha, Mississippi, for Montgomery, Alabama, as Faulkner told his class, because "she was still too involved in" the old code to "accept" Bayard's actions "morally" (42). Bayard actively denies what Sharpe calls "the ineluctable 'truth' of the planter society, that heritage is fate, that it not merely indicates but coins the future" (94), but Drusilla actively retains that "truth." In consequence, he cannot countenance Drusilla's full statement, her repeated insistence that "you could smell [verbena] above the smell of horses and courage" (469), that she has "smelled it above the odor of courage" (481). Bayard drops all references to "courage," and *The Unvanquished* ends without mention of supposed bravery, with the odor of verbena filling Bayard's room—a smell that "she said you could smell alone above the smell of horses" (492).

To repeat, more than outdoing the old signals, Bayard has overturned them. The olfactory signal of verbena testifies to this upheaval. The definition of verbena now signifies the opposite. "When Roman heralds-in-arms were dispatched to other nations with messages of peace," write Lehner and Lehner, "they bore crowns of verbena" (49). In this guise, relates Steven Olderr, verbena signifies "fertility; sanctity; peace" (213). In effect, Bayard has not just leveled the old antinomies, constructs in which the upper terms had suppressed their lower counterparts, but has inverted them.[16] John Sartoris's death, a passive suicide that is neither expiatory nor redeeming, has left his son free to act according to his own principles, which promote a wider and less self-interested interpretation of duty. These principles, which recognize the manner of his Southern preconditioning, and which subject that social construction to epistemological enlightenment, lower the boundaries between lives by rejecting discrimination. While the self-interest theory "can be directly collectively self-defeating," as Parfit counsels in *Reasons and Persons*, "this is not true of an agent-neutral morality" (191).

Bayard vanquishes the unvanquished by at once accepting and peacefully enacting his own vanquishment. Cooperation rather than defection characterizes his unarmed victory in Richmond's office. Bayard's act carries with it a sense of player-neutrality that foregrounds both a principle and the practice of that principle:

> [I]f there was anything at all in the Book, anything of hope and peace for His blind and bewildered spawn which He had chosen above all others to offer immortality, *Thou shalt not kill* must be it, since maybe he [Professor Wilkins] even believed that he had taught it to me except that he had not, nobody had, not even myself since it went further than just having been learned. But I did not tell him. He was too old to be forced so, to condone even in principle such a decision; he was too old to have to stick to principle

in the face of blood and raising and background, to be faced without warning and made to deliver like by a highwayman out of the dark: only the
young could do that—one still young enough to have his youth supplied
him gratis as a reason (not an excuse) for cowardice. (466–67)

Nonetheless, while Bayard's adherence to the Golden Rule *is* consistent
with the post-Kantian efforts that Parfit promulgates in *On What Matters*,
Bayard requires the non-Kantian sacrifice of his father to facilitate this
promotion.

Political solutions to each–we dilemmas tend to be easier to realize than
their psychological alternatives are, but those alternatives tend to be more
durable because they are opinions held by, rather than laws directed
toward, the individual. This distinction supports Arthur Ripstein's conclusion in "Private Order and Public Justice" (2006) concerning Sidgwick's
discussion of justice in *The Methods of Ethics:* that discussion "remains the
clearest and most forceful statement of the view that law and justice impose
general rules in order to achieve a moral good that makes no reference
whatsoever to anything rule-like" (1393 n.7). Philosophy undoubtedly
improves, and literature might stand still, as Parfit believed, but if literature fails to progress, this is because poets, dramatists, and novelists have
already interrogated the province that philosophers are struggling to
penetrate.

"Literary criticism," opines Derrida in "Force and Signification," "is
structuralist in every age, in its essence and destiny. Criticism has not
always known this, but understands it now, and thus is in the process of
thinking itself in its own concept, system and method" (5). Applying
game-theoretic notions to literary texts is a particularly structuralist
approach to interpretation, but one particularly suited to interrogating
Faulkner's different strategies in delineating human interaction. "Morality
is not an invention of philosophers," notes Bernard Williams. "It is the
outlook, or, incoherently, part of the outlook, of almost all of us" (174).
Indeed, "moral obligation applies to people even if they do not want it to"
(178); this "critical view of morality," as Eileen John concludes, is itself
"inescapable" (295); consequently, literature cannot help but "gravitate
toward moral concerns" (287). Martha C. Nussbaum, in effect, agrees.
"If our moral lives are 'stories' in which mystery and risk play a central and
a valuable role," she reasons in *Love's Knowledge* (1990), "then it may well
seem that the 'intelligent report' of those lives requires the abilities and
techniques of the teller of stories" (142).

The novelist and philosopher Iris Murdoch produced many such reports. "It is important to remember that language itself is a moral medium, almost all uses of language convey value," she counsels in "Literature and Philosophy" (1997). "This is one reason why we are almost always morally active. Life is soaked in the moral, literature is soaked in the moral." The novelist "is particularly bound to make moral judgements in so far as his subject-matter is the behaviour of human beings" (27). The presence of morality within the novel is implacable. On the one hand, as Jacques Derrida famously remarks in *Of Grammatology* concerning the "critical production" of hermeneutics, "*there is nothing outside of the text*" (158). On the other hand, as Bernard Williams asserts, "from the perspective of morality, there is nowhere outside the system, or at least nowhere for a responsible agent" (178). Related economies of inclusiveness inscribe the systems of language and morality; as a result, literature and moral philosophy share coincidental reserves.

Faulkner dared to suggest as much in *The Unvanquished* in leaving behind one part of the paradigm of modernity, the aesthetics of structuralism, in favor of another part of that paradigm, the sociological move from each to we. "Since we take nourishment from the fecundity of structuralism," writes Derrida in "Force and Signification," "it is too soon to dispel our dream" (4). That dream nourished Faulkner, but held his art in formal deadlock, until his cooperation with the ethical broke the impasse with *The Unvanquished*. In this novel, as its strategic games suggest, he extended his approach to the structures of human interaction, as expressed in the Shreve–Quentin negotiations of *Absalom*, with structural articulations of the human environment taking precedence over structuralist aesthetics. The ethics to which *Absalom* gravitated exerted a stronger pull on *The Unvanquished*. Both novels are intelligent reports, but the former has received far more plaudits than the latter, and this critical asymmetry deserves some redress because *The Unvanquished* conducts, with its own philosophical form of retrospective anticipation, a noteworthy foray into the domain of moral mathematics.

Notes

1. *The Methods of Ethics* supplies this chapter with all its quotations from Sidgwick.
2. Joseph Blotner's manifest of William Faulkner's Library (22) lists a copy of Catton's book.

3. "So long, sucker" (159), explains Martin Shubik, expresses the defector's cynical relief at his opponent's naïve decision.

4. In referring to the research of Albert Bigelow Paine, Joe B. Fulton traces Twain's lifelong interest in Lecky's volume. "According to Paine, Twain first read Lecky's *History of European Morals from Augustus to Charlemagne* in 1874, but," adds Fulton, "he certainly reread the book many times in the years to come" (21).

5. Reviewing *Knight's Gambit* (1949) for the Greenville *Delta Democrat-Times* (13 November 1949), Shelby Foote regrets that Faulkner's latest publication "has probably the lowest specific gravity of any book by this author since *The Unvanquished*, his thirteenth, or possibly even since *Mosquitoes*, his second" (18). Foote's judgment of *The Unvanquished* exemplifies the critical attitude toward the novel. Even Barnard DeVoto's early praise from February 1938, which commends Faulkner's overall clarity, condemns the concluding episode. "An Odor of Verbena," laments DeVoto, "employs the supersaturated lachrymatory gas under high pressure that is Mr. Faulkner's most irritating medium" (5). Ironically, what DeVoto praises, rather than what he condemns, has elicited persistent critical misjudgment. As Daniel Hoffman summarizes in *Faulkner's Country Matters* (1989), "*The Unvanquished* is among Faulkner's most accessible books, since its straightforward narration has neither the warpings of time nor the complications of style characteristic of his denser fictions. Accordingly, among some of its author's most devoted critics, this book has not enjoyed much respect" (35).

6. Indeed, as late as September 1965, Vladimir Nabokov would rejoice in decrying "Faulkner's corncobby chronicles" (57).

7. Episodes one to three, "Ambuscade," "Retreat," and "Raid," date to 1934. Episodes four and five, "Riposte in Tertio" (originally "The Unvanquished") and "Vendée," date to 1936. Episode six, "Skirmish at Sartoris" (originally "Drusilla"), dates to 1935. Episode seven, "An Odor of Verbena," dates to 1938.

8. Ringo could be John Sartoris's son. "Ringo and I had been born in the same month and had both fed at the same breast and had slept together and eaten together for so long that Ringo called Granny 'Granny' just like I did," muses Bayard, "until maybe he wasn't a nigger anymore or maybe I wasn't a white boy anymore" (323).

9. Faulkner was historically accurate in delineating this gambit. "Ordinary citizens of Mississippi, Union policy initially dictated, were to be presumed loyal citizens of the United States," explains Doyle. "Therefore, any property the U.S. Army confiscated from citizens could be reclaimed, or its value reimbursed, later" (210).

10. "Sidgwick was unusually good at seeing the force of objections to his views," writes Parfit in *On What Matters*. "After hearing Sidgwick defend a paper, William James remarked: 'Sidgwick displayed that reflective candour that can at times be so irritating'" (1:xxxix).

11. "Christians have been glad to appeal to the Self-interest Theory," continues Parfit, "since on their assumptions S implies that knaves are fools. Similar remarks apply to Moslems, many Buddhists, and Hindus" (130).

12. The first six volumes of *The Collected Papers of Charles Sanders Peirce* are *Principles of Philosophy* (1931), *Elements of Logic* (1932), *Exact Logic* (1933), *The Simplest Mathematics* (1933), *Pragmatism and Pragmaticism* (1934), and *Scientific Metaphysics* (1935). The remaining two volumes are *Science and Philosophy* (1958) and *Reviews, Correspondence, and Bibliography* (1958). Faulkner is unlikely to have read Peirce. The argument here simply suggests that the posthumous publication of *The Collected Papers of Charles Sanders Peirce*, starting in the 1930s, was proof of Peirce's prescience; that Peirce and Faulkner, as published authors, were (in effect) contemporaries; and that Faulkner's philosophical turn of mind was also prescient. On occasion, as Richard Godden implies in *William Faulkner: An Economy of Complex Words* (2009), the philosophical approaches of Faulkner and Peirce do coincide. For, in describing Labove's metaphoric conceptualization of Eula Varner in *The Hamlet* (1940), Godden turns to Peirce: "Eula, set within the mind's eye of Labove's metaphor, is both land and 'parts,' and as such she is, at the moment 'he saw it,' autochthony iconicized. Charles Saunders Peirce stressed that 'icons stand for something because they resemble it'" (53).

13. This imperative also answers both the question of canonical importance and the question of compositional form. In the first case, as Marjorie Pryse opines of "most commentators" on *The Unvanquished*, "the novel, or collection of stories, or whatever it is, is a small work" (343). In the second case, as Hans H. Skei writes in "William Faulkner's Short Stories" (2007), "*The Unvanquished* is certainly not a mere collection of short stories, but the question is whether it should be called a short story cycle or a novel" (403). The present argument asserts that *The Unvanquished* is a significant novel.

14. The mocking bird, which foregrounds its presence by singing throughout "An Odor of Verbena," provides the accompanying aural signal: "it was the day song" (484). Drusilla's "yellow ball gown" (468, 476, 478) provides the accompanying visual signal. The old moral formulations appear to be conspiring in their mockery of Bayard's (supposed) cowardice.

15. Benbow's Missourian canvassers were "human beings," Bayard tells Drusilla. "They were Northerners," she replies, "foreigners who had no business here." Were not their lives "worth anything?" he asks incredulously. Drusilla's response is uncompromising: "No. Not anything" (471). Mention of supremacist groups occurs across Faulkner's cannon: *Soldiers' Pay* (1926), *Mosquitoes* (1927), and *Light in August* (1932) reference the K.K.K. (224, 444, and 451, respectively); and *The Mansion* (1959) references the "Silver Shirts" as well as the K.K.K. (476, 602).

16. The aural and visual signals also mark this overhaul. In the first case, Bayard hears a "mockingbird singing in the magnolia," but "the night song now, the drowsy moony one" (491). In the second case, Drusilla and her ball gown are gone: she has left. The colors of Jenny's wisdom now overwrite Drusilla's formerly taunting yellow: "There was no light in the drawing room except the last of the afterglow which came through the western window where Aunt Jenny's colored glass was; I was about to go on up stairs when I saw her sitting there beside the window. She didn't call me and I didn't speak Drusilla's name, I just went to the door and stood there. 'She's gone,' Aunt Jenny said" (491–92).

CHAPTER 7

Benevolence (II): *Intruder in the Dust*

Henry Sidgwick's thoughts in *The Methods of Ethics* on the benevolence of gifting open from a historical perspective. "In earlier ages of society a peculiar sacredness was attached to the tie of hospitality, and claims arising out of it were considered peculiarly stringent," he relates, "but this has changed as hospitality in the progress of civilisation has become a luxury rather than a necessary, and we do not think that we owe much to a man because we have asked him to dinner" (246). Conversely, while "the duty of requiting benefits seems to be recognised wherever morality extends" (259), and "the general force of the obligation is not open to doubt (except of the sweeping and abstract kind with which we have not here to deal), its nature and extent are by no means equally clear" (259–60). Such doubts leave open to question "whether we are only bound to repay services, or whether we owe the special affection called Gratitude; which seems generally to combine kindly feeling and eagerness to requite with some sort of emotional recognition of superiority, as the giver of benefits is in a position of superiority to the receiver." On the one hand, common sense suggests "that, in so far as any affection can possibly be a duty, kindly feeling towards benefactors must be such: and yet to persons of a certain temperament this feeling is often peculiarly hard to attain, owing to their dislike of the position of inferiority; and this again we consider a right feeling to a certain extent, and call it 'independence' or 'proper pride'; but this feeling and the effusion of gratitude do not easily mix, and the moralist finds it difficult to recommend a proper combination of the two." On

M. Wainwright, *Faulkner's Ethics*,
https://doi.org/10.1007/978-3-030-68872-1_7

the other hand, common sense suggests that "if the benefit be coldly given, the mere recognition of the obligation and settled disposition to repay it seem to suffice," with "'independence' alone [...] prompt[ing] a man to repay the benefit in order to escape from the burden of obligation." Indeed, as Sidgwick observes, "it is partly this impatience of obligation which makes a man desirous of giving as requital more than he has received; for otherwise his benefactor has still the superiority of having taken the initiative" (260). In trying "to define [the] notion of 'equal return,' obscurity and divergence begin," and "though it is more plausible to say that we ought to requite an accepted service without weighing the amount of our benefactor's sacrifice, still when we take extreme cases the rule seems not to be valid." For example, "if a poor man sees a rich one drowning and pulls him out of the water, we do not think that the latter is bound to give as a reward what he would have been willing to give for his life. Still, we should think him niggardly if he only gave his preserver half-a-crown" (261).

Like Sidgwick's, Jacques Derrida's thoughts in *Given Time: I. Counterfeit Money* on the benevolence of gifting open from a historical perspective, returning to "the anthropologies, indeed the metaphysics of the gift." By doing so, however, Derrida departs more explicitly than Sidgwick does from the cycle of restitution, which treats the gift and the debt as a unified system. "For there to be a gift," explains Derrida, "*it is necessary* [*il faut*] that the donee not give back, amortize, reimburse, acquit himself, enter into a contract, and that he never have contracted a debt." Indeed, the economics of gifting insists that the donee must fail to recognize the gift as a gift, because "if the gift *appears to him as such*, if the present is present to him *as present*, this simple recognition suffices to annul the gift" (13; emphasis original). A symbolic equivalent enforces this cancellation. "It suffices therefore for the other to *perceive the gift*— not only to perceive it in the sense in which, as one says in French, 'on perçoit,' one receives, for example, merchandise, payment, or compensation—but to perceive its nature of gift, the meaning or intention, the *intentional meaning* of the gift, in order for this simple *recognition* of the gift *as* gift, *as such*, to annul the gift as gift even before *recognition* becomes *gratitude*" (13–14; emphasis original). Put simply, "identification of the gift seems to destroy it" (14). In Faulkner's *Intruder in the Dust* (1948), the impatience of obligation, the dislike of inferiority in a perceived exchange, misplaced debt, and a resistance to gratitude that nonetheless evokes gratitude, all appear within the rubric of the strange benevolence of (un)recognized gifting.

BENEVOLENCE (II): *INTRUDER IN THE DUST*

The duty of requiting benefits seems to be recognised wherever morality extends. (Henry Sidgwick, *The Methods of Ethics*, 259)

In 1948, banking on his publisher's continued interest in his work, and apparently speculating on the possible award of the Nobel Prize for Literature, the gifted William Faulkner, struggling with the atypical *A Fable* and with a perilously low bank balance, temporarily but concertedly reinvested himself in Yoknapatawpha County. The first major publication from this creative expenditure, which Faulkner would initially describe as "the best I have ever written" (qtd. in Patrick H. Samway 1), was *Intruder in the Dust*.[1] Published in 1948, the novel repaid Faulkner's reinvestment not only artistically, as its author's own appraisal testified, but also financially, as his bank balance attested, with the $40,000 that MGM paid for the film rights supplemented by the 25 percent on sales of the 37,040 copies that Random House printed of the first edition.[2] "*Intruder in the Dust*," as Michael Millgate reports, "sold more copies (about 18,000 in the first year) than any of his previous books" (47). At last, as Samway remarks, "Faulkner began to know a sense of financial security" (36).

Beyond these considerations, *Intruder in the Dust* reasserted Faulkner's literary presence, helping to secure him the 1949 Nobel Prize for Literature. In addition to the esteem of this award, the prize carried a substantial honorarium, which secured Faulkner's financial future for good. As *Intruder in the Dust* suggests, however, this combination of rewards is fundamentally unstable: while the conferral of esteem engages the *economy of the gift*, the transfer of capital engages the *economy of money*. Jacques Derrida, whose *Given Time: I. Counterfeit Money* capitalizes on the notion and possibilities of the gift, confirms this basic instability: each economy describes a figure of circulation, but unlike the economy of money, the economy of the gift demands neither exchange nor return of payment; indeed, the attempted transference of the gift seems to annul that very gift. The following analysis of the intractable relationship between the gift and money in *Intruder in the Dust* owes, therefore, an outstanding debt to Derrida's philosophical gift. By anchoring the resultant intellectual exchange to the accredited history of American foundation to which *Intruder in the Dust* occasionally but unarguably defers, a historical lineage spawned by the financial transactions encompassing the Middle Passage, economic concepts circulate between Faulkner's novel and

Derrida's philosophical treatise. This circulation, which parses the account of gifting opened at the beginning of *Intruder in the Dust* and intentionally never closed by the novel, provides a valuable account of a work that Faulknerians have hitherto underappreciated, a work that effectively sees beyond what Jean-Luc Marion laments as Derrida's reductive fixation with the "horizon of exchange."[3]

"Among its irreducible predicates or semantic values," expounds Derrida, "economy no doubt includes the values of law (*nomos*) and of home (*oikos*)." *Nomos* signifies not only "the law in general, but also the law of distribution (*nemein*), the law of sharing or partition [*partage*], the law as partition (*moira*), the given or assigned part, participation."[4] *Oikos* signifies not only the "home," but also "property, family, the hearth, the fire indoors" (*Given Time* 6).[5] These irreducible predicates contentiously define the social standing of Lucas Beauchamp in *Intruder in the Dust*, as an African-American farmer of mixed-race lineage, who lives and works in Yoknapatawpha County. Indeed, Chick Mallison assumes that Lucas Beauchamp is indebted to Carothers Edmonds, "on whose place Lucas lived seventeen miles from town" (285), even though the history and topography of Lucas's home proclaim otherwise. In historical terms, "Edmonds' father had deeded to his Negro first cousin and his heirs in perpetuity the house and the ten acres of land it sat in—an oblong of earth set forever in the middle of the two-thousand-acre plantation like a postage stamp in the center of an envelope" (289). In topographical terms, Lucas's home sits like a crown, central to the surrounding land, making his rectangle of native soil the center of Edmonds's place. This compound provenance is suited to fostering a benevolent outlook—"especially in modern times, since the revival of independent ethical speculation," to repeat Henry Sidgwick from *The Methods of Ethics*, "there have always been thinkers who have maintained, in some form, the view that Benevolence is a supreme and architectonic virtue, comprehending and summing up all the others, and fitted to regulate them and determine their proper limits and mutual relations" (238)—in its inheritor.

In assuming the failure of such fostering in Lucas's case, Chick's supposition bolsters his sense of socioeconomic superiority, and despite the admission that "he knew Lucas [...] as well that is as any white person knew him" (285), Chick cannot help but read Lucas's property as part of the economy of money. That Lucas remains "independent and intractable" (289) reaffirms, however, that he himself reads his inheritance otherwise. For Lucas, the Edmonds bequest is a gift; and the gift, as Faulkner's novel insists, is a contradictory phenomenon. "One cannot treat the gift, this goes without saying, without treating this relation to economy, even to the money economy," concedes Derrida in *Given Time*. "But is not the gift, if there is any, also that which interrupts economy?" (7). Lucas's appreciation of the contesting aspects of benevolence mean that his presence and actions in Yoknapatawpha County constantly agitate and interrupt Southern evaluations of law and home, distribution and partition. "Economy implies the idea of exchange, of circulation, of return. The figure of the circle is obviously *at the center*, if that can still be said of a circle" (6; emphasis original)," observes Derrida; and Lucas's hat—that crowning sign of hereditary authority ("a broad pale felt hat such as his grandfather had used to wear" [287])—marks its owner's central locus within such a figurative circumference. The figurative circle, which reinforces the symbolic position of Lucas's home, "stands at the center of any problematic of *oikonomia*," to appropriate Derrida, "as it does of any economic field: circular exchange, circulation of goods, products, monetary signs or merchandise, amortization of expenditures, revenues, substitution of use values and exchange values" (*Given Time* 6).

The novel opens with the enmeshment of Lucas's and Chick's socioeconomic circles. Chick's "breaking" (286) through the "ice" (286) when accidentally falling head over heels into a "creek" (286) is the tipping point that anticipates the turning "upside down" (286, 387, 434) of his racially inculcated thoughts—and Lucas is the benevolent agent who will underwrite this inversion. The attempts of the African-American boy Aleck Sander to help Chick out of the creek—"Aleck Sander rammed down at him the end of a long pole, almost a log whose first pass struck his feet out from under him and sent his head under again"—actually keep him immersed (287). It requires a disembodied voice, like that of God, to dissolve the two boys' antics: this "voice said: 'Get the pole out of his way so he can get out'—just a voice." This announcement comes from Lucas, who does not intervene physically, but whose passive involvement nonetheless enables Chick to make dry land. The inversion of racial assumptions in this tableau, with the African-American man standing above and looking down on the American boy, is obvious: events have contrived to upset the accustomed socioeconomic order. To Chick, annoyed with Lucas's passivity, Aleck's pole was "the one token toward help" (287). In consequence, Chick inserts Lucas and Aleck into the economy of money and the economy of the gift, respectively, with what Derrida calls "the relation of the gift to the 'present,' in all the senses of this term," coming to the fore (*Given Time* 9–10).

Unlike a present, which is monetary, fiduciary, or commercial, a gift implicitly recognizes its recipient with a different form of presentation. This acknowledgment is one of the necessary conditions for the act of gifting. "The line between virtues and other excellences of behaviour is commonly drawn," notes Sidgwick, "by this characteristic of voluntariness" (*Methods* 220). For benevolence to be unconditional, as Derrida explains, "it is necessary that the gift not even appear, that it not be perceived or received as gift" (*Given Time* 16); this munificence is at once unbidden and undemanding. Chick does not consciously realize this truth—accidental immersion and subsequent restitution have not broken through the socioeconomic ice of his majoritarian pretensions—but his use of the word "token" does reveal a subconscious recognition of false symbolism. The pole, as token, is a counterfeit gift; Lucas's alternative offering, his gift in the form of apportioning self-responsibility, was not entirely wasted.

Having rationalized his denial of Lucas's help in extracting him from the creek, Chick has simply to turn into Edmonds's drive when following the homeward-bound Lucas, but with his world turned upside down, Chick does not "even check when they passed the gate" (288). That failure implies that Chick is both prepared (he does not check or interrupt his movements) and unprepared (the accompanying narration is grounded in the discourse of the economy of money) to accept Lucas's prolonged benevolence. For, on entering Lucas's home, Chick at once partakes of the economy of the gift and the economy of money, but seemingly recognizes only the latter. "He could smell that smell which he had accepted without question all his life as being the smell always of the places where people with any trace of Negro blood live" (290). This odor, which "was a part of his inescapable past" (291–92), "a rich part of his heritage as a Southerner" (292), signifies the sweat of surplus value extracted from African Americans, a legacy that dates back to the days of the Middle Passage. Chick's assumption of narratorial control, despite his (already quoted) admission of lacking such mastery ("he knew Lucas [...] as well that is as any white person knew him" [285]), reinforces this significance, which the novel consistently underwrites by withholding the gift of narratorial interiority from Beauchamp himself.

Dozing in front of the fire, wrapped in a quilt (that symbol of African-American housewifery), and thereby subconsciously enjoying the economy of unconditional benevolence he consciously denies, Chick registers a flicker of enlightenment. The gifting of time, as part of this economy, enables this momentary pause for reflection. "Apparently and according to common logic or economics," as Derrida relates in *Given Time*, "one can only exchange, one can only take or give, by way of metonymy, what is *in* time" (3; emphasis original). This "somewhat simplifying representation" would suggest "that wherever there is time, wherever time predominates or conditions experience in general, wherever *time as circle* (a 'vulgar' concept Heidegger would therefore say) is predominant, the gift is impossible" (9; emphasis original). By the alternative way of metaphor, however, "one can only be blind to time, to the essential *disappearance* of time even as, nevertheless, in a certain manner nothing *appears* that does not require and take time" (6; emphasis original). According to this formulation, God in *Intruder in the Dust*, as already conjured by Lucas's disembodied voice at the creek, is without time, and the gifted, such as William Faulkner, gain their powers from this timeless benevolence.

Ultimately, as Derrida implies in *Given Time*, and as the quilt that cozens Chick suggests, the gift is female in origin. Nature, specifically parturition, tears time apart. "A gift could be possible, there could be a gift only at the instant an effraction in the circle will have taken place, at the instant all circulation will have been interrupted and *on the condition* of this instant"—and Lucas initially appeared as if from nowhere, but actually from the home superintended by his wife Molly. With this miraculous, but femininely countersigned, appearance, Lucas passively forces himself into Chick's life. "There would be a gift only at the instant when the *paradoxical* instant (in the sense in which Kierkegaard says of the paradoxical instant of decision that it is madness) tears time apart" (9; emphasis original). Lucas's prolongation of benevolence exploits the "gap between the impossible and the thinkable" as a dimension that "opens up where *there is* gift—and even where *there is* period, for example time, where *it gives* being and time" (10; emphasis original). Hereafter, the relation of the gift to the present (in spatial as well as temporal forms) becomes essential to the interlaced economies of the novel. The background image of knitting, as variously undertaken by Molly, the "kinless spinster of seventy" (340) Miss Eunice Habersham, and Chick's mother, hereby suits the "structure of *nodal* coiling" that "Heidegger names the *Geflecht*" (9; emphasis original) or woven network.

Lucas's benevolence relates intimately to the economic *oikos*, or the keeping of hearth and home, which Molly passively yet undeniably superintends: this, then, is the gift of hospitality. "In earlier ages of society," remarks Sidgwick, "a peculiar sacredness was attached to the tie of hospitality, and claims arising out of it were considered peculiarly stringent," but with the development of civilization, this kind of benevolence "has become a luxury rather than a necessary" (*Methods* 246). For Lucas, however, this necessity remains unalloyed, and from this hospitable basis, Lucas just keeps gifting, so that Chick finds himself eating "what obviously was to be Lucas' dinner" (292–93). Lucas's generosity is of a (Sidgwickian) earlier age. Nor does Chick's flicker of enlightenment flood ratiocinative time; he remains indebted to the economy of money; and his thoughts are still speculative:

> he was in the chair again in front of the now bright and swirling fire, enveloped in the quilt like a cocoon, enclosed completely now in that unmistakable odor of Negroes—that smell which if it were not for something that was going to happen to him within a space of time measurable now in minutes he would have gone to his grave never once pondering speculating if perhaps that smell were really not the odor of a race nor even actually of poverty but perhaps of a condition: an idea: a belief: an acceptance, a passive acceptance by them themselves of the idea that being Negroes they were not supposed to have facilities to wash properly or often or even to wash bathe often even without the facilities to do it with; that in fact it was a little to be preferred that they did not. (291)

Chick's further speculations, which he bases on the poverty of a warrantee's agrarian background, cannot help but highlight Lucas's symbols of wealth: "the gold-framed portrait-group on its gold easel" (293) contrasts with "the man in the gum boots and the faded overalls," whose clothes contrast, in turn, with the "heavy gold watch-chain looping across the bib of the overalls" (292).

These bursts of speculation—expressive of the circulation of the economy of money—soon blanket Chick's emerging enlightenment—expressive of the circulation of the economy of the gift—in darkness. Hence, despite subconscious reservations, Chick offers to pay for Lucas's gift: "his dumb hand open and on it the four shameful fragments of milled and minted dross" (294). Chick attempts to transform Lucas's one-sided benevolence into a two-sided exchange. The youngster falls foul of what Sidgwick in *The Elements of Politics* describes as the difficulty "of distinguishing a statement of a benevolent intention, not intended as a pledge, from a promise really understood as such on both sides," a pledge based on "'preappointed' evidence" (95). Lucas's initial response to Chick's attempt to exchange gift for money is silence. The farmer then asks, "What's that for?" Each of these reactions to the manner in which Chick "extended the coins" prolongs (or extends) Lucas's gift of extended presence. "In the same second in which" Chick knew that Molly would have taken the money, "he knew that only by that one irrevocable second was he *forever* now too late, *forever* beyond recall, standing with the *slow* hot blood *as slow as minutes* themselves up his neck and face, *forever* with his dumb hand open." In response, Lucas was "not even moving, not even tilting his face downward to look at what was on his palm," non-acts of denial that last "for another *eternity*" (294; emphasis added); and with his incipient enlightenment eclipsed, Chick finally reacts in an inculcated fashion to the extended presence of Lucas's denial: he drops the coins on the floor. Lucas, however, remains firm in rejecting the exchange between two related but distinct economies, ordering the two other youths present (Aleck Sander and Edmonds's boy) to pick up and return Chick's money.

Chick had tried to repay; Lucas had refused that repayment; so Chick symbolically reimburses Lucas: on his way home he "walked steadily to the creek and drew the four coins from his pocket and threw them out into the water" (296). The coins replace (or repay) Chick's earlier presence in that water. Such acts, however, do not wipe clean the relevant memory banks, and the day's additions to Chick's subconscious reserves continue to worry him. This anxiety expresses another of the necessary conditions for the benevolence of gifting. "For there to be gift," as Derrida expounds, "not only must the donor or donee not perceive or receive the gift as such, have no consciousness of it, no memory, no recognition; he or she must also forget it right away." Furthermore, "this forgetting must be so radical that it exceeds even the psychoanalytic categoriality of forgetting" (*Given Time* 16). Chick, who is not that radical, suffers a "sleepless" night over Lucas's benevolence, with the farmer's gift retaining an infelicific aspect. He realizes that "he had gone out there this morning as the guest not of Edmonds but of old Carothers McCaslin's plantation and Lucas knew it when he didn't and so Lucas had beat him" (296). In fact, although he still cannot quite admit it, Chick had been Lucas's guest, and repayment will remain at the economic heart of the novel.

Faulkner states as much in his 1 February 1948 letter to Harold Ober. "The story is a mystery-murder though the theme is more [the] relationship between Negro and white, specifically or rather the premise being that the white people in the south, before the North or the govt. or anyone else, owe and must pay a responsibility to the Negro" (262). In effect, as Erik Dussere relates, "Faulkner was worrying about how the debt of what James Baldwin called 'more than two hundred years in slavery and ninety years of quasi-freedom' would be paid back, and by whom" (43).[6] In "Teaching *Intruder in the Dust* through Its Political and Historical Context" (2001), Robert W. Hamblin reports how Faulkner's friendship with (William) Hodding Carter, whom he entertained at Rowan Oak while working on the novel, partly shaped his immediate response to these issues. Two years earlier, Carter had won a Pulitzer Prize for "his editorials condemning racial injustice and inequality" (154), and Faulkner tacitly acknowledged his fellow Mississippian's influence. "Carter's a good man," he told John K. Hutchens in October 1948, "and he's right when he says the solution of the Negro problem belongs to the South" (60).

The cycles of presents, by which Chick seeks to repay Lucas's positively unredeemable benevolence, and counterpresents, by which Lucas checks Chick's desire for the foreclosure of that benevolence, relate to another of the necessary conditions for the act of gifting. "For there to be gift," states Derrida, "*it is necessary* [*il faut*] that the donee not give back, amortize, reimburse, acquit himself, enter into a contract, and that he never contracted a debt" (*Given Time* 13). An exchange of gifts breaks this necessity. "An exchanged gift is only a tit for tat, that is, an annulment of the gift," insists Derrida. "By underscoring this, we do not mean to say that *there is no* exchanged gift. One cannot deny the *phenomenon*, nor that which presents this precisely phenomenal aspect of exchanged gifts. But the apparent, visible contradiction of these two values—gift and exchange—must be problematized" (37; emphasis original). The exchange of gifts, as *Intruder in the Dust* affirms, translates them into presents. The immediacy of money in Chick's act within Lucas's home attempts to prosecute this translation. "If the other *gives* me *back* or *owes* me or has to give me back what I give him or her," as Derrida maintains, "there will not have been a gift, whether this restitution is immediate or whether it is programmed by a complex calculation of a long-term deferral" (12; emphasis original). A gift silently presents an excess beyond the presentation of a present, an excess that any moderated, calculated, or measured present cannot reimburse.

One can surmise the excessiveness of Lucas's benevolence, and something of the nature of that indulgence, from the white community's desire for Lucas's payment of his racial dues: "Every white man in that whole section of the county had been thinking [this] about him for years: *We got to make him be a nigger first. He's got to admit he's a nigger. Then maybe we will accept him as he seems to intend to be accepted"* (296). Yet, the majoritarians of Yoknapatawpha County fail to recognize, let alone acknowledge, that Lucas proffers a gift of enlightenment. Lucas continues, therefore, to look at white men "with a calm speculative detachment" (297), with a gaze that relates to, but is at the same time separate from, the economics of speculation; in other words, with a gaze that concerns a reward that is beyond the monetary, a foresight that oversees the horizon of exchange, a transcendence that exceeds majoritarian comprehension.

In the meantime, Chick acts according to inculcation, with his attempt at psychological repression provoking a symbolic acknowledgement of his onetime host's detached disregard for the economy of money. Repression operates either systemically or topologically. "It always consists of keeping by exchanging places," states Derrida. "And, by keeping the meaning of the gift, repression annuls it in symbolic recognition" (*Given Time* 16). Chick's psyche tries to exchange Lucas's benevolence for a monetary symbol, one that nonetheless retains the significance of that benevolence in attempting to cancel it, and one of an inflated size that recalls the asymmetric racial foundation of American capital:

> Now not only his mistake and its shame but its protagonist too—the man, the Negro, the room, the moment, the day itself—had annealed vanished into the round hard symbol of the coin and he would seem to see himself lying watching regretless and even peaceful as day by day the coin swelled to its gigantic maximum, to hang fixed at last forever in the black vault of his anguish like the last dead and waneless moon and himself, his own puny shadow gesticulant and tiny against it in frantic and vain eclipse: frantic and vain yet indefatigable too because he would never stop, he could never give up now who had debased not merely his manhood but his whole race too. (298–99)

That debasement involves a specific relation to Southern propriety. Gift giving was central to the code of honor. On the one hand, the exchange of gifts cemented kith and kin relations. On the other hand, presenting an unrequitable gift confirmed the social status of both the giver (superior) and the recipient (inferior). "The language of the gift," avers Kenneth S. Greenberg, "was frequently the language of mastery," and this usage even mitigated the act of manumission. "The gift relation was just as deeply implicated in emancipation as it was in slavery," asserts Greenberg;

"masters could liberate individual slaves only by awarding them freedom as a gift" (66). Goodhue Coldfield, the Methodist steward of *Absalom, Absalom!*, who banked his altruism for future requital, partook of this pernicious economy: he manumitted two slaves "as he came into possession of them," but put them "on a weekly wage which he held back in full against the discharge of the current market value" (69). In fine, as Greenberg concludes, "slaves could never purchase themselves in market transactions because they could give nothing to their masters. Masters might permit slaves to purchase themselves, but that was only a round-about way of giving slaves a valuable gift" (66).

This racial history, according to Chick's conscious speculation, demands redress. He rather than Lucas should be the benevolent power. "The duty of requiting benefits seems to be recognised wherever morality extends," remarks Sidgwick. "Still, though the general force of the obligation is not open to doubt (except of the sweeping and abstract kind with which we have not here to deal), its nature and extent are by no means equally clear" (*Methods* 259–60); and Chick, in his determination to pay Lucas back, falls foul of this uncertainty. "In the first place," ponders Sidgwick, "it may be asked whether we are only bound to repay services, or whether we owe the special affection called Gratitude; which seems generally to combine kindly feeling and eagerness to requite with some sort of emotional recognition of superiority, as the giver of benefits is in a position of superiority to the receiver." Two thoughts come to mind. "We seem to think that, in so far as any affection can possibly be a duty, kindly feeling towards benefactors must be such." Yet, to people "of a certain temperament this feeling is often peculiarly hard to attain," as in Chick's relationship to Lucas, "owing to their dislike of the position of inferiority; and this again we consider a right feeling to a certain extent, and call it 'independence' or 'proper pride'; but this feeling and the effusion of gratitude do not easily mix, and the moralist finds it difficult to recommend a proper combination of the two" (260).

Independence dominated Chick's immediate attitude toward Lucas's benevolence. He wanted to be free of his status as a child; he wanted to prove his (supposed) racial superiority; but Lucas forestalled each of these desires. Chick's initial attempt at redress comprised "the four two-for-a-quarter cigars for Lucas and the tumbler of snuff for his wife" (299) that he sent as "Christmas presents" (302). Yet, in exemplifying conspicuous consumption, these items retained exchange value within the monetary economy; consequently, "there still remained the dead monstrous heatless disc which hung nightly in the black abyss of [Chick's] rage and impotence" (299).[7] Chick's subsequent attempt—for three months he saves "the twenty-five cents his father gave him each week as allowance and the twenty-five cents his uncle," the lawyer Gavin Stevens, "paid him as office salary," so that "in May he had enough and with his mother helping him chose the flowered imitation silk dress and sent it by mail to Molly Beauchamp"—provides "something like ease." Certainly, "the disc still hung in the black vault," but that coin was "almost a year old now and so the vault itself was not so black with the disc paling and he could even sleep under it" (300).

Chick's sense of relaxation has emerged, however, from Lucas's gift of time. "The gift only gives to the extent it *gives time*," as Derrida elucidates in *Given Time*:

> The difference between a gift and every other operation of pure and simple exchange is that the gift gives time. *There where there is gift, there is time.* What it gives, the gift, is time, but this gift of time is also a demand of time. The thing must not be restituted *immediately and right away.* There must be time, it must last, there must be waiting—without forgetting [*l'attente— sans oubli*]. It demands time, the thing, but it demands a delimited time, neither an instant nor an infinite time, but a time determined by a term, in other words, a rhythm, a cadence. (41; emphasis original)

Hence, Lucas waits four months before undermining Chick's sense of ease, with Chick returning home one afternoon to find "a gallon bucket of fresh homemade sorghum molasses" from the farmer (300). What is more, as if to emphasize the detachment between his initial gift and this present, Lucas had paid "a white boy" to deliver it. In terms of conventional honor, Chick remains in the unorthodox position of social inferiority to an African American, and in terms of cyclical economics, the two agents are "right back where they had started" (300), with Lucas's act of unconditional benevolence still unsullied, unassuaged, and unredeemed.[8]

Chick repeatedly thinks he has laid the economy of the gift to rest by bringing it full circle, but Chick's repeated presents to Lucas simply express his repression of donee status; and repression, to repeat, does not erase but retains through exchange. For Chick, who remains inculcated by a monetary economics once sustained by slavery, the gift of time means not only that "it was all to do over again," but also that "it was even worse this time," because "Lucas had commanded a white hand" to "give it back to him." Chick cannot help but feel a slave to Lucas's apparent whims: "Whatever would or could set him free was beyond not merely his reach but even his ken" (300). The necessary solution eludes Chick's current grasp because the economy of the gift is beyond the economy of money, but part of Lucas's benevolence to Chick remains ratiocinative time, time in which the boy's thoughts can circulate. Whereas Lucas's gift, to borrow the Derridean formula, "must not circulate, it must not be exchanged, it must not in any case be exhausted, as a gift, by the process of exchange, by the movement of circulation of the circle in the form of return to the point of departure," circular figuration is "essential to economics" (*Given Time* 7), and the aneconomic gift, according to this seemingly contradictory logic, can circulate without exchange. Such benevolence does not remain "foreign to the circle" but keeps "a relation of foreignness to the circle, a relation without relation of familiar foreignness" (*Given Time* 7), and the African-American Lucas embodies the familiarly foreign to the almost, but not completely, exhausted Chick.

In an economics that exploits racial difference, masters evaluate subalterns in the conferral of use- and exchange-value, but the complementary economics that shadows these evaluations places subalterns in the ideal position to offer a complimentary gift. This freedom under duress enables Lucas to invert the existing constructs of binary logic. The circulation put in motion by the gift, as Derrida states, "allows all the values to be inverted: The gift of life amounts to the gift of death, the gift of day to the gift of night" (*Given Time* 54). Chick's "four shameful fragments of milled and minted dross" (Faulkner, *Intruder*, 294), the "four two-for-a-quarter cigars" (299), and Molly's (albeit imitation) silk dress find their complement in the "four years" (291) that elapse before Chick realizes "the extent of its ramifications and what it had done to him" (291). Furthermore, "he would be a man grown before he would realise, admit that he had accepted it" (291), that "whatever" (300) of Lucas's gift. That acceptance will amount to a denial (however tacit) of the improper pride of self-sufficiency. "For a gift to be given," to draw on John McAteer's summary of Marion's thoughts, "we must reject our view of ourselves as self-sufficient subjects. For me to give you a gift, I must admit that I have some surplus, something given to me from outside myself (otherwise I have nothing to give)" (61). One such surplus is the legacy of slavery, and the ledgers of all southerners, whatever their ethnicity, carry this external debt.

That Lucas has "killed Vinson Gowrie" (303), that he is in custody, and that the Gowries and their friends from Beat Four ("where as a local wit said once the only stranger ever to enter in with impunity was God and He only by daylight and on Sunday" [310]) are expected to lynch him, promises to foreclose that debt. "Even as a child," Vinson "had shown an aptitude for trading and for money, so that now, though dead at only twenty-eight, he was not only said to own several small parcels of farmland about the county but was the first Gowrie who could sign his name to a check" (409). This Gowrie personified the monetary economy, and although his murderer erased this embodiment, the economy of money seems to have retained the upper hand: "the Lord Himself would have to stop to count the Gowries and Ingrums and Workitts" (304) willing to lynch Lucas.

Chick now believes that he can settle his outstanding balance with Lucas, and the prospective reestablishment of economic superiority underwrites Chick's sense of freedom. He now repeatedly avows himself "free" (302, 304, 306, 307, 309, 312) of Lucas's gift. Yet, immersed in the economy of money, all this thinking and convincing, and all these repetitions of surety—"Lucas was no longer his responsibility, he was no longer Lucas' keeper; Lucas himself had discharged him" (315)—fall outside the economy of unconditional benevolence. Memories of Lucas's home on the day of Chick's icy submergence keep returning: waiting in his uncle's office, Chick notices Gavin's "colored mug from the Heidelberg *stube* […] like the vase sitting on Lucas' mantel that day" (305). What is more, Chick's prejudices inflate these memories, so that he recalls Lucas as a "figure straddled baronial as a duke or a squire or a congressman before the fire hands clasped behind it and not even looking down at them but just commanding two nigger boys to pick up the coins and give them back to him" (310). Lucas's tactic of inverting the existing constructs of binary logic is paying aneconomic dividends, and even Stevens implicitly recalls that formative day for Chick in stating how "your friend Beauchamp seems to have done it this time" (307).

Chick, immersed in the economy of money, imagines Lucas's acceptance of a majoritarian gift. Visualizing his onetime host under arrest, Chick thinks how "the constable's wife had served their supper," and how "Lucas with a good appetite" was "sharp set for his since he […] wouldn't have to pay for it" (308). Yet, there is an underlying sense that Lucas is exploiting Vinson Gowrie's murder as the decisive means of relaying the economy of the gift to majoritarian agency. The reason for the murder is currently of little concern "least of all to Lucas since apparently he had been working for twenty or twentyfive years with indefatigable and unflagging concentration toward this one crowning moment." This ultimate achievement, which exploits the assumptions of his accusers, builds on their final indebtedness to Lucas: when the constable arrested him, separating his charge from a growing crowd, Lucas "made no resistance whatever, merely watching this too with that same calm detached not even scornful interest" (311).

That Chick recounts Lucas's arrest secondhand, with the report of the farmer's passive compliance separated from the rest of Chick's account by ellipses, adumbrates Lucas's essence as an agent who differentiates between related economies. A similar differentiation within Chick's secondhand account further suggests how the crowd awaiting Lucas's lynching operates according to the economy of money: "(and he gathered one car full had even gone back last night, yawning and lounging now and complaining of lack of sleep: and that to be added to Lucas' account too)" (313). This operation appears to be without, but is actually within, normal economics. "Then suddenly the empty street was full of men," reports the heterodiegetic narrator, "the ones who could be seen all week long in or around the poolhall who did nothing at all that anyone knew, who owned automobiles and spent money nobody really knew exactly how they earned on weekends in Memphis or New Orleans brothels." These men, according to Chick's uncle, "were in every little Southern town"; they "never really led mobs nor even instigated them but were always the nucleus of them because of their mass availability" (315). Walking from the car to the Jefferson jail, with this crowd watching, Lucas remains "detached, impersonal, almost musing, intractable and composed" (316). Notwithstanding this detachment, Lucas pinpoints Chick among the spectators ("Lucas even knew where he was in the crowd before he turned, looking straight at him before he got turned around even, speaking to him" [317]), because of the growing reciprocity between them. Chick's notable maturation partly accounts for this nascent mutuality. When making Chick's present of "molasses," Lucas had "remembered how a boy's always got a sweet tooth" (301), but now he asks the "young man" (317) to bring lawyer Stevens to the jail.

In addition to the jailer Mr. Tubbs, Lucas's security relies on the farmer Will Legate, as deputized by Sheriff Hope Hampton, for his protection. That Lucas "aint 'quainted with no Will Legate" (330)—a temporary officer whose first and last names resonate with the economy of money—comes as little surprise. That Tubbs has no confidence in Legate bodes ill. The jailer complains about Legate reading "the colored comic section of today's Memphis paper" (322). He wonders if "Hampton think[s] that funny paper's going to stop them folks from Beat Four?" To which Legate replies, "I dont think he's worrying about Beat Four yet," adding "this here's just for local consumption" (323). That Legate sits on guard, with the "front door [...] open, standing wide to the street," which Chick "had never seen before" (322), makes this "comic display" yet another instance of conspicuous, and somewhat unnerving, consumption. The whole situation is almost too much for Tubbs, who sums up the danger of this departure from his normal duties in financial terms: "Me get in the way of them Gowries and Ingrums for seventy-five dollars a month? Just for one nigger? And if you aint a fool," he tells Legate, "you wont neither." Yet, as Tubbs implicitly accepts, whatever the economics of the situation, the law (or *nomos*) holds sway: "Dont mind me," he tells Stevens, "I'm going to do the best I can; I taken an oath of office too" (323–24).

Concerning Chick's account with Lucas, uncovering a body of evidence will prove the farmer's innocence, but by entering the jail, Chick and his uncle Gavin pass "out of the world of man"—white men, that is, "people who worked and had homes and raised families and tried to make a little more money than they perhaps deserved" (325). Indeed, the interior of the jail, which Chick associates almost exclusively with the incarceration of African Americans, is alien to the economy of money: the prisoners form a self-contained collective, and this environment is the site of Lucas's ultimate gamble. "Beauchamp and not the county attorney holds the cards" (114), as Jay Watson remarks in *Forensic Fictions* (1993), but in exploiting Vinson's murder, and in braving a possible lynching, Lucas is willing to risk the noose, willing to "risk entering into" what Derrida calls "the destructive circle" of the untranslatable gift (*Given Time* 30).

Lucas appears to have kept some gifting in reserve, or in the black, for this emergency. "Liberality appears to require an external abundance in the gift even more than a self-sacrificing disposition," to repeat Sidgwick. "It seems therefore to be possible only to the rich: and, as I have hinted, in the admiration commonly accorded to it there seems to be mingled an element rather aesthetic than moral. For we are all apt to admire power, and we recognise the latent power of wealth gracefully exhibited in a certain degree of careless profusion when the object is to give happiness to others" (*Methods* 324). Lucas's wealth is aneconomic. Indeed, any supposition that doubts the unconditional nature of Lucas's benevolence is deceptive in partaking of the economy of money, and Lucas, as his verbal exchange with Stevens underlines, carefully separates the economy of the gift from the *nomos* of his legal defense. Lucas, who appreciates rational calculation as Stevens's supreme quality, plays on that asset: "I'm gonter pay you," he assures the attorney. "You dont need to worry" (328). Retaining an economic reserve of the gift would open that gift to the prospect of a countergift; such an annulment encapsulates payment and discharge; that discharge would be the negative gift by which Vinson's family would repay Lucas. "For there to be gift," as Derrida avers, "there must be no reciprocity, return, exchange, countergift, or debt." Otherwise, "from the moment the gift puts the other in debt," that gift is "bad, poisonous," and giving amounts to harming. "Here one need hardly mention the fact that in certain languages, for example in French, one may say as readily 'to give a gift' as 'to give a blow' [*donner un coup*], 'to give life' [*donner la vie*] as 'to give death' [*donner la mort*], thereby either dissociating and opposing them or identifying them" (*Given Time* 12).

In the problematic logic of indebtedness, "the circulation of a good or of goods is not only the circulation of the 'things' that we will have offered to each other," explains Derrida, "but even of the values or the symbols that are involved there [*qui s'y engagent*] and the intentions to give, whether they are conscious or unconscious" (*Given Time*, 12–13). Although social anthropologists "have *quite rightly and justifiably*, treated *together*, as a system, the gift and the debt, the gift and the cycle of restitution, the gift and the loan, the gift and credit, the gift and the countergift, we are here *departing*, in a peremptory and distinct fashion, from this tradition." Lucas constantly prosecutes this departure. He has already done so in annulling Chick's Christmas presents, because that tradition relegates African Americans to subalterns for whom presents are carnivalesque, masterly sleights of hand intended to offset temporarily, without alleviating permanently, the burden of oppression. For "there is gift, if there is any," as Derrida observes, "only in what interrupts the system as well as the symbol, in a partition without return and without division [*répartition*], without being-with-self of the gift-counter-gift" (*Given Time* 13; emphasis original).

Lucas effects such an interruption while incarcerated by exploiting that exemplar of both forced African-American production and conspicuous consumption, tobacco, to engineer Chick's return to the jail without Stevens. "You might send me some tobacco," he tells the boy, "if them Gowries leaves me time to smoke it" (332). Chick reciprocates Lucas's feint in returning to the jail empty-handed. Now, sealed in an exchange of looks between Chick and the imprisoned Lucas, the transference of the gift overwrites the economy of money, translating Chick's search for Lucas's innocence into an acceptance of further tuition. In effect, the benevolent Lucas passes on (rather than exchanges) the economy of the gift, which Chick's maturation into what the heterodiegetic narrator calls "Charles Mallison junior" (335), a moniker used nowhere else in the novel, acknowledges. Charles, who "wasn't even thinking anymore" (335) as Chick, whose dawning independence accompanies a proper pride, has passed Lucas's latest test. Although separated by racial constructs, as symbolized by the bars of the prison cell, Charles can accept Lucas's gift. This transference goes beyond a reductive obsession with the horizon of exchange. "Givability," as Marion expounds in *The Visible and the Revealed* (2008), "arises around the potential giver when [he], first of all in relation to [himself] alone, recognizes that the principle 'I owe no one anything' may (and must) admit at least one exception. The gift begins and in fact ends as soon as the giver envisions that he owes something to someone, when he admits that he could be a debtor, and thus a recipient. The gift begins when the potential giver suspects that another gift has already preceded [him], to which [he] owes something, to which [he] owes [himself] to respond" (91).[9]

What maintains Charles's attention in Lucas's gaze is that "whatever" (300), that divine immanence (or *quidditas*) of the gift, and "that something—whatever it was—[holds] him [t]here" (335). Lucas's transference of the gift occupies an elongated present that unhinges the common (or majoritarian) notions of Chick's upbringing. What Charles must credit, as Lucas intends, goes beyond the economics of a single agent to the wider and profounder implications of racial politics. Faulkner's synesthetic description of Charles "hear[ing] the mute unhoping urgency of [Lucas's] eyes" (335) connotes the resulting derangement of socioeconomic norms. Agreeing to disinter Vinson Gowrie is lunacy; insanity "is a certain excess of the gift," as Derrida warns (*Given Time* 45), and the intensity of this madness "begins to burn up the word or the meaning 'gift' itself and to disseminate without return its ashes" (47)—or, in the related Faulknerian discourse, its dust.

Beyond testifying that his gun is "a fawty-one Colt" (335)—the weapon that killed Vinson Gowrie will be identified as "a German Luger automatic" (419)—Lucas tells Charles nothing. This silence appears to signify the imprisoned Lucas's withdrawal from the narrative. As such, according to Samway, "Lucas becomes a major character more by his absence than by his presence" (253), but more accurately adduced, Lucas's metaphysical rather than his physical presence secures his status as the preeminent character in the novel.[10] Similarly, although Lucas leaves Charles incredulous ("he thought in a kind of raging fury: *Believe? Believe what?* because Lucas was not even asking him to believe anything" [338; emphasis original]), Charles cannot help but recollect, or circulate past thoughts, concerning Mrs. Downs. For a price, this local woman "didn't merely tell fortunes and cure hexes but found things" (337). Mrs. Downs had once divined the whereabouts of a friendship ring (or circle) that Charles's mother had received in kind from "her room-mate at Sweetbriar Virginia," but which she had subsequently lost. According to the economy of money, this ring was "a cheap thing with an imitation stone," but according to the economy of the gift, the two friends had "exchanged to wear until death" (336). Recalled with pertinence to the relationship between Charles and Lucas, this anecdote suggests that the former will locate what the latter asks him to find, and not from a financial incentive.

Appropriately to Charles's tuition in the economy of the gift, but annoyingly for the start of his mission, which involves trying to "convince" his uncle to "find a J.P." willing to sanction a disinterment, an immediate impediment confronts him. Parked outside the family house is a pickup truck. Charles assumes Gavin is busy with a farmer whose stray animal "had been impounded by a neighbor who insisted on collecting a dollar pound fee before he would release it" (339).[11] Interrupting this meeting, Charles discovers the owner of the truck to be the benevolent Miss Habersham, rather than a financially minded farmer. Charles tells his uncle of Lucas's alibi, which Gavin interprets as a lie, because its obviousness belies credibility. Notwithstanding this rebuff, Charles holds his ground, and Miss Habersham, who knows Lucas better than Gavin does, silently supports Charles's stance. Miss Habersham not only employs "Molly's brother and Lucas' brother-in-law" (374), but also boasts close links with Molly herself. Lucas's wife "had been the daughter of one of old Doctor Habersham's, Miss Habersham's grandfather's, slaves." Molly and Miss Habersham, who were "the same age, born in the same week and both suckled at Molly's mother's breast," had "grown up together almost inextricably like sisters" (349). No wonder, then, that as the young Charles's complement, the aged Miss Habersham has already determined to prove Lucas's alibi, and secretly offers her help. The only other recruit is Aleck Sander. Like Charles, Aleck rejects the offer of money, but unlike the silent Charles, Aleck is plain speaking in this rejection. "Lucas is going to pay you," Charles informs him. Aleck "laugh[s], without mirth or scorn or anything else: with no more in the sound of it than there is anything in the sound of breathing but just breathing." Whereas people wedded to the economy of money need money, Aleck is amenable to the economy of the gift: "I aint rich," he tells Charles. "I dont need money" (348).

As the white members of this triumvirate, Miss Habersham and Charles effectively command the mission, "like two people who have irrevocably accepted a gambit they are not at all certain they can cope with" (350). Owing to the quietness and stillness of the graveyard, reasons Charles, "they would have some warning" of possible detection when disinterring Vinson. This reassurance fails to reassure them, however, because their actions are sure to break these conditions, and Charles finds himself "not speculating on who the warning could help since they who would be warned were already six and seven miles from the jail and still moving away from it as fast as he dared push the horse" (354). The equivocal nature of this warning seems, therefore, to link any possible comfort from it to the economy of the gift.

Charles additionally muses on the reaction of local African Americans to Lucas's arrest for the murder. Very few have been in evidence since Lucas's arrest. This cautiousness attests to what the economy of the gift has always demanded of them: "they had not fled," they were "just waiting, biding since theirs was an armament which the white man could not match nor—if he but knew it—even cope with: patience"; and their lawful homes accommodate the just waiting of their patience. The presence of absent African Americans ("this land was a desert and a witness, this empty road its postulate") equates to "one irremediable invincible inflexible repudiation"—irremediable because that disavowal places subaltern over master, making the warrantee the only one who can donate the gift of forgiveness. Such benevolence will forgive majoritarians for counting on "the whole dark people" for "the very economy of the land itself," a reliance that, in turn, counts on the minimum of repayment. Only the economy of the gift, when thoroughly disseminated, can afford this valid absolution for the economy of the Middle Passage: that circulation of enslaved peoples, raw materials, goods, and monies for the benefit of the majoritarians of the American Republic and Old World empires. That Charles consciously considers these issues—even if "it would be some time yet before he would realise how far he had come" (356)—further testifies to his growing enlightenment.

The prominence of Lucas's absence throughout the central portions of the novel, which shadows that of his African-American confrères, echoes this repudiation. His ever-present disappearance hints at the divide between the metaphysical (even the theological) economy of the gift and the secular (even the atheistical) economy of money. The exhumation conducted by Charles, Aleck, and Miss Habersham, which reveals not Vinson Gowrie's body, but that of the "jackleg timber buyer" (370) Jake Montgomery, relates these divided economies. Lucas *got the whole county upset trying to pretend he murdered a white man*" (427; emphasis original), as Miss Habersham recognizes, but this benevolent gamble, as a potentially self-sacrificing act, has revealed the circulation of dead bodies.[12] This revelation leaves the gifted Charles feeling "responsible for having brought into the light and glare of day something shocking and shameful out of the whole white foundation of the county" (388), the South, and the United States. The crowd outside the jail knows nothing of Montgomery's death and the circulation of dead bodies, but as rumors circulate, Charles begins to gain further enlightenment when one of the throng unwittingly invokes the theme of surplus labor peremptorily and forever usurped by supposed mastery. This man notes that Sheriff Hope Hampton has drafted two African-American convicts to help in the graveyard. "If he's depending on anybody named Gowrie to dig a hole or do anything else that might bring up a sweat," shouts the man, "he'll sure need them" (389).

Joining Gavin to witness the re-exhumation, Charles experiences an epiphany on their journey, which assures his enlightenment. He again observes an empty landscape, one without African-American farmers, that "formal group of ritual almost mystic significance identical and monotonous as milestones tying the county-seat to the county's ultimate rim as milestones would" (395), before seeing, "with an incredulous an almost shocked amazement" (395), a solitary African-American ploughman "eye to eye" (396). This look, which passes from "the face black and gleamed with sweat and passionate with effort" (396) to the chauffeured Charles, recalls the gaze that passed from Lucas to Chick in the jail; and this compound vision underwrites Charles's acceptance of the economy of the gift.

Charles's uncle, observing this economy from without, understands it at a number of levels. Stevens understands how "all man had was time" (305). Stevens understands how "only a few of us know that only from homogeneity comes anything of a people or for a people of durable and lasting value—the literature, the art, the science, that minimum of government and police which is the meaning of freedom and liberty" (400).

Stevens understands how, after the dissemination of these gifts, "we would prevail." The commonalty "would dominate the United States; we would present a front not only impregnable but not even to be threatened by a mass of people who no longer have anything in common save a frantic greed for money and a basic fear of a failure of national character" (402). Stevens understands how "outlanders […] will fling" the cause of the subaltern "decades back" (437), because they do the south the injustice of "forcing on us laws based on the idea that man's injustice to man can be abolished overnight by police" (438). His dismissal of northern interference exposes the narcissism to which the donor is prone. Such self-interest turns a gift into a present. "The simple intention to give," as Derrida warns, "suffices to make a return payment to oneself. The simple consciousness of the gift right away sends itself back the gratifying image of goodness or generosity, of the giving-being who, knowing itself to be such, recognizes itself in a circular, specular fashion, in a sort of auto-recognition, self-approval, and narcissistic gratitude" (*Given Time* 23). In this sense, as Walt Whitman's "A Song of the Rolling Earth" (1881) avers, "the gift is to the giver, and comes back most to him," just as "the murder is to the murderer, and comes back most to him" (179).

Notwithstanding this exposure, and despite his multivalent understanding of the economy of the gift, Stevens assumes "the privilege of setting" the subaltern "free" (400); in doing so, the lawyer exposes his own narcissistic needs. From the minoritarian perspective, the legacy of the economy of money, as expressed in the economics of slavery, withholds the status of specular donor from Lucas. For Derrida, narcissistic gratitude "is produced as soon as there is a subject, as soon as donor and donee are constituted as identical, identifiable subjects, capable of identifying themselves by keeping and naming themselves" (*Given Time* 23), but the act of transference between Lucas and Charles precludes self-reverence. The movement invested in that transfer constitutes an effraction to the circulation of the gift and its trustee. The distinction of setting subalterns free lies not with southerners "ourselves" (400), as Stevens would have it, but with subalterns themselves. In other words, the gift of that release is for the subaltern to give once that subaltern has identified a warrantor capable of trusteeship. Charles Mallison, as a junior citizen whose credit in the economy of money has yet to fully mature, and Miss Habersham, as a senior citizen whose credit in the economy of money awaits the capitalization accounted for by death, are the only potential trustees among Lucas's acquaintances. While the former has a creditable future, the latter's future is practically written off.[13] The young Charles is, then, the only viable trustee of "the gift of his time" in "man's enduring chronicle" (430), as this, the sole use of the word "gift" in the novel, confirms. As a trustee, "a locus of giving-and-receiving" who rejects "the ontology of will in favor of an ontology of gift" (McAteer 65), Charles experiences a positive advancement beyond the horizon of exchange.

The evidence uncovered by Charles, Aleck, and Miss Habersham in Lucas's defense exposes Vinson's brother Crawford as the guilty party. Crawford, whom the army cashiered (or discredited) for desertion, but who remains dedicated to the economy of money, has latterly usurped the right of gifting by stealing timber. He killed Vinson because he cannot afford to be discredited a second time. Indeed, with his murders of Vinson and Montgomery, double homicide has paid out on Crawford's double-dealing. With this confirmation of Crawford's guilt, the majoritarians of Jefferson try to draw Lucas back into the monetary economy by regularly and unendingly recompensing him with an item that is neither a gift nor a present but a reminder of the colonial past: tobacco. Stevens understands this aspect of masterly behavior: "Lucas will ultimately get his can of tobacco," he tells Charles, "they will insist on it, they will have to. He will receive installments on it for the rest of his life in this county whether he wants them or not and not just Lucas but *Lucas: Sambo*" (434).

Unwittingly recalling the incident at the creek that overturned Chick's worldview, Stevens adds, "he wont want it of course and he'll try to resist it. But he'll get it and so we shall watch right here in Yoknapatawpha County the ancient oriental relationship between the savior and the life he saved turned upside down" (434; emphasis original). As Charles comes to realize of the wider picture, Lucas's freedom remains "*in check going on a hundred years after Lee surrendered*" (447; emphasis original), because the economy of money guarantees that check. Charles "had no more expected Lucas to be swept out of his cell shoulder high on a tide of expiation and set for his moment of vindication and triumph on the base say of the Confederate monument (or maybe better on the balcony of the postoffice building beneath the pole where the national flag flew) than he had expected such for himself and Aleck Sander and Miss Habersham" (429–30). Indeed, Charles "not only had not wanted that but could not have accepted it since it would have abrogated and made void the whole sum of what part he had done which had to be anonymous else it was valueless" (430). Like Lucas, the trustee before him, Charles eschews the economic circularity of auto-recognition, self-approval, and narcissistic gratitude.

Despite and because of this disengagement, Charles "hadn't expected [...] the grudging pretermission of a date" for the "all *now*" of the gift (430; emphasis original): "Because you escape nothing, you flee nothing; the pursuer is what is doing the running and tomorrow night is nothing but one long sleepless wrestle with yesterday's omissions and regrets" (431). That "all *now*" is the "going to begin" of a gifted dissemination that would return America to the unsullied dream, "the moment in 1492 when somebody thought *This is it*: the absolute edge of no return, to turn back now and make home or sail irrevocably on and either find land or plunge over the world's roaring rim." The economy of the gift remains, therefore, autotelic in the contradictory manner of never returning to its origin: "It was still there or at least his unfinished part in it which was not even a minuscule but rather a minutecule of his uncle's and the sheriff's in the unfinishability of Lucas Beauchamp and Crawford Gowrie" (433). The unfinishability of a gifted dissemination heralds the ultimate, self-effacing character of benevolence, which Derrida describes as "an absolute forgetting—a forgetting that also absolves, that unbinds absolutely and infinitely more, therefore, than excuse, forgiveness, or acquittal" (*Given Time* 16). "Some things," as Stevens counsels Charles, "you must always be unable to bear": these unbearable issues include "injustice and outrage and dishonor and shame. No matter how young you are or how old you have got. Not for kudos and not for cash: your picture in the paper nor money in the bank either. Just refuse to bear them" (439). While this advice reveals the partial extent of Stevens's enlightenment, his middle-aged resignation to the unrealizable nature of the gift confronts yet encourages Charles's determination to reach for the unattainable—unattainable because the act of absolution in forgetting rests with African Americans alone. This radical kenosis of inscape requires the self-undoing of personal attitudes, knowledge, and history by entering into, or letting oneself go at, the traumatic heart of their causation.

"The American," opines Stevens, "really loves nothing but his automobile." He does not love "his wife his child nor his country nor even his bank-account first (in fact he doesn't really love that bank-account nearly as much as foreigners like to think because he will spend almost any or all of it for almost anything providing it is valueless enough) but his motorcar" (463). Charles, inspired by his trusteeship, denies his uncle's contention, and although Gavin is without or beyond the gift, he recognizes his nephew's potential creditability in that other economy: "and even when you are fifty and plus," urges Stevens, "still refuse to believe it" (464). During this exchange, the authorities having released him with no case to answer, Lucas appears in Stevens's office, and this visit insures and ensures the continued circulation of the economy of the gift. Lucas first invokes the gift that sparked the slow emergence of Chick's release from prejudice: "You aint fell in no more creeks lately, have you?" he asks (465). In answer to Charles's rejoinder, "I'm saving that until you get some more ice on yours," Lucas reminds him of the ever-immanence of that gift: "You'll be welcome without waiting for a freeze" (465). Lucas then changes the subjective focus of the economy of the gift, not only freeing himself from a specific instance of the economy of money, but also indicting Stevens for his lack of sociopolitical perception. Thinking himself a man of enlightenment, Stevens admits that Americans "are willing to sell liberty short at any tawdry price" (467); yet justice, *nomos*, the law as equal partition, should eschew the economy of money: justice should be within the economy of the gift.

"I believe you got a little bill against me," states Lucas (468). "I didn't do anything," replies Stevens. As Lucas insists, however, as if accepting and resisting Stevens's check, or unenlightened state, "I authorised you." At the outset of his incarceration, Lucas had intentionally inserted both client (himself) and lawyer (Stevens) into the economy of money, and the cost Lucas assumes of "two dollars to have a new point put in" (468) Stevens's fountain pen is a fee that demands reimbursement. This sum is small, but is, nevertheless, a monetary charge; and while Gavin believes Lucas owes Miss Habersham a present for proving his innocence, Charles's uncle has already bought the flowers that Lucas will deliver to her. Stevens's bouquet is nothing other, therefore, than another token (or counterfeit) gift. Lucas, having tested the lawyer throughout the negotiations in Gavin's office, is well aware of this fact. Thus, he first covers the lawyer's charge in monetary kind, but then with bodily gestures. His gaze speaks of, but is separate from, the economy of money: "Lucas blinked rapidly once" (465); Lucas, looking at Stevens, "blinked twice this time" (466); "once more Lucas blinked twice"; "he blinked twice again"; and, finally, "he blinked twice again" (468). In this manner, Lucas repeatedly casts out his glance, but unlike his earlier projection of the quidditas of the gift with Chick, this casting produces no effect on Stevens. Acknowledging Gavin's indifference, Lucas "now [...] just blinked once, then he did something with his breath: not a sigh, simply a *discharge* of it." With this act, which attempts to close his financial account with Stevens, Lucas repays the lawyer for the "expense [of] sitting here last Tuesday trying to write down all the different things you finally told me in such a way that Mr Hampton could get enough sense out of it to *discharge* you from the jail" (468; emphasis added).

Lucas extends this recompense in a timely fashion, taking back a quarter from his original payment and exchanging it for fifty pennies, which come from "a knotted soiled cloth tobacco sack" (469). The significance of this bag is twofold: expressing both conspicuous consumption and Lucas's freedom, as an African American, to fill the colonial sign with his own choice of signifying content. This compound worth also fails, however, to strike the lawyer, who makes Lucas count the coins out one by one. Only then, when Stevens finally assumes that this "business" (469) transaction is over, does Lucas emphasize Steven's enslavement to an economy of which he himself has "wiped his hands" (470). "What are you waiting for now?" asks the exasperated lawyer. "My receipt," replies the equitable farmer. Lucas's denial of Chick's payment for his hospitality at the beginning of *Intruder in the Dust* has found its counterpart, but while the economy of money has come full circle, the economy of the gift remains unclosed.

To repeat, Lucas's generosity is of an earlier age, and this virtue approaches what Sidgwick calls chivalry. This more specific understanding of generosity somewhat eclipses that of liberality. "In so far as the sphere of Generosity coincides with that of Liberality," explains Sidgwick, "the former seems partly to transcend the latter, partly to refer more to feelings than to outward acts, and to imply a completer triumph of unselfish over selfish impulses." In its wider sense, generosity "is strikingly exhibited in conflict and competition of all kinds. Here it is sometimes called Chivalry." The essence of this noble virtue, as Lucas's case illustrates, "is the realisation of Benevolence under circumstances which make it peculiarly difficult and therefore peculiarly admirable." For, "Chivalry towards adversaries or competitors seems to consist in showing as much kindness and regard for their well-being as is compatible with the ends and conditions of conflict." In sum, Lucas's generosity, as chivalry in its strictly ethical sense, denotes "the virtue of Benevolence (perhaps including Justice to some extent) as exhibited in special ways and under special conditions" (*Methods* 326).

That conspicuous consumption, as signaled by the "uproar" (470) that washes over Stevens's office from the "valueless enough" (463) automobiles that fill the town square, accompanies the quietus of Lucas's settling of his monetary debt to Stevens is entirely apt. Stevens, as the temporary exchange (or hierarchical inversion) in sociopolitical order sealed by the two men's spoken exchange implies, ought to think over or outside or without the economy of money, beyond not only the *nomos* of the law in general, but also the *nemein* of the law of distribution. The African-American gift must turn toward the African-American giver, and the present imminence of the accumulated interest on this benevolence, as figured at once in Charles's ability and Gavin's inability to accept the trusteeship of the economy of the gift, encapsulates the tragedy of postbellum America. Stevens must take responsibility, but blinded by his own narcissistic needs, he fails to do so.

"On what condition is responsibility possible?" asks Derrida in *The Gift of Death*. "On the condition that the Good no longer be a transcendental objective, a relation between objective things, but the relation to the other, a response to the other; an experience of personal goodness and a movement of intention" (50). In *Intruder in the Dust*, that conditional relationship involves the gift of forgiveness, a gift that demands the acknowledgement of an original sin. For America, that realm of Manifest Destiny, that capital chance (offered by a supposedly *de novo* site) for the expansion of western capital, this sin pertains to the horrific assumptions and acts of colonialism. "The deed of gift," as Robert Frost acknowledges in "The Gift Outright" (1941), "was many deeds of war" (316). "The doctrine of original sin suggests an ancient and infinite guilt that requires rectification," writes Eric R. Severson. "Finite human beings are incapable of compensating for infinite guilt, and must instead receive justification as the miracle of a gift. The idea of *grace* therefore functions as the cornerstone for any Christian theology of forgiveness. The origin of this gift is God, who is also the origin of responsibility. In this way, responsibility is wrested away from the cult of reason and returned to the realm of secrecy and mystery, but not without first being radically transformed." By analogy, the origin of this gift in *Intruder in the Dust* is the substantially insubstantial Lucas Beauchamp, whose God-like voice dominates the opening scene, and who ultimately wrests responsibility from the figure of inculcated deliberation, Gavin Stevens, with the obscurities and clarities of benevolence emerging from the novel's philosophical transformation of mystery-murder conventions. Neither the ratiocination of a Gavin Stevens nor the enthusiasm of a religious zealot can elicit such a gift. "Goodness happens *to* the self," observes Severson, "but it is not a performance or achievement of the self" (5; emphasis original).

In "A Song of the Rolling Earth," to quote more extensively from Whitman's poem, the narrator speaks of redounding acts. "The murder is to the murderer, and comes back most to him, / The theft is to the thief, and comes back most to him, / The love is to the lover, and comes back most to him, / The gift is to the giver, and comes back most to him—it cannot fail" (179).[14] In a similar vein, Quentin Compson in *Absalom* recalls his father telling him of an axiom espoused by Quentin's grandfather: "a man always falls back upon what he knows best in a crisis—the murderer upon murder, the thief thieving, the liar lying" (197). The analogy from *Intruder in the Dust* concerns the unconditional benevolence of the African American. That gift must turn toward the African-American giver, but the present imminence of the accumulated interest on that gift, as figured at once in Charles Mallison's ability and Gavin Steven's inability to accept the trusteeship of the economy of the gift, encapsulates the tragedy of postbellum America. While African Americans seek through the gesture of the gift to constitute the identity and unity born of self-possession, orthodox majoritarians, through a combination of inculcated arrogance, ignorance, and generational precedence, maintain that embodiment as a tantalizing prospect.

Intruder in the Dust renders the gifted William Faulkner's account of that gesture to posterity. "What has been said of Virtue, seems to me still more manifestly true of the other talents, gifts, and graces which make up the common notion of human excellence or Perfection," avers Sidgwick. "However immediately the excellent quality of such gifts and skills may be recognised and admired, reflection shows that they are only valuable on account of the good or desirable conscious life in which they are or will be actualised, or which will be somehow promoted by their exercise" (*Methods* 395). As the novel foretells at an authorial level beyond, but in relation to, its narratorial levels, Faulkner's gift to literature engaged the economic cycle from which it, like its author, would have preferred to remain apart. The Nobel Prize for Literature exacerbated the resulting conflict. The excess and dislocation of the gift repaid the gifted Faulkner with a madness that was, to borrow the Derridean phrasing, "at once reason and unreason" (*Given Time* 36). That insanity manifested the "madness of the rational *logos* itself, that madness of the economic circle the calculation of which is constantly reconstituted, logically, rationally, annulling the excess that itself [...] entails the circle, makes it turn without end, gives it its movement, a movement that the circle and the ring can never comprehend or annul" (36–37). This incomprehension is always a matter of psychic expenditure. The economic dislocation of the gift "folds back in a contradictory manner toward the subject who utters it (for example, 'do not listen to me,' 'do not read me'), it engenders that schism in the response or the responsibility in which some have sought to recognize the schizopathogenic power of the double bind" (56–57). Four years after Faulkner's death, when "Helen Tartakoff coined the term 'Nobel Prize complex'" to describe narcissistic analysands, "she undoubtedly," as Julie Des Jardin states, "had scientists rather than poets or peace activists in mind" (175), but the 1949 Nobel Prize for Literature, as Faulkner's continuing struggles with *A Fable* evinced, undoubtedly stimulated a contradictory foldingback for its recipient too.[15] The Nobel Prize Committee had gifted an unrequitable predicament to the gifted author's psychological ledger, an entry indebted to the ongoing cost of the colonial past, an entry that no amount of esteem or money could ever repay.

NOTES

1. Although Faulkner completed "Notes on a Horsethief" in November 1947, some two months before he started work on *Intruder in the Dust*, this episode from the forthcoming *A Fable* would not appear in print until 1951.
2. "Random House sold the movie rights of *Intruder* to M-G-M for $50,000," Samway explains, "with Faulkner receiving $40,000 of this. The rest being Random House's commission" (36). Lawrence H. Schwartz documents the number of first editions printed (70). "Each copy of this edition […] cost $2.50," details Samway, and Faulkner received "25% of that" (25).
3. Marion's contention appears in both *Being Given* (2002) (82) and *The Visible and the Revealed* (2008) (88). The critical undervaluation of *Intruder* has held relatively firm since the 1950s. "*Intruder in the Dust*," writes William Van O'Connor in *The Tangled Fire of William Faulkner* (1954), "has many of the virtues, although in a lesser degree, of Faulkner's earlier work: the wit, the virtuosity in language, the quality of living figures, the luminous scenes. But the reader does not feel that the true center of the novel is in the relationship between Lucas Beauchamp […] and the white citizens of Jefferson" (141). Although Donna Gerstenberger excludes the novel from "Edmund Wilson's condemnation of Faulkner's carelessness in constructing the design of his books," her study of "Meaning and Form in *Intruder in the Dust*" (1961) still dismisses the author's creative framework as a "somewhat-contrived murder mystery" (223). In

"Gradual Progress and *Intruder in the Dust*" (1986), John E. Bassett finds much to praise in the novel, but cannot help classifying it as "a transitional work in Faulkner's career" (208), aligning the evolution of the novelist's approach to literary creation with the slow emergence of majoritarian enlightenment in the south. "*Intruder*, correctly grouped with Faulkner's lesser works," opines Robert W. Hamblin in *A William Faulkner Encyclopedia* (1999), "is a very uneven novel." For Hamblin, "the Hollywood-style 'whodunit' action […] seems incompatible with the stream-of-consciousness, high modernist style that is Faulkner's hallmark," and "the story is frequently set aside (as in chapters 7, 9, and 10) for the effusive propagandizing of Gavin Stevens on the issues of race and sectionalism" (200).

4. "As soon as there is law," explains Derrida, "there is partition: as soon as there is *nomy*, there is economy" (*Given Time* 6).

5. "In Faulkner's previous stories and novels," notes Samway, "there are certain elements which seem to find further expression in *Intruder*" (236). In other words, these motifs (or *figurations*) come back with renewed interest. The term *oikos*, for example, immediately recalls "The Fire and the Hearth" section of *Go Down, Moses* (1942), in which Lucas Beauchamp's earlier engagement with the economy of money comes to a head. For at least a generation, Lucas had treated majoritarians with "cold and deliberate calculation" (81). What is more, as "The Fire and the Hearth" makes clear from the outset, Lucas "already had more money in the bank now than he would ever spend" (26). His twenty-first birthday had secured his "financial independence" (81) because Theophilus (Buck) and Amodeus (Buddy) McCaslin had "made an especial provision (hence a formal acknowledgment, even though only by inference and only from his white half-brothers) for their father's negro son. It was a sum of money, with the accumulated interest, to become the negro son's on his verbal demand but which Tomey's Turl, who elected to remain even after his constitutional liberation, never availed himself of" (82). "The Fire and the Hearth" recounts Lucas's related actions on coming of age. Isaac McCaslin, who has transferred the relevant account, accompanies Lucas to the bank. Lucas immediately writes a check, withdraws the entire sum, counts the money, and then returns it all to his account (84–85). Nonetheless, the chance discovery of "a single [gold] coin" (30), which Lucas links to a hoard that "old Buck and Buddy had [supposedly] buried almost a hundred years ago" (31), is enough to destabilize his circulation. Lucas's febrile thoughts induce nightly perambulations in search of gold. Only Molly's determination to divorce Lucas cures him of this obsession. "I reckon to find that money aint for me," he concedes (101). The motif of extended presence—so prominent in *Intruder in the Dust*—precedes this admission. When

Lucas finally decides against a divorce, he tells Edmonds to wait outside the county courthouse from which they have just emerged, so that he can buy Molly "a nickel's worth" (100) of candy. "'Wait a minute?' Edmonds said. 'Hah!' he said. 'You've bankrupted your waiting. You've already spent—' But Lucas had gone on. And Edmonds waited" (99–100). Importantly for a reading of *Intruder in the Dust*, not only are Chick Mallison, Gavin Stevens, and the Gowries outside the domestic and familial contexts that circumscribe "The Fire and the Hearth," but thanks to Molly, Lucas's gold fever is also spent by the end of this episode.

6. The Baldwin quotation comes from his essay "Faulkner and Desegregation" (118) (1961).

7. From Stevens's "burning cob pipe" (342) to "the neat trim colored maids in frilled caps" (374) to the "valueless enough" (463) motorcars, *Intruder in the Dust* repeatedly illustrates the circumambience of conspicuous consumption.

8. Samway's study of the typescripts of the novel emphasizes Faulkner's growing interest in the unanswerable gift: "The second chapter of the setting copy, which had also been part of the first chapter of the original draft, structures more carefully Chick's [attempts at] repayment and Lucas' gift of molasses delivered to Chick by a white boy" (257).

9. The gifted Molly's cure of Lucas's gold fever in "The Fire and the Hearth" (see note 5 above) is one of these preceding gifts.

10. Few critics, if any, understand Lucas to be the eponymous intruder, let alone the leading character, in the novel. While suggesting that "dust refers to a void in Chick's life" (250), Samway contents himself with the conclusion that "the ambiguity of the title [...] does not reveal the novel's main concerns" (252). "The title of *Intruder in the Dust* is ambiguous," agrees Hyatt H. Wagoner. "Both a radical naturalism and a Biblical view of man are consistent with the implications of the phrase." In the first sense, man is "an 'intruder' in nature in the sense of a biological accident, an 'unnatural,' temporary, incidental offshoot of the convolutions of the nebulae." In the second sense, "the Bible and the Prayer Book caution man to remember that he is dust and will return to dust, that unless he be regenerated he lives only toward death" (214). Joseph Gold argues that the violation of corpses in the novel, as if digging up the dust of bodily decomposition, is a necessary intrusion into the American past. Almost forty years later, William H. Rueckert effectively returned to Gold's argument. "An intruder in the dust is someone who disturbs the dead," he states. "But the title is more violent and specific than that because 'intrude' carries the sense of the uninvited, of forced entry"; as a result, "it is not just a matter of disturbing the dead but of violating the grave—two actions which have always had a profound significance for Faulkner" (262). Readers who fail to grasp

that Lucas's literal intrusion into the dust of a lumberyard makes him the eponymous protagonist do not appear to have followed Faulkner's own conceptual journey. His initial approach to *Intruder in the Dust* as a detective story changed under Lucas Beauchamp's direction. "Once I thought of Beauchamp," Faulkner told participants in the "Graduate Course in the Novel" at the University of Virginia (13 May 1957), "then he took charge of the story and the story was a good deal different from the idea [...] of the detective story that I had started with" (142).

11. Stevens lives with his sister's family.

12. For Philip M. Weinstein in "'*And you are*———?'" (2014), "Lucas Beauchamp is not genuinely menaced." Indeed, "all readers gather (this is the implicit narrative contract embedded in the genre) that his innocence will be revealed. Rather than menaced, Lucas remains encased in his dignity, a throwback to earlier mores. His plight, external only, is designed to engage white Jeffersonians and the white reader as an unmistakable call to come to his aid. Put otherwise, by 1948 Faulkner had come to respect, enshrine, and reify black difference. He envisaged it as a sturdy composite of Southern-white-liberal-approved traits: minority traits in no need of alteration" (17). Faulkner, however, was always an author who was willing to break the narrative contract embedded in a genre, and while Lucas's gambit assumes Chick's engagement, that gamble *is* risky. Most Jeffersonians have some scruples, but the Gowries and other inhabitants Beat Four have few, if any. "The sense of mobs, not waiting to lynch but waiting passively to watch a lynching," as Walter Allen observes, "is superbly rendered" (106).

13. "Grandparents and grandchildren (keeping in mind Aleck Sander)," as Samway remarks, "are able to view life from a larger context and not become imitators of the prejudices of their parents" (268). All told, Miss Habersham proves to be an eccentric figure of circulation, as her journey home after the townsfolk's acceptance of Lucas's innocence attests. She pulls her pickup truck into the traffic leaving the town square, but the weight of vehicles carries her out of Jefferson, and she must ask for return directions. In effect, she describes a circle, one with its center offset from the town square.

14. "The poem that eventually became 'A Song of the Rolling Earth' was first included in the 1856 edition of *Leaves of Grass*, under the title 'Poem of The Sayers of The Words of The Earth,'" writes Burton Hatlen. "It later became 'To the Sayers of Words' (in the 1860 and 1867 editions) and 'Carol of Words' (in the 1871 and 1876 editions), before acquiring its final title in the 1881 edition" (665).

15. Ernest Hemingway's reaction to receiving the 1954 Nobel Prize for Literature, as his recourse to ECT intimates (see Chap. 2), manifested a similar contradiction.

CHAPTER 8

Responsibility (II): *A Fable*

"For as in ordinary deliberation we have to consider what is best under certain conditions of human life, internal or external," reasons Henry Sidgwick in *The Methods of Ethics*, "so we must do this in contemplating the ideal society. We require to contemplate not so much the end supposed to be attained—which is simply the most pleasant consciousness conceivable, lasting as long and as uninterruptedly as possible—but rather some method of realising it, pursued by human beings; and these, again, must be conceived as existing under conditions not too remote from our own, so that we can at least endeavour to imitate them." This contemplative responsibility brings the extent to which one can modify present circumstances under scrutiny; "a very difficult question," admits Sidgwick, "as the constructions which have actually been made of such ideal societies show." A classical example remains telling. "The *Republic* of Plato seems in many respects sufficiently divergent from the reality, and yet he contemplates war as a permanent unalterable fact, to be provided for in the ideal state, and indeed such provision seems the predominant aim of his construction." In contrast, "the soberest modern Utopia would certainly include the suppression of war. Indeed the ideal will often seem to diverge in diametrically opposite directions from the actual, according to the line of imagined change which we happen to adopt, in our visionary flight from present evils" (21).

Common opinion usually relies on historical analyses to counsel on past evils, but in "This Strange Institution Called Literature," Jacques Derrida

M. Wainwright, *Faulkner's Ethics*,
https://doi.org/10.1007/978-3-030-68872-1_8

wonders whether the novelist, poet, or artist "doesn't 'treat' history in the course of an experience which is more significant, more alive, more *necessary* in a word, than that of some professional 'historians.'" Although such treatment is not "a moral or political duty (but it can also become one), this experience of writing is 'subject' to an imperative: to give space for singular events, to invent something new in the form of acts of writing which no longer consist in a theoretical knowledge, in new constative statements, to give oneself to a poetico-literary performativity at least analogous to that of promises, orders, or acts of constitution or legislation." Literary performance is more engaging than factual repetition. Historical awareness can, however, enhance this potential. "In order for this singular performativity to be effective, for something new to be produced, historical competence is not indispensable in a certain form (that of a certain academic kind of knowledge, for example, on the subject of literary history), but it increases the chances." Derrida emphasizes this responsibility to the past. "In his or her experience of writing as such, if not in a research activity, a writer cannot not be concerned, interested, anxious about the past, that of literature, history, or philosophy, of culture in general. S/he cannot not take account of it in some way and not consider her- or himself a responsible heir, inscribed in a genealogy, whatever the ruptures or denials on this subject may be." The commitment necessitated by this responsibility increases in proportion to the seriousness of these breaches. "The sharper the rupture is," explains Derrida, "the more vital the genealogical responsibility. Account cannot not be taken, whether one wish it or not, of the past. Once again, this historicity or this historical responsibility is not necessarily linked to awareness, knowledge, or even the themes of history. What I have just suggested is as valid for Joyce, that immense allegory of historical memory, as for Faulkner, who doesn't write in such a way that he gathers together at every sentence, and in several languages at once, the whole of Western culture" (55; emphasis original).

The issue of responsible heirs arose in 1952 when William Faulkner spoke to Loïc Bouvard of the human condition. "'Man,' he said gravely, 'is free and he is responsible, terribly responsible. His tragedy is the impossibility—or at least the tremendous difficulty—of communication'" (70). Faulkner's commitment to terrible responsibility, as a writer aware of his genealogical responsibilities and as a modernist in dialogue with the contingency of his own artistic vision, is never more apparent than in *A Fable* (1954), a novel that not only anticipates the Derridean call from *The Other Heading* (1992) to recall "what has been promised under the name of

Europe" (76), but more especially points uncompromisingly yet implicitly through both the future anterior and the lacunary to the fundamental reason for that promise: the Holocaust.

RESPONSIBILITY (II): *A FABLE*

In some ages and countries Patriotism and Loyalty have been regarded as almost supreme among the virtues; and even now Common Sense gives them a high place. (Henry Sidgwick, *The Methods of Ethics*, 244)

The following discussion pursues an interpretive trajectory similar to that which emerges, on the one hand, from Jürgen Habermas's understanding of modernity and, on the other hand, from Jean-François Lyotard's definition of postmodernity. For Habermas, whose interpretation in "Modernity versus Postmodernity" (1981) begins with a consideration of the phrase "the Ancients and the Moderns," modernity has been constantly renewing itself since antiquity. "The word 'modern' in its Latin form 'modernus,'" he writes, "was used for the first time in the late 5th century in order to distinguish the present, which had become officially Christian, from the Roman and pagan past. With varying content, the term 'modern' again and again expresses the consciousness of an epoch that relates itself to the past of antiquity, in order to view itself as the result of a transition from the old to the new" (5). The drive inherent to modernity promotes the emergence of a new modernism (or cultural expression) from current modernist practice.

For Lyotard, whose explanation from "Answer to the Question, 'What is the Postmodern?'" (1982), also references the ancients, postmodernity describes this immanent force. The postmodern "is undoubtedly part of the modern," he affirms. "Everything that is received must be suspected, even if it is only a day old ('Modo, modo,' wrote Petronius). What space does Cézanne challenge? The Impressionists'. What object do Picasso and Braque challenge? Cézanne's. What presupposition does Duchamp break with in 1912? The idea that one has to make a painting—even a cubist painting. And Buren examines another presupposition that he believes emerged intact from Duchamp's work: the place of the work's presentation" (12). A movement "can become modern only if it is first postmodern. Thus understood, postmodernism is not modernism at its end, but in a nascent state, and this state is recurrent" (13). What distinguished the early twentieth century from previous eras was the pace of cultural renewal:

"the 'generations,'" as Lyotard states, "flash[ed] by at an astonishing rate" (12–13).

This dramatic speed helped to underscore the constantly present, but barely perceived, paradox of modernity: its dynamis seeks stasis; as such, regeneration follows regeneration until the totalizing accumulation of perspectives and narratives realizes that aim. Eventually, this "Law of Totalitarianism," as defined by Igor Golomstock in *Totalitarian Art* (1990), produces cultural petrification—"however diverse the historical and cultural traditions of the countries in question, there arises a style that one can justifiably term the international style of totalitarian culture: total realism" (xiv)—and during the interwar years, European modernity eventually met this end. "Modernity," confirms Jacques Derrida in *The Other Heading* (1992), "is an imperative for totalitarianism" (42). In short, the paradox of modernity was "crucial to creating the ethos of dynamism and transformation" necessary for the creation of "totalitarian regime[s]" (24), as Roger Griffin summarizes, with the various modernisms of the period bearing some degree of responsibility for political authoritarianism and its subsequent petrification of usurped cultures.

The Third Reich exemplifies this paradox. "The Nazis," as Henry A. Turner outlines in "Fascism and Modernization" (1972), "practiced modernization inadvertently in order to pursue their fundamentally anti-modern aims" (558), and this contradictory practice elicited "a disturbing complicity," as Mark C. Taylor traces in *Disfiguring: Art, Architecture, Religion* (1992), "between modernism and fascism" (12). "This claim might initially seem implausible," as Taylor admits, "for many Fascist leaders were extraordinarily hostile to modern art," and "some of the most creative twentieth-century artists and architects were ruthlessly persecuted by Fascist governments" (12). For, as Franz Schulze explains, "right-wing *völkisch* sentiment saw the modern arts as pernicious and pathological, the expressions of a rootless *undeutsch* urbanism for which the International Jew was made the most readily fitting symbol" (187). Modernisms "expressed," as Vicki Mahaffey avers, "the euphoria of exploring human potential through experimental innovation." As such, these cultural expressions "ran headlong into the politics of xenophobia, the fear of proliferating differences in a rapidly changing and increasingly global world." Nazism, in particular, "tended to conflate any divergence from an idealized national and racial norm with 'foreignness' and 'degeneracy'"—and this conflation transformed originality into "a defect" (59).

Notwithstanding such cogent, robust, and historically validatable arguments, "the vehemence of the Nazi attack" on contemporary artistic practices, as Taylor cautions, should not overshadow the "ambivalent relation between national socialism and modern art" (132). Golomstock instances (Paul) Joseph Goebbels, Adolf Hitler's propaganda minister, whose "personal ambitions had clashed with the iron laws of the development of totalitarian culture" (79). Promoted to the newly created post of Minister for Public Enlightenment and Propaganda in 1933, as Gösta Werner reports, Goebbels "lost no time in preparing a large-scale drive to 'renew' German film production" (25). He admired Sergei Eisenstein's technique of montage in *The Battleship Potemkin* (1925), appreciated "the power with which a political idea permeated the film" (26), and thought Eisenstein had "set an example for the new, ideologically conscious and politically engaged film that he expected from all German producers, directors and manuscript writers—though of course the political overtones would have to be different!" (26). Taylor instances Hitler and Albert Speer, the most prominent of Hitler's architects (and later minister for armaments), whose tastes were principally classical, but who "shared modernism's longing for order and, perhaps more important, desire for purity" (132). Indeed, as D. K. Ching, Mark M. Jarzombek, and Vikramaditya Prakash observe, Speer's designs "espoused a kind of stripped-down modernist classicism" (750), which the Zeppelinfeld in Nuremberg and the Reich Chancellery in Berlin typified.

As the brief examples cited by Golomstock and Taylor imply, "there is a subtle and undeniable ontological and ideological relationship between certain strands in modern aesthetics and art on the one hand, and, on the other, authoritarian and totalitarian forms of sociopolitical organization" (Taylor 12). Put succinctly, dictatorial demands for order, which sanctioned the dynamic of destruction as an almost philosophical prerequisite, freely exploited what Eileen John calls the "delusory, destructive, humanity-denying tendencies" of modernisms (293). One of the first commentators to examine this accommodation was the English novelist (and later politician) C. P. Snow. In his early version of "The Two Cultures" (1956), Snow expresses his "contempt" for modernists, "who use a deep insight into man's fate to obscure the social truth—or to do something prettier than obscure the truth, just to hang on to a few perks." Having castigated Fyodor Dostoevsky for "sucking up to the Chancellor Pobedonotsev, who thought the only thing wrong with slavery was that there was not enough of it," Snow decries "the political decadence of the *avant-garde* of 1914, with Ezra Pound finishing up broadcasting for the Fascists; Claudel agreeing sanctimoniously with the Marshal about the virtue in others' suffering; [and] Faulkner giving sentimental reasons for treating Negroes as a different species" (414).[1] Two years later, in "Challenge to the Intellect" (1958), Snow argues that the modernist "desire to contract out of society" was irresponsible: "abdication of the generalizing intellect" amounted to "the alienation of the intellectual" from social responsibility (iii). That abdication, as Griffin's overarching conclusion implies, was tragic: the avant-garde was "crucial to creating the ethos of dynamism and transformation needed to establish [...] totalitarian regime[s]," but "once power [was] securely in the hands of the new ruling elite," that influence and importance "quickly wane[d]" (24). In Germany, the Nazis channeled the dynamic of modernity into the crystallization of the Third Reich, a monolith of "total realism," which they intended to maintain for one thousand years. To that comprehensive end, the regime sought to expunge alterity, and modernists, despite their invalidation under cultural petrification, bear some responsibility for this final solution.

The destructive potential of twentieth-century modernity, with its fixations on mechanization, productivity, and efficiency, found advocates in the Futurists. They seemingly championed the pathological strains of the era. "The slogan of the First Futurist Manifesto of 1909—'*War is the world's only hygiene*'—led directly, though thirty years later," argues Paul Virilio, "to the shower block of Auschwitz-Birkenau" (16). Virilio posits "this connection," as Griffin explains, "on a latent nexus that links the cold-hearted experimentalism evident in some variants of modernism—particularly those which apparently reduce the human body to an object to be manipulated for the amoral purposes of aesthetic pleasure—to the episodes of mass murder, state torture, and systematized cruelty that litter modern European history" (24). Griffin extols Virilio's argument. "Virilio turns on its heads the assumption that a truly avant-garde art form such as Futurism can have no genuine affinity with a fascist regime. Instead the wholesale aestheticization of reality allegedly advocated by modernists is seen as both symptomatic of and contributing to the failure of compassion and erosion of *pity*—'pitié' is a key concept in Virilian world-view—which makes modern states capable of wholesale crimes against humanity for the 'good of the people'" (25).

Griffin highlights the pitiless nature of that "reactionary modernist" (187) Ezra Pound, who intentionally surrenders authorial responsibility, thereby freeing himself to advocate "a virulent form of anti-Semitism focused on the Jews' alleged economic parasitism." This advocacy "could express itself [...] with a eugenic ferocity" (217). Pound's "What is Money for?" (1939) exemplifies this savagery. "USURY is the cancer of the world, which only the surgeon's knife of Fascism can cut out of the life of nations" (300), he rails. Such "perceptions are the common heritage of all men of good will, and only the Jewspapers and worse than Jewspapers, try now to obscure them" (299). That the pitiless Pound, prosecuted for treason and confined in 1946 to long-term incarceration, reappears in *The Two Cultures* (1959), Snow's Rede Lecture based on his paper from 1956, comes as little surprise. "I remember being cross-examined by a scientist of distinction," relates Snow. "'Why do most writers take on social opinions which would have been thought distinctly uncivilised and démodé at the time of the Plantagenets? Wasn't that true of most of the famous twentieth-century writers? Yeats, Pound, Wyndham Lewis, nine out of ten of those who have dominated literary sensibility in our time—weren't they not only politically silly, but politically wicked? Didn't the influence of all they represent bring Auschwitz that much nearer?'" (7).[2] For Snow, "the correct answer was not to defend the indefensible. It was no use saying that Yeats, according to friends whose judgment I trust, was a man of singular magnanimity of character, as well as a great poet. It was no use denying the facts, which are broadly true" (7–8). Snow's self-professed "honest answer" was to acknowledge the "connection, which literary persons were culpably slow to see, between some kinds of early twentieth-century art and the most imbecile expressions of anti-social feeling" (8).

Was William Faulkner, one of Snow's earlier targets, but whom he does not mention in his Rede Lecture, as indefensible as the compassionless Ezra Pound? Links between Faulkner and Pound are undoubted. "Faulkner's poetry, published and unpublished, and his early critical essays," as Carvel Collins remarks in "About the Sketches," his introduction to Faulkner's *New Orleans Sketches*, "show how much he had been interested in the work of, among others, Shelley, Keats, Verlaine, Housman, Eliot, Pound—and Swinburne" (14). As Faulkner's Parisian letter of 18 August 1925 testifies, the "very very modernist," the "futurist and vorticist" (13), captured his imagination, and that reverence embraced Pound. Indeed, a month earlier, when boarding the Genoa-bound *West Ivis* at New Orleans, Faulkner had carried letters of introduction. Pound was among the intended recipients, and although Faulkner did not approach him at the time, Pound would firmly reappear in Faulkner's sights some thirty years later. As chair of the writers' section of the People-to-People Program—President Dwight D. Eisenhower's endeavor to promote cultural exchange between the United States of America and the Union of Soviet Socialist Republics—Faulkner had accepted a role of sociopolitical responsibility. His "Distillate" (2 January 1957) of the committee meeting of 29 November 1956 ends with a specific proposal—"we should free Ezra Pound"—an appeal couched in reference to Faulkner the Nobel laureate. For, "while the Chairman of this Committee, appointed by the President, was awarded a prize for literature by the Swedish Government and was given a decoration by the French Government, the American Government locks up one of its best poets" (54).

Even Faulkner's pity for Pound was, in some people's estimation, indefensible. Saul Bellow had left the November 1956 committee meeting before the remaining attendees discussed (let alone) ratified the call for Pound's release. When Bellow read Faulkner's "Distillate," he was incensed, as his reply attests. "Pound advocated in his poems and in his broadcasts enmity to the Jews and preached hatred and murder. Do you mean to ask me to join you in honoring a man who called for the destruction of my kinsmen?" he asks incredulously. "I can take no part in such a thing" (83). The influence of Pound's modernism on the young Faulkner, and the influence of Pound's personal difficulties on the mature Faulkner, cannot be denied. For Snow, as his early version of "The Two Cultures" specifically testifies, Faulkner's sociopolitical culpabilities rank alongside those of his incarcerated coeval. For Bellow, Faulkner's chairmanship of the writers' section of the People-to-People Program failed to defuse such charges.

The growing recognition in Faulkner's works of the *assumed* permanence of authoritarian order and the maturing author's artistic acceptance of the complicities of modernisms in accommodating totalitarianism help to mitigate these failures of responsibility. The importance of structural order and control certainly arises early in Faulkner's canon. In "Wealthy Jew," the vignette that opens his *New Orleans Sketches*, and as the second chapter of the present volume relates, Faulkner's subject begins and ends his short oration by admitting his "love [of] three things: gold; marble and purple; splendor, solidarity, color" (37, 38). "These three qualities," to requote Lothar Hönnighausen, "recall the parnassian ideals of the three French forefathers of modernism, Théophile Gautier, Charles Baudelaire, and Gustave Flaubert" (565), and that recollection somewhat mitigates the racist overtone to Faulkner's Jewish caricature: Parnassian principles undercut casual prejudice. Furthermore, these protomodernist ideals dovetailed with the wholeness, harmony, and radiance of Thomism, a concurrence that James Joyce develops in *A Portrait of the Artist as a Young Man* (1916), with Stephen Dedalus's understanding of modernism acknowledging the same scholastic precepts by carefully subsuming them. This approach, while apparently escaping the authoritarian shadow of scholasticism, manages to retain radiance as a numinous bulwark against the modernist erosion of compassion, and a decade later, in an admittedly small way, Faulkner commits to this strategy in *Mosquitoes* (1927): Julius Kaufmann utters the same phrase as the "Wealthy Jew" does in *New Orleans Sketches*—"(The semitic man nursed the bottle against his breast. 'I love three things: gold, marble and purple—')" (533)—but Faulkner encases, and thereby subsumes, this utterance in ellipses.

The orderly and structural constraints of which Eileen John accuses modernisms find their highest expression in Faulkner's oeuvre in *As I Lay Dying* (1930), which "Faulkner actually facets," as Panthea Reid Broughton observes, "like a cubist painting" (93). On the one hand, these facets reveal what John T. Matthews in *William Faulkner: Seeing through the South* (2009) calls "Faulkner's fascination—even if it's sometimes skeptical—with the way modern technology might create new structures of human feeling, new relations to one's own body and place, and new possibilities for human imagination" (62). On the other hand, this occasional skepticism, as if recognizing the self-interested, irresponsible, and inhumane sides to these sculptural possibilities, comes to the fore in his next novel, *Sanctuary* (1931), which acknowledges how an obsession with structure can distract from, and even overwhelm, moral concerns. The novel traces the Apollonian purity of Temple Drake as this exemplar of classical integrity falls prey to the Dionysian monstrosities of Popeye Vitelli. The simple composure or contours of the "too pure" (241) seventeen-year-old virgin disintegrate into "precarious dissolute angle[s]" (217) under the gangster's violation, with Vitelli, a person "all angles, like a modernist lampstand" (183), inflicting Temple's dissolution in a practically formless, or "broken-backed" (207), barn.

Almost twenty years later, in "Knight's Gambit" (1949), Faulkner would return to the dangers of structure, questioning them in a subtler and less violent manner than in *Sanctuary*. During the contretemps between Melisandre Harriss's daughter and Miss Cayley in Gavin Stevens's office, the chessboard on which the lawyer's game with his nephew Chick Mallison sits is overturned. When Mallison returns to the room, having ensured the departure of the two women, he finds "his uncle now sat among the scattered chessmen" (199). The dispersal of the pieces discloses the breaking of restrictive stipulations, and the effect of this poststructuralist revelation is especially pronounced on Stevens because his professional life concerns the implementation of rules, laws, and judgments. In metafictional terms, the structural approach to literature and the Saussurean approach to language tend to habituate and thereby anaesthetize the powers of perception, and the knocking over of Stevens's chessboard in "Knight's Gambit" becomes a crucial episode in Faulkner's aesthetic maturation, an event that signals the upsetting for good of structural constraints, restrictions that the author's modernisms had sometimes rigidly imposed.[3]

That upheaval highlights withal the interstitial space between structural delimitations. Interpreted temporally, this space marks the fleeting but repetitive gap between modernisms, an uncanny no place or disfiguring medium that facilitated the rapid succession of artistic strategies of which Lyotard writes. "On the most obvious level, *to disfigure*," as Taylor explains, "means 'to mar the figure or appearance of, destroy the beauty of; to deform or deface.'" On a less obvious level, "to disfigure also means 'to disguise' or 'to carve.'" *Disfigurement*, therefore, "designates a defacement, deformity, blemish, or flaw" (6). Thus, somewhat paradoxically, a prolonged period of stasis across an unoccupied space—namely, the impasse across no-man's-land during World War I—provided a major sociopolitical manifestation of this disfiguring space. Donald Mahon in Faulkner's *Soldiers' Pay* (1926) embodies both the immediate and the ultimate results of inhabiting this uncanny no place: Mahon's "young face with a dreadful scar across his brow" (17) manifests the immediate consequence; Joe Gilligan's confession to Margaret Powers about that countenance—"if ever I seen death in a man's face, its in his" (28)—correctly predicts the ultimate consequence.

Who owned (up to) the responsibility of disfigurement effected within this interstrategic medium? This question began to haunt Faulkner, and his modernist project, to appropriate Peter Eisenman, "was well into a confrontation with the contingency of its vision and consequent futility of its optimism when, in 1945, it received its final blow[s]," with "the scientifically orchestrated horror of Hiroshima and the consciousness of the human brutality of the Holocaust" (212). Faulkner, the responsible modernist, not at all at ease with this new dispensation, felt a responsibility for countermanding the totalitarian usurpation and petrification of culture. In addressing this task, he resurrected the uncanny no place of no-man's-land, the space he had made significant in *Soldiers' Pay* through its narrative absence, in *A Fable* (1954). Of significance in this regard are the corporeal spaces of Corporal Stefan Demont. From a religious perspective, "the 'fable' of the title is Christ's passion," as John Sykes notes. "The Christ figure is a corporal who manages to bring World War I to a halt for a period of days until he is executed by those in authority" (49). The identification of Demont with Christ informs David L. Minter's compounded complaints "that *A Fable's* basic affinity as well as much of its obtrusive framework l[ies] with the New Testament," and that that association signals an authorial "move toward a fiction of ideas" (228), but beyond this identification, and thus beyond Minter's grievances, is Faulkner's responsibility to the necessary repetition promised by the relentless prospect of Christianity.

"In the middle of that war," as he explained to Robert K. Haas (15 January 1944) of his basic premise for the novel, "Christ (some movement in mankind which wished to stop war forever) reappeared and was crucified again" (180), and "it may be for this reason," as Barbara Ladd suggests, "that [the corporal] is so fluid a figure" (126). The Generalissimo, as "the Commander-in-Chief of all the Allied Armies in France" (970), has called together representatives of these forces to court martial Demont. Unaware that Demont is the Generalissimo's son, but seemingly haunted by Demont's avatars, these three aides are nonplussed by "his" presence before them. The corporal "seems to have lived and died in several different places and in different bodies" (Ladd 126). Demont was or is also "Boggan" (921); Boggan was or is also "Brzonyi" (923, 925); and Brzonyi was or is also "Brzewski" (923). As Derrida writes in "Force of Law" from *Acts of Religion* of Walter Benjamin's *Zur Kritik der Grewalt* (1921), so of Faulkner's *A Fable*: "*this text is haunted by the themes of exterminating violence,*" because "*it is haunted by haunting itself, by a quasi-logic of the ghost which, because it is the more forceful one, should be substituted for an ontological logic of presence, absence or representation*" (259; emphasis original). For Minter, *A Fable* evinces a "greater moral directness" (228) than Faulkner's previous writings do, and this thrust is both obvious and discreditable, but read otherwise, this ethical sincerity is at once obvious, obscure, and creditable, with the novel manifesting a responsible act of religion.

Taylor's analysis of the term "disfigure" furthers this contention. The prefix *dis* connotes "negation, lack, invalidation, or deprivation." The suffix *figure* connotes "form, shape; an embodied (human) form; a person considered with regard to visible form or appearance; the image, likeness, or representation of something material or immaterial." Employing this etymology suggests that Demont disfigures Boggan as Boggan disfigures Brzonyi as Brzonyi disfigures Brzewski. Indeed, "disfiguring can figure a disguise," as Taylor observes, "whose efficacy is measured by the failure to decipher or comprehend it" (6), and such an inability disorients the officers before whom Demont stands. "'That puts us all in a fix, doesn't it?' the American captain said. 'All three of us; I dont know who's worst off. Because I didn't just see him dead: I buried him, in the middle of the Atlantic Ocean. His name is—was—no, it cant be because I'm looking at him—wasn't Brzonyi. At least it wasn't last year. It was—damn it—I'm sorry sir—is Brzewski'" (922–23). Only the Generalissimo and Demont, whose relationship recalls the betrayal of ethics by the biblical Abraham that both Søren Kierkegaard and Jacques Derrida find so disturbing, remain impassive.

To the uninitiated, the incarnations of the corporal disfigure, distort, deface, and deform their complements in at once representing and misrepresenting one another. The Freudian term for this effect is *Verneinung*. For Taylor, the synonym *denegation* best "captures the irresolvable duplicity of *Verneinung*, in which affirmation and negation are conjoined without being united or synthesized." *Verneinung* means "at once an affirmation that is a negation and a negation that is an affirmation." Put otherwise, "to de-negate is to un-negate," where "un-negation is itself a form of negation." Disfiguring "enacts denegation in the realm of figure, image, form, and representation. As such, disfiguring is a formation that is a deformation and a deformation that is a formation." The process of disfiguring interweaves revelation and concealment "in such a way that every representation is both a re-presentation and a de-presentation" (7). Georges Didi-Huberman classifies this process as a torn function (*fonction déchirée* [178]) that leaves vestiges of both presence and absence. In this sense, the torn or disfiguring function of Demont, a figure whom an entire French regiment followed in refusing to prosecute an attack across no-man's-land, a soldier who has then stood before an Allied court martial for inciting mutiny, and whose sentence is death, but whose imminent return thereafter is seemingly promised, critiques the destructive and widespread intention toward alterity. Demont's incarnations trace a lingering denial of that intention. For, despite the most concerted efforts of the perpetrators of destruction, the haunting vestiges, remainders, and traces of effacement, as the avatars (or revenants) before the court marshal attest, defy eradication.

But should the responsible author delineate even these remains? "To write poetry after Auschwitz," insists Theodor W. Adorno in "Cultural Criticism and Society" (1967), "is barbaric" (34). Culture must find a particularly fitting response. To Adorno, as he states in *Negative Dialectics* (1973), the postwar Samuel Beckett alone has met this challenge. "Beckett has given us the only fitting reaction to the situation of the concentration camps—a situation he never calls by name, as if it were subject to an image ban. What is, he says, is like a concentration camp" (380). Beckett's "narratives, which he sardonically calls novels," expounds Adorno in *Aesthetic Theory* (1970), "no more offer objective descriptions of social reality than—as the widespread misunderstanding supposes—they present the reduction of life to basic human relationships, that minimum of existence that subsists *in extremis.*" Instead, they "touch on fundamental layers of experience *hic et nunc,* which are brought together into a paradoxical dynamic at a standstill" (42). This coalescence recalls that flickering space between cultural expressions, the empowering vacuum of modernity— and that seemingly broken yet seemingly functional recollection meets the representational demands of the Holocaust.

Faulkner's confrontation with the contingency of his own artistic vision prepared the ground for similarly meeting these requirements. Most obviously, as a forewarning, *Light in August* (1932) had already proffered the disfiguring figure of Percy Grimm, who completes his murder of Joe Christmas with his victim's castration. "I didn't realise until after Hitler got into the newspapers," Faulkner wrote to Malcolm Cowley on 20 September 1945, "that I had created a Nazi before he did" (202). The author of the "Wealthy Jew," who had somewhat diluted the racist nature of this caricature with that character's deference to Parnassian ideals, and whose mastery of conditional secrets in "Barn Burning" (1939) resists the undemocratic power of conditional secrecy, was assuredly maturing into a responsible author. The Faulkner of the 1940s was at once critical of his own art and resistant to artistic self-satisfaction. Even if Faulkner, the man, often failed to live up to his responsibilities, his oeuvre evolved, and ethical considerations played an important role in that evolution. "I am a veteran member of a living literature," to repeat his comments to Albert Erskine (May 1959). "In my synonymity, 'living' equals 'motion, change, constant alteration,' equals 'evolution,' which in my optimistic synonymity equals 'improvement'" (429). For Adorno, as he argues in "Cultural Criticism and Society," the literary mind is unequal to the challenge of the Holocaust "as long as it confines itself to self-satisfied contemplation" (34), and *A Fable*, which answers that challenge through responsible distancing, evinces the mature Faulkner's artistic creed. "To write on universal threats and fears, such is the responsibility of the artist" (421), as François Pitavy recognizes in "The Two Orders in *A Fable*," and Faulkner assumed that responsibility in this work, which thus becomes of seminal importance to his canon.

In his "Chronology of William Faulkner's Life and Works" (1995), Philip M. Weinstein states that *A Fable* is Faulkner's "most premeditated novel" (xix), and Catherine Gunther Kodat rightly emphasizes Weinstein's deployment of "that single word, 'premeditated'—implying, as it does, that the book represents the scene of some monstrous crime, and that the perpetrator knew exactly what he was doing" (83). Faulkner's psychical expenditure on this horrific scenario was protracted. "He wrote it," as Richard Godden traces in *William Faulkner: An Economy of Complex Words* (2009), "over the ten years between 1943 and 1954" (156). Relatively early in this period of mental expenditure, on 19 March 1945, Faulkner noted in a letter to Harold Ober that this project "may be my epic poem" (191),and the following year, he informed Malcolm Cowley (23 April 1946) that he was "working on what seems now to me to be my magnum o" (233). Soon thereafter, in two letters to Robert K. Haas (5 May 1946; 3 June 1946), Faulkner foretold of the realization of his hopes. "I think it is all right," he averred in May. "It may be my best. It's not a novel at all. I think it's more than just a fable" (234). In June, he added, "I believe I see a rosy future for this book, I mean it may sell, it will be a War and Peace close enough to home, our times, language, for Americans to really buy it" (238).

Faulkner's high expectations, allied to his determined commitment, mean that the Foucauldian "author function" (41), as expounded by Robert Eaglestone in *The Broken Voice. Reading Post-Holocaust Literature* (2017), relates to *A Fable* as it does to no other Faulkner novel. In texts informed by the Holocaust, "the role of the historical author," as Eaglestone argues, is impossible to ignore. In these cases, "it is legitimate to ask about their identity, about their relationship to the events or material and about their responsibilities, in a way that is not perhaps, so normal or legitimate in relation to other forms of writing" (102). This legitimacy allows one to inquire about Faulkner's major source of Holocaust testimony and how he mediated that narrative of witness. The barely hidden significance of *A Fable* rests in no small measure, then, on Faulkner's relationship with his stepson Malcolm Franklin.

On 5 December 1942, "with eloquent bravado, Faulkner implored his stepson to enlist," as Louis Daniel Brodsky chronicles in "Faulkner's Wounded Art" (1987), "asserting his own desire to participate directly, actively, physically in the war. More significantly, Faulkner actually spelled out his fundamental reason for insisting Malcolm not allow himself any outs; going to fight was a matter of manhood" (57). The war "is the biggest thing that will happen in your lifetime," he informed his stepson. "All your contemporaries will be in it before it is over, and if you are not one of them, you will always regret it." Faulkner made enlistment a matter of duty to the conscientious Malcolm. "It's a strange thing how a man, no matter how intelligent, will cling to the public proof of his masculinity: his courage and endurance, his willingness to sacrifice himself for the land which shaped his ancestors" (166). His stepfather's influence was decisive; Franklin joined the US Army Medical Corps, and shortly after the Third Army under Major-General George S. Patton helped to liberate Buchenwald concentration camp on 11 April 1945, that corps set to work aiding the survivors and advising on postmortem hygiene. Franklin found himself, as Victoria Fielden Johnson (Franklin's niece and Faulkner's stepgranddaughter) recalls to Brodsky in *William Faulkner: Life Glimpses* (1990), "right behind Patton, as they opened up the death camps, and the horrors that he saw really screwed up his mind" (153). Johnson recalls her mother Melvina Victoria Fielden (née Franklin) "holding him while he sobbed over the horrors he had seen firsthand. He cried all the time; he had horrible nightmares" (154). That sobbing told of Franklin's own disfigurement.

Faulkner appreciated his stepson's horrific grief, with *A Fable* effectively registering, interpreting, and transfiguring Franklin's *smothered words*. Sarah Kofman, a second-generation Holocaust survivor whose father died in Auschwitz, employs this term, which derives from the English translation of the title of her *Paroles suffoquées* (1987), in a poststructuralist manner, so that smothered words, as Eaglestone expounds, "describe the aporia which lies between the inability of Holocaust survivors to put into words the evil they survived—its traumatic breakage of the very possibility of narrative—and their duty and often compulsion to do so, which would reform the events into a comprehensible narrative. The accounts are 'smothered words' which both 'say' and 'unsay' the events" (*Broken* 135). Technically speaking, Franklin had not survived the

Holocaust, but he had witnessed its outcome firsthand, and sobbing smothered his narrative of witness. The resultant utterances coalesced around aporias and absences. In "Knight's Gambit," Gavin Stevens talks of the "rendering [of] a whole race into fertilizer and lubricating oil" (255), a rendering of all Jewish children, women, and men to almost nothing. This (un)thinkable vacancy manifests what Gil Anidjar calls "Derrida's insistent preoccupation with the Holocaust and with the 'final solution'" (228), and in "Force of Law," Derrida indicates the result of this preoccupation, writing how "it was normal, foreseeable, and desirable that studies of deconstructive style should culminate in the problematic of right, of law [*loi*] and justice" (235). Put succinctly, "*deconstruction is justice*" (243; emphasis original), which "while seeming not to 'address' the problem of justice, has done nothing else while unable to do so directly but only in an oblique fashion. I say *oblique*, since at this very moment I am preparing to demonstrate that one cannot speak *directly* about justice, thematize or objectivize justice, say 'this is just,' and even less 'I am just,' without immediately betraying justice, if not law" (237; emphasis original). Inextricable ties bind the postmodern to the poststructural: the aporias and absences around which the smothered words of the Holocaust coalesce demand justice.

For Lyotard, "the modern aesthetic is an aesthetic of the sublime. But it is nostalgic; it allows the unpresentable to be invoked only as absent content, while form, thanks to its recognizable consistency, continues to offer the reader or spectator material for consolation and pleasure" ("Answer to the Question" 14). In terms of absent content, *A Fable* cannot and does not speak of the Holocaust directly; rather, the novel testifies to this event through responsible distancing. This strategy, as a torn function that necessarily disfigures fresh horrors, pays respect at once through the future anterior and via the lacunary. In terms of form, however, *A Fable* both accepts and denies Lyotard's contention. On the one hand, Faulkner drew comfort from, and on, his enclosed writing space at Rowan Oak. "He was so obsessed with *A Fable*'s structure," relates Theresa M. Towner, "that he outlined it on his study walls" (24). On the other hand, Faulkner's confrontation with the costs attributable to modernity appealed to the Holocaust, as absent content, to bear formal witness in his novel, with *A Fable* assuming an inconsistent, torn, doubly shattered, and hence disfigured structure: the "Notes on a Horse Thief" (1951) section of the novel, an analeptic episode set in the southern states of America, breaking with the overarching *mise en scène*, which is France during and after the final year of World War I. Faulkner's self-avowed magnum opus was a psychologically and an artistically taxing project, and while Faulkner required formal consolation and pleasure to complete that enterprise, the resultant form of that work denied those authorial desires.

That denial was an absolute necessity. The formalist techniques of modernisms, as carefully and consistently applied in so many of Faulkner's previous works, had to be toned (or even torn) down in favor of an *avant-la-lettre* approach (that anticipated poststructuralism). The disconsolate and unpleasurable disfiguring that molds the form of *A Fable* could then invoke the unpresentable as absent content: World War I could figure World War II in anticipative retrospect. The outcome is so successful that Hannah Arendt—whose meditations on misused power in *The Origins of Totalitarianism* (1951) are frequently and rightly lauded—praises Faulkner's novel in confining it to an examination of the past. "After the First World War," she writes in *Men in Dark Times* (1968),

> we experienced the 'mastering of the past' in a spate of descriptions of the war that varied enormously in kind and quality; naturally, this happened not only in Germany, but in all the affected countries. Nevertheless, nearly thirty years were to pass before a work of art appeared which so transparently displayed the inner truth of the event that it became possible to say: Yes, this is how it was. And in this novel, William Faulkner's *A Fable*, very little is described, still less explained, and nothing at all 'mastered'; its end is tears, which the reader also weeps, and what remains beyond that is the 'tragic effect' or the 'tragic pleasure,' the shattering emotion which makes one able to accept the fact that something like this war could have happened at all. (20)

Faulkner's invocation of the unpresentable as absent content helps to question, as Derrida does in *The Gift of Death* in following Jan Patočka's lead, "what is it that ails 'modern civilization' inasmuch as it is European?" (3–4). Facilitated and confronted not only by the ambiguous gift of hindsight in writing of the horrors of World War I but also by the limited gift of the present in adumbrating the terrors of World War II, Faulkner (in effect) poses the subsequent Derridean query as to why Europe "suffer[s] from ignorance of its history, from a failure to assume its responsibility, that is, the memory of its history *as* history of responsibility?" Crucially, as Derrida emphasizes, "it is not in fact a sin of ignorance or lack of knowledge" that is to blame; rather, "their historical knowledge occludes, confines, or saturates those questions, grounds, or abysses," which ought to be asked, "naively presuming to totalize or naturalize them" (4; emphasis original).

In shedding light on these occlusions, *A Fable* delineates how the stratification of identification with the enemy during World War I is responsible at once for challenging and maintaining the war. Privates across the divide of no-man's-land mutually cooperate on two separate occasions. Demont incites the first mutiny. In this instance, a French regiment remains passive, refusing to prosecute an attack. The regiment's German counterpart behaves similarly. The battalion runner, as the Demont's disciple, incites the second mutiny. While Demont instigated passivity, the battalion runner encourages his followers to emerge actively but peaceably into no-man's-land. Their German counterparts again behave similarly. These frontline mutinies, which manifest live-and-let-live stages in warfare evolution, rely on the lowest military class, and these nonaggressive actions initially baffle their respective high commands. "Social conflict," states John Bowlby in "A Psycho-Analytic Approach to Conflict and its Regulation," "is universal in the sense that wherever there are social organizations with an authority structure there are causes for conflict" (168), and there are two axes in the strategic dynamic portrayed in *A Fable*, with each army exhibiting a hierarchy of non-cooperation, which is stratified by planes of cooperation across no-man's-land. Hence, while the lowest military classes on both sides manage to prosecute two interruptions to the fighting, the high commands reciprocate in managing to restart hostilities on each occasion.

Significantly, scientific and technological developments between the two world wars instigated an exceptional alteration to combatant relations, to responsibility toward the other, and to transcendent alterity. On the battlefield, the architectonic status of the fronts (east, south, and west) as practically impassable barriers during World War I presaged a military determination to forestall the establishment of such unbreachable lines in future conflicts. Together, these advances in alienation ensured a loss of identification with the enemy in World War II, and this dehumanization of the conflict helped to facilitate the atrocities of SS-Einsatzgruppen, execution squads for whom an impasse at close quarters—a situation that might engender some respect for alterity—was intolerable.[4] Both the temporal and the spatial registers of *A Fable* acknowledge this loss of confrontational identification. "The old Roman citadel" (983), which by 1918 houses the headquarters of the Generalissimo, dominates the city of

Chaulnesmont. The significance of the fortress "is connected with, and enforced by, the allusions to Caesar and to Roman history found throughout the novel," as Keen Butterworth notes, and that connection compounds historical sense with spatial stolidity. "Evidently," remarks Butterworth, "Faulkner intends for the Roman citadel to remind us of that tradition of war, conquest and rapacity that is so constant a part of our Western history" (60). The future anterior casts not only Ancient wars as anticipatory of World War I but also World War I as anticipatory of World War II, with this proleptic potential positing Hitler and his totalitarian coevals as the latest versions of that "blackguard" (669) from "inglorious history" (693), whose figurations include "Hannibal" (673), "Caesar" (673), and "Napoleon" (669).

Faulkner's "Address to the Graduating Class, University High School, Oxford, Mississippi" (28 May 1951)—which names Caesar and Napoleon alongside the twentieth-century dictators connoted by, but purposefully excised from, *A Fable*—confirms this pervasion of the novel by the future anterior:

> Never be afraid to raise your voice for honesty and truth and compassion, against injustice and lying and greed. If you, not just you in this room tonight, but in all the thousands of other rooms like this one about the world today and tomorrow and next week, will do this, not as a class or classes, but as individuals, men and women, you will change the earth. In one generation all the Napoleons and Hitlers and Caesars and Mussolinis and Stalins and all the other tyrants who want power and aggrandisement, and the simple politicians and time-servers who themselves are merely baffled or ignorant or afraid, who have used, or are using, or hope to use, man's fear and greed for man's enslavement, will have vanished from the face of it. (123–24)

In *A Fable*, Faulkner not only responded to World War I but "also wrote in response to a different political moment," as Ladd confirms: "mid-twentieth century totalitarianism" (117). Faulkner's temporal strategy implements a form of historicization, one of redirection via the future anterior, which effectively recognizes the Third Reich as an exceptionally undesirable but extremely complex mutation in social evolution that "normal" historical studies cannot accommodate.

One avatar of the future anterior appears during Division Commander General Gragnon's interview with the Generalissimo. Having requested the execution of his entire regiment for mutiny, Gragnon leaves the Commander-in-Chief's office flanked by the Generalissimo's personal aide, "the very tall elegantly thin captain of twenty-eight or thirty with the face and body of a durable matinee idol, who might have been a creature from another planet, anachronistic and immune, inviolable, so invincibly homeless as to be completely and impregnably at home on this or any other planet where he might find himself." This anachronism is "not even of tomorrow but of the day before it, projected by reverse avatar back into a world where what remained of lost and finished man struggled feebly for a moment yet among the jumbled ruins of his yesterdays" (883).

The Quartermaster General, in untangling the early army career of his erstwhile fellow trainee, the Generalissimo, repeatedly invokes a sense of reversal. The Generalissimo was "not only the nephew of a Cabinet Minister, but the godson of the board chairman of that gigantic international federation producing munitions" (893). Desirous of being a self-made man, however, he never drew on these connections. Indeed, when he took up a position at Oran, "a station as famous in its circles as the Black Hole of Calcutta," it appeared to the Quartermaster General "that earth itself had faltered, rapacity itself had failed, when regardless of whatever had been the nephew's old defalcation from his family's hope or dream seven or eight or ten years ago, even that uncle and that godfather had been incapable of saving him." This picture of failure was incorrect, however, and the Quartermaster General corrected his mistake, "pick[ing] up the whole picture and revers[ing] it" (900). The heterodiegetic narrator then compounds this sense of reversal—heaping metaphor on metaphor; "hierarchate and superposed" (900)—remarking how the Generalissimo took his own history, and the people within that chronicle, "like so many paper dolls and turned them around and set them down again in the same positions and attitudes but obversed" (901).[5]

In a broader sense, and as Faulkner surely intends, the registers of temporal and spatial reversal in *A Fable* disorient the reader. Disorientation brings the Generalissimo, with the eastern provenance of his wilderness years, and the effects of the disastrous war he now wages on the Western front, with its "wreckage of the disaster" (1071), together. "In his youth," explains Pitavy in "The Two Orders," "the future general had chosen as his first appointment an unlikely forgotten post in the African desert, and then had retired to a Tibetan lamasery for thirteen years." The Generalissimo's time in Tibet is "a complete blank in his life" (408) so that for Pitavy, "there seems to be some contradiction in the general's character, when the ascetic young man becomes the cynical generalissimo" (409 n.38). In truth, however, no contradiction pertains. The Generalissimo wrestled with notions of altruism and asceticism during his monastic retreat, but came away unaltered. Those years of internal debate simply served no future account.

Disorientation also brings the "east" and the "disaster" together etymologically. Eaglestone's work on *The Broken Voice* helps to situate this meeting within the colonial past and the future anterior of the Holocaust. The fourth chapter of his monograph, "Disorientalism," "takes its title from the etymological coincidence of 'the orient' and what Blanchot calls 'the disaster.'" These appropriations place "together, as a handful of critics are beginning to do, the Holocaust and the colonial and postcolonial past" (7). This imbrication emphasizes the trope of inversion as a complement to that of reversal. "The worlds of the Holocaust and the worlds of colonial and postcolonial genocides are the worlds of the disaster." In these dystopias "everything is inverted: doctors torture and do not heal; midwives bring children into the world to let them die or kill them; progress is death" (95). Yehuda Bauer describes the Holocaust as "a mysterious event, an upside-down miracle, so to speak, an event of religious significance in the sense that it is not man-made as that term is normally understood" (31). These inversions informed Walter Benjamin's posthumously published "Theses on the Philosophy of History" (1942). For Benjamin, one cannot responsibly contemplate the cultural products of civilization without feelings of horror. These dubious treasures "owe their existence not only to the efforts of the great minds and talents who have created them, but also to the anonymous toil of their contemporaries." In consequence, "there is no document of civilization which is not at the same time a document of barbarism" (248).

One finds Faulkner's most concise censure of civilized barbarity in "Ad Astra" (1931). The German prisoner relates to his Allied captors the episode of his youthful homecoming after his years as a university student: "I return home; I say to my father, in the University I haf learned it iss not good; baron I will not be. He cannot believe. He talks of Germany, the fatherland; I say to him, It iss there; so. You say fatherland; I, brotherland, I say, the word *father* iss that barbarism which will be first swept away; it iss the symbol of that hierarchy which hass stained the history of man with injustice of arbitrary instead of moral; force instead of love" (417; emphasis original). Faulkner re-presents an unalloyed and unrelenting sense of civilized barbarity in *A Fable*. Group Commander General Lallemont, in conversation with General Gragnon, admits how the Allied high command "can permit even our own rank and file to let us down on occasion; that's one of the prerequisites of their doom and fate as rank and file forever." The same is true of the Central Powers. The other ranks "may even stop the wars, as they have done before and will again; ours merely to guard them from the knowledge that it was actually they who accomplished that act" (715). The unmolested sanctity of a single word ensures that guardianship. "The simple effacement from man's memory of a single word will be enough. But we are safe. Do you know what that word is?" he asks (715–16). Gragnon looks to his colleague for enlightenment: "Fatherland" (716) is Lallemont's answer.

No-man's-land effectively erases fatherland. Any unsanctioned coming together in this non-space threatens the high commands. The battalion runner's mutiny breaches their hallowed topographical demarcations. The respective artillery barrages that counter this combined mutiny manifest the civilized barbarity of the conflict. This measure reveals not the obvious separation between "us" and "them," but the subtler difference between "we" and "us." The pronoun counters its objective form. Aggression reacts against peacefulness within a structure supposedly unified for war. "We did it," the Quartermaster General declares almost incredulously to the Generalissimo when they next confer.

> We. Not British and American and French we against German them nor German they against American and British and French us, but We against all because we no longer belong to us. A subterfuge not of ours to confuse and mislead the enemy nor of the enemy to mislead and confuse us, but of We to betray all since all has had to repudiate us in simple defensive horror; no barrage by us or vice versa to prevent an enemy running over us with bayonets and hand grenades or vice versa, but a barrage by both of We to prevent naked and weaponless hand touching opposite naked and weaponless hand. We, you and I and our whole unregenerate and unregenerable kind; not only you and I and our tight close jealous unchallengeable hierarchy behind this wire and our opposite German one behind that one, but more, worse: our whole small repudiated and homeless species about the earth who not only no longer belong to man but even to earth itself since we have had to make this last base desperate cast in order to hold our last desperate and precarious place on it (969).

This subterfuge is "the real horror of the story" for Ladd: *A Fable* "deals with a betrayal of momentous proportions, and the mutineers are not the betrayers" (117).

In the future anterior of World War II, the most momentous of human betrayals occurs at the death camps, with the name of Auschwitz summoning up that egregiousness. In *The Gift of Death*, Derrida proffers the phrase "burnt offering" as a suitable definition of the term "Holocaust." Moreover, as Hebraic sacrifice, or burnt offering, the Holocaust invokes the Old Testament story to which *A Fable* repeatedly alludes, the case that so exercises Kierkegaard, Derrida, and Faulkner: Abraham's unreasonable authority over Isaac. "God will provide," as Derrida's interpretation of Genesis 22.8 reads, "a lamb for the holocaust" (59). In this sense, then, *A Fable* is Holocaust literature. "The reading, interpretation, and tradition of the sacrifice of Isaac," avers Derrida, "are themselves sites of bloody, holocaustic sacrifice" (70). That Gerald David Levine, one of the responsible suicides in *A Fable*, is Jewish carries, therefore, unquestionable import.

Butterworth, in reporting a story from Shelby Foote, confirms the authorial intention behind this significance. Jill Faulkner, William's daughter, married Paul D. Summers, Jr., on 21 August 1954. "At the reception," writes Butterworth, "Foote told Faulkner that he had read his new book *A Fable*." Faulkner asked for Foote's opinion. "Foote said that he did not like it so much: he could tell Faulkner that because Faulkner knew how much Foote admired his other work." To Foote, "the characters did not seem to be impelled to act as they did by fate or some personal destiny as the characters in the other novels had been." In particular, "there seemed to be no real reason for the young pilot to commit suicide." Faulkner, by way of prompting Foote, asked for that character's name. "Foote said, David. Faulkner said, No, he meant his last name. Foote thought for a moment, then said that he could not remember, but that the pilot was a Jew." His interlocutor's response was emphatic: "Yes, Faulkner said, That's it!" (43).

Foote later admitted that "although he was sure Faulkner had some intricate connection between Levine's religion and his suicide in mind, he did not get the point," and Butterworth echoes Foote: "I am not sure that I do either" (43). Derrida's preoccupation with the Holocaust helps to answer this difficulty. In addition to his meditation on the burnt offering in *The Gift of Death*, Derrida considers the postwar Jewish condition in "Hospitality" (1997), stating:

A Jew, a Jew of any time but, above all, in this century, is also someone who undergoes the test and the ordeal of the impossibility of forgiveness, of its radical impossibility. Besides, who would give this right to forgive? Who would give—and to whom—the right to forgive for the dead, and to forgive the infinite violence done to them, depriving them of burial and of name, everywhere in the world and not only in Auschwitz? And thus everywhere the unforgivable would have occurred? Besides, regarding everything for which Auschwitz remains both the proper name and the metonymy, we would have to speak of this painful but essential experience which consists in reproaching oneself as well, in front of the dead, as it were, with having survived, with being a survivor. (382)

In the future anterior of *A Fable*, Levine effectively reproaches himself for avoiding the fate of his fellow Jews under Nazism. "How does one give *oneself* death [*se donner la mort*]?" asks Derrida in *The Gift of Death*. "How does one give it to oneself in the sense that putting oneself to death means dying while assuming responsibility for one's own death, committing suicide but also sacrificing oneself for another, *dying for the other*, thus perhaps giving one's life by giving oneself death, accepting the gift of death, such as Socrates, Christ, and others did in so many different ways" (10; emphasis original). Levine assumes this ultimate responsibility. His suicide is an expression of Jewish solidarity.

"The modernist project failed miserably and tragically," concludes Taylor. "The apocalypse became a Holocaust that left Western culture in ruins. Within a few short years, the dream of modernity became a nightmare from which we are still struggling to awaken" (12). Lyotard's conclusion in "Apostil on Narratives" (1984) concerning the "project of modernity" is, however, subtly different to Taylor's assertion of modernist failure. In coincidently using a term that recalls Gavin Stevens's use of the word "rendering" in "Knight's Gambit," Lyotard argues that "the realization of universality" at which the project of modernity aimed "has not been forsaken or forgotten but destroyed, 'liquidated.'" Of the "several modes of destruction, several names that are symbols for them," Lyotard chooses one: "'Auschwitz' can be taken as a paradigmatic name for the tragic 'incompletion' of modernity" (18). The responsibility for a concept unknown and unnamed until 1944, "genocide," can be laid with those responsible for the death camps. "At 'Auschwitz,' a modern sovereign, a whole people was physically destroyed. The attempt was made to destroy it." The Holocaust was "a crime of *lèse-souveraineté* [violated sovereignty]—not regicide this time, but populicide (as distinct from ethnocide)" (19).

According to Faulkner's figuration in *A Fable* in which World War I stands for World War II in anticipative retrospect, the hellish conditions of the first conflict, which lie under the auspices of "Dis" (718), only intensify during the second, with the Roman God of the underworld becoming, as Pitavy observes, "Moloch himself, the cruel god of the Ammonites and the Phoenicians to whom children were offered and burned in his fiery brazen maw" (396). In this future anterior, which Pitavy does not consider, but which encapsulates both the barbarism of Nazism and the irresponsible failures and complicities of modernity, that becoming manifests a crematorium for the Jewish race. Adorno, Derrida, Lyotard, and Virilio name this crematorium Auschwitz. The analogous site for William Faulkner, as for his stepson Malcolm Franklin, was Buchenwald, and Demont's mutineers in *A Fable* are imprisoned in a compound that "had been a factory once" (786), but which hereafter resembles a concentration camp. The factory has been converted "into a man-proof pen for the mutinied regiment, by the addition of barricades of electrified wire and searchlight towers and machine-gun platforms and pits and an elevated catwalk for guards." Now, for the only time in the novel, and in a figural reversal that accompanies the sense of temporal projection, the word "holocaust" appears. Recalling the dead bodies Franklin witnessed at Buchenwald, a remembrance the horror of which his smothered words must have conveyed to his stepfather, the relatives and friends of the mutineers line the electrified barrier that separates them from the compound, "like victims being resurrected after a holocaust, staring through the taut, vicious, unclimbable strands beyond which the regiment had vanished" (787).

The staging, or spatial setting, "in which outside becomes inside so that French civilians may become Jewish," as Godden notes, "stresses chiasmus, or the formal figure of inversion" (*Complex Words* 165). The Senegalese prison guards—whom the racial politics of the era would normally regard as inferior to their colonial counterparts—reiterate this figuration. These African sentinels literally stand watch over their European prisoners. The guards, "lounging haughtily overhead along the catwalks," appeared "to muse down at them, contemplative, inattentive, inscrutable, and not even interested" (787). The term "inscrutable," with its racially freighted sense of the eastern face and mind, further augments the play of disorientation, and as construction of the compound continues, this disorientation spreads, with the "Senegalese, lounging in lethargic disdain among their machine guns above both the white people engaged in labor inside the fence and the ones engaged in anguish outside it" (788).

In *The Broken Voice*, Eaglestone remarks how relating the Holocaust to disorientalism and colonial texts "has proved to be controversial and deeply politicized" (99). Such attempts often suffer under the pressure of what David Moshman calls "conceptual constraints" (431) and A. Dirk Moses terms "conceptual blockage[s]" (22). Moses turns fleetingly to game theory to explain these difficulties: "the problem with Holocaust–indigenous genocide discourse is that it is structured as a zero-sum game"; where some scholars regard Native American analogies "with the Jewish Holocaust as antisemitic and as the occlusion of its world-historical meaning," others regard "the resistance to precisely such analogies as anti-Native American and the enabling condition for the continuing rape of the world by the western spirit" (18). For Eaglestone, one of the worrying possibilities of this zero-sum game is "that the *memory* of one terrible event would drive out or reduce the 'memory-space' of another" (99) so that a responsible analysis of one atrocity unintentionally undervalues another. In terms of Faulkner studies, and the new memory-spaces opened by World War II, Eaglestone's concern would question whether the Holocaust in *A Fable* drives out the memory of the Trail of Tears (in *Requiem for a Nun* [1951]), with that earlier memorialization driving out an even earlier one, the Middle Passage in *Intruder in the Dust* (1948), and so on. The final and most reductive accumulation of this process might then be linked to the (open) question of Faulkner's ECT during the 1950s and the possible reduction of his available memory-spaces.

Conflicts of memorialization might elicit, however, a non-zero-sum game. More (not less) remembrance might result. *A Fable* offers this hope. The "Notes on a Horse Thief" section recalls the racial history of America, and with World War I figuring World War II in anticipative retrospect, the process of writing the novel could be understood as having revitalized and thereby increased Faulkner's memory-spaces. "The task is to relate each genocide to others in a way that allows them to retain their distinctive features," as Moses argues, and *A Fable* effectively affords such allowances. "What is striking about the Holocaust," writes Moses,

> is that it was a project of racial cleansing and self-assertion that sought *consciously* to achieve for Germans what the imperial endeavours of rival European powers had achieved in a largely haphazard manner before the

First World War: permanent security and well-being for the domestic population conceived as the citadel and bearer of a superior European culture.
The dispersion of agency and consciousness in the period of 'classical' colonialism is gathered up and located centrally in a totalitarian state, notwithstanding recent research about the importance of peripheral initiatives in the
first phase of killing in 1941. Here was the most radical genocidal moment
of the racial century, the culmination of the violence directed towards inner
and outer enemies. (35; emphasis original)

In *A Fable*, the unforgotten history of regimental mutinies—in "'Ad
Astra' through New Haven" (1990), Collins writes of "*A Fable* with its
featuring of an invented [...] mutiny" (118), but Faulkner knew his early-
twentieth-century history and would have been aware of the well-
documented French Army revolts of 1917—links the past to the present.[6]
In the past, "one of the glorious blackguards who later became Napoleon's
marshals [...] delivered the regiment into the Emperor's own hand, and
along with it became one of the fiercest stars in that constellation which
filled half the sky with its portent and blasted half the earth with its lightning" (669). In the present, General Gragnon delivers Demont's regiment—they have been betrayed by Polchek, whose subsequent Judas
misery adumbrates, according to the homophonic associations of his name
and Faulkner's strategy of reversal, the misery of the betrayed Poles and
Czechs of World War II—into the Generalissimo's hands.

"Once to each period of his inglorious history," Gragnon had mused
on the evening after the Demont mutiny, "one of us appears with the stature of a giant, suddenly and without warning in the middle of a nation as
a dairymaid enters a buttery, and with his sword for paddle he heaps and
pounds and stiffens the malleable mass and even holds it cohered and purposeful for a time" (693). Gragnon almost appears to be talking of Hitler.
Pitavy thinks similarly. "Power—here a near-fascist military power—cannot even consider the individual. Though this is the view of one of those
chiefs whose very reason for being is the existence of that abject, dehu-
manized mass made the instrument of their designs, the simile points to a
military order that uses and reifies individuals subjected to a will-power
that scorns their very abjection" ("Two Orders" 395–96). Having
accepted finally that the German fight for Stalingrad was lost, Hitler promoted the general commanding the German 6th Army, Friedrich Paulus,
to field marshal. Both Hitler and Paulus knew that no German field marshal had been captured alive; Hitler expected Paulus to commit suicide;

Paulus defied him. "How can one be so cowardly? I don't understand it," fumed Hitler. "What is life? Life is the Nation. The individual must die anyway. Beyond the life of the individual is the Nation" (qtd. in William L. Shirer 933). Unlike Hitler, Gragnon does appreciate, as the continuation of his speech makes clear, that even the human demigod cannot mold the malleable mass "for always, nor even for very long: sometimes before he can even turn his back, it has relinquished, dis-cohered, faster and faster flowing and seeking back to its own base anonymity" (693). Paulus surely knew this too.

In *A Fable*, and much as Hitler wished to do at Stalingrad, the supreme commander spares the men (excepting Demont), but sacrifices their general. Having become the fiercest star in the European constellation during the 1930s, Hitler blasted half the earth with his blitzkrieg, accounting for more than sixty percent of the Jews (or Stars of David) on the war-torn continent. According to the future anteriority of Faulkner's novel, which extrapolates from the anterior description of a French sergeant—"a thick man of forty, moustached like a Sicilian brigand and wearing the service and campaign ribbons of three continents and two hemispheres on his tunic, whose racial stature Napoleon had shortened two or three inches a hundred years ago as Caesar had shortened that of the Italians and Hannibal that of the nameless pediment-pieces of his glory" (673)— Hitler severely foreshortened the presence (or stature) of the Jews. One of the first critical anticipations of the connoted site of this foreshortening in *A Fable* arises in its annotated reading by Nancy and Keen Butterworth: "Buchwald," the name of an American GI in the novel, "may be intended as an ironic anachronistic reference to Buchenwald, a village in central Germany near Weimar, which was used as a concentration and extermination camp for political and racial prisoners, especially Jews, from 1933" (220). A later critical anticipation, building on the first, comes from Godden in "*A Fable* ... Whispering about the Wars" (2002): "one of the three killers of General Gragnon is called Buchwald," and "Buchenwald," as Godden adds, "was liberated by American forces in 1945" (39).

Ian Sayer and Jeremy Dronfield detail the history of the site. "Buchenwald was one of the Reich's oldest concentration camps, founded in the early years of the Nazi regime," and soon became "a sprawling complex, a small city of ninety thousand souls in torment, carved out of the beech forest from which it took its name" (17). Faulkner would not take responsibility for Burch Grove in 1932, because the permanent union of Lucas Burch and Lena Grove in *Light in August* was unconscionable, but the unconscionable Holocaust made him confront the beech grove of Buchenwald in *A Fable*. Two cynical rallying cries greeted the incoming prisoner to the camp. "The main gate," note Sayer and Dronfield, "bore the slogan *Jedem das Seine*: literally 'to each his own,' although it could also be read as 'everyone gets what he deserves'." Internment, treatment, and possible release were supposedly the prisoner's responsibility. Above *Jedem das Seine* was another slogan, one that resonates in the Faulknerian context with the German prisoner's execration in "Ad Astra," a motto that "reflect[ed] the ethos expected of all Germans under Nazism: 'My fatherland, right or wrong'" (17). Ironically, the architect and graphic designer Franz Ehrlich, who was imprisoned at Buchenwald as a communist, designed the camp gates according to the modernist principles he had learned at the Bauhaus in Dessau. The Nazis supposedly despised the Bauhaus, but Ehrlich used a font for the slogans that was typical of that school, thereby defying (or disfiguring) those mottos through their very style.

In *A Fable*, Faulkner shadows the aporias of survivors, the aporias that "bear witness" to Buchenwald, through kindred devices of disfigurement. Hence, with a subtlety akin to Ehrlich's, the loss of an en dash ("en"), a puncturation that disfigures the word "Buchenwald," produces the name "Buchwald." This typographical loss elevates one of Faulkner's customary tactics—the absence of punctuation, a "device Faulkner uses very extensively," as Eberhard Boecker relates, "in order to reinforce the effect of fluidity and uninterrupted motion which his hypotactic sentences convey" (175)—to ethical significance. The disfiguring figure of Grimm anticipates this significance in *Light in August*, but whereas he prefigured the paramilitary Nazis, the disfiguring figure of Buchwald in *A Fable* manifests the future anterior of an Einsatzkommando (or Einsatzgruppe subunit) leader. Buchwald is tacitly tasked with the execution of the politically undesirable General Gragnon, whose divisional command was fatally compromised by the regimental mutiny under Demont. Moreover, in another instance of disorientation (or disfigurement) in the novel, Buchwald not only heads the group but also does so as a man who carries the generational weight of anti-Semitism: he is "a Russian-American Jew," as Godden notes, "whose grandfather (a rabbi) died in a pogrom in Minsk" ("Whispering" 39).

The other two Einsatzkommando members are a Mississippian named Beauchamp and an unnamed Iowan farmer. The heterodiegetic narrator does not name Beauchamp, but introduces him in both racial and sexual terms as "a Negro, of a complete and unrelieved black," and an "epicene," who appears "at once masculine and girlish" (1011). Nor does Buchwald, in announcing his own racist credentials, have any compunction in calling the Mississippian "Sambo." In response to such pejorative disfigurements, however, Beauchamp retains his pride in announcing his name, "Philip Manigault Beauchamp" (1013), and in revealing his postwar desire to be an "undertaker" (1014). Towner describes (and somewhat disfigures) the Iowan as a "military grunt/tourist clown" (36). A farmer in civilian life, "fated to love his peaceful agrarian heritage," as the heterodiegetic narrator remarks, the Iowan is devoted to rearing pigs. Yet, in another disorienting (or disfiguring) mixture of metaphors, the personal qualities of this porcine lover appear distinctly bovine. "He was quite young, with brown eyes as trustful and unalarmed as those of a cow, in an open reliant invincibly and incorrigibly bucolic face" (1010), and these bovine but humane eyes contrast sharply with the inhumane, "pale, almost colorless eyes" (1011) of Buchwald.

Gragnon is the Einsatzkommando's sheep for the slaughter, and his executioners comprise, to varying figurative and moral degrees, animals in human form. *A Fable* meets the major criterion of a classical fable, as defined by J. A. Cuddon, through this means of disfigurement: "(L *fabula*, 'discourse, story') A short narrative in prose or verse which points a moral. Non-human creatures or inanimate things are normally the characters. The presentation of human beings as animals is the characteristic of the literary fable" (322). If the mixed metaphor that introduces the Einsatzkommando—the honking horn of their military vehicle "bleated its snaillike passage" (1010)—is a disfiguring tactic appropriate to this definition of a fable, then the end of their mission—with Buchwald telling Beauchamp to "keep on yelling until you find a Frog" (1019)—is similarly apposite. In fine, the Einsatzkommando scene is bookended by the animalistic or the fabulous.

Mystery cloaks the group's task—only Buchwald has guessed their mission—and this mantle is in keeping with what Eaglestone calls the engagement of post-Holocaust literature "with secrecy and complicity" (*Broken* 98).[7] The Nazi perpetration of mass murder exploited the enigmatic nature of secrecy. "There is a secret of denial and a denial of the secret," explains Derrida in "How to Avoid Speaking." "The secret as such, *as secret*, separates and already institutes a negativity; it is a negation that denies itself. It de-negates itself. This denegation does not happen to it by accident; it is essential and originary. And in the *as such* of the secret that denies itself because it appears to itself in order to be what it is, this de-negation gives no chance to dialectic." This torn function facilitates the double-natured *"sharing of the secret."* On the one hand, passing a secret to another—"my partner in a sect or in a secret society, my accomplice, my witness, my ally" (95)—denies that secret through revelation. On the other hand, retaining a secret denies that secret through dispersion, with Derrida referring "to the secret shared *within itself*, its partition 'proper,' which divides the essence of a secret that cannot even appear to one alone except in starting to be lost, to divulge itself, hence to dissimulate itself, as secret, in showing itself" (95; emphasis original).

The opening of the Einsatzkommando scene in *A Fable*, with the beeping of the murder squad's car horn, certainly announces the group's arrival, but does so "not pettishly nor fretfully nor even irritatedly but in fact with a sort of unwearyable blasé Gallic *detachment.*" Moreover, this car is of little note, even as a military vehicle. "It was not a big car. It flew no general's pennon nor in fact any insignia of any kind" (1009; emphasis added). There is nothing to draw an onlooker's attention. Mundanity preempts the entrance of men on a secret mission. Then, when their car reaches the Hôtel de Ville, which serves as the headquarters of Allied command, where Gragnon awaits his execution and where questions might be asked, the blasé attitude immediately evaporates. No longer at a snail's pace, with unusual dexterity preempting the entrance of men on a secret mission, the car is quickly concealed: "darting its way among the other vehicles at a really headlong speed," "it dashed on around to the extreme rear of the baroque and awesome pile" (1010).

Just as the archetypes of katabatic descent (a journey into the underworld) and anabatic ascent (a journey out of the underworld) underpin many modernist novels, such as Joseph Conrad's *Heart of Darkness* (1902) and Joyce's *Ulysses* (1922), so they inscribe numerous Holocaust testimonies, such as Primo Levi's account of his survival of internment in Auschwitz in *If This Is a Man* (1947), and so they appear in the Einsatzkommando episode in *A Fable*. An American military policeman leads the three soldiers "to the areaway and descend[s] into it, the Iowan following with his eyes the building's soaring upward swoop" (1012). Buchwald, as a soon-to-be member of the postwar criminal underworld— "within two years after the passage of the American prohibition law, with nothing in his bare hands but a converted army-surplus Lewis machine gun, he himself was to become czar of a million-dollar empire covering the entire Atlantic coast from Canada to whatever Florida cove or sandspit they were using that night" (1011)—follows directly behind the policeman. A sergeant-major meets the group in an anteroom. He becomes their guide to hell (or classical *Nekyia*). An unnervingly disinterested geological record tells of the physical, and by implication the immoral, depths to which the three men are sinking. "The whitewashed stone sweating in furious immobility beneath the whole concentrated weight of history, stratum upon stratum of dead tradition impounded by the *Hôtel* above them—monarchy revolution empire and republic, duke farmer-general and sans culotte, levee tribunal and guillotine, liberty fraternity equality and death and the people the People always to endure and prevail, the group, the clump, huddled now, going quite fast" (1017). What amounts to an explosion of light, "the single unshaded electric light" (1017), greets their entrance into the subterranean death cell. To use Roland Barthes's terms from *Camera Lucida* (1980)—a fitting hermeneutical reference for a novel that "is," according to Stefan Solomon, "the product of nothing less than an intermedial dialectic between literature and cinema" (116)—this punctum (or foreground burst) at once presages the disfiguring gunfire of Gragnon's execution and illuminates the tawdry studium (or background) of his "cubicle fierce with whitewash" (1017).[8] As of forthcoming blood, another punctum—"the splash of ribbons" (1017–18) on Gragnon's tunic—makes the condemned man stand out against this backcloth.

Under Faulkner's anticipative strategy, just as the death squad in *A Fable* implicates a range of Americans, so Nazism and the Holocaust implicated a range of Germans.[9] The Butterworths's reading of the novel confirms this interpretation: Buchwald, Beauchamp, and the Iowan "represent a cross-section of the American population," and "are an ironic inversion of the motif" (219) of the "trinity of conscience" (43), whom Levine, the battalion runner, and the Quartermaster General represent. As already argued, the demarcations of trench warfare often kept killing at a distance during World War I, but no such boundaries hampered the face-to-face murderers of the Einsatzkommandos, and Gragnon's physical closeness barely registers with Buchwald. At the same time, there is about Beauchamp something of that troubling predictability, willingness, and facileness of which Arendt writes in *Eichmann in Jerusalem: A Report on the Banality of Evil* (1963). Arendt notes how the deeply disturbing thing about (Otto) Adolf Eichmann, the arch facilitator of the Holocaust, "was precisely that so many were like him, and that the many were neither perverted nor sadistic, that they were, and still are, terribly and terrifyingly normal" (253).

The Iowan, however, is somewhat different to his companions, as Buchwald's enjoyment of the man's innocence implies. "Dont you know what you volunteered for?" Buchwald asks. The Iowan responds with what would become known as the Nuremberg Defense: "in the army, you dont ask what you are going to do: you just do it" (1013). Notwithstanding this answer, and although inured to the slaughtering of pigs, the Iowan will find Gragnon's murder unconscionable. The pencil marks this naïve tourist has been making on his map of France to trace his wartime odyssey are as nothing compared with the fatal mark the Einsatzkommando is meant to leave on Gragnon: "what was going to happen to [the farmer] inside the next thirty minutes would haunt him [...] as nightmares haunt" (1010), and the Iowan's refusal to participate in the Einsatzkommando operation—he has to be knocked semiconscious by Buchwald—enables Faulkner to delineate a nuanced approach to conformity. The farmer's dissent, though neither vigorous opposition nor active resistance, eschews apathy or silent resignation. He is a state servant, but one who awakens to the horror of that service in extremis and who expresses (however ineffectively) his dissent.

Nonetheless, Faulkner rightly understands the dutiful obedience behind the Einsatzkommando mission, with the Iowan's behavior anticipating one of the reasons why such operations, as Eaglestone notes in *The Holocaust and the Postmodern* (2004), were inapplicable to race extermination. The disfiguring function of face-to-face execution redounded when perpetrating mass murder: "the killing was psychologically damaging for many of the men involved at the bottom end of the genocidal chain of command" (312). In *A Fable*, the single execution of Gragnon is harrowing enough, with the general's body having to suggest that he died leading an attack, rather than survived in witnessing a mutiny. The mortal wound, as if the enemy had shot him, must penetrate his forehead. Gragnon defies this whitewash. He wants the bullet to penetrate occipitally. This wound, as if inflicted by his own side as he entered no-man's-land, would signify his men's disobedience. Hence, "the round hole" from Buchwald's first shot, which "was actually behind the ear," requires filling. This misplaced disfigurement must leave no trace. "'All right, all right,' Buchwald said. 'Now we got to plug that one up and shoot him again.' 'Plug it up?' the Negro said. 'Yes,' Buchwald said. 'What the hell sort of undertaker will you make if you dont know how to plug up a hole in a bastard that got shot in the wrong place? Wax will do it. Get a candle'" (1019). The second puncture, with the infliction of which the scene ends, thus leaves two small holes of an illuminating caliber, with not only the disfiguring and puncturing of Gragnon but also the tracings of that unholy (because the last rites are left unadministered) disfigurement leaving an aporetic shadow, creating what Fredric Jameson calls "the codification of affect" (45) in which "the realm of the visual begins to separate from that of the verbal and conceptual and to float away in a new kind of autonomy" (55).

In *A Fable*, that autonomous realm concerns a lacunary figuration that mitigates Faulkner's modernist practice in extending a lineage of such disfiguring holes from a number of the author's previous works. The first major disfigurement in Faulkner's modernisms occurs with Donald Mahon's wartime injury in *Soldiers' Pay*. The "scar across his brow" (17) is so "dreadful" (17) that his fiancée Cecily Saunders "c-cant bear to think of it" (74), and this eventually fatal disfigurement, which is too gruesome to describe in detail, is never fully revealed. In *Sanctuary*, the murderous hole in Red's forehead, which was plugged with painted wax to leave no trace, cannot help but reappear—the bearers drop his coffin during the wake; the plug drops out; the bullet wound gapes; and the bearers must cover this evidence by pulling down the dead man's cap. The dubious Harriss in "Knight's Gambit" also seems to have been murdered, but in this case no trace of a hole appears. "Maybe he really did die at the desk; maybe it was even a desk in an office," reports the narrator. "Because you can be shot just as discreetly across a desk in an office as anywhere else. And maybe he really did just die sitting at it, because prohibition was even legally dead by then and he was already rich when it ended, and the casket wasn't opened again after the lawyer and eight or ten of the butlers in their sharp clothes and arm-pitted pistols brought him home to lie in state" (167–68). Whatever the explicitness of their disclosures, all these disfigurements from Faulkner's canon culminate in *A Fable*, the text in which he figures the disfiguring horror of the Holocaust in anticipative retrospect, the text in which he concertedly confronts the artistic vision of his modernist period—and in this confrontation, the author shadows one of his most disturbing creations, with the Semitic Einsatzkommando Buchwald figuring Faulkner's effort to disfigure disturbing modernisms for good.

Notes

1. Snow had perhaps read William Faulkner's "Interview with Russell Howe" in which he had counselled African Americans to "Go slow" (258) on the issue of suffrage.

2. Snow, who had earned a PhD in physics and who had initially worked as a physical chemist, makes no mention of similarly culpable scientists, "yet Nazi thought could just as easily identify itself with modernity, with science, and with advanced technology" (Schulze 187).

3. Although Faulkner initially based Stevens on Phil Stone, many critics, including Cleanth Brooks (*Yoknapatawpha Country* 279), Michael Grimwood (220), and John Kenny Crane (11), have interpreted the fictional lawyer as Faulkner's own shadow.

4. Einsatzgruppen were employed behind the frontlines in the eastern campaigns. The first indictment in the *Trials of War Criminals before the Nuernberg Military Tribunals* (October 1946–April 1949) is "Crimes against Humanity," and the third part of this indictment concerns the Einsatzgruppen: "Beginning in May 1941, on the orders of Himmler, special task forces called 'Einsatzgruppen' were formed from the personnel of the SS, the SD, the Gestapo, and other police units. The primary purpose of these groups was to accompany the German Army into the eastern territories, and exterminate Jews, gypsies, Soviet officials, and other elements of the civilian population regarded as racially 'inferior' or 'politically undesirable'" (15).

5. The temporal register of reversal retains its presence during the formal break produced by the "Notes from a Horse Thief" section. The lawyer believes that the outcome to the Reverend Tobe Sutterfield's arrest is wrong. "It's backwards," he complains. "The law spirits a nigger prisoner out of jail and out of town, to protect him from a mob that wants to take him out and burn him. All these folks want to do is to set this one free" (830).

6. "The 1917 mutinies on the French front," confirms Pitavy, "were immediately known in France and abroad" ("Two Orders" 414 n.41).

7. "The inadequacy of the sources, reflecting in good measure the secrecy of the killing operations and the deliberate unclarity of the language employed to refer to them," explains Ian Kershaw, "has led to historians drawing widely varying conclusions from the same evidence about the timing and the nature of the decision or decisions to exterminate the Jews" (132).

8. "In its long process of composition, the work stages the representational conflict between two competing media," as Solomon elucidates: "beginning life as a screenplay, *A Fable* was always held in tension between potential manifestation as novel or film" (116).

9. "The apparent need to find a supreme culprit," as Kershaw warns of equating Nazism with Hitlerism, "comes close to trivializing" historical debate. This desire "divert[s] attention from the active forces in German society which did not have to be given a 'Führer Order' to turn the screws of Jewish persecution one thread further until extermination became the logical (and only available) 'solution'" (121). In a small way, Faulkner's Einsatzkommando members contribute to the history of everyday life, or *Alltagsgeschichte*, which German historians developed during the 1980s in their studies of the Third Reich.

CHAPTER 9

Conclusion: The Levine Shadow

The Utilitarian basis of current morality, which I have endeavoured to exhibit in the present chapter, seems to be rather less than more distinctly apprehended by the common moral consciousness. Thus (e.g.) Aristotle sees that the sphere of the Virtue of Courage (ἀνδρεία), as recognised by the Common Sense of Greece, is restricted to dangers in war, and we can now explain this limitation by a reference to the utilitarian importance of this kind of courage, at a period of history when the individual's happiness was bound up more completely than it now is with the welfare of his state, while the very existence of the latter was more frequently imperilled by hostile invasions: but this explanation lies quite beyond the range of Aristotle's own reflection.
—Henry Sidgwick, *The Methods of Ethics* (456)

"An excellence which we think no effort of will could at once enable us to exhibit in any appreciable degree," writes Henry Sidgwick in *The Methods of Ethics*, "is called a gift, grace, or talent, but not properly a virtue" (220). William Faulkner, though often failing to be a virtuous man, turned his gift to ethical account. "However immediately the excellent quality of such gifts and skills may be recognised and admired," adds Sidgwick, "reflection shows that they are only valuable on account of the good or desirable conscious life in which they are or will be actualised, or which will be somehow promoted by their exercise" (395). The life of Faulkner

© The Author(s), under exclusive license to Springer Nature
Switzerland AG 2021
M. Wainwright, *Faulkner's Ethics*,
https://doi.org/10.1007/978-3-030-68872-1_9

the man seldom profited from his talent. Pecuniary worries only ended with his Nobel laureateship, and the mental losses he accrued from employing his gift frequently resulted in deleterious or unconscionable behavior, which appeared to be the shameful price for the excellent qualities of his artistic output. Nevertheless, owing to Faulkner's literary promotion of life as conscionable practice, as the preceding chapters in this volume evince, the overall balance of this account was undoubtedly positive.

"Both [Søren] Kierkegaard and Faulkner," as George C. Bedell observes, "decry the tendency of modern men to run off into abstraction. Kierkegaard complains about the lack of passion and action, Faulkner about the tendency to reduce everyone to an impersonal and mechanical level" (16). Abstraction of the sort Faulkner decried presaged the failure of President Dwight D. Eisenhower's People-to-People Program, the writers' section of which Faulkner had chaired. "What doomed it," averred Faulkner to the "The English Club. A Word to Young Writers" at the University of Virginia on 24 April 1958,

> was an evil inherent in our culture itself; an evil quality inherent in (and perhaps necessary though I for one do not believe this last) in the culture of any country capable of enduring and surviving through this period of history. This is the mystical belief, almost a religion, that individual man cannot speak to individual man because individual man can no longer exist. A belief that there is no place anymore where individual man can speak quietly to individual man of such simple things as honesty with oneself and responsibility toward others and protection for the weak and compassion and pity for all, because such individual things as honesty and pity and responsibility and compassion no longer exist, and man himself can hope to continue only by relinquishing and denying his individuality into a regimented group of his arbitrary, factional kind, arrayed against an opposite opposed arbitrary, factional, regimented group, both filling the same air at the same time with the same double-barreled abstractions of "peoples' democracy" and "minority rights" and "equal justice" and "social welfare"—all the synonyms which take all the shame out of irresponsibility by not merely inviting but even compelling everyone to participate in it. (241–42)

The individual's responsibility toward others demands respect for them as individuals. Faulkner, as a man of intuitive morality rather than theoretical abstraction, understood this necessity. "Man," as he told Loïc Bouvard in 1952, "is free and he is responsible, terribly responsible. His tragedy is the impossibility—or at least the tremendous difficulty—of communication" (70). Sidgwick, as a man of moral contemplation rather than abstract theorization, understood this necessity too. Universalistic hedonism must mitigate egoistic hedonism. Self-interest must respect alterity. The inner self must own an outward prospect.

"The man of real inwardness is a man of character," as Bedell explains of Kierkegaard's notion of authenticity, "a man who acts on his inner convictions" (18). Authentic individuals have moral sense. "To be neither moral nor immoral is merely ambiguous," states Kierkegaard in *The Present Age: On the Death of Rebellion* (1846), "and ambiguity enters into life when the qualitative distinctions are weakened by a gnawing reflection" (43). Theorization blurs the differences between the moral and the immoral. "When too much thought is given to the problem, all inwardness is lost, and to that extent no vital antagonism is maintained between good and evil," expounds Bedell. "Instead, a 'stasis' is produced which signals the end of moral contradiction" (18–19). In contrast, authenticity avoids a "theoretical knowledge of evil" (Kierkegaard, *Present Age* 44), and the resultant moral struggle is genuine and intense. In their own distinct ways, and despite the extent, complexity, and in some cases lubriciousness of their thoughts, Søren Kierkegaard, Henry Sidgwick, Jacques Derrida, and William Faulkner, as men of "real inwardness," experienced the methods of ethics.

Among some of Sidgwick's contemporaries, and in this instance from *The Methods of Ethics* Sidgwick references the Herbert Spencer of *Social Statics* (1851), "Ethics ought to deal with ideally perfect human relations, just as Geometry treats of ideally straight lines and perfect circles," but Sidgwick appropriates Spencer's analogy to support his own reasoning. "The irregular lines which we meet with in experience have spatial relations which Geometry does not ignore altogether." Indeed, "it can and does ascertain them with a sufficient degree of accuracy for practical purposes: though of course they are more complex than those of perfectly straight lines" (19). Thus, as Sidgwick maintains,

in Astronomy, it would be more convenient for purposes of study if the stars moved in circles, as was once believed: but the fact that they move not in circles but in ellipses, and even in imperfect and perturbed ellipses, does not take them out of the sphere of scientific investigation: by patience and industry we have learnt how to reduce to principles and calculate even these more complicated motions. It may be useful for purposes of instruction to assume that the planets move in perfect ellipses: but what we want, as astronomers, to know is the actual motion of the stars, and its causes: and similarly as moralists we naturally inquire what ought to be done in the actual world in which we live. In neither case can we hope to represent in our general reasonings the full complexity of the actual considerations: but we endeavour to approximate to it as closely as possible. It is only so that we really grapple with the question to which mankind generally require an answer: "What is a man's duty in his present condition?" (19).

The reasonable duty of terribly responsible humankind haunted Faulkner; the gifted artist struggled with this specter; and the self-sacrifice demanded by this intense confrontation bore a canon of ethical significance. "Some souls," relates Derrida in *On the Name*, "believe themselves to have found in Deconstruction ['*la*' *Déconstruction*]—as if there were one, and only one—a modern form of immorality, of amorality, or of irresponsibility." Other souls, "more serious, in less of a hurry, better disposed toward so-called Deconstruction, today claim the opposite; they discern encouraging signs and in increasing numbers (at times, I must admit, in some of my texts) which would testify to a permanent, extreme, direct, or oblique, in any event, increasingly intense attention, to those things which one could identify under the fine names of 'ethics,' 'morality,' 'responsibility,' 'subject,' etc." True to his poststructuralist faith, and "so that one not be in too much of a hurry to say that it is in the name of a *higher* responsibility and a more intractable [*intraitable*] moral exigency," Derrida "declares [his] distaste, uneven as it may be, for both moralisrns" (15; emphasis original). That unevenness, or asymmetry, however, cannot help but weigh in favor of the fine names.

Faulkner's canon, when considered from this perspective, which considers the methods of ethics before interpretative deconstruction, poses moral exigencies that are as numerous as they are intractable—but their number and ungovernable nature, as Derrida himself would have admitted, ought not to preclude their investigation. For Sidgwick, as for Derrida, the questions of self-love and reasonable egoism are multifaceted, and for both Sidgwick and Derrida, unmitigated self-interest is an unreasonable form of hedonism. *Absalom, Absalom!* consummately figures that unreasonableness in Thomas Sutpen. Faulkner recognized his responsibility to literary inheritance in penning the best novel until then written by an American; and that bequest interrogates the dangers that attend self-interest and the possibilities universalism offers for moderating these dangers. Sometimes, as *Pylon* intimates, social pressures undercut the chances for the most basic form of human-to-human attachment, with parents failing in their duties toward their children. Faulkner's novel and John Bowlby's theory bring their authors together in a summary lesson for the related non-zero lesson, which counsels that parents must recipro-cate their children's desire for attachment. The responsibilities of duty may, as *The Unvanquished* adumbrates, demand acts of reconciliation. The underlying concerns of the maturing Bayard Sartoris implicitly capture the questions wrought by this requirement in the aftermath of the American Civil War. In *Intruder in the Dust*, unease over a supposed obligation, dis-like of inferiority in a perceived exchange, aversion to an unrequited gift, and maturation of conscience all lie under the rubric of benevolence. *Light in August* shows that individual dedication to human liberty, the sort of freedom that democracy supposedly champions, may occasionally require the benevolence of unconditional self-sacrifice. Consciousness of freedom and concomitant responsibility may call on the economics of secrecy, as "Barn Burning" illustrates, to defy the undemocratic power of inviolable secrets.

A Fable dedicates its democratic responsibility to the effacement of totalitarianism. Group Commander General Lallemont argues that humankind is unavoidably enslaved to the generic manifestation of egois-tic hedonism at its worst. "It wasn't we who invented war," the group commander tells Division Commander General Gragnon. "It was war which created us. From the loins of man's furious ineradicable greed sprang the captains and the colonels to his necessity. We are his responsi-bility" (715). This argument is fallacious; Sidgwick explodes this fallacy in *The Methods of Ethics* in demonstrating the virtuousness of universalism; as such, no better philosophical framework exists for exploring the related illustration in *A Fable*. That demonstration climaxes in the "Tomorrow" of the final chapter. The task of recovering the remains of an unknown soldier in the spring of 1919 reiterates and intensifies the concentration camp imagery of the prison compound at Chaulnesmont. Sergeant Landry is in nominal charge of the small force detailed to this task. "The job, mis-sion, was going to be an unpleasant one, now that peace and victory had really come to Western Europe in November (six months after the fake armistice in May, that curious week's holiday which the war had taken which had been so false that they remembered it only as phenomena) and a man, even though still in uniform, might have thought himself free, at least until they started the next one, of yesterday's cadavers" (1039). The taskforce must get a body from "the catacombs beneath the Fort of Valaumont" (1045). This retrieval involves, as did the earlier three-man Einsatzkommando mission, a journey into hell. Approaching Valaumont, following

> the curve of the Meuse Heights, the sergeant at least could watch beyond the open door the ruined and slain land unfold—the corpse of earth, some of which, its soil soured forever with cordite and human blood and anguish, would never live again, as though not only abandoned by man but repudiated forever by God Himself: the craters, the old trenches and rusted wire, the stripped and blasted trees, the little villages and farms like shattered skulls no longer even recognisable as skulls, already beginning to vanish beneath a fierce rank colorless growth of nourishmentless grass coming not tenderly out of the earth's surface but as though miles and leagues up from Hell itself, as if the Devil himself were trying to hide what man had done to the earth which was his mother. (1043)

Nearing the fort, as Malcolm Franklin must have experienced approaching Buchenwald concentration camp, the taskforce members are "already smelling it: who had not thought they would have to begin that until they were actually inside the fort; though once the sergeant had kicked and cursed the last of them out of the lorry, they saw why—a midden of white bones and skulls and some still partly covered with strips and patches of what looked like brown or black leather, and boots and stained uniforms and now and then what would be an intact body wrapped in a fragment of tarpaulin" (1043).

At Buchenwald, as Dan Stone chronicles, "many of the US infantrymen were there for just a brief length of time, but it was long enough to sear itself into their minds forever" (71). Stone reports that an eighteen-year-old soldier, Louis Blatz, "said that on seeing Buchenwald's inmates on 12 April it occurred to him that the Nazis 'didn't care one way or another. They treated them as animals. It was just horrible. Because it was hard to breathe. The odor, the smell, the air. The crematoriums, some of them still had bodies burning in 'em, so you could still smell it. And it was a relief on our part to get away from it, but you couldn't forget, you couldn't forget'" (71). Nor can one imagine the taskforce members in *A Fable* forgetting their mission. As they look on inside the fort, "two more soldiers in butchers' aprons and with pieces of cloth bound over their nostrils and lower faces, emerged from the low entrance carrying between them a two-man wheel-less barrow heaped with more scraps and fragments of the fort's old 1916 defenders" (1043–44). The two soldiers turn "to look at" the taskforce "for a moment above the taut rags over their nostrils and mouths with the fixed exhaustless unseeing unrecognising glares of sleep-walkers in nightmares before descending the steps again," the steps that Landry and his men must descend; "and over all, permeant and invincible, the odor, the smell" (1044). In preparation for their katabatic descent, the taskforce members "could see one another binding across their nostrils and lower faces what soiled handkerchiefs and filthy scraps of rag which they found on themselves" (1045–46). Ominously, their *Nekyia*, "a corporal carrying an electric torch and a folded stretcher," has withal "a gas-mask slung about his neck" (1046).

In the "Tomorrow" of years later, "there would be a vast towered chapel, an ossuary, visible for miles across the Heights like the faintly futuristic effigy of a gigantic gray goose or an iguanodon created out of gray stone." This edifice will be erected "not by a sculptor but by expert masons" and will sit "over the vast deep pit into which the now clean inextricable anonymous bones of what had been man, men, would be shoveled and sealed." The future experience of visiting this site will be one of familiarity and disorientation. Facing the chapel "would be the slope white with the orderly parade of Christian crosses bearing the names and regimental designations of the bones which could be identified." Beyond this bank would be "that other slope ranked not with crosses but with rounded headstones set faintly but intractably oblique to face where Mecca was, set with a consistent and almost formal awryness and carved in cryptic and indecipherable hieroglyph because the bones here had been identifiable too which had once been men come this far from their hot sun and sand, this far from home and all familiar things" (1044). The implication (or future anterior sense) of these unfamiliar eastern markers evokes the necessary memorialization of the Jews (and other supposed aliens) of Eastern Europe lost to the Holocaust.

The almost inconspicuous nature of this historical resonance in *A Fable* matches Samuel Beckett's praiseworthy response to genocide. The problem of objectivity toward the Holocaust affected, and continues to affect, artists and historians alike. Considerable detachment characterizes Beckett's and Faulkner's considerable attachment to their subject matter. One major impulse behind Faulkner's well-documented storytelling as a child was the overwhelming presence of the American Civil War in the "unvanquished" land of his upbringing. In middle age, he again sensed the cognitive overload of wartime events, and again resorted to storytelling, treating contemporary events in *A Fable* in a more apposite manner than historians and other novelists of the time did. The future anterior atrocities projected by Faulkner's novel adumbrate those of the Holocaust. In accordance with this implication, Faulkner's intuitive morality resonates to such a degree with Sidgwick's contemplative ethics that self-effacement characterizes that hermeneutic; as such, the nonappearance of *The Methods of Ethics* in the main body of the preceding chapter intensifies rather than diminishes that resonance. "To be self-effacing," as Derek Parfit insists in *Reasons and Persons*, "is not to be self-defeating." The aim of a theory is not belief in that theory. "If we personify theories, and pretend that they have aims, the aim of a theory is not to be believed, but to be true, or to be the best theory. That a theory is self-effacing does not show that it is not the best theory" (24).

Corporal Stefan Demont's obliteration appears to leave the novel with no remains of the east, and that complete sense of disorientation, the rendering of a final solution to the future anterior condition of the Jews, includes the demise of the character whose surname bespeaks the Levantine, the eighteen-year-old ("he wouldn't be nineteen for another year yet" [746]) pilot, Gerald David Levine. As with Buchwald and Demont, Levine dies within the confines of the novel, but Levine is the Jewish inverse of the Jewish Buchwald.[1] Their upbringings suggest root causes for the men's notable differences. Levine's parents hailed from London, where "he had been born," and where he had "lived ever since" (775). Levine's father, "until he died ten years ago," worked in the City, where he "manage[d] the London office of a vast American cotton establishment" (775). This link to the history of colonial exploitation helps to account for Levine's unassuageable desire to realize an act of expiation. Though born in or around 1900, and thus too young to have been called up, Levine dutifully volunteers for military service.

In doing so, Levine also meets the Sidgwickian concession from *The Elements of Politics* that recognizes "crises of national life in which it is the duty of the present generation of citizens, the actually living human beings who compose any political community, to make important sacrifices of personal happiness for the 'good' or 'welfare of their country'" (38). And so, in 1918, Second Lieutenant Levine of the Royal Flying Corps finds himself stationed at Villeneuve Blanche; less than a month earlier he had been "in England, waiting in Pilot's Pool for posting to the front—a certificated stationary engine scout pilot" (746). That certificate bears the inscription "*We Reposing Trust and Confidence in Our Trusty and Well-Beloved Gerald David*" (746–47; emphasis original). Significantly, in ordinary usage, Levine has dropped his first name—"Gerald is a name of Germanic origin," note Nancy and Keen Butterworth, "meaning to rule with spear" (74)—instead, as with the signature on what will be his final letter home, he uses the forename "David" (761). This appellation compounds his Jewish surname. "David is of Hebrew origin (King David of the Old Testament)," remark the Butterworths, "thus connecting Levine with the warrior tradition of the ancient Jews" (74). In a sense, then, Levine self-compounds his name because he is dutiful; and his duty amounts to taking complete responsibility for his Jewish origins.

Enemy action cannot wing (or hole) Levine. Desperate for active participation in the war, one "morning when he had been supposed simply to be out practicing, contour chasing probably," Levine flies "right down on the carpet with the unarmed aeroplane over the hun trenches or at least what he thought was the hun front line" (761). On his return Major Bridesman, his flight commander, is incredulous. He cannot believe that Levine is unharmed. "You didn't get even one bullet hole?" asks Bridesman. "No," replies Levine (762). Levine's desperation is such that the ceasefire instigated by Demont, the cessation of hostilities across the uncanny no place of no-man's-land, troubles him deeply. To Levine, a negative, or apophatic sense of "no dust no murk no gout and drift of smoke purposeless and unorigined and convoluted with no sound out of nothing and already fading and already replaced, no wink of guns" (763), marks this hiatus. Aporias of silence fill this intermission, "allow[ing] the unpresentable," to requote Jean-François Lyotard from "Answer to the Question," "to be invoked only as absent content" (14). The ceasefire as absence speaks loudly to Levine of his dutiful lack. "His trouble was probably very simple, really," Levine tells himself: "he simply had never heard silence before; he had been thirteen, almost fourteen, when the guns began, but perhaps even at fourteen you still could not bear silence: you denied it at once and immediately began to try to do something about it" (754). This attempt at self-consolation fails. Indeed, his disorientation triggers an apophatic response from his own senses, "hearing the silence still falling like a millstone into a well" (751), "leaving audibility with nothing now to lean against, outbursting into vacuum as the eardrums crack with altitude" (751–52).

The mutiny of Gragnon's regiment has, in effect, punctured the frontline, so French headquarters plug that hole. "They pulled the regiment out and replaced it and moved up guns and put down a heavy barrage all along their front," Captain Cowrie tells Levine, "just like we did this afternoon. To give ourselves time to see what was what" (756). A non-peace mission then forges an alliance between two fundamentally similar, and hence inseparable, adversaries. The Germans fly a general across no-man's-land to broker the deal; and Levine and Bridesman find themselves engaging this officer's aircraft in supposed combat. Like the bovine Iowan at the outset of his Einsatzkommando mission, Levine is unaware of his actual assignment, but while the hidden intent of the former task is murderous, the hidden intent of latter task is peaceful. The Allied and Central Powers wish to forge an inviolably secret compact; this covenant is murderous; Levine's naïve determination to give of his best recommended his involvement; and that innocence will stamp the meeting with a seal of unwarranted authenticity. Bridesman, as his surname suggests, is Levine's innocent attendant at these nuptials. He and Levine cross "right over the upper British balloon, heading straight for the German one," from which come "a white salvo bursting well below them and in front and then four single bursts pointing away eastward like four asterisks" (763). These bursts, with their orientation and shape, are akin to Stars of David; as such, they cannot wing (or hole) Levine; indeed, these shots are just for show, purposefully leaving no trace on either Allied pilot.

Sighting the German aircraft, Levine follows "Bridesman going almost straight down, the German right under them now, going west; he could see Bridesman's tracer going right into it until Bridesman pulled out and away" (763). In his turn, Levine "pressed the button and nudged and ruddered the tracer right onto it, walking the tracer the whole length of it and return—the engine, the back of the pilot's head then the observer sitting as motionless as though in a saloon car on the way to the opera, the unfired machine gun slanting back and down from its quadrant behind the observer like a rolled umbrella hanging from a rail" (764–75). That observer then "turned without haste and looked right into the tracer, right at him, and with one hand deliberately raised [his] goggles" (765). The future anterior of *A Fable* associates this passenger, who happens to be the German negotiator, with the Holocaust. Levine, who "had seen too many caricatures of the Hohenzollern Crown Prince in the last three years," notes the man's "Prussian face, a Prussian general's face" (765). Members of the Jewish community of Hohenzollern, a former Prussian province in Southern Germany, resided in the towns of Hechingen and Haigerloch. The Jewish Virtual Library records their fate under the Nazis.

In Hechingen, "the synagogue was demolished" during Kristallnacht (9–10 November 1938), and thirty-two inhabitants were later "deported and murdered." In Haigerloch, "the synagogue, school, and communal center were demolished" during Kristallnacht, "windows were smashed in shops and homes, and the men arrested and interned in Dachau." More townsfolk were arrested on the first anniversary of Kristallnacht, and "during the war Jews from Wuerttemberg were transferred to Haigerloch and at least 192 were deported."

Levine and Bridesman cannot wing (or hole) the enemy because such an embodiment of anti-Semitism is already a shell (or hollow within). Indeed, as later revealed, the German officer has a vacant eye socket: the general "put up a monocle at him and looked at him through it, then removed the monocle and faced front again" (765); there was "nothing behind the monocle at all" (767); "in fact there had been no eyeball behind it: no scar nor healed suture even: only the lidless and empty socket" (948). Bemused and desperate at failing to hole the German aircraft, and having finally guessed that his machinegun carries blank ammunition, Levine finally tries the weapon on his own battery, and even shoots at (as it turns out) the battalion runner:

> from the tight vertical turn he could look straight down at the gunners, shaking his hand at them and yelling: 'Come on! Come on! This is your last chance!' and slanted away and came back diving, walking the tracer right through the gun and the pale still up-turned discs of the faces watching him about it; as he pulled up he saw another man whom he had not seen before standing just on the edge of the wood behind the battery; the gentlest nudge on stick and rudder brought this one squarely into the Aldis itself this time and, pulling up at last to get over the trees, he knew that he should have got something very close to a possible ten somewhere about that one's navel. (765)

Levine fails both to incommode the battery and to hole the man's anatomical hole. Now sure that his machinegun had been loaded, without his prior knowledge, with tracer bullets, Levine wants incontrovertible proof of this deception. "Take your own word for it," Bridesman tells him. "I watched your tracer rake him from the engine right on back through the monocle" (768). Notwithstanding this testimony, Levine insists on double checking, "facing the little black port out of which the gun shot"

(769), as Bridesman pulls the trigger. Levine hereby confirms his guess: the bullets are phosphorized wooden pellets.

In comparison, the German general does carry live ammunition, which he uses on his own pilot once they have landed. This sacrificial lamb is, in many respects, including his age, Levine's counterpart. The general "drew a pistol from somewhere and even aimed it for a second while the rigid pilot (he looked about eighteen himself) stared not even at the pistol's muzzle but at the monocle and shot the pilot through the center of the face and turned almost before the body jerked and began to fall and swapped the pistol to the other gloved hand" (766). The German general explains at dinner to his British counterparts: "'I could have done it at your aerodrome this afternoon by using on myself the pistol which I employed to preserve even in defeat the integrity of what this—' he made a brief rapid gesture with one hand; with barely a motion of it he indicated his entire uniform—belts brass braid insigne and all '—represents" (950). Levine asks Bridesman why the general executed his pilot. What is offered as a precept of World War I stands in stark contrast to the Holocaust of World War II. "Germans fight wars by the rulebooks," explains Bridesman. "By the book, a German pilot who lands an undamaged German aeroplane containing a German lieutenant general on an enemy aerodrome is either a traitor or a coward, and he must die for it" (771).

An addition to the lineage of disfiguring holes in Faulkner's canon, the German pilot's execution underscores the current peace, and Levine's flying jacket, left with burning holes after his experiment with the phosphorized wooden pellets, symbolizes how this intermission remains his burning issue: "in the pitch dark there was nothing to see: only the slow thick invisible burning" (771). Levine's sacrificial wish, as a reversal of the survival instinct of concentration and death camp prisoners, now becomes apparent. Whereas Levine's flying suit (or Sidcott) amounts to his burnt offering, "he had heard that [...] a man in B Flight last year [...] had got a tracer between the bones of his lower leg and they were still whittling the bone away as the phosphorus rotted it" (771–72). This man's ongoing sacrifice appeals to the young second lieutenant, but the "Notes on a Horse Thief" section of the novel interrupts Levine's story, intentionally effecting both a formal dislocation and a narratorial disfiguration. This double intention expresses the postmodern within Faulkner's responsible modernism, with the mature author refusing the consolation of formal control. "The postmodern would be that which in the modern invokes the unpresentable in presentation itself," writes Lyotard in "Answer to the

Question," "which refuses the consolation of correct forms, refuses the consensus of taste permitting a common experience of nostalgia for the impossible, and inquires into new presentations—not to take pleasure in them, but to better produce the feeling that there is something unpresentable" (15).

The fabled horse in *A Fable* is a thoroughbred. In 1912, "even the price which the Argentine hide-and-wheat prince paid for it at the Newmarket sale, although an exceptional one, was not an outrageous one" (805), but within two years "it was bought by a United States oil baron for a price which even the Argentine millionaire could not refuse" (806). The thoroughbred horse, like the "Wealthy Jew" of *New Orleans Sketches*, whose "blood is old, but strong," unlike that of "mixed races, with your blood mingled and thinned and lost" (38), is lineally akin to Levine. Crippled in an accident, but cared for by the Reverend Sutterfield, Mister Harry, and Sutterfield's son, the horse evades capture for months. When captivity beckons, however, Mister Harry shoots the horse dead: "the foreigner, the Englishman leaning in the doorless frame of the fallen stable," as if forever associated with a corrupt version of Christ's birthplace, "the butt of the still-warm pistol protruding from the waistband of his filthy jodhpurs." Behind him lies the dead horse. That prostate body—the groom shot the thoroughbred "neatly once through *the star* on its forehead" (815; emphasis added)—is a portent.

Another such symbol, the burnt offering of Levine's flying suit, then reanimates the main narrative: "for a moment he toyed with the idea of unrolling the sidcott to see how far the burning had spread." At one point, Levine tries to cleanse himself of, or dispense with, the flying suit, but he cannot forsake this premonitory item. He "picked up the sidcott again and went to the washroom." With "the sidcott stinking peacefully under his arm, he could see movement about the mess, remembering suddenly that he had not eaten since lunch yesterday. But then there was the sidcott, when suddenly he realised that the sidcott would serve that too, turning and already walking" (965). Recalling the suicidal Quentin Compson stepping into or "finding my shadow" (939) in *The Sound and the Fury*, Levine, as if submerging himself in his conscience, now immerses himself in his own shadow. "They—someone—had brought his bus back and rolled it in, so he trod his long shadow toward only the petrol tin and put the sidcott into it and stood peaceful and empty while the day incremented, the infinitesimal ineluctable shortening of the shadows" (965).

Levine enters the mess and enjoys what appears to be the last meal of a self-condemned man: "eating steadily on in the empty mess until at last the orderly told him there was simply no more toast" (966). Since being stationed at Villeneuve Blanche, and somewhat reminiscent of the young Thomas Sutpen's recourse in *Absalom* to the canebrake where "an oak tree had fallen across it and made a kind of cave" (192), Levine has taken to sitting in "an old tree with two big roots like the arms of a chair on the bank" (966). He spends time there now. Despite all his consumption, and without requiring the repeated emeses that characterize Joe Christmas in *Light in August*, Levine emerges from this retreat "empty and peaceful." His subsequent behavior appears to be a race to save the (t)race. "He was looking at evening, the aftermath of sun, treading no shadow at all now to the petrol tin," as if he has already forsaken his body. "Though almost at once he began to hurry a little, remembering not the sidcott but the burning; it had been more than twelve hours now since he left it in the tin and there might not be anything left of it. But he was in time: just the tin itself too hot to touch so that he kicked it over and tumbled the sidcott out, which would have to cool a little too. Which it did: not evening incrementing now but actual night itself" (967). Levine makes his way to the toilet block.

Now, sitting in the latrine, "the tree" in his mind's eye, the old tree of spiritual repose, "was no longer green" (967). All that remains is "the stink of the sidcott." He drops the smoldering suit "into the sink where it unfolded as of its own accord into visibility, into one last repudiation—the slow thick invincible smell of the burning itself visible now in creeping overlaps, almost gone now—only a beggar's crumb but perhaps there had been an instant in the beginning when only a crumb of fire lay on the face of darkness and the falling waters" (967). The irony of Levine's imminent everlasting peace is its violent inauguration. "You didn't get even one bullet hole?" Bridesman had asked, faced with his second lieutenant's desperation for active service. This time, however, Levine makes sure; the bullet is live; all the disfigurements from Faulkner's earlier works reach their culmination; and the young pilot does not miss. "At the very point where Levine voids himself," writes Richard Godden, "the signatory image for that cancellation is a miniature 'holocaust,' or an extended burning in the enclosed space of a temporary 'incinerator.' To strain the logic of the image: an Englishman burns, releasing a residual Jew encoded as fire, stink, and shit" (*Complex Words* 169). Godden's logic is not strained. Levine's fate echoes that of two other "Jews" assimilated by the novel: Stefan Demont and the thoroughbred horse.

"If we ask, therefore, how far forgiveness is practically possible," muses Sidgwick in *The Methods of Ethics*, "the answer seems admittedly to depend on two considerations: (1) how far the punishment to which resentment prompts is really required in the interests of society, and (2) how far, if so, it will be adequately inflicted if the person wronged refrains from inflicting it" (322). The Holocaust pushed such considerations to their limits. For, as Derrida writes of the postwar Jewish condition in "Hospitality":

> There would be, there sometimes is, a feeling of guilt, muted or acute, for living, for surviving, and therefore an injunction to ask for forgiveness, to ask the dead or one knows not who, for the simple fact of being there [*être là*], alive, that is to say, for surviving, for being here, still here, always here, here where the other is no longer-and therefore to ask for forgiveness for one's being-there [*être-là*], a being there originarily guilty. Being-there: this would be asking for forgiveness; this would be to be inscribed in a scene of forgiveness, and of impossible forgiveness. (382–83)

At the Arc de Triomphe, where the Generalissimo's coffin pauses on its way to Les Invalides, the battalion runner execrates the continued divide between the "we" of war and the "us" of peace. From the Derridean perspective of *The Other Heading*, this execration concerns "the European, and *uniquely* European, heritage of an idea of democracy," a bequest inherited by America, a gift that recognizes "that this idea, like that of international law, is never simply given." This idea is "something that remains to be thought and to come [*à venir*]: not something that is certain to happen tomorrow, not the democracy (national or international, state or trans-state) of the *future*, but a democracy that must have the structure of a promise—*and thus the memory of that which carries the future, the to-come, here and now*" (78; emphasis original). The acts of witnessing of Demont and Levine cannot, of course, guarantee a victimless future. The Quartermaster General's reaction to the battalion runner's display of anger suggests as much. Indeed, the old man's "tremble" (1072) of fearful "tears" (1072), with which the novel ends, indicates the ineffectiveness of most (if not all) such acts. "That whatever is to be will be better than what is, we all hope," avers Sidgwick in *The Methods of Ethics*, "but there seems to be no more reason for summarily identifying 'what ought to be' with 'what certainly will be,' than for finding it in 'what commonly is,' or 'what originally was'" (83).

*   *   *

After *A Fable*, Faulkner would complete three more novels: the remaining two parts of the Snopes Trilogy, comprising *The Town* (1957) and *The Mansion* (1959), and *The Reivers* (1962). These final works offer much from an ethical perspective. In *The Mansion*, for example, the Jewish sculptor Barton Kohl, who marries Linda Snopes, sacrifices himself for republican democracy during the Spanish Civil War. By this time, Linda's father Flem, whose self-interest had reached its zenith in *The Town*, implicitly admits the self-defeating nature of his egoistic hedonism: in another instance of passive suicide in Faulkner's canon, Flem lets his cousin Mink Snopes murder him, thereby snuffing out his personification of self-interest. By contrast, *The Reivers* offers a particular interpretation of the psychological and ethical differences between growth and maturation. The teenager Otis, who celebrates his fifteenth birthday during the narrative, has grown up too quickly: he has practical experience of alcohol and voyeuristic experience of prostitution. The eleven-year-old Lucius Priest, who is at once younger and less grown up than Otis, having never imbibed alcohol nor previously been inside a bordello, exhibits a far healthier maturation. That maturity appears most obviously in Lucius accepting responsibility for taking his grandfather's car, but also less obviously (yet just as tellingly) in Lucius identifying Otis as a "demon child" (852).

Notwithstanding these (admittedly cursory) observations, and the possibilities they open for further research, a tentative judgment concludes that *The Town*, *The Mansion*, and *The Reivers* struggle to emerge from the shadow cast by *A Fable*. The manner in which the gifted Faulkner's duty of authorial responsibility resonates with that of the responsibly gifted Sidgwick coalesces to maximum effect in his self-avowed magnum opus, the novel for which he sacrificed ten years of his life. In his "Interview with Jean Stein vanden Heuvel," which includes a lengthy discussion of *A Fable*, Faulkner uses (as previously cited) Christianity as an analogue for a moral outlook that appreciates but mitigates self-interest. This perspective ought to be "every individual's individual code of behavior by means of which he makes himself a better human being," a better member of the human collective, "a better human being than his nature wants to be if he followed his nature only" (246–47). Faulkner even disorients his analogy in destabilizing its symbolism: "whatever its symbol—cross or crescent or whatever—that symbol is man's reminder of his duty inside the human race," his individual duty to universalism. Unlike Sidgwick, Faulkner felt that this symbol "cannot teach man to be good as the text book teaches him mathematics," but like Sidgwick, Faulkner felt that this symbol "shows him how to discover himself, evolve for himself a moral code and standard within his capacities and aspirations, by giving him a matchless example of suffering" (247).

"Faulkner appears to have felt, in 1943, at the heart of a second war his own country had joined," remarks François Pitavy in "The Two Orders in *A Fable*," "the necessity to stage his story of an apocalypse-haunted world in a Europe wounded by war rather than in the United States that had experienced only a civil war but had not retained in its memory nor in its sites of memory the experience of devastation by foreign forces violating the home-land." Faulkner realized that he must both retain and leave his central ground. "Faulkner had to *de-center* his subject, to leave his familiar territory so as to distance his reflection and *re-center* it, away from the prevailing ideological discourse on the Cold War and the official verities he would soon feel Nobel-obliged to utter" (421; emphasis original). For Pitavy, this de-centering suffers from two obvious weaknesses, which comprise "the heightened language and over-powered rhetoric" of *A Fable*. This linguistic combination is "probably meant to signal the importance of the fictional and metafictional stakes at the core of Faulkner's fable," but this strategy fails, not as "the result of its author's decreasing powers but of his being somewhat of a stranger in this foreign territory (and he stages characters, not ideas), with a considerable elephant to handle" (413). I would argue, however, that the mature Faulkner appreciates that he is a stranger exploring the foreign territory of the extraordinary, unthinkable, ineffable, and ultimately unimaginable horror of the Holocaust, and that the heightened language and powerful rhetoric of his magnum opus succeed in emphasizing the aporia that facilitate their functioning. The importance of the novel lies in and around an emphatic silence. To repeat Hannah Arendt from *Men in Dark Times*, "very little is described, still less explained, and nothing at all 'mastered'" (20) in a work of responsible irresponsibility, and that "failure" is of ethical significance.

For Pitavy, Faulkner's de-centering suffers from another obvious fault: "the corporal is the absent center of the novel." Demont lacks a significant presence, and "when he is physically present, and vocal, the Christian allegory (made even more insistent with Faulkner's last minute revisions) becomes detrimental to the credibility of a character now too matter-of-fact, bereft of his aura, for a would-be hero."[2] Pitavy fails to appreciate the intention behind this central absence. Demont is not meant to be the hero; his actions do not recognize heroics; Demont discounts deference to standards that do not matter. Demont, whose Jewish origins are questionable, steps aside for Levine, whose Jewish origins are undoubted.[3] Rather than "a backward glance on his [canon] at a time when he experienced a weakening of inspiration" ("Two Orders" 422), and despite related moments of avowed uncertainty during the composition of his magnum opus, Faulkner was effectively shifting his center of canonical gravity in bearing silent witness to the Holocaust.

A Fable further supports this assumption of responsibility from *Absalom* by moving directly from the Einsatzkommando episode to the crucifixion scene. This move brings the narrative back to explicit martyrdom. The interior and constrained setting of Gragnon's cell, bathed as it is in artificial light, transforms into the exterior and open setting of the parade ground, bathed as it is in what "bade fair to be another bright and perennial lark-filled vernal morning" (1020). The crucifixion of Stefan Demont and two criminals (Lapin and Casse-tête), an artifice that many commentators disparage, seemingly wipes the memory of the presentation of the unpresentable in the preceding episode. "I do not intend to analyze in detail here the way the various avant-gardes have, as it were, humiliated and disqualified reality by their scrutiny of the pictorial techniques used to instill a belief in it," states Lyotard in "Answer to the Question." "Local tone, drawing, the blending of colors, linear perspective, the nature of the support and of tools, 'execution,' the hanging of the work, the museum: the avant-gardes continually expose the artifices of presentation that allow thought to be enslaved by the gaze and diverted from the unpresentable" (12). In *A Fable*, however, the seeming artifice of presentation cannot help but carry the trace of the previous scene: the Einsatzkommando members have been promised a trip to Paris; Lapin has promised Casse-tête the same excursion. What is more, as with Gragnon's murder, and again for utilitarian reasons, extra holes complete the parade ground executions, with "the sergeant-major" in charge of the firing squad making sure of each death by subsequently "setting the pistol's muzzle against the ear" (1023).

Demont's death adds to a roster of responsible suicides both in the novel, which includes Levine and the priestly confessor who succumbs to Stefan's standard of ethics, and in Faulkner's canon, which already includes

Joe Christmas from *Light in August* and will later include Flem Snopes from *The Mansion*. The duty of Stefan's burial falls on his half sisters Marthe and Marya, and on Stefan's former fiancée, who leave Chaulnesmont forever via "the old eastern city gate" (1027). "They didn't look back at it, though for a while it remained, squatting above the flat plain, supreme still, gray and crowned by the ancient Roman citadel" (1028). Their ultimate destination is beyond the family home: "the cart moving again, crossing the field now rank with weeds and wild poppies, skirting the occasional craters, on for perhaps half a kilometre to a bank beneath an ancient beech tree which also had escaped the shells" (1034). This specimen, "the finest beech tree in this country" (1059), recalls the motif of the beech wood (or Buchenwald). They bury Stefan in the bank under this rare survivor, but after the next artillery barrage, "at first they couldn't even find the bank." Then, "when they did at last, the beech tree had vanished: no mark, nothing remained to orient by" (1037). Eventually, "they found a few […] shards and fragments of the coffin, but the body itself was gone" (1038). All trace of Stefan seems to have been wiped out, and when Polchek in his postwar Judas misery seeks Demont's burial marker ("Marya said. 'This one is looking for a tree.'/'A tree?' the sister said./'Yes, Sister. Cant you see him?'" [1061]), he can find nothing. Buchenwald, "which had been built in the old ducal hunting forest on the summit of the Ettersberg, consuming the hill's woods and stone in the building" (Sayer and Dronfield 17), thus finds a fictional counterpart in the sacrifice of Stefan's beechwood headstone to the reanimation of war.

The erasure of the Jewish trace is, however, more difficult than anti-Semites imagine. The mission of recovering the remains of an unknown soldier in the spring of 1919 proves this difficulty. The body the taskforce members remove from the catacombs beneath the Fort of Valaumont is Stefan's, and the reinterment of these remains eventually occurs on 11 November 1920 under the Arc de Triomphe. In a significant sense, then, Quartermaster General Erich Ludendorff's "problem" with the English, as expressed by Levine, anticipates Hitler's "problem" with the Jews: "because," whatever he tried, "he would still have to envelop and reduce every tree in every wood and every stone in every wall in all England" (776). Hence, and in spite of himself, Pitavy shares the sense of canonical shift from *Absalom, Absalom!* to *A Fable*, suggesting that Faulkner's magnum opus "may paradoxically remain—despite the elephant-like 'enormity' of its aim—the de-centered center of the whole work, and its reading, not always easy, may open the way to a better comprehension of the

Faulkner canon and of the author's overall design" ("Two Orders" 423), a design in which moral considerations play an intense part, a role that this book celebrates in inviting others to further investigate Faulkner's ethics.

NOTES

1. Alfred J. Kutzik notes how the young Faulkner "used the Jew as a symbol of the rapacity and inhumanity of modern industrial society" (224). The mature Faulkner, regretting that earlier usage, worked "to suppress his anti-Semitic rhetoric," as Thomas Peyser observes, with "the admirable Jews in his later work, like Gerald David in *A Fable*, hardly seem[ing] anomalous, since they can be construed, as Alfred J. Kutzik has hypothesized, as a kind of public apology" (9).

2. For Pitavy, "The 'Judas' material, concerning Polchek's visit to the corporal's sisters, was added when the galleys had already been set" ("Two Orders" 422 n.56) and is intended to bolster Demont's supposed heroics. Alternatively, read through Faulkner's strategy of reversal in the novel, this material is intended to emphasize Polchek's misery.

3. Pitavy helps to clarify this point. "Stefan's mother comes from some indefinite place in the Balkans (she is not Tibetan, as some critics have said). Marthe, Stefan, Polchek, Pierre Bouc, all speak that rough 'mountain' language, full of consonants, of the fictitious Zsettlanis" ("Two Orders" 405 n.33). Jewish history in the Balkans predates that of the Serbians, so Stefan's maternal ancestors could be Jewish.

WORKS CITED

Adorno, Theodor W. *Aesthetic Theory*. 1970. Ed. Gretel Adorno and Rolf Tiedemann. Trans. Robert Hullot-Kentor. London: Bloomsbury, 2012.

———. "Cultural Criticism and Society." *Prisms*. 1967. Trans. Samuel Weber and Shierry Weber. Cambridge, MA: MIT P, 1983. 17–34.

———. *Negative Dialectics*. 1973. Trans. E. B. Ashton. London: Routledge and Kegan Paul. 1996.

Ali, Seemee. "Faulkner's Augustinian Sense of Time" *Augustine and Literature*. Ed. Robert Peter Kennedy, Kim Paffenroth, and John Doody. Lanham, MD: Lexington, 2006. 287–300.

Allen, Walter. "Mr Faulkner's Humanity." 15 October 1949. *William Faulkner: Critical Assessments*. Ed. Henry Claridge. Vol. 4. Mountfield, UK: Helm, 1999. 104–7.

Alvard, Michael S., and David A. Nolin. "Rousseau's Whale Hunt? Coordination among Big-Game Hunters." *Current Anthropology* 43.4 (August/October 2002): 533–59.

Anidjar, Gil. "A Note on 'Force of Law.'" *Acts of Religion*. By Jacques Derrida. New York: Routledge, 2002. 228–29.

Arendt, Hannah. *Eichmann in Jerusalem: A Report on the Banality of Evil*. 1963. New York: Penguin, 1994.

———. *Men in Dark Times*. London: Harcourt Brace, 1968.

Atkins, Richard Kenneth. *Peirce and the Conduct of Life: Sentiment and Instinct in Ethics and Religion*. Cambridge, UK: Cambridge UP, 2016.

Bacigalupo, Massimo. "New Information on William Faulkner's First Trip to Italy." *Journal of Modern Literature* 24.2 (2000/2001): 321–25.

© The Author(s), under exclusive license to Springer Nature   289
Switzerland AG 2021
M. Wainwright, *Faulkner's Ethics*,
https://doi.org/10.1007/978-3-030-68872-1

Backman, Melvin. *Faulkner: The Major Years: A Critical Study.* Bloomington, IN: Indiana UP, 1966.

Baldwin, James. "Faulkner and Desegregation." *Nobody Knows My Name: More Notes of a Native Son.* New York: Dial P, 1961. 117–26.

Barnhart, Robert K., ed. *Chambers Dictionary of Etymology.* Edinburgh: Chambers, 2001.

Barrow, R. H. *Introduction to St Augustine.* The City of God. *Being Selections from the* De Civitate Dei *Including Most of the XIXth Book.* London: Faber and Faber, 1950.

Barthes, Roland. *Camera Lucida: Reflections on Photography.* 1980. Trans. Richard Howard. London: Vintage, 1982.

Bassett, John E. "Gradual Progress and *Intruder in the Dust.*" *College Literature* 13.3 (Fall 1986): 207–16.

Baudelaire, Charles. "La fausse monnaie." *Petits poèmes en prose.* My translation. Ed. Melvin Zimmerman. Manchester, UK: Manchester UP, 1968. 48–50.

———. *Les Fleurs du mal.* 1857. Trans. Richard Howard. Boston, MA: David R. Godine, 1982.

Bauer, Yehuda. *The Holocaust in Historical Perspective.* Seattle, WA: U of Washington P, 1978.

Bedell, George C. *Kierkegaard and Faulkner: Modalities of Existence.* Baton Rouge, LA: Louisiana State UP, 1972.

Bellow, Saul. "To William Faulkner." 7 January 1957. "Lost Classic: The People-to-People Project." Introd. and ed. Caroline Henze-Gongola and Jeb Livingood. *Meridian: The Semi-Annual from the University of Virginia* 18 (January 2007): 83.

Benjamin, Walter. "Theses on the Philosophy of History." 1942. *Illuminations.* Trans. Harry Zohn. Ed. Hannah Arendt. New York: Harcourt, Brace and World, 1968. 245–55.

Berton, Pierre. *The Dionne Years: A Thirties Melodrama.* 1977. Toronto: Penguin, 1991.

Binion, Rudolph. *Hitler among the Germans.* New York: Elsevier, 1976.

Blanshard, Brand. *Reason and Goodness.* 1961. Abingdon, UK: Routledge, 2014.

Blotner, Joseph. *Faulkner: A Biography. One-Volume Edition.* 1984. Jackson, MS: UP of Mississippi, 2010

———. *Faulkner: A Biography.* 2 vols. London: Chatto and Windus, 1974.

———. *William Faulkner's Library: A Catalogue.* Charlottesville, VA: UP of Virginia, 1964.

Blum, Deborah. *Ghost Hunters: William James and the Search for Scientific Proof of Life after Death.* London: Penguin, 2006.

Bobro, Marc Elliott. *Self and Substance in Leibniz.* 2004. New York: Springer, 2005.

Boecker, Eberhard. *William Faulkner's Later Novels in German: A Study in the Theory and Practice of Translation.* Tübingen, Ger.: Niemeyer, 1973.

Bouyer, Louis. *The Christian Mystery: From Pagan Myth to Christian Mysticism.* 1990. Trans. Illtyd Trethowan. London: Clark, 2004.

Bowlby, John. "The Abnormally Aggressive Child." *The New Era in Home and School* 19 (September–October 1938): 230–34.

———. *Attachment and Loss.* Vol. 1. *Attachment.* 1969. 2nd. ed. New York: Basic, 1990a.

———. *Attachment and Loss.* Vol. 3. *Loss: Sadness and Depression.* 1980. 2nd. ed. New York: Basic, 1990b.

———. "Commentary: Where Science and Humanism Meet." *Group Analysis* 21.1 (1988a): 81–82.

———. "Forty-Four Juvenile Thieves: Their Characters and Home Life." *International Journal of Psycho-Analysis* 25 (1944): 1–57, 207–28.

———. "The Influence of Early Environment in the Development of Neuroses and Neurotic Character." *International Journal of Psycho-Analysis* 21 (1940): 154–78.

———. *Maternal Care and Mental Health: A Report Prepared on Behalf of the World Health Organization as a Contribution to the United Nations Programme for the Welfare of Homeless Children.* Geneva, Switz.: World Health Organization, 1951.

———. "A Psycho-Analytic Approach to Conflict and its Regulation (A Seminar Delivered to Members of the Stanford Conflict Seminar, January, 1958)." *Trauma and Loss: Key Texts from the John Bowlby Archive.* Ed. Robbie Duschinsky and Kate White. London: Routledge, 2020. 167–72.

———. "Research into the Origins of Delinquent Behaviour." *The British Medical Journal* 1.4653 (11 March 1950): 570–73.

———. "The Roots of Human Personality." *Readings in General Psychology.* Ed. Paul Halmos and Alan Iliffe. 1959. Abingdon, UK: Routledge, 2002. 108–29.

———. *A Secure Base: Parent-Child Attachment and Healthy Human Development.* New York: Basic, 1988b.

Bradley, F. H. "My Station and Its Duties." *Ethical Studies: Selected Essays.* London: King, 1876. 145–92.

Brams, Steven J. *Biblical Games: Game Theory and the Hebrew Bible.* Cambridge, MA: MIT P, 1980.

Brasch, James D. *That Other Hemingway: The Master Inventor.* Victoria, BC: Trafford, 2009.

Bretherton, Inge. "The Origins of Attachment Theory: John Bowlby and Mary Ainsworth." *Developmental Psychology* 28.5 (September 1992):759–75.

Broad, C. D. *Five Types of Ethical Theory.* 1930. London: Routledge, 2002.

Brodsky, Louis Daniel. "Faulkner's Wounded Art: The Aftermath of Hollywood and World War II." *Special Issue: William Faulkner and the Military.* Spec. issue of *The Faulkner Journal* 2.2 (Spring 1987): 55–66.

———. *William Faulkner: Life Glimpses.* Austin, TX: U of Texas P, 1990.

Brooks, Cleanth. "The Community and the Pariah." *Virginia Quarterly Review* 39.2 (Spring 1963): 236-53.

———. *On the Prejudices, Predilections, and Firm Beliefs of William Faulkner.* Baton Rouge, LA: Louisiana State UP, 1987.

———. *William Faulkner: The Yoknapatawpha Country.* 1963. Baton Rouge, LA: Louisiana State UP, 1990a.

———. *William Faulkner: Toward Yoknapatawpha and Beyond.* 1978. Baton Rouge, LA: Louisiana State UP, 1990b.

Broughton, Panthea Reid. "Faulkner's Cubist Novels." *A Cosmos of My Own.* Ed. Doreen Fowler and Ann J. Abadie. Jackson, MS: UP of Mississippi, 1981. 59–94.

Brown, David. *Divine Humanity: Kenosis Explored and Defended.* London: SMC, 2011.

Budd, Susan. "'No sex, please—we're British': Sexuality in English and French Psychoanalysis." *Sexuality: Psychoanalytic Perspectives.* Ed. Celia Harding. Hove, UK: Taylor and Francis, 2001. 52–68.

Butler, Joseph. *Analogy of Religion, Natural and Revealed, to the Constitution and Course of Nature.* 1736. London: George Bell & Sons, 1897.

———. "Sermon III. Upon Human Nature." 1726. *Human Nature and other Sermons.* London: Cassell, 1887. 44–53.

Butterworth, Keen. *A Critical and Textual Study of Faulkner's* A Fable. Ann Arbor, MI: U of Michigan Research P, 1983.

Butterworth, Nancy, and Keen Butterworth. A Fable *Annotated by Nancy Butterworth and Keen Butterworth.* New York: Garland, 1989.

Byng-Hall, John. "An Appreciation of John Bowlby: His Significance for Family Therapy." *Journal of Family Therapy* 13 (1991): 5–16.

Cannariato, Christy A. "Rise and Fall: Degeneration, Historical Determinism, and William Faulkner's *Absalom, Absalom!*" *Darwin in Atlantic Cultures: Evolutionary Visions of Race, Gender, and Sexuality.* Ed. Jeannette Eileen Jones and Patrick B. Sharp. New York: Routledge, 2010. 111–27.

Caputo, John D. *The Prayers and Tears of Jacques Derrida: Religion without Religion.* Bloomington, IN: Indiana UP, 1997.

Catton, Bruce. *This Hallowed Ground: The Story of the Union Side of the Civil War.* Garden City, NY: Doubleday, 1956.

Ching, D. K., Mark M. Jarzombek, and Vikramaditya Prakash. *A Global History of Architecture.* Hoboken, NJ: Wiley, 2011.

Clarke, Deborah. *Robbing the Mother: Women in Faulkner.* Jackson, MS: UP of Mississippi, 1994.

Coats, R. H. *Types of English Piety.* Edinburgh: Clark, 1912.

Collins, Carvel. "About the Sketches." *New Orleans Sketches.* By William Faulkner. 1925. New Brunswick, NJ: Rutgers UP, 1958. 7–34.

————. "'Ad Astra' through New Haven: Some Biographical Sources of Faulkner's War Fiction." *Faulkner and the Short Story.* Ed. Evans Harrington and Ann J. Abadie. Jackson, MS: UP of Mississippi, 1992. 108–27.

Coughlan, Robert. *The Private World of William Faulkner.* New York: Harper, 1954.

Crane, John Kenny. *The Yoknapatawpha Chronicle of Gavin Stevens.* Selinsgrove, PA: Susquehanna UP, 1988.

Crawford, Vincent. "A Survey of Experiments on Communication via Cheap Talk." *Journal of Economic Theory* 78.2 (1998): 286–98.

Cross, F. L., and E. A. Livingstone, ed. *The Oxford Dictionary of the Christian Church.* 3rd. ed. Oxford, UK: Oxford UP, 2005.

Cuddon, J. A. *A Dictionary of Literary Terms and Literary Theory.* 3rd. ed. London: Penguin, 1991.

Davis, David A. *World War I and Southern Modernism.* Jackson, MS: UP of Mississippi, 2018.

Davis, Thadious M. *Games of Property: Law, Race, Gender, and Faulkner's* Go Down, Moses. Durham, NC: Duke UP, 2003.

Derrida, Jacques. "Before the Law." 1982. *Acts of Literature.* Ed. Derek Attridge. New York: Routledge, 1992a. 183–220.

————. "Cogito and the History of Madness." 1963. *Writing and Difference.* Trans. Alan Bass. Chicago, IL: U of Chicago P, 1978a. 36–63.

————. *Glas.* Trans. John P. Leavey and Richard Rand. Lincoln, NE: U of Nebraska P, 1986.

————. "How to Avoid Speaking: Denials." 1989. Trans. Ken Frieden. Ed. Harold Coward and Toby Foshay. Albany, NY: State U of New York P, 1992. 73–142.

————. "That Dangerous Supplement." *Of Grammatology.* 1974. Trans. Gayatri Chakravorty Spivak. Baltimore, MD: Johns Hopkins UP, 1997a. 141–64.

————. *Dissemination.* 1981. Trans. Barbara Johnson. London: Athlone, 2000.

————. "Faith and Knowledge: The Two Sources of 'Religion' at the Limits of Reason Alone." 1998. *Acts of Religion.* Trans. Samuel Weber. Ed. Gil Anidjar. New York: Routledge, 2002a. 42–101.

————. "The First Session." *Acts of Literature.* 1981. Ed. Derek Attridge. New York: Routledge, 1992. 129–80.

————. "Following Theory." *Life.After.Theory.* Ed. Michael Payne and John Schad. London: Continuum, 2003. 1–51.

————. "Force and Signification." 1967. *Writing and Difference.* Trans. Alan Bass. Chicago, IL: U of Chicago P, 1978b. 3–30.

————. "Force of Law: The 'Mystical Foundation of Authority.'" 1990. *Acts of Religion.* Trans. Mary Quaintance. Ed. Gil Anidjar. New York: Routledge, 2002b. 230–98.

————. *The Gift of Death.* Trans. David Wills. Chicago, IL: U of Chicago P, 1995a.

————. *Given Time: I. Counterfeit Money.* Trans. Peggy Kamuf. Chicago, IL: U of Chicago P, 1992b.

————. "Hospitality." 1997. *Acts of Religion.* Trans. and ed. Gil Anidjar. New York: Routledge, 2002c. 358–420.

————. *Of Grammatology.* 1974. Trans. Gayatri Chakravorty Spivak. Baltimore, MD: Johns Hopkins UP, 1997b.

————. *On the Name.* Trans. John P. Leavey. Ed. Thomas Dutoit. Stanford, CA: Stanford UP, 1995b.

————. *The Other Heading: Reflections of Today's Europe.* Trans. Pascale-Anne Brault and Michael B. Naas. Bloomington, IN: Indiana UP, 1992c.

————. "Remarks on Deconstruction and Pragmatism." *Deconstruction and Pragmatism.* Ed. Chantal Mouffe. London: Routledge, 1996. 77–88.

————. *Spurs: Nietzsche's Styles.* 1978. Trans. Barbara Harlow. Chicago, IL: U of Chicago P, 1979.

————. "This Strange Institution Called Literature: An Interview with Jacques Derrida." 1989. *Acts of Literature.* Ed. Derek Attridge. New York: Routledge, 1992d. 33–75.

————. "Structure, Sign, and Play in the Discourse of the Human Sciences." 1966. *Writing and Difference.* Trans. Alan Bass. London: Routledge, 1978c. 278–93.

————. "Violence and Metaphysics: An Essay on the Thought of Emmanuel Levinas." 1964. *Writing and Difference.* Trans. Alan Bass. Chicago, IL: U of Chicago P, 1978d. 79-153.

Des Jardin, Julie. *The Madame Curie Complex: The Hidden History of Women in Science.* New York: Feminist P at City U of New York, 2010.

DeVoto, Bernard. "'Faulkner's South.' Review of William Faulkner, *The Unvanquished.*" *Saturday Review of Literature.* 19 February 1938: 5.

Dewey, John. "Review of *Henry Sidgwick: A Memoir* by Arthur Sidgwick and Eleanor Mildred Sidgwick." 1907. *The Middle Works of John Dewey, 1899–1924.* Vol. 4. *Journal Articles and Book Reviews in the 1907–1909 Period, and* The Pragmatic Movement of Contemporary Thought *and* Moral Principles in Education. 1977. Introd. Lewis E. Hahn. Ed. Jo Ann Boydston. Carbondale, IL: Southern Illinois UP, 2008. 242–44.

Didi-Huberman, Georges. *Devant l'image: Question posée aux fins d'une histoire de l'art.* Paris: Éditions de Minuit, 1990.

Dionysius the Areopagite. *Dionysius the Areopagite on* The Divine Names *and* The Mystical Theology. Trans. C. E. Rolt. 1920. Berwick, ME: Hays, 2004.

Dixon, Angela. "'At All Costs Let Us Avoid Any Risk of Allowing Our Hearts to be Broken Again': A Review of John Bowlby's *Forty-Four Juvenile Thieves.*" *Clinical Child Psychology and Psychiatry* 8.2 (April 2003): 278–89.

Donagan, Alan. "History of Western Ethics: 12. Twentieth-Century Anglo-American." *Encyclopedia of Ethics.* Ed. Lawrence C. Becker and Charlotte B. Becker. New York: Routledge, 2001. 765–73.

Douglass, Frederick. "The Mission of the War." 1863. *The American Civil War: An Anthology of Essential Writings.* Ed. Ian Frederick Finseth. New York: Routledge, 2006. 264–76.

Doyle, Don H. *Faulkner's County: The Historical Roots of Yoknapatawpha, 1540–1962.* Chapel Hill, NC: U of North Carolina P, 2001.

Drever, Matthew. *Image, Identity, and the Forming of the Augustinian Soul.* Oxford, UK: Oxford UP, 2013.

Dubilet, Alex. *The Self-Emptying Subject: Kenosis and Immanence, Medieval to Modern.* New York: Fordham UP, 2018.

Durbin, E. P. M., and John Bowlby. *Personal Aggressiveness and War.* 1939. Abingdon, UK: Routledge, 2001.

Dussere, Erik. "The Debts of History: Southern Honor, Affirmative Action, and Faulkner's *Intruder in the Dust.*" *The Faulkner Journal* 17.1 (Fall 2001): 37–57.

Dutoit, Thomas. "Translating the Name?" *On the Name.* By Jacques Derrida. Trans. John P. Leavey. Ed. Thomas Dutoit. Stanford, CA: Stanford UP, 1995. ix–xvi.

Duvall, John N. *Faulkner's Marginal Couple: Invisible, Outlaw, and Unspeakable Communities.* Austin, TX: U of Texas P, 1990.

Derrida, Jacques. "'A Strange Nigger': Faulkner and the Minstrel Performance of Whiteness." *The Faulkner Journal* 22.1/2 (Fall 2006/Spring 2007): 106–19.

Eaglestone, Robert. *The Broken Voice: Reading Post-Holocaust Literature.* Oxford, UK: Oxford UP, 2017.

———. *The Holocaust and the Postmodern.* Oxford, UK: Oxford UP, 2004.

Eagleton, Terry. *Literary Theory: An Introduction.* 1983. 2nd ed. Minneapolis, MN: U of Minnesota P, 1996.

Earle, David M. "Faulkner and the Paperback Trade." *William Faulkner in Context.* Ed. John T. Matthews. Cambridge, UK: Cambridge UP, 2015. 231–45.

Eisenman, Peter. "Misreading." *Eisenman Inside Out: Selected Writings, 1963–1988.* New Haven, CT: Yale UP, 2004. 208–25.

Eliot, T. S. "The Love Song of J. Alfred Prufrock." 1917. *Selected Poems.* London: Faber and Faber, 1954. 11–16.

———. "Philip Massinger." 1920. *Selected Essays.* London: Harcourt, Brace, 1950. 181–95.

Evans, David H. *William Faulkner, William James, and the American Pragmatic Tradition.* Baton Rouge, LA: Louisiana State UP, 2008.

Fargnoli, A. Nicholas, Michael Golay, and Robert W. Hamblin. *Critical Companion to William Faulkner: A Literary Reference to His Life and Work.* New York: Infobase, 2008.

Faulkner, John. *My Brother Bill: An Affectionate Reminiscence.* New York: Trident, 1963.

Faulkner, William. "Ad Astra." 1931. *Collected Stories of William Faulkner.* New York: Vintage, 1995a. 407–29.

———. "Address to the Graduating Class, University High School, Oxford, Mississippi." 28 May 1951. *William Faulkner: Essays, Speeches and Public Letters.* Ed. James B. Meriwether. New York: Random House, 2004a. 122–24.

———. "Address upon Receiving the Nobel Prize for Literature." 10 December 1950. *William Faulkner: Essays, Speeches and Public Letters.* Ed. James B. Meriwether. New York: Random House, 2004b. 119–21.

———. "Appendix: The Compsons." *The Portable Faulkner.* 1946. Ed. Malcolm Cowley. Harmondsworth, UK: Penguin, 1977a. 704–21.

———. "Barn Burning." 1939. *Collected Stories of William Faulkner.* New York: Vintage, 1995b. 3–25.

———. "Carcassonne." 1926. *Collected Stories of William Faulkner.* New York: Vintage, 1995c. 895–900.

———. "Classroom Statements at the University of Mississippi." 1947. *Lion in the Garden: Interviews with William Faulkner, 1926–1962.* Ed. James B. Meriwether and Michael Millgate. New York: Random, 1968a. 52–58.

———. "Department of Psychiatry." 7 May 1958. *Faulkner in the University.* Ed. Frederick L. Gwynn and Joseph L. Blotner. New York: Vintage, 1959a. 267–69.

———. "Distillate." 2 January 1957. "Lost Classic: The People-to-People Project." Introd. and ed. Caroline Henze-Gongola and Jeb Livingood. *Meridian: The Semi-Annual from the University of Virginia* 18 (January 2007): 54.

———. *Elmer. Mississippi Quarterly* 36.1 (Winter 1983): 337–460.

———. "The English Club. A Word to Young Writers." 24 April 1958. *Faulkner in the University.* Ed. Frederick L. Gwynn and Joseph L. Blotner. New York: Vintage, 1959b. 241–48.

———. *Faulkner at West Point.* 1964. Ed. Joseph L. Fant and Robert Ashley. Jackson, MS: UP of Mississippi, 2002.

———. "Faulkner in Manila." 1955. *Lion in the Garden: Interviews with William Faulkner, 1926–1962.* Ed. James B. Meriwether and Michael Millgate. New York: Random House, 1968b. 199–214.

———. "Funeral Sermon for Mammy Caroline Barr." 5 February 1940. *William Faulkner: Essays, Speeches and Public Letters.* Ed. James B. Meriwether. New York: Random House, 2004c. 275–76.

———. "Graduate Course in the Novel." 13 May 1957. *Faulkner in the University.* Ed. Frederick L. Gwynn and Joseph L. Blotner. New York: Vintage, 1959c. 135–45.

————. "Interview with Betty Beale." 1957. *Lion in the Garden: Interviews with William Faulkner, 1926–1962*. Ed. James B. Meriwether and Michael Millgate. New York: Random House, 1968c. 267–69.

————. "Interview with Cynthia Grenier." 1955. *Lion in the Garden: Interviews with William Faulkner, 1926–1962*. Ed. James B. Meriwether and Michael Millgate. New York: Random House, 1968d. 215–27.

————. "Interview with Jean Stein vanden Heuvel." 1956. *Lion in the Garden: Interviews with William Faulkner, 1926–1962*. Ed. James B. Meriwether and Michael Millgate. New York: Random House, 1968e. 237–56.

————. "Interview with John K. Hutchens." October 1948. *Lion in the Garden: Interviews with William Faulkner, 1926–1962*. Ed. James B. Meriwether and Michael Millgate. New York: Random House, 1968f. 59–60.

————. "Interview with Loïc Bouvard." 1952. *Lion in the Garden: Interviews with William Faulkner, 1926–1962*. Ed. James B. Meriwether and Michael Millgate. New York: Random House, 1968g. 68–73.

————. "Interview with Russell Howe." 4 March 1956. *Lion in the Garden: Interviews with William Faulkner, 1926–1962*. Ed. James B. Meriwether and Michael Millgate. New York: Random House, 1968h. 257–64.

————. "Interview with Simon Claxton." 23 March 1962. *Lion in the Garden: Interviews with William Faulkner, 1926–1962*. Ed. James B. Meriwether and Michael Millgate. New York: Random House, 1968i. 270–81.

————. "Interviews in Japan: Colloquies at Nagano Seminar." 1955. *Lion in the Garden: Interviews with William Faulkner, 1926–1962*. Ed. James B. Meriwether and Michael Millgate. New York: Random House, 1968j. 101–63.

————. "Knight's Gambit." *Knight's Gambit*. New York: Vintage, 1978a. 147–258.

————. "Law School Wives." 16 May 1957. *Faulkner in the University*. Ed. Frederick L. Gwynn and Joseph L. Blotner. New York: Vintage, 1959d. 153–70.

————. *The Marionettes*. 1920. Introd. Noel Polk. Charlottesville, VA: UP of Virginia, 1978b.

————. "Notes on a Horse Thief." Greenville, MS: Levee, 1951.

————. "On Privacy (The American Dream: What Happened to It?)." July 1955. *William Faulkner: Essays, Speeches and Public Letters*. Ed. James B. Meriwether. New York: Random House, 2004d. 62–75.

————. "A Rose for Emily." 1930. *Collected Stories of William Faulkner*. New York: Vintage, 1995d. 119–30.

————. "To Albert Erskine." c. 7 May 1959. *Selected Letters of William Faulkner*. Ed. Joseph Blotner. London: Scolar, 1977b. 429–30.

————. "To Harold Ober." 19 March 1945. *Selected Letters of William Faulkner*. Ed. Joseph Blotner. London: Scolar, 1977c. 190–91.

————. "To Harold Ober." 1 February 1948. *Selected Letters of William Faulkner*. Ed. Joseph Blotner. London: Scolar, 1977d. 262.

———. "To Malcolm A. Franklin." 5 December 1942. *Selected Letters of William Faulkner.* Ed. Joseph Blotner. London: Scolar, 1977e. 165–66.

———. "To Malcolm Cowley." 20 September 1945. *Selected Letters of William Faulkner.* Ed. Joseph Blotner. London: Scolar, 1977f. 202–3.

———. "To Malcolm Cowley." 23 April 1946. *Selected Letters of William Faulkner.* Ed. Joseph Blotner. London: Scolar, 1977g. 233.

———. "To Mrs. M. C. Falkner." 18 August 1925. *Selected Letters of William Faulkner.* Ed. Joseph Blotner. London: Scolar, 1977h. 13.

———. "To the President of the League of American Writers." 1938. *William Faulkner: Essays, Speeches and Public Letters.* Ed. James B. Meriwether. New York: Random House, 2004e. 198.

———. "To Robert K. Haas." 15 January 1944. *Selected Letters of William Faulkner.* Ed. Joseph Blotner. London: Scolar, 1977i. 180.

———. "To Robert K. Haas." 5 May 1946. *Selected Letters of William Faulkner.* Ed. Joseph Blotner. London: Scolar, 1977j. 233–34.

———. "To Robert K. Haas." 3 June 1946. *Selected Letters of William Faulkner.* Ed. Joseph Blotner. London: Scolar, 1977k. 237–38.

———. "Undergraduate Course in Contemporary Literature." 9 March 1957. *Faulkner in the University.* Ed. Frederick L. Gwynn and Joseph L. Blotner. New York: Vintage, 1959e. 37–44.

———. "Undergraduate Course in Contemporary Literature." 11 March 1957. *Faulkner in the University.* Ed. Frederick L. Gwynn and Joseph L. Blotner. New York: Vintage, 1959f. 45–56.

———. "University and Community Public." 23 May 1958. *Faulkner in the University.* Ed. Frederick L. Gwynn and Joseph L. Blotner. New York: Vintage, 1959g. 285–86.

———. "Visitors from Virginia Colleges." 15 April 1957. *Faulkner in the University.* Ed. Frederick L. Gwynn and Joseph L. Blotner. New York: Vintage, 1959. 83–88.

———. "Wealthy Jew." *New Orleans Sketches.* 1925. Introd. Carvel Collins. New Brunswick, NJ: Rutgers UP, 1958. 37–38.

———. *William Faulkner Novels 1926–1929:* Soldiers' Pay, Mosquitoes, Flags in the Dust, The Sound and the Fury. Ed. Joseph Blotner and Noel Polk. New York: Library of America, 2006.

———. *William Faulkner Novels 1930–1935:* As I Lay Dying, Sanctuary, Light in August, Pylon. Ed. Joseph Blotner and Noel Polk. New York: Library of America, 1985.

———. *William Faulkner Novels 1936–1940:* Absalom, Absalom!, The Unvanquished, If I Forget Thee, Jerusalem, The Hamlet. Ed. Joseph Blotner and Noel Polk. New York: Library of America, 1990.

———. *William Faulkner Novels 1942–1954:* Go Down, Moses, Intruder in the Dust, Requiem for a Nun, A Fable. Ed. Joseph Blotner and Noel Polk. New York: Library of America, 1994.

———, William. *William Faulkner Novels 1957–1962:* The Town, The Mansion, The Reivers. Ed. Joseph Blotner and Noel Polk. New York: Library of America, 1999.

Fenton, Charles. *The Apprenticeship of Ernest Hemingway: The Early Years.* New York: Farrar, Straus and Young, 1954.

Foote, Shelby. "Five Stories, One Novella and Crime Themes Comprise Faulkner's Newest Collection." Greenville *Delta Democrat-Times.* 13 November 1949: 18.

Fowler, Doreen. "Eleusinian Mysteries in *The Sound and the Fury.*" *Faulkner and Religion.* Ed. Doreen Fowler and Ann J. Abadie. Jackson, MS: UP of Mississippi, 1991. 140–56.

Franklin, Benjamin. *Writings:* The Autobiography, Poor Richard's Almanack, *Bagatelles, Pamphlets, Essays, and Letters.* Ed. Joseph A. Leo Lemay. New York: Library of America, 1987.

Frazer, James George. *The Golden Bough: A Study in Magic and Religion.* 1890. 12 vols. London: Macmillan, 1911–15.

Frost, Robert. "The Gift Outright." 1941. *Robert Frost: Collected Poems, Prose, and Plays.* Ed. Richard Poirier and Mark Richardson. New York: Library of America, 1995. 316.

Fruscione, Joseph. "Rivalry and Influence in the Afternoon: Faulkner, Hemingway, and *If I Forget Thee, Jerusalem.*" *South Atlantic Review* 71.4 (Fall 2006): 78–98.

Fulton, Joe B. *Mark Twain's Ethical Realism: The Aesthetics of Race, Class, and Gender.* Columbia, MO: U of Missouri P, 1997.

Gautier, Théophile. *Mademoiselle de Maupin.* 1835. Paris: Charpentier, 1892.

Gerhardt, Uta. "Charismatische Herrschaft und Massenmord im Nationalsozialismus. Eine soziologische These zum Thema der freiwilligen Verbrechen an Juden." *Geschichte und Gesellschaft* (October–December 1998): 503–38.

Gerstenberger, Donna. "Meaning and Form in *Intruder in the Dust.*" *College English* 23.3 (December 1961): 223–25.

Glover, Jonathan. *I: The Philosophy and Psychology of Personal Identity.* London: Allen Lane, 1988.

Godden, Richard. "*A Fable* … Whispering about the Wars." *The Faulkner Journal* 17.2 (Spring 2002): 25–88.

———. *William Faulkner: An Economy of Complex Words.* Princeton, NJ: Princeton UP, 2007.

Goff, Stan. *Borderline: Reflections on War, Sex, and Church.* Eugene, OR: Wipf and Stock, 2015.

Gold, Joseph. *William Faulkner: A Study in Humanism from Metaphor to Discourse.* Norman, OK: U of Oklahoma P, 1966.

Golomstock, Igor. *Totalitarian Art: In the Soviet Union, the Third Reich, Fascist Italy and the People's Republic of China*. New York: HarperCollins, 1990.

Grant, Julia. *Raising Baby by the Book: The Education of American Mothers*. New Haven, CT: Yale UP, 1998.

Green, Mitchell. "How and What We Can Learn from Fiction." *A Companion to the Philosophy of Literature*. Ed. Garry L. Hagberg and Walter Jost. Chichester, UK: Wiley, 2010. 350–66.

Greenberg, Kenneth S. *Honor and Slavery: Lies, Duels, Noses, Masks, Dressing as a Woman, Gifts, Strangers, Humanitarianism, Death, Slave Rebellions, the Proslavery Argument, Baseball, Hunting, and Gambling in the Old South*. Princeton, NJ: Princeton UP, 1996.

Gresset, Michel. *Fascination: Faulkner's Fiction, 1919–1936*. Durham, NC: Duke UP, 1989.

Gresset, Michel, and Noel Polk. *Intertextuality in Faulkner*. Jackson, MS: UP of Mississippi, 1985.

Griffin, Roger. *Modernism and Fascism: The Sense of a Beginning under Mussolini and Hitler*. Basingstoke, UK: Palgrave Macmillan, 2007.

Grimwood, Michael. *Heart in Conflict: Faulkner's Struggles with Vocation*. 1987. Athens, GA: U of Georgia P, 2009.

Habermas, Jürgen. "Modernity versus Postmodernity." 1981. Trans. Seyla Ben-Habib. *Modernity: Critical Concepts*. Vol. 4. *After Modernity*. Ed. Malcolm Waters. London: Routledge, 1999. 5–16.

Hale, Grace Elizabeth, and Robert Jackson. "'We're Trying Hard as Hell to Free Ourselves': Southern History and Race in the Making of William Faulkner's Literary Terrain." *A Companion to William Faulkner*. Ed. Richard C. Moreland. Malden, MA: Blackwell, 2007. 28–45.

Hamblin, Robert W. "*Intruder in the Dust*." *A William Faulkner Encyclopedia*. Ed. Robert W. Hamblin and Charles A. Peek. Westport, CT: Greenwood, 1999. 199–201.

———. *Myself and the World: A Biography of William Faulkner*. Jackson, MS: UP of Mississippi, 2016.

———. "Teaching *Intruder in the Dust* through Its Political and Historical Context." *Teaching Faulkner: Approaches and Methods*. Ed. Stephen Hahn and Robert W. Hamblin. Westport, CT: Greenwood, 2001. 151–62.

Hamilton, Victoria. "Personal Reminiscences of John Bowlby." *Tavistock Gazette* (Autumn 1991): 18.

Hanks, Patrick, Flavia Hodges, and Kate Hardcastle. *A Dictionary of First Names*. Oxford, UK: Oxford UP, 2006.

Hassan, Ihab. "Fundamentalism and Literature." *The Georgia Review* 62.1 (Spring 2008): 16–29.

————. "The Privations of Postmodernism: Faulkner as Exemplar (A Meditation in Ten Parts)." *Faulkner and Postmodernism*. Ed. John N. Duvall and Ann J. Abadie. Jackson, MS: UP of Mississippi, 2002. 1–18.

Hatlen, Burton. "'Song of the Rolling Earth, A' (1856)." *Walt Whitman: An Encyclopedia*. Ed. J. R. LeMaster and Donald D. Kummings. Abingdon, UK: Routledge, 1998. 665–66.

Hays, Peter L. "Modernism and the American Novel." *A Companion to the American Novel*. 2012. Ed. Alfred Bendixen. Chichester, UK: Wiley-Blackwell, 2015. 60–75.

Healy, W., A. F. Bronner, E. M. H. Baylor, and J. P. Murphy. *Reconstructing Behavior in Youth: A Study of Problem Children in Foster Families*. New York: Knopf, 1929.

Hemingway, Ernest. "American Bohemians in Paris." 25 March 1922. *Dateline: Toronto. The Complete* Toronto Star *Dispatches, 1920–1924*. 1985. Ed. William White. New York: Simon and Schuster, 2002. 148–50.

————. "The Art of the Short Story." 1959. *New Critical Approaches to the Short Stories of Ernest Hemingway*. Ed. Jackson J. Benson. Durham, NC: Duke UP, 1990. 2–13.

————. "The Battler." 1925. *The Complete Short Stories of Ernest Hemingway*. 1987. Foreword John, Patrick, and Gregory Hemingway. Preface Charles Scribner, Jr. New York: Scribner, 2003. 97–104.

————. *Death in the Afternoon*. New York: Scribner, 1932.

————. *A Moveable Feast*. New York: Scribner, 1964.

Henze-Gongola, Caroline, and Jeb Livingood. "Introduction." "Lost Classic: The People-to-People Project." Ed. Caroline Henze-Gongola and Jeb Livingood. *Meridian: The Semi-Annual from the University of Virginia* 18 (January 2007): 48–89.

Hinkle, James C., and Robert McCoy. *Reading Faulkner*. The Unvanquished: *Glossary and Commentary*. Jackson, MS: UP of Mississippi, 1995.

Hlavsa, Virginia V. "The Crucifixion in *Light in August*: Suspending Rules at the Post." *Faulkner and Religion*. Ed. Doreen Fowler and Ann J. Abadie. Jackson, MS: UP of Mississippi, 1991. 127–39.

————. "*The Golden Bough*." *A William Faulkner Encyclopedia*. Ed. Robert W. Hamblin and Charles A. Peek. Westport, CT: Greenwood, 1999. 152–54.

Hoffman, Daniel. *Faulkner's Country Matters: Folklore and Fable in Yoknapatawpha*. Baton Rouge, LA: Louisiana State UP, 1989.

Holmes, Jeremy. *John Bowlby and Attachment Theory*. London: Routledge, 1993.

The Holy Bible. Revised Standard Edition. New York: Collins, 1973.

Hönnighausen, Lothar. "The Impact of the Arts on Faulkner's Writing." *Special Issue: William Faulkner: German Responses*. Spec. issue of *Amerikastudien/ American Studies* 42.4 (Winter 1997): 559–71.

Horowitz, Daniel. *The Morality of Spending: Attitudes toward the Consumer Society in America, 1875–1940*. Baltimore, MD: Johns Hopkins UP, 1985.

Howe, Irving. "The Southern Myth and William Faulkner." *American Quarterly* 3.4 (Winter 1951): 357–62.

Hughes, Henry Trevor. *The Piety of Jeremy Taylor*. London: Macmillan, 1960.

Hulbert, Ann. *Raising America: Experts, Parents, and a Century of Advice about Children*. New York: Knopf, 2003.

Irwin, John T. *Doubling and Incest/Repetition and Revenge: A Speculative Reading of Faulkner*. 1975. Baltimore, MD: Johns Hopkins UP, 1996.

Issroff, Judith. "Bowlby and Winnicott: Differences, Ideas, Influences." *Donald Winnicott and John Bowlby: Personal and Professional Perspectives*. Ed. Judith Issroff. London: Karnac, 2005a. 115–78.

———. "Winnicott and Bowlby: Personal Reminiscences." *Donald Winnicott and John Bowlby: Personal and Professional Perspectives*. Ed. Judith Issroff. London: Karnac, 2005b. 13–69.

Jacobi, Mary Putnam. "The Prophylaxis of Insanity." *Archives of Medicine* 6.2 (October 1881): 120–35.

Jameson, Fredric. *The Antinomies of Realism*. London: Verso, 2013.

Jewish Virtual Library. "Hohenzollern." Web. 4 January 2020. https://www.jewishvirtuallibrary.org/hohenzollern.

John, Eileen. "Literature and the Idea of Morality." *A Companion to the Philosophy of Literature*. Ed. Garry L. Hagberg and Walter Jost. Chichester, UK: Wiley, 2010. 285–99.

Johnson, Robert L. "William Faulkner, Calvinism and the Presbyterians." *Journal of Presbyterian History* 57.1 (Spring 1979): 66–81.

Johnson, Susie Paul. "*Pylon*: Faulkner's Waste Land." *The Mississippi Quarterly* 38.3 (Summer 1985): 287–94.

Jones, Kathleen W. *Taming the Troublesome Child: American Families, Child Guidance, and the Limits of Psychiatric Authority*. Cambridge, MA: Harvard UP, 1999.

Kahan, Alan S. "Checks and Balances for Democratic Souls: Alexis de Tocqueville on Religion in Democratic Societies." *American Political Thought* 4.1 (Winter 2015a): 100–19.

Kahan, Alan S. *Tocqueville, Democracy, and Religion: Checks and Balances for Democratic Souls*. Oxford, UK: Oxford UP, 2015b.

Karen, Robert. *Becoming Attached: First Relationships and How They Shape Our Capacity to Love*. Oxford, UK: Oxford UP, 1998.

Karl, Frederick R. *William Faulkner: American Writer. A Biography*. New York: Weidenfeld and Nicolson, 1989.

Kartiganer, Donald M. "*Absalom, Absalom!*: The Discovery of Values." *On Faulkner: The Best from American Literature*. Ed. Louis J. Budd and Edwin H. Cady. Durham, NC: Duke UP, 1989. 42–57.

Kazin, Alfred. "William Faulkner and Religion: Determinism, Compassion, and the God of Defeat." *Faulkner and Religion*. Ed. Doreen Fowler and Ann J. Abadie. Jackson, MS: UP of Mississippi, 1991. 3–20.

Kermode, Frank. "Endings, Continued." *Languages of the Unsayable: The Play of Negativity in Literature and Literary Theory*. Introd. and ed. Sanford Budick and Wolfgang Iser. New York: Columbia UP, 1989. 71–94.

———. *The Genesis of Secrecy: On the Interpretation of Narrative*. Cambridge, MA: Harvard UP, 1979.

———. *Pleasure and Change: The Aesthetics of Canon*. Introd. and ed. Robert Alter. Oxford, UK: Oxford UP, 2004.

Kershaw, Ian. *The Nazi Dictatorship: Problems and Perspectives of Interpretation*. London: Bloomsbury, 2000.

Kierkegaard, Søren. *Either/Or: A Fragment of Life*. 1843. 2 vols. Ed. David Ferdinand Swenson, Lillian Marvin Swenson, and Walter Lowrie. Princeton, NJ: Princeton UP, 1949.

———. *Fear and Trembling*. 1843. Trans. Alastair Hannay. London: Penguin, 1985.

———. *The Present Age: On the Death of Rebellion*. 1846. Trans. Alexander Dru. 1940. New York: HarperCollins, 1962.

———. *The Sickness unto Death*. 1849. Trans. Alastair Hannay. London: Penguin, 1989.

King, Richard H. "*A Fable*: Faulkner's Political Novel?" *The Southern Literary Journal* 17.2 (Spring 1985): 3–17.

———. "World-Rejection in Faulkner's Fiction." *Faulkner and Religion*. Ed. Doreen Fowler and Ann J. Abadie. Jackson, MS: UP of Mississippi, 1991. 65–84.

Kloppenberg, James T. "Rethinking Tradition: Sidgwick and the Philosophy of the Via Media." 1992. *Essays on Henry Sidgwick*. Ed. Bart Schultz. Cambridge, UK: Cambridge UP, 2002. 369–96.

Kloppenberg, James T. *Uncertain Victory: Social Democracy and Progressivism in European and American Thought, 1870–1920*. Oxford, UK: Oxford UP, 1986.

Kodat, Catherine Gunther. "Writing *A Fable* for America." *Faulkner in America*. Ed. Joseph R. Urgo and Ann J. Abadie. Jackson, MS: UP of Mississippi, 2001. 82–97.

Kofman, Sarah. *Paroles suffoquées*. Paris: Éditions Galilée, 1987.

Kristeva, Julia. *Powers of Horror: An Essay on Abjection*. Trans. Leon S. Roudiez. New York: Columbia UP, 1982.

Kutzik, Alfred J. "Faulkner and the Jews." *YIVO Annual of Jewish Social Science* 13 (1965): 213–26.

Lacan, Jacques. *The Four Fundamental Concepts of Psycho-Analysis*. 1973. Trans. Alan Sheridan. Ed. Jacques-Alain Miller. London: Penguin, 1977.

Ladd, Barbara. "Faulkner's Paris: State and Metropole in *A Fable*." *Special Issue: Faulkner and the Metropolis*. Spec. issue of *The Faulkner Journal* 26.1 (Spring 2012): 115–28.

Law, David R. *Kierkegaard's Kenotic Christology*. Oxford, UK: Oxford UP, 2013.

Lecky, William. *History of European Morals from Augustus to Charlemagne*. 2 vols. New York: Appleton, 1869.

Lehner, Ernst, and Johanna Lehner. *Folklore and Symbolism of Flowers, Plants and Trees*. 1960. New York: Courier, 2003.

Lenski, R. C. H. *The Interpretation of St. John's Gospel 11–21*. Minneapolis, MN: Augsburg Fortress, 1942.

Lentricchia, Frank. *After the New Criticism*. Chicago, IL: U of Chicago P, 1980.

Lester, Cheryl. "'What the Future Will Now Bring Forth': Reminiscing for Posterity in *The Reivers*." *Fifty Years after Faulkner*. Ed. Jay Watson and Ann J. Abadie. Jackson, MS: UP of Mississippi, 2016. 274–87.

Lewisohn, Ludwig. *A Modern Book of Criticism*. New York: Boni and Liveright, 1919.

Livingston, Paisley. *Literature and Rationality: Ideas of Agency in Theory and Fiction*. Cambridge, UK: Cambridge UP, 1991.

Lowe, John. "*The Unvanquished*: Faulkner's Nietzschean Skirmish with the Civil War." *Special Issue: William Faulkner*. Spec. issue of *The Mississippi Quarterly* 46.3 (Summer 1993): 407–36.

Lyotard, Jean-François. "Answer to the Question, 'What is the Postmodern?'" 15 May 1982. *The Postmodern Explained: Correspondence 1982–1985*. 1992. Trans. Don Barry et al. Ed. Julian Pefanis and Morgan Thomas. Minneapolis, MN: U of Minnesota P, 2003a. 1–16.

———. "Apostil on Narratives." 6 February 1984. *The Postmodern Explained: Correspondence 1982–1985*. 1992. Trans. Don Barry et al. Ed. Julian Pefanis and Morgan Thomas. Minneapolis, MN: U of Minnesota P, 2003b. 17–21.

———. "Note on the Meaning of 'Post-'." 1 May 1985. *The Postmodern Explained: Correspondence 1982–1985*. 1992. Trans. Don Barry et al. Ed. Julian Pefanis and Morgan Thomas. Minneapolis, MN: U of Minnesota P, 2003c. 75–80.

Madden, Deborah, and David Towsey. "Derrida, Faith and St Paul." *Literature and Theology* 16.4 (December 2002): 396–409.

Mahaffey, Vicki. *Modernist Literature: Challenging Fictions?* Malden, MA: Blackwell, 2007.

Margolis, Maxine L. *Mothers and Such: Views of American Women and Why They Changed*. Berkeley, CA: U of California P, 1984

Marion, Jean-Luc. *Being Given: Toward a Phenomenology of Givenness*. Trans. Jeffrey L. Kosky. Stanford, CA: Stanford UP, 2002.

———. *The Visible and the Revealed*. Trans. Christina M. Gschwandtner. New York: Fordham UP, 2008.

Marrone, Mario. *Attachment and Interaction: From Bowlby to Current Clinical Theory and Practice*. 1998. 2nd ed. London: Kingsley, 2014.

Martin, Christopher D. "Ernest Hemingway: A Psychological Autopsy of a Suicide." *Psychiatry: Interpersonal and Biological Processes* 69.4 (Winter 2006): 351–61.

Martin, Jay. "Faulkner's 'Male Commedia': The Triumph of Manly Grief." *Faulkner and Psychology.* Ed. Donald M. Kartiganer and Ann J. Abadie. Jackson, MS: UP of Mississippi, 1994. 123–64.

———. "'The Whole Burden of Man's History of His Impossible Heart's Desire': The Early Life of William Faulkner." *American Literature* 53.4 (January 1982a): 607–29.

Martin, Stoddard. *Wagner to* The Waste Land*: A Study of the Relationship of Wagner to English Literature.* London: Macmillan, 1982b.

Matthews, John T. Introduction. *William Faulkner in Context.* Ed. John T. Matthews. Cambridge, UK: Cambridge UP, 2015. 1–7.

———. "The Marriage of Speaking and Hearing in *Absalom, Absalom!*" *English Literary History* 47.3 (Autumn 1980): 575–94.

———. *William Faulkner: Seeing through the South.* Chichester, UK: Wiley, 2009.

McAteer, John. "The Gifts of God for the People of God: Communion as Derrida's Impossible Gift." *Gift and Economy: Ethics, Hospitality and the Market.* Ed. Eric R. Severson. Newcastle upon Tyne, UK: Cambridge Scholars, 2012. 59–74.

McElrath, Joseph R. "*Pylon*: The Portrait of a Lady." *Special Issue: William Faulkner.* Spec. issue of *The Mississippi Quarterly* 27.3 (Summer 1974): 277–90.

McNicoll, Geoffrey. "Review of *Reasons and Persons* by Derek Parfit." *Population and Development Review* 10.3 (September 1984): 545–47.

Millgate, Michael. *The Achievement of William Faulkner.* New York: Random House, 1966.

Minter, David L. *William Faulkner: His Life and Work.* 1980. Baltimore, MD: Johns Hopkins UP, 1997.

Mitchell, Andrew J., and Sam Slote. Introduction. "Derrida and Joyce: On Totality and Equivocation." *Derrida and Joyce: Texts and Contexts.* Ed. Andrew J. Mitchell and Sam Slote. New York: State U of New York P, 2013. 1–16.

Moore, Mark E. *Kenotic Politics: The Reconfiguration of Power in Jesus' Political Praxis.* London: Bloomsbury, 2013.

Morgenstern, Oskar. "Perfect Foresight and Economic Equilibrium." 1935. *Selected Writings of Oskar Morgenstern.* Trans. Frank Knight. Ed. Andrew Schotter. New York: New York UP, 1976. 169–83.

Moses, A. Dirk. "Conceptual Blockages and Definition Dilemmas in the 'Racial Century': Genocides of Indigenous Peoples and the Holocaust." *Patterns of Prejudice* 36.4 (2002): 7–36.

Moshman, David. "Conceptual Constraints on Thinking about Genocide." *Journal of Genocide Research* 3.3 (2001): 431–50.

Mumford, Lewis. "What Is a City?" 1939. *The City Reader.* Ed. Richard T. LeGates and Frederic Stout. Abingdon, UK: Routledge, 1996. 183–88.

Murdoch, Iris. "Literature and Philosophy: A Conversation with Bryan Magee." *Existentialists and Mystics: Writings on Philosophy and Literature.* 1997. Foreword George Steiner. Ed. Peter J. Conradi. London: Penguin, 1998. 3–30.

———. *Metaphysics as a Guide to Morals.* 1992. London: Vintage, 2003.

Murphet, Julian. *Faulkner's Media Romance.* Oxford, UK: Oxford UP, 2017.

Nabokov, Vladimir. "TV-13 NY." September 1965. *Strong Opinions.* New York: McGraw Hill, 1973. 51–61.

Nelson, Paul David. "Cost of the Civil War." *American Civil War: The Definitive Encyclopedia and Document Collection.* Ed. Spencer C. Tucker. 6 vols. Santa Barbara, CA: ABC-CLIO, 2013. 442.

Newhouse, Wade. "'Aghast and Uplifted': William Faulkner and the Absence of History." *The Faulkner Journal* 21.1/2 (Fall 2005/2006): 145–165.

Nichols, Aidan. *Lost in Wonder: Essays on Liturgy and the Arts.* 2011. Abingdon, UK: Routledge, 2016.

Nussbaum, Martha C. *Love's Knowledge.* New York: Oxford UP, 1990.

———. "Perceptive Equilibrium: Literary Theory and Ethical Theory." 1987. *A Companion to the Philosophy of Literature.* Ed. Garry Hagberg and Walter Jost. Chichester, UK: Wiley, 2010. 241–67.

O'Connor, William Van. *The Tangled Fire of William Faulkner.* Minneapolis, MN: U of Minnesota P, 1954.

Olderr, Steven. *Symbolism: A Comprehensive Dictionary.* Jefferson, NC: McFarland, 2012.

O'Neill, Barry. *Honor, Symbols, and War.* 1999. Ann Arbor, MI: U of Michigan P, 2001.

Paddock, Lisa. "'Trifles with a tragic profundity': The Importance of 'Mistral.'" *Special Issue: William Faulkner.* Spec. issue of *The Mississippi Quarterly* 32.3 (Summer 1979): 413–22.

Parfit, Derek. *On What Matters.* 3 vols. Oxford, UK: Oxford UP, 2011–2017.

———. *Reasons and Persons.* 1984. Oxford, UK: Oxford UP, 1987.

Parini, Jay. *One Matchless Time: A Life of William Faulkner.* New York: HarperCollins, 2004.

Peirce, Charles Sanders. *Principles of Philosophy.* 1931. Vol. 1 of *The Collected Papers of Charles Sanders Peirce.* Ed. Charles Hartshorne and Paul Weiss. 6 vols. Cambridge, MA: Harvard UP, 1931–1935

———. *Reviews, Correspondence, and Bibliography.* Vol. 8 of *The Collected Papers of Charles Sanders Peirce.* Ed. Arthur W. Burks. 2 vols. Cambridge, MA: Harvard UP, 1958.

Peyser, Thomas. "Faulkner, Jews, and the New Deal: The Regional Commitments of 'Barn Burning.'" *The Cambridge Quarterly* 42.1 (March 2013): 1–19.

Pitavy, François. "Le Reporter: Tentation et derision de l'ecriture." *Ranam* IX (Summer 1976): 95–108.

————. "The Two Orders in *A Fable*: A Reappraisal of Faulkner's 'Elephant.'" *Special Issue: William Faulkner.* Spec. issue of *The Mississippi Quarterly* 62.3 (Summer 2009): 381–425.

Polk, Noel. *Faulkner and Welty and the Southern Literary Tradition.* Jackson, MS: UP of Mississippi, 2008.

————. "William Faulkner's *Marionettes.*" *Special Issue: William Faulkner.* Spec. issue of *The Mississippi Quarterly* 26.3 (Summer 1973): 247–80.

Posada, Germán. "Attachment." *Social and Emotional Development in Infancy and Early Childhood.* Ed. Janette B. Benson and Marshall M. Haith. Denver, CO: Elsevier, 2009. 30–40.

Pound, Ezra. "What is Money for?" 1939. *Ezra Pound. Selected Prose 1909–1965.* Ed. William Cookson. New York: New Directions, 1973. 290–302.

Poundstone, William. *Prisoner's Dilemma: John von Neumann, Game Theory, and the Puzzle of the Bomb.* Oxford, UK: Oxford UP, 1993.

Pryse, Marjorie. "Miniaturizing Yoknapatawpha: *The Unvanquished* as Faulkner's Theory of Realism." *Special Issue: William Faulkner.* Spec. issue of *The Mississippi Quarterly* 33.3 (Summer 1980): 343–54.

Rawls, John. Foreword. 1982. *The Methods of Ethics.* By Henry Sidgwick. 1874. 7th ed. 1907. Indianapolis, IN: Hackett, 1981. v–vi.

Reedy, Elizabeth A. *American Babies: Their Life and Times in the 20th Century.* Westport, CT: Greenwood, 2007.

Ripstein, Arthur. "Private Order and Public Justice: Kant and Rawls." *Virginia Law Review* 92.7 (November 2006): 1391–438.

Riviere, Joan. "On the Genesis of Psychical Conflict in Earliest Infancy." 1936. *The Inner World and Joan Riviere: Collected Papers, 1920–1958.* Ed. Athol Hughes. London: Karnac, 1991. 272–300.

————. "The Unconscious Phantasy of an Inner World Reflected in Examples from Literature." 1952. *The Inner World and Joan Riviere: Collected Papers, 1920–1958.* Ed. Athol Hughes. London: Karnac, 1991. 302–30.

Robinson, Owen. *Creating Yoknapatawpha: Readers and Writers in Faulkner's Fiction.* Abingdon, UK: Routledge, 2006.

Rollyson, Carl E. "Faulkner, William." *The New Encyclopedia of Southern Culture.* Vol. 9. *Literature.* Ed. M. Thomas Inge. Chapel Hill, NC: U North Carolina P, 2014. 257–60.

Rommel, Lylas Dayton. "A Poetics of Shame and the Literary Meaning of Kenosis." PhD diss., U of Dallas, 2004.

Rorty, Richard. *Contingency, Irony, and Solidarity.* Cambridge, UK: Cambridge UP, 2005.

Rousseau, Jean-Jacques. *Émile, or On Education.* 1763. Trans. and ed. Christopher Kelly and Allan Bloom. Hanover, NH: UP of New England, 2010.

Rueckert, William H. *Faulkner from Within: Destructive and Generative Being in the Novels of William Faulkner.* West Lafayette, IN: Parlor P, 2004.

Russell, Bertrand. *Common Sense and Nuclear Warfare,* 1959. London: Routledge, 2013.

Samway, Patrick H. *Faulkner's* Intruder in the Dust: *A Critical Study of the Typescripts.* Troy, NY: Whitson, 1980.

Sarkar, Husain. *Kant and Parfit: The Groundwork of Morals.* New York: Routledge, 2018.

Sayer, Ian, and Jeremy Dronfield. *Hitler's Last Plot: The 139 VIP Hostages Selected for Death in the Final Days of World War II.* New York: Hachette, 2019.

Schneewind, Jerome B. *Sidgwick's Ethics and Victorian Moral Philosophy.* Oxford, UK: Clarendon, 1977.

Schulze, Franz. *Mies von der Rohe: A Critical Biography.* Chicago, IL: U of Chicago P, 1985.

Schwartz, Lawrence H. *Creating Faulkner's Reputation: The Politics of Modern Literary Criticism.* 1988. Knoxville, TN: U of Tennessee P, 1990.

Sedgwick, Timothy F. "The Anglican Exemplary Tradition." *Anglican Theological Review* 94.2 (Spring 2012): 207–31.

Segal, Alex. "Deconstruction, Radical Secrecy, and *The Secret Agent.*" *Modern Fiction Studies* 54.2 (Summer 2008): 189–208.

Sensibar, Judith L. *Faulkner and Love: The Women Who Shaped His Art.* New Haven, CT: Yale UP, 2009.

Severson, Eric R. "Introduction: Economy, Gift and Mystery." *Gift and Economy: Ethics, Hospitality and the Market.* Ed. Eric R. Severson. Newcastle upon Tyne, UK: Cambridge Scholars, 2012. 1–8.

Shakespeare, Alex. "Reading Hemingway's Baudelaire." *Literary Imagination* 14.2 (July 2012): 237–44.

Sharpe, Peter. "Bonds that Shackle: Memory, Violence, and Freedom in *The Unvanquished.*" *Special Issue: Faulkner, Memory, History.* Spec. issue of *The Faulkner Journal* 20.1/2 (Fall 2004/Spring 2005): 85–110.

Shirer, William L. *The Rise and Fall of the Third Reich: A History of Nazi Germany.* New York: Simon and Schuster, 1959.

Shoemaker, Sydney. "Review of *Reasons and Persons* by Derek Parfit." *Mind* 94.375 (July 1985): 443–53.

Shorter, Edward, and David Healy. *Shock Therapy: A History of Electroconvulsive Treatment in Mental Illness.* New Brunswick, NJ: Rutgers UP, 2007.

Shubik, Martin. "Game Theory at Princeton, 1949–1955: A Personal Reminiscence." *Towards a History of Game Theory.* Ed. E. Roy Weintraub. Durham, NC: Duke UP, 1992. 151–63.

Sicherman, Barbara. "The Paradox of Prudence: Mental Health in the Gilded Age." *The Journal of American History* 62.4 (March 1976): 890–912.

Sidgwick, Henry. "Alexis de Tocqueville." *Macmillan's Magazine* 5.25 (November 1861): 37–45.

———. *The Elements of Politics.* 1891. 2nd ed. London: Macmillan, 1897.

———. *The Methods of Ethics.* 1874. 7th ed. 1907. Foreword John Rawls. Indianapolis, IN: Hackett, 1981a.

———. *Outlines of the History of Ethics.* 1886. 5th ed. London: Macmillan, 1902.

———. "Preface to the First Edition." 1874. *The Methods of Ethics.* 1874. 7th ed. 1907. Foreword John Rawls. Indianapolis, IN: Hackett, 1981b. vii–viii.

———. "Preface to the Second Edition." 1877. *The Methods of Ethics.* 1874. 7th ed. 1907. Foreword John Rawls. Indianapolis, IN: Hackett, 1981c. ix–xiii.

———. "Preface to the Sixth Edition." 1901. *The Methods of Ethics.* 1874. 7th ed. 1907. Foreword John Rawls. Indianapolis, IN: Hackett, 1981d. xvi–xxiii.

———. *The Principles of Political Economy.* 1883. 2nd ed. London: Macmillan, 1887.

Singer, Marcus G. "The Many Methods of Sidgwick's Ethics." *Special Issue: Sidgwick and Moral Philosophy.* Spec. issue of *The Monist* 58.3 (July 1974): 420–48.

Skei, Hans H. *Reading Faulkner's Best Short Stories.* Columbia, SC: U of South Carolina P, 1999.

———. "William Faulkner's Short Stories." *A Companion to William Faulkner.* Ed. Richard C. Moreland. Malden, MA: Blackwell, 2007. 394–409.

Smith, Adam. *The Theory of Moral Sentiments, or, An Essay towards an Analysis of the Principles by which Men Naturally Judge, First of Their Neighbours, and afterwards of Themselves.* 1759. London: Bohn, 1853.

Smith, Barry, Hans Albert, David Armstrong, Ruth Barcan Marcus, Keith Campbell, Richard Glauser, Rudolf Haller, Massimo Mugnai, Kevin Mulligan, Lorenzo Peña, Willard van Orman Quine, Wolfgang Röd, Edmund Ruggaldier, Karl Schuhmann, Daniel Schulthess, Peter Simons, René Thom, Dallas Willard, and Jan Wolenski. "Derrida Degree a Question of Honour." Letter to the Editor. *The Times,* 9 May 1992, 13.

Snead, James A. "Litotes and Chiasmus: Cloaking Tropes in *Absalom, Absalom!*" *Faulkner's Discourse: An International Symposium.* Ed. Lothar Hönnighausen. Tübingen, Ger.: Niemeyer, 1989. 16–24.

Snow, C. P. "Challenge to the Intellect." *The Times Literary Supplement,* 15 August 1958, iii.

———. "The Two Cultures." *New Statesman,* 6 October 1956, 413–14.

———. *The Two Cultures.* 1959. Introd. Stefan Collini. Cambridge, UK: Cambridge UP, 2012.

Snyder, Glenn H., and Paul Diesing. *Conflict among Nations: Bargaining, Decision Making, and System Structure in International Crises.* Princeton, NJ: Princeton UP, 1977.

Sobolewski, Dorette. "The 'Grand Design' of Southern Class: Race and Class Constructs in Southern Society and William Faulkner's Literature." *Bonds and Borders: Identity, Imagination and Transformation in Literature.* Ed. Rebecca DeWald and Dorette Sobolewski. Newcastle upon Tyne, UK: Cambridge Scholars, 2011. 63–72.

Solomon, Stefan. "Faulkner and the Masses: A Hollywood Fable." *Faulkner and Film*. Ed. Peter Lurie and Ann J. Abadie. Jackson, MS: UP of Mississippi, 2014. 98–119.

Spivak, Gayatri Chakravorty. "Translator's Preface." *Of Grammatology*. 1974. By Jacques Derrida. Trans. Gayatri Chakravorty Spivak. Baltimore, MD: Johns Hopkins UP, 1997. ix–lxxxvii.

Spratling, William. "Chronicle of a Friendship." *Sherwood Anderson and Other Famous Creoles*. 1926. By William Spratling and William Faulkner. Austin, TX: U of Texas P, 1966. 11–16.

Stearns, Henry Putnam. *Insanity: Its Causes and Prevention*. New York: Putnam's, 1883.

Stone, Dan. *The Liberation of the Camps: The End of the Holocaust and Its Aftermath*. New Haven, CT: Yale UP, 2015.

Stoneback, H. R. "Golden Land." *A William Faulkner Encyclopedia*. Ed. Robert W. Hamblin and Charles A. Peek. Westport, CT: Greenwood, 1999. 155.

Stonum, Gary Lee. *Faulkner's Career: An Internal Literary History*. Ithaca, NY: Cornell UP, 1979.

Surette, Leon. *The Birth of Modernism: Ezra Pound, T. S. Eliot, W. B. Yeats, and the Occult*. London: McGill-Queen's UP, 1994.

Suttie, Ian D. *The Origins of Love and Hate*. London: Kegan Paul, 1935.

Sykes, John. "Faulkner, Calvinism, and Religion." *The Journal of Presbyterian History* 75.1 (Spring 1997): 43–53.

Taylor, Jeremy. *Holy Living and Dying: Together with Prayers: Containing the Whole Duty of a Christian, and the Parts of Devotion Fitted to All Occasions, and Furnished for All Necessities*. 1650. London: Duncan, 1837.

———. "Sermon X. The Minister's Duty in Life and Doctrine." 1672. *The Whole Works of the Right Rev. Jeremy Taylor*. Ed. Charles Page Eden. Vol. 8. London: Longmans, 1850. 499–518.

Taylor, Mark C. *Disfiguring: Art, Architecture, Religion*. Chicago, IL: U of Chicago P, 1992.

Tocqueville, Alexis de. *Democracy in America: Historical-Critical Edition of* De la démocratie en Amérique. 1835–40. Trans. James T. Schleifer. Ed. Eduardo Nolla. 4 vols. Indianapolis, IN: Liberty Fund, 2010.

———. *Journey to America*. 1831–32. Trans. George Lawrence. Ed. J. P. Mayer. London: Faber and Faber, 1959.

Towner, Theresa M. *Faulkner on the Color Line: The Later Novels*. Jackson, MS: UP of Mississippi, 2000.

Trials of War Criminals before the Nuernberg Military Tribunals under Control Council Law No. 10, Nuernberg, October 1946–April 1949. Vol. 4. Washington, DC: U.S. Government Printing Office, 1949.

Turner, Henry A. "Fascism and Modernization." *World Politics* 24.4 (July 1972): 547–64.

Urgo, Joseph R., and Noel Polk. *Reading Faulkner: Absalom, Absalom!* Jackson, MS: UP of Mississippi, 2010.

Valverde, Mariana. "Families, Private Property, and the State: The Dionnes and the Toronto Stock Derby." 1994. *Sexing the Maple: A Canadian Sourcebook.* Ed. Richard Cavell and Peter Dickinson. Peterborough, ON: Broadview P, 2006. 50–71.

Vicedo, Marga. "The Social Nature of the Mother's Tie to Her Child: John Bowlby's Theory of Attachment in Post-War America." *The British Journal for the History of Science* 44.3 (September 2011): 401–26.

Vickery, Olga W. *The Novels of William Faulkner: A Critical Interpretation.* Baton Rouge, LA: Louisiana State UP, 1959.

Virilio, Paul. *Art and Fear.* Trans. Julie Rose. London: Continuum, 2006.

Von Neumann, John. "Zur Theorie der Gesellschaftsspiele." December 1928. "On the Theory of Games of Strategy." Trans. Sonya Bargmann. *Annals of Mathematics Studies* 40 (1959): 13–42.

Wagoner, Hyatt H. *William Faulkner: From Jefferson to the World.* 1959. Lexington, KY: U of Kentucky P, 2014.

Watson, Jay. *Forensic Fictions: The Lawyer Figure in Faulkner.* 1993. Athens, GA: U of Georgia P, 2008.

———. *Reading for the Body: The Recalcitrant Materiality of Southern Fiction, 1893–1985.* Athens, GA: U of Georgia P, 2012.

Watt, Donald Cameron. How War Came: The Immediate Origins of the Second World War, 1938–1939. 1989. London: Random House, 2001.

Weinstein, Philip M. "'*And you are——*?': Faulkner's Mysteries of Race and Identity." *Faulkner and Mystery.* Ed. Annette Trefzer and Ann J. Abadie. Jackson, MS: UP of Mississippi, 2014. 3–18.

———. "Chronology of William Faulkner's Life and Works." *The Cambridge Companion to William Faulkner.* Ed. Philip M. Weinstein. Cambridge, UK: Cambridge UP, 1995. xv–xix.

Welling, Bart. "More News from Faulkner's Library." *The Mississippi Quarterly* 53.4 (Fall 2000): 583–89.

Werner, Gösta. "Fritz Lang and Goebbels: Myth and Facts." *Film Quarterly* 43.3 (Spring 1990): 24–27.

Whitman, Walt. "A Song of the Rolling Earth." 1881. *Leaves of Grass.* Philadelphia, PA: McKay, 1891–92. 176–80.

Williams, Bernard. *Ethics and the Limits of Philosophy.* 1985. London: Routledge, 2006.

Williams, John Davis. *The Compleat Strategyst: Being a Primer on the Theory of Games.* New York: McGraw-Hill, 1954.

Williams, Scott G. "Eating Faulkner Eating Baudelaire: Multiple Rewritings and Cultural Cannibalism." *The Faulkner Journal* 25.1 (Fall 2009): 65–84.

Williams, Trevor L. "History over Theology: The Case for Pinkie in Greene's *Brighton Rock*." *Special Issue: Dickens, Dostoevsky, Fielding, Golding, Greene, Lewis, Meredith*. Spec. issue of *Studies in the Novel* 24.1 (Spring 1992): 67–77.

Wyatt-Brown, Bertram. *Honor and Violence in the Old South*. Oxford, UK: Oxford UP, 1986.

Young, Philip. "Adventures of Nick Adams." *Nick Adams*. Introd. and ed. Harold Bloom. Philadelphia, PA: Chelsea House, 2004. 7–25.

Zaretsky, Eli. "Melanie Klein and the Emergence of Modern Personal Life." *Reading Melanie Klein*. Ed. Lyndsey Stonebridge and John Phillips. London: Routledge, 1998. 32–50.

Zeitlin, Michael. "*Pylon* and the Rise of European Fascism." *The Faulkner Journal* 26.1 (Spring 2012): 97–114.

———. "*Pylon*, Joyce, and Faulkner's Imagination." *Faulkner and the Artist*. Ed. Donald M. Kartiganer and Ann J. Abadie. Jackson, MS: UP of Mississippi, 1996. 181–207.

INDEX[1]

---

[1] Note: Page numbers followed by 'n' refer to notes.

Printed by Printforce, the Netherlands